The sociological domain

The Durkheimians and the founding of French sociology

T0381564

The sociological domain

The Durkheimians and the founding of French sociology

Edited by
PHILIPPE BESNARD

With a preface by
LEWIS A. COSER

CAMBRIDGE UNIVERSITY PRESS

Cambridge
London   New York   New Rochelle   Melbourne   Sydney

& EDITIONS DE LA MAISON DES SCIENCES DE L'HOMME

Paris

CAMBRIDGE UNIVERSITY PRESS
Cambridge, New York, Melbourne, Madrid, Cape Town, Singapore, São Paulo, Delhi

Cambridge University Press
The Edinburgh Building, Cambridge CB2 8RU, UK

With Editions de la Maison des Sciences de l'Homme
54 Boulevard Raspail, 75270 Paris Cedex 06, France

Published in the United States of America by Cambridge University Press, New York

www.cambridge.org
Information on this title: www.cambridge.org/9780521108034

First published 1983
This digitally printed version 2009

A catalogue record for this publication is available from the British Library

Library of Congress Catalogue Card Number: 82-9485

ISBN 978-0-521-23876-2 hardback
ISBN 978-0-521-10803-4 paperback

Contents

Contents

Notes on contributors

PHILIPPE BESNARD is a Senior Research Fellow with the Centre National de la Recherche Scientifique in Paris, and a member of the Groupe d'Etude des Methodes de l'Analyse Sociologique and teacher at the Institut d'Etudes Politiques de Paris. As the secretary of the Groupe d'Etudes Durkheimiennes, an international network created by the Maison des Sciences de l'Homme, Paris, he has published mainly in the field of the history of sociology. His other current interests include a study on the concept of anomie and the sociology of fashion.

MOHAMED CHERKAOUI is a Senior Research Fellow with the Centre National de la Recherche Scientifique in Paris. He is the author of numerous articles and two books concerning education, mobility and methodology: *Les Paradoxes de la réussite scolaire: sociologie comparée des systèmes d'enseignement* (1979) and *Les Changements du système éducatif en France 1950–1980* (1982). His publications also include essays on Durkheim and the Durkheimian School.

JOHN E. CRAIG is Associate Professor of the History of Education and Director of the Comparative Education Center at the University of Chicago. He is the author of *Scholarship and Nation-Building: the Universities of Strasbourg and Alsatian Society, 1870–1939* (forthcoming) and of articles on social mobility in Germany and the development of educational systems. His current research is on the causes and consequences of educational expansion in Europe and North America, from 1830 to the present.

PIERRE FAVRE is Professor of Political Science at the University of Clermont-Ferrand, working at present at the Centre National de la Recherche Scientifique in Paris. He has written books and articles on the history of political ideas, political theory, electoral sociology, and methodological issues, and has contributed to the major French journals of sociology and political science. He is at present working on the history of political science in France from 1871 to the present day.

Notes on contributors

ROGER GEIGER is a Research Associate in the Yale University Institution for Social and Policy Studies. He has written on the history of sociology in France in his Ph.D. dissertation 'The Development of French Sociology, 1870–1905', and in articles for *Societas* and *Revue française de sociologie*. Articles on higher education in France, past and present, have been contributed to *Historical Reflections/Réflexions historiques*, *Higher Education* and the *European Journal of Education*. He has recently completed a comparative study of private higher education in eight countries, and is currently investigating the development of American research universities in the twentieth century.

VICTOR KARADY was educated in Budapest, Vienna and Paris. He is a Senior Research Fellow with the Centre National de la Recherche Scientifique in Paris and held a visiting fellowship at Wolfson College, Oxford, from 1980 to 1982. He has edited several classics of French sociology (Durkheim, Mauss, Halbwachs) and published extensively on the institutionalisation of the social sciences, the post-Napoleonic university system and problems of Jewish assimilation in Hungary. His present research focuses on the historical uses of schooling both in France and in Central Europe.

FRANÇOIS A. ISAMBERT is Professor at the Ecole des Hautes Etudes en Sciences Sociales, Paris, and heads the research group 'Ethique et pratiques symboliques'. He has published extensively in the fields of the sociology of religion, the history of sociology, and sociological methodology. He is currently working on medical ethics.

W. PAUL VOGT is a member of the Department of Educational and Social Thought at the State University of New York at Albany. His articles have appeared in *History and Theory*, the *Revue française de sociologie*, *Research in the Sociology of Knowledge*, *Science and Art* and other journals. He is currently writing a comparative historical sociology of the theory and practice of. toleration in Western Europe and the United States.

GEORGE WEISZ is Associate Professor of the History of Medicine at McGill University, Montreal. He is the author of *The Emergence of Modern Universities in France 1860–1914* (forthcoming) and of articles on the history of education, medicine and the social sciences in France. He is the editor (with Robert Fox) of *The Organization of Science and Technology in France 1808–1914* (Cambridge, 1980).

Preface

Having had the privilege to have been a student of the Sorbonne in the middle thirties, of Paul Fauconnet and Célestin Bouglé, central members of the Durkheimian school, it is a special pleasure to be given the opportunity to write a preface to this volume. To be sure, both men were then near the end of their academic careers. They no longer displayed the missionary spirit and enthusiasm that characterised them in earlier years when they collaborated with Durkheim in bringing out the twelve prewar volumes of the *Année sociologique* that were the foundation stones of the Durkheimian school. By then the charisma of Durkheim had become routinised, and one perceived only an afterglow of his overpowering personality in Bouglé's and Fauconnet's lectures. But they still managed to some degree to convey the excitement and sense of discovery that had once animated the Durkheimian movement.

It is the merit of this book that it evokes the spirit of the early Durkheimian movement even more vividly than the lectures of such contemporaries as Bouglé or Fauconnet. It permits readers to have a privileged seat from which they can witness the creation and development of some of the paradigms of the Durkheimian school. Philippe Besnard and his collaborators judicially have chosen to intersperse with direct testimony a number of papers on key figures and on the relationship of the school with other academic disciplines. The publication of until recently unknown letters between some of the Durkheimians as well as a remarkable autobiographical statement by Marcel Mauss makes it possible to check current interpretations against the voices of the actors themselves.

This volume allows both an appreciation of the inner dynamics of the relations between the key members of the brilliant team that Durkheim succeeded in assembling around himself in an amazingly short time, and the context in which the Durkheimian movement operated. It shows that an earlier view that all the members of the school were sworn to Durkheimian orthodoxy has been vastly overstated. To be sure, Durkheim overshadowed all his collaborators and impressed the mark of his mind on all of them, yet there were many internal divergencies. Some members of the school, such as Bouglé, would never be fully reconciled with what they perceived to be Durkheim's extreme anti-psychologism; others such as Halbwachs and Simiand pursued enquiries that were only peripherally concerned with the religious phenomena that were central to Durkheim in the mature phase of his work. Durkheim was surely the sociometric star of the group, as he was also the key link between the geographically dispersed members, but he never, not even in the period just before World War I when he had consolidated his central position, dominated the group in a manner reminiscent of that of Freud in the early years of the psychoanalytical movement. This also accounts for the fact that, though there were some individual defections, there were never major splits similar to those among erstwhile Freudians.

This volume shows again the irrelevance of the current disputes about internalist or externalist criteria in the sociology of science. To be sure, internal discussions among the Durkheimians and between them and other social scientists were significant in their intellectual orientation, but the external constellations of power in the world of academic politics, inter-disciplinary rivalries, and connections to political decision-makers on the national level were also responsible for the future course of Durkheimian sociology. That most Durkheimians, for example, had been trained as philosophers, and mainly relied on the sponsorship of philosophers rather than, say, historians, may have been of considerable help in the beginning but proved to be a brake to further expansion of Durkheimian thought. In similar ways, its close ties to the politically dominant tendencies in pre World War I France became a liability under the very different political circumstances after the war. The Durkheimian message was not received in a political vacuum but was shaped by the specific political and academic milieu of the prewar years.

Several contributions to this volume help explain not only why the Durkheimians chose certain paths of enquiry, but also why they neglected others or soon abandoned still others that at first had seemed promising. Here again, both internal and external criteria seem to have played a central role, and scholarly and prudential criteria were often intertwined. The marked reluctance, for example, to develop political sociology seems at least in part to have been motivated by fear of being drawn into political controversies that seemed to threaten scientific objectivity.

Philippe Besnard's fine introduction so well characterises the various contributions to this volume that it would be redundant to comment on them in this preface. Let me only say that the remarkable unity of this volume, despite the very different subject-matters to which the various collaborators address themselves, seems to be largely the result of the collective effort of the members of the Paris-based Groupe d'Etudes Durkheimiennes, which in recent years has renewed the study of Durkheim and other members of his school and encouraged the other contributors to this volume. While it would be an exaggeration to compare the importance of this group to that of the Durkheimian group to which it devotes its intellectual energies, it is not far-fetched to assert that once again a similar collective effort has borne fruits that lonely scholarly work could hardly have achieved.

The English and American readers to whom this volume is addressed are conversant with the work of Durkheim. But for the most part they are likely to be ignorant of some of the members of the Durkheimian group. I find it understandable that the work of, say, Bouglé and Fauconnet is largely forgotten, if it ever was well known, in England and America. But I am astonished that even Marcel Mauss, Maurice Halbwachs, and Marcel Granet seem so little known, and, if known, often misunderstood. Thus Paul Hirst, to give just one especially glaring example, in his book, *Durkheim, Bernard and Epistemology* (London: Routledge and Kegan Paul 1975, p. 176) talks of 'an absolute sociologism which submerges the individual, which determines even his biological capacities – this sociologism [was] adopted by Mauss after Durkheim's death'. This despite the well-documented fact that Mauss argued again and again (see his recently translated *Sociology and Psychology* published by Routledge and Kegan Paul in 1979) that only a close collaboration of psychology, biology and sociology can bring about a fully-fledged 'total' study of the human animal. (See also his similar formulations in his intellectual self-portrait in this volume.) In the writing of the history and systematics of sociology almost anything seems admissible. If the present volume will have contributed only to reducing such misrepresentations, it will be worthy of admission for that alone.

This book is both a contribution to the history of the Durkheimian movement and a study of the institutionalisation of a new discipline in the French academic system. But it also serves, Philippe Besnard remarks in his introduction, as a reminder that 'the Durkheimians can still teach us many things'. Their work is important for contemporary sociological enquiry. Durkheim and his co-workers are in many respects our contemporaries, and this splendid volume does not let us forget it.

LEWIS A. COSER
Distinguished Professor of Sociology
SUNY at Stony Brook

Acknowledgements

I would like to thank the Editions du Centre National de la Recherche Scientifique, Paris, for permission to reproduce the following: from the *Revue française de sociologie*, vol. 20, no. 1, 1979, chapters 1 (pp. 7–31), 3 (pp. 83–112), 4 (pp. 257–67), 5 (pp. 209–20), 7 (pp. 123–39), 9 (pp. 239–55), and 12 (pp. 273–91); letters of Lapie, Parodi and Fauconnet to Bouglé (pp. 33–44), and letters on the 'Lapie affair' (pp. 268–72); from the *Revue française de sociologie*, vol. 17, no. 2, 1976, the letters of Durkheim to Bouglé dated 14 December 1895, 14 May 1900, 13 June 1900, and 6 July 1900; and from the *Archives de sciences sociales des religions*, vol. 23, no. 1, 1978, p. 120, the map in chapter 6 of this book.

I would also like to thank the Editions de Minuit for the permission to reproduce the letters of Durkheim to Bouglé and to Simiand from the *Textes d'Emile Durkheim*, vol. 2, *Religion, morale, anomie* (Paris: Editions de Minuit, 1975), pp. 390–4, 399–402, 419–21, 443, 445–8; and M. J.-C. Filloux for the right to reproduce the photograph on the jacket.

Paris, January 1982   PHILIPPE BESNARD

Introduction

Several highly talented co-workers assembled around Durkheim; all were united in their goal – the founding of sociology. Their association was a unique event in the history of the discipline. The Durkheimian group represents something very close to an ideal type of a 'school', and everyone agrees in recognising its decisive role in establishing the field of sociology. Yet no thorough and systematic study has been devoted to this 'Durkheimian school', which was more commonly called 'the French school of sociology' at the time. After so many studies dealing with Emile Durkheim, the uncontested leader of the group, this is the first book to introduce the individual and collective work of the other members of the group and to analyse not only the way in which they conceived of the domain of sociology, but also, and above all, how they constructed it in practice. This book, which examines a collective undertaking, is itself the product of a collective effort. The various contributions focus simultaneously on two subjects: the group of Durkheim's collaborators and disciples, and how they constituted the discipline of sociology.

It was not possible within the limits of this volume to provide a complete description of the scientific work of all the group's members. But the essential elements of the intellectual biographies of the most significant among them will be found here. Thus, Mauss, Hubert, Bouglé, Simiand, Halbwachs, Lapie, and Hertz are the object of specific contributions, while the most important aspects of the work of others – Davy, Fauconnet, Richard – are taken up in more general articles; and still others – H. Bourgin, Parodi, Huvelin, Gernet, etc.[1] – are referred to more or less extensively.

The principal purpose of this book is not, however, to introduce the work of the Durkheimians, although certain papers do draw attention to forgotten

---

[1] If the work of important authors such as Louis Gernet or Marcel Granet is dealt with only slightly in this volume, that is because it grew up after Durkheim's death. The majority of the contributions presented here are concerned with the era of the formation and the establishment of the Durkheimian school, although the interwar years are not neglected.

or misunderstood authors. The various contributions are mainly oriented toward analysing the way the Durkheimian group, as it constituted itself, affirmed sociology's right to exist and defined the sociological domain. For, if Durkheim wanted to form a team under his leadership, that was not only to obtain the advantages of the 'school effect' – which, as can still be seen today in intellectual and artistic life, remains one of the best ways to attract attention – it was also, and more so, to recruit brilliant young academics who would specialise in the diverse branches of the nascent discipline. This collective organisation of labour was rendered all the more necessary by the Durkheimians' territorial ambitions, which put them in competition with existing social and human sciences. We will see below how Durkheimian sociology affirmed itself in regard to other disciplines and fields of study, and we will examine the relationships, generally conflictual relationships, it established with philosophy, psychology, history, archaeology, human geography, economics, legal scholarship, religious studies, folklore studies, etc.[2]

The examination of the Durkheimians' texts in this volume is thus not separate from the analysis of the social and intellectual context in which the group attempted to create a new discipline. We will see what strategies the Durkheimians utilised to impose sociology in the face of certain external constraints and the ways they strove to substantiate the idea that this new science was capable of dealing with practically all human events from its own point of view. And the new science in question was *their* sociology, since the Durkheimians took care at the same time to discredit competing undertakings.[3]

The first part of this volume is focused on the Durkheimian group as a group, its role in the institutionalisation of sociology in French Academe, and the social and ideological context in which the group's activities were situated.

The object of the first paper is to present the Durkheimian group as it formed itself around its organ, the *Année sociologique*. It provides information about the academic careers of all those who collaborated on that journal

---

[2] This list is certainly not exhaustive as one can confirm by examining the content of the *Année sociologique*. For example, aesthetics, literature, philology, and technology were areas in which the Durkheimians were interested. One could also devote a study to the relationships between Durkheimian sociology and linguistics. The great linguist, Antoine Meillet, contributed rather regularly to the *Année sociologique*: and André Durkheim, the son of the leader of the group who died in the war, would have become the group's linguist. However, the Durkheimians' interest in the sociology of language was more virtual than real and had on the whole rather little impact on the subsequent development of linguistics.

[3] On contemporary and parallel attempts to create a social science in France, see the recent special number of the *Revue française de sociologie*, vol. 22, no. 3, 1981: 'Sociologies françaises au tournant du siècle. Les concurrents du groupe durkheimien'.

during Durkheim's lifetime and on the part that each took in the collective labour. It would certainly be excessive, and even erroneous, to consider all of the contributors to the *Année sociologique* to be Durkheimians. Some of them contributed very infrequently. Yet all of Durkheim's important fellow-workers and disciples (with the exceptions of Granet and Czarnowski in the prewar years) collaborated very actively on the journal. The *Année sociologique* was, in sum, the instrument permitting the creation of the group and, at the same time, the principal means for promoting it. Our study of the recruitment and functioning of the team, of its different sub-groups, and of its internal stratification, corrects the widespread image of a clan or a coterie that had closed ranks around a man and a doctrine. But, the doctrinal heterogeneity that existed from the outset did not prevent the *Année sociologique* from being an incontestable success as a collective undertaking and as a means of annexing territories that sociology could occupy and exploit. A selection of letters between several members of the group, recently discovered and published here for the first time in English, makes the debates, the difficulties, and the various events marking the existence of the *Année sociologique* come alive once more.

As a counterpoint to that internal study of the group, Victor Karady, in an essay synthesising his previous work, paints a general picture of the external constraints to which the Durkheimians had to adapt as they strove to increase the value of sociology's assets. He demonstrates in particular that the new discipline, while indeed responding to a social demand, could acquire only a limited degree of institutional legitimation. This contradicts the image one has often had of sociology's great academic success in France. On the other hand, the unprecedented effort at intellectual innovation made by the Durkheimians was fully efficacious in conferring a scientific legitimacy upon sociology.

Karady's study of the overall social and academic context of the Durkheimian enterprise is complemented by two case studies. The first, by George Weisz, deals with the rise of sociology's institutionalisation. It examines the particular circumstances leading to the creation of a course in the history of social economy – the first subject matter recognised as being sociological at the Paris faculty of letters – and how the Durkheimians, Bouglé that is, came to take possession of it in 1907. These episodes in the academic institutionalisation of sociology enable one to grasp more clearly the ideological debates provoked by sociology's success and the stakes in the rivalries it incited, rivalries first between the law faculties and the faculties of letters, and subsequently between sociologists and historians.

The year 1907 can be considered as marking a decisive stage in the academic success of the Durkheimian group. Durkheim himself had just

Introduction

definitively become a titled professor at the Sorbonne, and Gaston Richard acceded to Durkheim's former chair of social science at Bordeaux[4] where Lapie was likewise named professor of philosophy. Fauconnet took over the chair of social philosophy at Toulouse left vacant by Bouglé's departure for the Sorbonne. The same year, Mauss became director of studies at the Ecole Pratique des Hautes Etudes, where Hubert obtained a similar position the next year. Finally, one could add that Lévy-Bruhl, who sympathised with Durkheimian sociology, was elected, also in 1907, professor of modern philosophy at the Sorbonne.

Less than twenty years later, what has been called the 'Lapie affair' marked the limits of what could have appeared as sociology's conquest of academic legitimacy and social recognition. Our second case study, by Roger Geiger, concerns the introduction of sociology into the curriculum of the training schools for primary teachers. This reform unleashed a counter-offensive by conservatives and reanimated old prejudices against sociology. Geiger recounts the controversy that began in 1923 and shows how the Durkheimians had to fall back on a defensive position, thus limiting their ambitions as to the social role of their discipline. His article is supplemented by two letters from two of the protagonists (Bergson and Bérard) in the 'affair'.

The second part of this volume, by presenting the work of the principal Durkheimians, shows how each contributed in his own way to delimiting the sociological domain and to occupying its various regions.

Of all the members of the group, Marcel Mauss was, after Durkheim, the one who held the most central position. It is not easy to synthesise his work, for it is abundant, multifarious and, as he himself confessed, somewhat discontinuous. Who could bring out the unity of his writings better than Mauss himself? This is what he attempted in an autobiographical text written in 1930 that I recently discovered. Drawing up a sort of balance-sheet of his work, Mauss clarifies his principal contributions to the discipline. He also stresses the necessarily shared character of the Durkheimians' efforts to constitute sociology and provides some specifics on his collaboration with Durkheim, Hubert, and other members of the group whose research he so often oriented and inspired.

One sees in the next paper a direct reflection of the way in which Mauss inspired the Durkheimian team. François Isambert discusses three Durkheimians less well known than Mauss but close to him in their central research interests as well as in their approaches to them: Robert Hertz, probably the most brilliant of the younger generation of Durkheimians;

---

[4] It is true that it was also in 1907 that Gaston Richard broke with the Durkheimian group. He was even to become one of its principal adversaries. See W. S. F. Pickering, 'Gaston Richard: collaborateur et adversaire', *Revue française de sociologie*, vol. 20, no. 1, 1979, pp. 163–82.

Stefan Czarnowski, who was to become a notable figure in Polish sociology; and Henri Hubert, a friend and close collaborator of Mauss, to whom Mauss referred as my 'work twin'. Hubert, because of his very close collaboration with Mauss, has too often been left in Mauss's shadow, although his own work and his contributions to the Durkheimian theory of religion were considerable.[5]

The sociology of religion, which can be considered the keystone of Durkheimian sociology, could not be the subject of a comprehensive study in this volume. Rather, Isambert approaches it from the particular perspective of folk religion. This example enables us to see how the Durkheimians appropriated an intellectual field, folklore studies, which at the time held a generally low rank in the hierarchy of disciplines in France. Each of the three authors he studies contributed in his own way to establishing folk religions as an object for sociological study. Hubert did so by integrating them into a general sociological theory of religion, Czarnowski by bringing together folk cults and national consciousness, and Hertz by going furthest in the sociological treatment of the subject in a study which, in addition, is the sole example of an ethnological study based on fieldwork ever conducted by a Durkheimian.

Along with the sociology of religion, the sociology of law was clearly the area most studied by the Durkheimians, an area characterised by the work of Paul Fauconnet, Georges Davy, Gaston Richard, Paul Huvelin, Emmanuel Lévy, to say nothing of the work of Durkheim and Mauss themselves. In his general study devoted to this sub-discipline, Paul Vogt shows that the central place accorded to the sociology of law by the Durkheimians is explained by the necessary ties they saw between law on the one hand and morality and religion on the other. Thus, the sociology of law is paradigmatic of the Durkheimians' penchant for totalising approaches, for subsuming all social phenomena under the same general model of explanation. A particular feature of the Durkheimians' work in this area is that their perspective had several aspects in common with that of certain eminent legal scholars of the time, such as Duguit and Hauriou. This similarity reinforced the Durkheimians' tendency to give priority to the ethnological approach to the study of law, especially the study of law's origins, since they found here a comparatively untrammelled field – one in which they made important scholarly contributions.

In thinking about the subsequent development of the sociology of law in

---

[5] How, for example, could English-speaking readers know that the work on magic was written collaboratively by Hubert and Mauss? *A General Theory of Magic*, published by Routledge and Kegan Paul, London, 1972, is presented as the work of Mauss alone; Hubert's name does not even appear in D. F. Pocock's preface. Yet it is indeed the work of Hubert, perhaps even more than it is the work of Mauss.

comparison to that of political sociology, one is struck by the essential place the Durkheimians gave to the former field of study and the very minor role they granted to the latter. Political sociology, as Pierre Favre shows in his paper, was all but absent from the Durkheimian classifications of the social sciences, both in Durkheim's programmatic writings where he outlined the divisions of sociology and in the classificatory plan of the *Année sociologique*, which was where the Durkheimians put into practice their ideas about the demarcation and the mapping of sociological territory. Favre mentions the various factors that could explain this singular absence, which was a not inconsiderable factor accounting for the fact that political sociology was relatively slow to constitute itself in France.

From the perspective of contemporary criteria, the absence of yet another area of study is no less striking: that is, the relationship between education and social mobility, which is today considered central to and typical of the discipline of sociology. The only Durkheimian directly interested in it was Paul Lapie, a rather marginal member of the team. The pioneering character of his work on the social effects of the school is brought to the fore in Mohamed Cherkaoui's article. The fact that Lapie's work found no echo in the era, that this area of study was excluded from the field of the 'sociologisable', probably came about because it seemed rather to belong to psychology. (Alfred Binet had conducted studies of a similar sort at the time.) Even Lapie's colleagues on the *Année sociologique* had no idea of the importance and originality of his work. This was undoubtedly unfortunate for the development of French sociology, for Lapie, who invented mobility tables, had he pursued that line of investigation, could certainly have conducted rigorous empirical research.[6] Instead, the lack of recognition from his peers probably contributed to orienting him toward an administrative career in the education system.

If Célestin Bouglé's name is better known today than that of his friend Lapie, his work, with the possible exception of his study of the caste system, is largely misunderstood. Because of his varied and extensive activities (as an academic, a lecturer, a journalist, etc.), he was one of the best known Durkheimians of the era. Paul Vogt conducts a general survey of his scholarly work as a whole and particularly insists upon Bouglé's contributions to the sociology of knowledge. He stresses the ambivalent position of Bouglé, who was determined to be a sociologist and yet who never broke completely with a neo-Kantian rationalism that was logically incompatible with Durkheimian sociologism. Doubtless because he embodied the antagonism between philosophic rationalism and sociologism, Bouglé's

---

[6] He was, for example, one of the rare readers of *Suicide* who well understood the most complex of the methodological procedures that Durkheim employed. See his book, *La Femme dans la famille*, Paris, Doin, 1908.

scientific work did not attain a level of originality and accomplishment commensurate with his talent.

François Simiand was another key member of the Durkheimian group whose work would merit an overall reassessment. The article devoted to him here deals primarily with his role in the epistemological battles in which the Durkheimians engaged with neighbouring social sciences (especially history, human geography, and economics) in order to impose the scientific legitimacy of sociology. Simiand's works in economic sociology, which were aimed at demonstrating that scientific economics could only be a branch of sociology, and his insistence that since there was only one scientific method, there had to be a (sociological) unity to all true social sciences, made him a salient figure in what has been called 'sociological imperialism'.

This imperialism could not fail to stimulate spirited resistance from those disciplines affected by it. In the interwar period, at which time the Durkheimians were less dominant, the main defender of sociology's claims was Simiand's friend and collaborator, Maurice Halbwachs. His post as professor at the new and innovating University of Strasbourg fitted well with his engagement in these interdisciplinary debates. John Craig examines how Halbwachs's discussions with colleagues in psychology, history and geography, as well as his knowledge of German and American sociologies, could have influenced his conception and practice in such a way as to make him the principal figure in the transition between the Durkheimians and contemporary French sociology.

The totality of studies and documents gathered here allows one to evaluate the true measure of the Durkheimian group's contribution to the birth and the establishment of the field of sociology. The present contours of the discipline are of course not exactly those that the Durkheimians had drawn in their programs and established by their practice. But the essential thing was that there be constructed a territory for sociology, a territory that was moreover virtually limitless since, in the final analysis, all aspects of human life in society ought to have been within the scope of a sociological explanation.

This formidable ambition could have developed and could have had a chance to end with favourable results only as a collective undertaking and only by drawing sustenance from a particular sort of intellectual and social context. In that respect, the study of the Durkheimian group has a significance far greater than a simple contribution to the history of sociology, for it is instructive about the birth and institutionalisation of academic disciplines in general. But, it also goes beyond the limits of a history of sociology in another way; studying the work of the Durkheimians has more than an historical interest. It would indeed be highly presumptuous to believe that sociology has progressed to such an extent that their work no

Introduction

longer has relevance for modern sociology. The Durkheimians can still teach us many things. They can above all be useful as guides to exploring the territory of sociology, an area in which so many virgin lands remain unmapped.

The realisation of this book was made possible by the existence of the Groupe d'Etudes Durkheimiennes, an international network of specialists in the history of French sociology created by the Fondation de la Maison des Sciences de l'Homme.[7] If this volume has, as I hope it does, the merit of presenting a coherent perspective, despite the large number of contributors, that is because it is not only a work studying a group endeavour, but also because it is itself in large part the result of a collective effort. While the responsibility for the conception of the volume is mine, all those who have participated in it have willingly accepted the constraints inherent in the genre and have aided me with their suggestions and encouragement. For this I would like to thank them and express my special gratitude to Paul Vogt who agreed to write two of the contributions and to take on the task of translating several texts (Chapters 8 and 11, the introduction and the majority of the correspondence). Equally I would like to thank the other translators, P. Fawcett (Chapters 6 and 9), Mark Aston (Chapter 1 and the letters of Durkheim to Bouglé), A. Bailey and J. R. Llobera (Chapter 5), as well as Mary Baffoni for her valuable help in the preparation of the manuscript. I am also very grateful to Marie-France Essyad, a research assistant at the Maison des Sciences de l'Homme, for her aid in the collection of documentation and in the preparation of the volume.

Some of these papers have already been published in French in the *Revue française de sociologie* vol. 20, no. 1, 1979. They have all been revised to a greater or lesser extent for inclusion in the present work. The majority of the documents (letters and Mauss's autobiographical text) were likewise published in the same issue of that journal or in an earlier number: vol. 17, no. 2, 1976. Some letters were taken from Durkheim's *Textes* published in 1975 by Victor Karady. I thank the Editions du Centre National de la Recherche Scientifique and Editions de Minuit for having authorised their publication in English. Finally, I should like to express my gratitude to all those who have made documents available to us or who have given us access to their private archives, especially the late Mlle Jeanne Bouglé, Mme P. Chatenet, and M. Pierre Olivier Lapie.

PHILIPPE BESNARD

[7] This group publishes a newsletter, *Etudes durkheimiennes*, which presents unpublished documents, information about research in progress, bibliographies, etc. It is sent upon request to all interested persons. Editor: Philippe Besnard, Groupe d'Etudes Durkheimiennes, Maison des Sciences de l'Homme, 54 boulevard Raspail, 75006 Paris.

Part I. The Durkheimian group and its context

1. The 'Année sociologique' team

PHILIPPE BESNARD

It is widely recognised that the Durkheimian school played an important, even decisive, role in the birth and institutionalisation of sociology as a discipline, but the way in which the school was first constituted has not so far been made the object of any detailed research. The *Année sociologique*, without any doubt, played an essential part in this respect, by fulfilling functions rather like those of a research centre (Clark 1968). Yet there has hardly been any study of the precise circumstances in which this review was created, of the way in which its collaborators were recruited and of the functioning of this collective enterprise.

The various data presented here fill this gap only in part. But they do contribute, in my opinion, new and relatively precise information on several matters, such as the birth of the *Année*, the 'sociological calling' of the young *agrégés* in philosophy[1] who decided to take part in it, the tensions within the team and its stratification. I believe these documents also question the commonly received image of the group of *Année* collaborators as forming a kind of sociological clan, homogeneous in its personnel and tightly knit around one man and one doctrine.[2]

If the information provided here is fragmentary and incomplete, it is because the data used come largely from work still in progress – and of long duration – consisting of tracking down unpublished documents (items of correspondence especially). Many of the documents so far collected concern a sub-group. (Bouglé, Lapie, Parodi) which is particularly heterodox as concerns Durkheimianism. However, this sub-group played an essential role in the creation of the *Année*. Furthermore, the extent of our ignorance of such a key aspect of the birth of sociology in France seemed justification enough for introducing and exploiting these few documents.

[1] *agrégé*: one who has been successful in the *agrégation*. The *agrégation* is a yearly national recruiting competition for teaching posts in secondary education (in literary and scientific subjects). For Law, the *agrégation* is a recruitment for higher education.
[2] This image was first accredited by the opponents of Durkheimian sociology and adopted later, in part, as their own, by certain Durkheimians (see, for example, the autobiographical text by Mauss in this volume); it remains the chief representation of the collaborators of the *Année*.

Philippe Besnard

The idea of the 'Année sociologique' and its antecedents

In a letter to Elie Halévy dated 13 January 1936, Célestin Bouglé wrote: 'Who would guess that it was I who, after a conversation with Paul Lapie, went and required Durkheim to set up the *Année sociologique*?'[3] Even allowing for the fact that Bouglé is reconstructing a time forty years past,[4] many clues show that Bouglé did play a great part in the creation of the *Année*. The meeting with Durkheim to which he refers can be dated, on the evidence of the letters, as April 1896, when both men must have met in Paris. The idea of founding the review was therefore launched very soon after the first contact Durkheim made with Bouglé by letter (letter dated 14 December 1895, below) and during what was very probably their first meeting. Durkheim kept Bouglé informed of his difficult negotiations with Alcan (letter dated 16 May 1896, below), and on 2 July, Bouglé, in a letter to Halévy, concluded: 'The *Année sociologique* has taken the plunge.' Even though he left to Durkheim the task of negotiating with Alcan, Bouglé, then only twenty-six, does seem to have been the moving force in this affair. His friend Lapie still saw him in November '96 as the true architect of the enterprise (see letter dated 20 November 1896, below). Durkheim himself confirmed as much when he wrote to Bouglé, on 22 March 1898, after the publication of the first volume: 'I reciprocate your congratulations about the *Année* since, on that point again, you are the one who spurred me on' (Durkheim 1975 : 424). Bouglé's role is better understood and appreciated if one remembers that, due to his friendly relations with Elie Halévy, indicated by the abundant correspondence between them, he was the intermediary between the budding *Année sociologique* and the *Revue de métaphysique et de morale*. It so happens that 'L'Année sociologique' ('The Sociological Year') was originally the title of an annual rubric (from 1895 to 1898) in that review which had been founded in 1893 by Xavier Léon with the help of Elie Halévy.

That this rubric had been created is rather surprising, considering the declarations of intent formulated in the first number of the review. The explicit project was to be distinct from Ribot's *Revue philosophique*,

[3] Correspondence Bouglé to Halévy, in the private archives of Mlle Bouglé and Mme Guy-Loé; extracts available for consultation at the Groupe d'Etudes Durkheimiennes, Maison des Sciences de l'Homme (hereafter designated by the acronym GED).

[4] Bouglé was less affirmative in a presentation he gave of the *Année sociologique* in 1907: 'Who first conceived the idea of our common enterprise? We do not really know. We like not to know. We like to think that the idea of the *Année sociologique*, as a good social phenomenon, was in the air and that it settled in several brains at the same time, round about 1895. I vaguely recall a conversation with Lapie ...' (Bouglé 1907:338). Note that, though he does not claim in this public presentation to be the initiator of the enterprise, Bouglé nonetheless suggests that his role was important, since he reveals that it was not Durkheim – though the undisputed head of the team – who alone conceived the idea of the *Année sociologique*.

12

considered too eclectic, and from Renouvier and Pillon's *Critique philosophique*, which was too much devoted to the 'moral and political applications' of a doctrine. What was thought necessary was to return to philosophy itself, that is to metaphysics, and to contribute not 'facts but ideas' and 'not to follow the movement of ideas but to try to channel it in some direction'.[5] Was there not some deviation from those initial intentions in publishing a sort of periodic balance-sheet of works far removed from metaphysics? Did not the review of sociological studies amount to following the movement of ideas and even obeying a fashion?

Quite clearly it was chiefly Bouglé who engineered the rapid opening of the *Revue de métaphysique et de morale* to the social sciences. In 1894 the review published two articles by Bouglé on Simmel and Wagner, as well as two articles brought forward by Bouglé, one by Simmel, the other by Lapie, on 'the definition of socialism'.[6] It was again through Bouglé that his friend Paul Lapie, who had just been appointed as teacher in the *lycée* of Tunis, was entrusted with the rubric 'L'Année sociologique'.

Lapie accepted, but not without scruples, as he did not feel competent to judge the sociologists of the day. Furthermore he found it necessary to make clear to Xavier Léon that he believed 'that it is possible to constitute a science of societies: consequently the judgements I could pass on attempts to constitute it would not be condemnations *a priori*'.[7] The statement gives a glimpse of the direction X. Léon and E. Halévy intended their chronicle to take, in accordance with the principles of their review as enunciated above[8] (see also Lapie's letter dated 30 January 1895, below).

As a matter of fact, *a priori* condemnations and destructive critical reviews were not Lapie's style. (Lapie was to be in charge of 'L'Année sociologique' for two years – Lapie 1895, 1896.) It will be noted, nevertheless, that in the first of the texts reviewing works published in 1894 by Bernès, Lacombe, Le Bon, Novicow, Tarde, etc., there is a rather harsh review of the 'Règles de la méthode sociologique', published the same year in the *Revue philosophique*: 'the assimilation of societies to organisms', wrote Lapie 'is sometimes of use to biology, never to sociology'. M. Durkheim 'interprets certain facts by

---

[5] *Revue de métaphysique et de morale*, vol. 1, 1893, pp. 1–3.
[6] A letter from Xavier Léon to Bouglé dated 9 May 1894 is enough to prove Bouglé's role in this matter. X. Léon wrote, in particular, 'I entirely agree with you; merely because the Review bears in its title the name Metaphysics, we should not systematically disregard those who, though not doing metaphysics, do serious philosophy, and, to judge from what you have said, Simmel is such a one ... I am counting greatly on you to speak to our readers about sociologists and sociology' (GED).
[7] Letter from Lapie to X. Léon dated 1 May 1894 (Xavier Léon Papers, the Victor Cousin Library). On Lapie's hesitancy, see also his letter to Bouglé dated 18 June 1894 (GED).
[8] The *Revue de métaphysique et de morale* had already indicated its opposition to Durkheim's conception of sociology, when reviewing *Division of Labour*. See Brunschvicg and Halévy 1894.

using facts in which constraint is manifest: he generalises to excess. All that sociological observation can offer is psychic facts suggested [i.e. to the actor] sometimes by force, sometimes by reason.'

Simiand succeeded Lapie in charge of this rubric, likewise for two years (1897, 1898). He was to fulfil the task in a more critical and selective manner than Lapie, denouncing in 1897 the fashion for sociology, and choosing to introduce in 1898, together with *Suicide*, authors 'who would willingly reject the title of sociologist' (such as Andler, Langlois and Seignobos). Would we not, he wrote, 'waste precious space if we were to reserve it for mediocre books merely because they call themselves sociological?' (1898 : 608). This way of proceeding was perhaps more in accord with the wishes of Léon and Halévy. Above all, when Simiand wrote this chronicle, which was to be the last of the series, the *Année sociologique* had already appeared, and Simiand was faithfully following the principles of this new enterprise by looking for material which could be used by sociology, instead of taking sides for labels.

The title *Année sociologique* was only a borrowing; neither were its principal characteristics an innovation. The new review found its inspiration in many models. *Années* presenting the main output of a sector of knowledge had been very fashionable for some time, for example (with date of foundation) the *Année artistique* (1878), the *Année médicale* (1878), the *Année archéologique* (1879), the *Année épigraphique* (1888), the *Année cartographique* (1890), the *Année biologique* (1897),[9] and two publications in particular – the *Année philosophique* and the *Année psychologique*.

The *Année philosophique*, under the direction of Pillon, was first published in 1868 and 1869, and reappeared in 1891 (from 1872 to 1889 it had been replaced by the *Critique philosophique* under the direction of Renouvier, first as a weekly, then as a monthly review). It was published by Alcan from 1891, which explains why he at first offered Durkheim a one-volume publication of the *Année philosophique* with the *Année sociologique*, a proposal considered unacceptable (see letter to Bouglé dated 16 May 1896, below). The *Année philosophique* consisted, on the one hand, of articles and, on the other, of a substantial bibliographic rubric divided into several sections reviewing the philosophical literature published during the previous year. However, two main differences from the future *Année sociologique* are to be noted: the bibliographic rubric dealt only with what had been published in France, and the analyses, rather brief, all seem to be the work of one man, Pillon.

It is more clearly the *Année psychologique* which can, in many respects, be regarded as the model from which Durkheim and his collaborators may have

[9] Durkheim (1975 : 403) mentions this last journal in a letter to Bouglé dated 25 July 1897.

drawn inspiration. It was first published in 1895 by Alcan, but as early as 1897 was published by Reinwald and Schleicher, then in 1904 by Masson.[10] Far from being the work of one man, it was a publication by a laboratory, the laboratory of physiological psychology of the Sorbonne, which Binet directed as well as being director of the review. The team of collaborators was remarkably stable from 1895 to 1901, and each volume was in three parts: (1) 'original articles' by members of the laboratory or outside collaborators, the former clearly distinguished from the latter; (2) analyses of the most important publications of the previous year, whether books or articles, French and foreign. These analyses were divided into rubrics and sub-rubrics; they were signed and their length, rather variable, averaged one page; (3) 'bibliographic tables' merely mentioning 'everything which is of greater or lesser interest to the psychologist'. The amount of space devoted to the articles was more or less equal to that devoted to the analyses.[11]

Clearly then, Durkheim did not have to look far to find the formal model for the *Année sociologique*. All was already in the *Année psychologique*, including the distinction between the authors of articles according to whether they belonged or not to the group, a distinction which Durkheim was to make explicitly in his letters,[12] though he did not go as far as materialising it in the *Année*. Since the influence of the German model of the research laboratory in the creation of the *Année* has often been stressed (Clark 1968), it seems fitting to recall the existence of a closer source of inspiration.

However, there was between the *Année psychologique* and the *Année sociologique* one essential difference: sociology did not exist. It was, therefore, necessary for sociology, in order to legitimate its scientific credentials, to progressively carve out its own field by taking over material originating in other disciplines. Such was, as we know, the explicit aim of the *Année* as spelt out by Durkheim in his preface to the first volume: to construct sociology with materials issuing 'from researches taking place in specialised sciences, history of law, customs, religions, moral statistics, economics etc.'.[13] As for studies which themselves claimed to be sociological,

[10] On these changes of publisher, see Durkheim's letter to Bouglé dated 25 May 1897 (Durkheim 1975 : 395).
[11] A modification can be noted in 1904, with the appearance of general reviews, annually or biennally, on subjects outside psychology *stricto sensu* (biology and moral sciences). At that point, the journal announced that Durkheim was to take charge of the 'sociology' rubric, a promise to remain unfulfilled.
[12] See, for example, Durkheim's letter to Simiand dated 15 February 1902, below. About the articles, Durkheim wrote, 'in what has been published, only what comes from ourselves is of value'. The articles coming from 'outsiders' were, in any case, rather rare (four out of a total of twenty-two, one each from Simmel, Ratzel, Steinmetz and Charmont) and there were no more from the fifth volume onwards (1902).
[13] Durkheim 1898 : i. On this theme, see V. Karady's article in this volume.

15

Philippe Besnard

they were, for the most part, to be analysed in the section 'General sociology', considered the least interesting by the collaborators of the *Année*.[14]

Having brought to light these antecedents and outside suggestions, we should not forget that the notion of a division of labour between social scientists collaborating in a common task, which is the principle of the *Année sociologique*, corresponded to a long-standing preoccupation of Durkheim. From his very first writings, he observed that sociology 'can only progress through work in common and a collective effort' and that it lent itself already to a 'useful division of labour' (Durkheim 1886 : 80). Likewise, in his doctoral thesis, he presented as an example of anomie the current situation of the moral and social sciences and, in accordance with his general thesis, stressed the necessity of bringing together the different specialists and of their realising that 'they work together for the same task' (Durkheim 1893 : 359, 363).

Recruitment of the 'Année' Team

During the second half of 1896, Durkheim finally convinced Alcan, and it was early in 1897 that the collaborators were recruited, the tasks shared out and the *Année*'s plan of classification elaborated.[15] The letters of that time bear the mark of these activities. They bear the mark too of doctrinal divergences over the conception of sociology, which Durkheim was to do his best to smooth over or put into brackets.

It is known that Bouglé had expressed, even more clearly than Lapie, serious reservations about the conception of sociology which emerged from the *Règles de la méthode sociologique*.[16]

March 1897 saw an exchange of letters between Durkheim, Bouglé and

[14] Simiand, reviewing the first volume, expressed satisfaction at the fact that sociology was becoming more extrovert, attributing a bare fifty pages to 'general sociology', 'that is to say to all the sociology of yesterday, all the sociology which gave the word its bad reputation' (Simiand 1898 : 652). Bouglé himself, though in charge of this section, judged it to be the one 'which provides the least amount of useful information' (Bouglé 1904 : 656).

[15] It will not be possible to tackle the study, still to be done, of this classificatory plan, of its successive transformations, of its lacunae and of the distribution of the texts reviewed into the various sections. Let us, nevertheless, note the fact that Durkheim regarded the issue as of the utmost importance. See, for example, his letter to Bouglé dated 6 July 1900, below: 'These questions of classification are important, for it is sociology itself which is organised therein. To give some order to this shapeless mass is no small matter. Maybe it is one of the things that will live on from the *Année*.' See also the criticisms formulated by Lapie on the organisation of the *Année* in the letters below, and likewise Bouglé 1904 and Mauss 1927.

[16] See the last chapter of his book *Les Sciences sociales en Allemagne* (Bouglé 1896a), which he had added to the article published in the *Revue de métaphysique et de morale*. Note that the book, though dated 1896, had in fact been published by October or November 1895. On the criticisms Bouglé addressed to Durkheim, see Paul Vogt's article in this volume.

16

Lapie, the 'great issue under litigation' (as Durkheim called it) being that of the relation between sociology and psychology.[17]

Despite some slight differences, Lapie and Bouglé agreed in identifying the social fact with the psychological fact. In Lapie's view, the object of sociology was to account for desires, these being social facts (see letters dated 30 January 1895 and 18 February 1895, below). At this point, Durkheim asked his collaborators to agree on 'the need to do sociology sociologically' (Lapie's letter dated 14 March 1897, below). Faced with the resistance shown by Bouglé and Lapie, who insisted on stressing the links between sociology and psychology and who would have liked to review works of 'social psychology', Durkheim argued, 'I never meant to say that one could do sociology without some psychological culture, nor that sociology was anything other than a psychology' (letter to Bouglé dated March 1897, below); and the formula he wrote to Lapie, viz. 'in sociology I see only a psychology, but a psychology *sui generis*', was enough to reassure the latter (letter from Lapie dated 24 January 1897, below).

The publication of Durkheim's *Suicide* in May or June of 1897, at the time when the team of collaborators was being constituted, was to bring fresh matter to these doctrinal arguments. This work left a favourable impression on such young philosophers as Lapie and Parodi, who had been less than enchanted by the *Règles de la méthode*. Lapie saw in it 'the desire to make concessions to us' on the importance of psychological causes (letter dated 9 July 1897, below). Parodi, though he judged the relations between the psychological and social domains still not defined clearly enough, considered nonetheless that Durkheim was right on that point (letter dated 1897, below). Bouglé seems to have been much more reticent, since he spoke, according to Lapie, of 'scientific narrow-mindedness'.[18]

Similarly, a reading of the reviews of *Suicide* by some of the *Année*'s first collaborators (Fauconnet, Richard, Simiand) enlightens us as to Durkheim's place in the then nascent group; it shows that Durkheim was not in any way a master gathering around himself zealous disciples burning to follow and honour him.

Admittedly, the review of *Suicide* published in the *Revue philosophique* (1898) by Fauconnet (who, as a young *agrégé*, was more likely to behave in such a way) was fairly uncritical and he gave a long and faithful summary of it; but, on the other hand, he did not display any obvious enthusiasm either.

As for Simiand (1898), after giving a substantial analysis of *Suicide*, he had little hesitation in questioning the value of certain statistics and particularly

---

[17] See letters of that period from Durkheim and Lapie to Bouglé, published below.
[18] See also Durkheim's answer to these objections in his letter dated 6 July 1897, below, which confirms that *Suicide* succeeded in removing Lapie's final reservations.

in attacking the conception of sociology which emerged from the book. In his eyes, 'sociology can be founded as a science far more economically'. When Durkheim claimed that collective tendencies were 'forces as real as cosmic forces', Simiand maintained that one might better have said 'as unreal', because 'science does not need to work on "realities"'. He rejected, in short, what he considered to be a 'metaphysics of sociology', a 'sociological realism' (1898 : 649–50). In no way did this radical criticism prevent Simiand, when a few pages later he reviewed the first volume of the *Année sociologique*, from wishing that the association of those people should be neither 'restricted nor ephemeral', so justifying the hope 'that sociology might some day rank among the sciences' (1898 : 653). Clearly Simiand, while identifying totally with the project of the *Année*, was very far from adopting a reverent attitude towards Durkheim.

The least benevolent review to come from a collaborator of the *Année* appeared in the *Année* itself, signed by Gaston Richard, who failed 'to understand what sociological explanation gains in clarity and strength' by denying 'individual action', and who shuddered 'at the thought of the abusive use some could make' of such a metaphor as 'currents which generate social facts'. In his view, the various forms of suicide are tied to 'psychological types' (Richard 1898 : 405).

Apparently, then, it was in no one's mind, not even Durkheim's, to create a school by creating a journal. As Durkheim wrote to Simiand on 15 February 1902 (see letter, below): 'I hardly dared hope for the moral homogeneity which has come about between us and I meant to make of the *Année* only a collection of works, admission to which would require nothing beyond scientific honesty.' The aim was therefore to set up a team of 'workers' (an expression which occurs very often in Durkheim's writing and in that of the Durkheimians) as opposed to 'amateurs' who boast of doing sociology because 'for some time since, sociology has become fashionable'.[19] Durkheim thought that, thanks to the *Année sociologique*, 'a distinction will be drawn in public opinion between the good workers and the others' (letter to Bouglé dated 13 June 1900, below).

These 'workers' also shared a belief in the possibility of a social science, even though they may not have agreed on its definition and its object. And an author such as Bouglé could be seen to engage, as early as 1896, in a virulent polemic with Andler, on that very point, in the *Revue de métaphysique et de morale*,[20] after having, nevertheless, made contact with Durkheim. Bouglé

[19] This is the first sentence of Durkheim's preface to *Suicide*. On the same theme, see Simiand 1897. One index of the fashion for sociology in the year 1897 is the creation of a chair in social philosophy at the Collège de France (see G. Weisz's article in this volume).

[20] See Andler 1896; Bouglé 1896b. See also a very sour letter from Andler to Bouglé dated 20 May 1896 (GED).

wrote to Halévy: 'Now that I have consulted Durkheim, it will prove to be I who will fight for the honour of sociology.'[21]

The sociological 'calling' felt by those young *agrégés* in philosophy, Bouglé and Lapie, thus seems to have been quite pronounced at the time the *Année* team was being constituted. But where did this calling originate? The letters provide some information on this point.

As far as Bouglé is concerned, his year of studying in Germany just after his *agrégation* (1893–4) turned him towards the 'social sciences' by acquainting him with the teachings and writings of Wagner, Lazarus, Ihering and particularly Simmel, with whom he felt a strong intellectual affinity.[22] Should one also take seriously an entirely negative motivation which he often expressed in his letters to Halévy? During the years 1893–4, he complained of his 'metaphysical impotence which turns into Ribotism' and thought he ought 'rather to turn to the collection of facts than to metaphysics'. In 1895, he stated he suffered from 'weakness of mind'. 'Fortunately', he added, 'good positivist sociology is around.'[23]

No doubt his own inclination was reinforced by advice on his career. Thus Georges Lyon wrote to him on 12 May 1894: 'I have often advised you to choose one city as your own from the wide province of philosophy; therefore I can only applaud your projected work in sociology. These are studies, still young, which will prove more and more attractive and you do well to stake your claim.' In similar vein, Bouglé wrote to Halévy in 1894 that Henry Michel was encouraging him to bring out articles 'bearing in their title the magic words "social sciences"', so as to enable him to apply 'for some sociology lecturing in a provincial university'. A little later one of his friends, Havard, wrote to him on 31 December 1896: 'The access to Higher Education these days is a myth, I think, unless one chooses a well-defined specialism. I think you were altogether right to choose sociology.'

Nevertheless, some advised against undue specialisation. Paul Janet, in a letter dated late 1895, advised him to abandon the idea of a Latin thesis in sociology. 'As far as your career is concerned, you should not lock yourself

---

[21] Undated letter (GED). Bouglé also states he would show the proofs of this text to Durkheim. Durkheim was to approve wholeheartedly: see his letter to X. Léon, 26 May 1896 (Durkheim 1975 : 462) and his letter to Bouglé dated 16 May 1896, below.

[22] Bouglé wrote to Halévy in 1894 (undated letter) that Simmel 'affects me like a Mephistopheles commissioned to express my own thoughts'.

[23] A letter Bouglé wrote to Halévy later typifies quite well his disenchanted attitude: 'What is the point of new ambitious plans? It seems I must abandon this style [of work, like the studies of *Castes*]. Not, I think, because of intellectual incapacity – I may get muddled with pure ideas but I still consider m self able to cope with facts – but because of physical incapacity. I cannot spend as many hours as I ought reading to accumulate the necessary notes ... My average output would do nicely for a "philosopher" but is not enough for a "sociologist"' (Undated letter, GED).

inside a single specialism.' And the supervisor of Bouglé's thesis, Henry Michel, who had been asked in 1896 to give a course of lectures at the Sorbonne in the history of political doctrines, was to view only with reluctance Bouglé's greater commitment to sociology and, even worse, to Durkheimianism. He was to voice serious reservations about the draft of Bouglé's thesis, and was to reproach him mainly with drawing too much inspiration from 'Durkheim's methods' (letter dated April 1899).

As to Lapie's 'sociological calling', it can be seen in his letters to Bouglé to have emerged under a two-fold influence: Bouglé's influence (particularly through his reading of Bouglé's articles on the social sciences in Germany) and that of his stay in Tunis (1893–7), the town where he had first been posted, as requested, to teach philosophy in a *lycée*. From the first letters he wrote to Bouglé, he showed interest in the social questions arising in Tunisia, in the consequences of the 'mixing of races', and engaged in the criticism, quite harsh, of French colonisation.[24] He laboured to constitute 'a small collection of social facts' (letter dated 11 November 1894, below). Finally, it was Bouglé's insistence which made him accept, as noted, the task of reviewing works of sociology in the *Revue de métaphysique et de morale*. That task obliged him to immerse himself in the literature. Nevertheless, Lapie was not to give up philosophy: if his first book *Les Civilisations tunisiennes* (1898) was presented as a 'study in social psychology', his thesis *La Logique de la volonté* (1902), highly rationalist in inspiration, was not at all sociological. As to his later works on education they were not, at the time, perceived as belonging to sociology.[25]

Bouglé had also a close relationship with another future collaborator of the *Année*, Dominique Parodi, who had been a student at the Ecole Normale Supérieure and had become an *agrégé* in philosophy at the same time as himself. Unlike Lapie and Bouglé, Parodi's sociological calling never really materialised. In the letters he was writing to Bouglé at that time he did not identify with the 'sociologists' despite the enthusiasm – mixed with irony – he manifested in his letter dated 1897 (published below).[26]

Why did young philosophers who inclined in various degrees towards sociology gather around Durkheim, although the conception of sociology found in their early works showed them more akin to a man like Tarde? The first reason is certainly that Tarde was not of the university. Another factor to be considered is that Durkheim was animated by a permanent wish to convince, and even proselytise, which was virtually lacking in Tarde. In this respect, it is enough to compare the letters that Durkheim and Tarde wrote

[24] It was not possible to include in the selection of letters published below these testimonies of Lapie's; though interesting in themselves, they fall outside the present subject.

[25] On this point, see M. Cherkaoui's article in this volume.

[26] Durkheim did not consider Parodi as a 'professional sociologist': see his letter to Bouglé dated 27 May 1900 (Durkheim 1976 : 173).

to Bouglé after receiving his book *Les Sciences sociales en Allemagne.*
Whereas Durkheim worked to 'lessen the distance there is, or appears to be,
between us', Tarde limited himself to writing that he was 'delighted by the
appreciation' of his ideas.[27] And when Tarde wrote again to Bouglé (letter of
3 December 1899) about *Les Idées égalitaires*, which was critical of the theory
of imitation, it was to let him know that he preferred not to answer his
objections 'for fear of boring you'.

Let us add that Durkheim's personality, even considered independently of
his standing as a scientist, appeared as altogether different in dimension. We
might quote this opinion of Tarde by Henry Michel in a letter to Bouglé
dated November 1895: 'I may surprise you by saying that this sociologist's
conversation is a great disappointment. He appears commonplace, somewhat pretentious and exceptionally provincial. I am convinced that, even in
Sarlat where he lived for a long time, there are people who do not in any way
give this impression.' Undoubtedly, Henry Michel was often savage,
particularly towards sociologists. But no one ever gave of Durkheim a
description of that sort.

As for Durkheim, as noted before, he was looking above all for talented
workers and had few illusions about the doctrinal homogeneity of the team,
even though he wanted to stress 'what we all have in common' (letter to
Bouglé dated March 1897, below). In the same letter, he made it clear that
the preface he was to write for the first volume of the *Année sociologique*
would 'not embarrass anyone', and he was actually to submit the preface to
the collaborators of the *Année*, at least to the main ones.[28] Up to the last
moment, he concentrated on erasing the chief divergences by suggesting
modifications to Bouglé, always on the issue of the relation between
psychology and sociology.[29]

Intellectual heterogeneity remained nonetheless, as one may see by
leafing through the first volume of the *Année*. Tarde's *Opposition universelle*
was the first book to be analysed by Bouglé: he had some sympathy for it. We
have already mentioned the lack of benevolence Richard manifested towards
Suicide. Richard himself was handled roughly by Simiand about his book *Le
Socialisme et la science sociale*. Finally, a sub-section, under the charge of
Muffang, was devoted to anthropo-sociology,[30] and Durkheim felt obliged to
write a foreword dissociating himself from this type of study and pointing out

---

[27] Letter from Durkheim to Bouglé dated 14 December 1895, below. Letter from Tarde to
Bouglé dated 26 November 1895 (GED).

[28] See Durkheim's letter to Bouglé dated 26 December 1897 (Durkheim 1975 : 416).

[29] He went as far as rewriting part of a review of Bouglé's, who took fairly full account of his
suggestions. See letter to Bouglé dated 27 September 1897 (Durkheim 1975 : 410). Cf. *Année
sociologique*, vol. 1, 1898, p. 157.

[30] ['Anthropo' here in the sense of physical anthropology, theory of racial characteristics etc.
Translator].

Philippe Besnard

that the *Année* had turned 'for this section to one of the school's partisans'.[31]

Who were the collaborators of the first volume and how had they been recruited?[32] Of the twelve reviewers (Durkheim included), there were, contrary to a widespread belief, only six former students of the Ecole Normale Supérieure. There were eight *agrégés* in philosophy (Durkheim, Richard, Lapie, Bouglé, Parodi, Mauss, Simiand, Fauconnet), two *agrégés* in history (Hubert and Milhaud) and a doctor of law (E. Lévy) (see Table 3). The *agrégation* in philosophy is therefore, by far, the dominant feature, especially when one considers that Milhaud and Muffang were to be but marginal and ephemeral collaborators. As for the networks of recruitment, even though full information is lacking, they can be more or less reconstructed. Bouglé played an important role in the constitution of the initial team, since it was through him that Lapie and Parodi were recruited as well as Muffang, a colleague of his at the *lycée* of Saint-Brieuc.[33] Marcel Mauss, who followed his uncle Durkheim to Bordeaux so as to finish his studies in philosophy, abandoning application for entry to the Ecole Normale Supérieure, was from the beginning a 'recruiting agent',[34] since he introduced to Durkheim Henri Hubert and very probably Paul Fauconnet.[35] We do not know precisely how François Simiand was made known to the rest of the team. He was probably in touch with the jurist Emmanuel Lévy, since they had studied law at the same time in Paris. As for Gaston Richard, who had been a fellow-student of Durkheim's at the rue d'Ulm (Ecole Normale Supérieure), he had in all likelihood been contacted directly by Durkheim, who had reviewed his first publications with approbation.[36] It is to be noted

[31] *Année sociologique*, vol. 1, 1898, p. 519. Bouglé had drafted a more controversial foreword: see Durkheim's letter to Bouglé dated 27 September 1897 (Durkheim 1975 : 411).

[32] I do not count among the collaborators to the *Année* those authors who wrote only 'original articles': Simmel, Steinmetz, Ratzel and Charmont. Bearing in mind what was said above (n. 12), such a principle is necessary even though it leads to retaining as among the collaborators the author of only one review and to excluding Charmont, who in 1912 subscribed to the bust of Durkheim, while recognising that he did 'not deserve to count as one of the *Année's* collaborators': see his letter to Simiand dated 14 February 1912, Simiand Papers in the Institut Français d'Histoire Sociale.

[33] On Bouglé's role in this matter, see Durkheim's letters to him, one dated 25 July on Muffang, and another dated 18 September 1897 on Parodi (Durkheim 1975 : 403, 408).

[34] This is the term he applies to himself in the autobiographical text published in this volume (p.140). His role as recruiting agent was to increase later.

[35] Bouglé (1907 : 340) suggests that Fauconnet might have been a student at Bordeaux too. However, nothing to confirm this suggestion has been found in the file on Fauconnet in the Archives Nationales, where he is mentioned as occasional student at the Sorbonne. Note that Mauss and Fauconnet passed their *agrégation* the same year.

[36] See Pickering 1979 on the relationship between Durkheim and Richard. It is to be remembered too that Richard's academic career was, in a way, linked with Durkheim's. Durkheim's departure for Paris in 1902 made available a post at the University of Bordeaux. Richard, who was then still teaching in a *lycée*, although he had been a doctor of letters since 1892, filled the post vacated by Durkheim, after some administrative palaver: see Pickering 1979: 166 n. 1; and n. 55 below.

that Durkheim seems to have met all the collaborators of the first volume of the *Année* in 1897.[37]

The later recruitment of new collaborators shows a clear break, corresponding to Durkheim's arrival in Paris late in 1902. The first period (volumes 2 to 6, 1899–1903) is characterised by a recruitment with 'a Bordeaux tendency'. During this period, of the thirteen new collaborators, four (Aubin, Hourticq, Foucault and Lalo, who were, moreover, the only *agrégés* in philosophy among the new recruits) had studied in Bordeaux and had been taught by Durkheim. This fact makes more understandable the name 'Bordeaux school', which was often applied to the Durkheimians at that time. H. Bourgin was recruited by Simiand and Huvelin by Emmanuel Lévy, his colleague from Lyons.[38] Mauss and Hubert certainly were important recruiting agents *via* their teaching posts at the Ecole Pratique des Hautes Etudes. Stickney and Chaillié were registered students of the Ecole, while Fossey, Isidore Lévy, Meillet and Moret taught there.[39] We must also mention, for a complete account, the participation in volume 3 of a foreign teacher, Sigel, lecturer at the University of Warsaw. Recruitment was therefore, all in all, still rather heterogeneous, and Bouglé no longer played any role in it. As a result, former students of the Ecole Normale Supérieure became a minority in the team, since there were only two new collaborators out of thirteen who had attended the rue d'Ulm (H. Bourgin and Fossey).

By contrast, during the Paris period of Durkheim's career, corresponding to volumes 7 to 12 (1904–13), recruitment was centred on former students of the Ecole Normale Supérieure. Among the twenty-two new collaborators, sixteen had been students of the ENS. The *Année* in that period did not recruit any *agrégés* who were not of the ENS. Out of the sixteen former students from the rue d'Ulm, nine were *agrégés* in philosophy (Halbwachs, Hertz, Maître, Reynier, Bianconi, Ray, David, Davy and Laskine), three were *agrégés* in history (Demangeon, Vacher and Jeanmaire), two were *agrégés* in grammar (Gernet and Gelly), one in letters (Roussel) and one in German (Poirot). There were also two former students of the Ecole des Chartes (G. Bourgin and Marx). Three other collaborators seem to have been only registered students at the Ecole Pratique des Hautes Etudes (Beuchat, De Felice and Lafitte). Finally there was Edmond Doutté, who taught at the faculty of letters in Algiers.

The concentration of the networks of recruitment is well-marked, for, though Simiand still played a role in that respect (Halbwachs and G. Bourgin), Durkheim and, *in tandem*, Mauss and Hubert appeared more and

---

[37] This is attested in the letters, as far as Bouglé, Lapie, Parodi and Muffang are concerned.
[38] On the recruitment of Bourgin, which Herr entrusted to Simiand, see Bourgin 1938 : 349; on Huvelin's offer of collaboration, see Durkheim's letter to Bouglé (1901), below.
[39] See Mauss's biographical articles on Meillet and Moret (Mauss 1969 : 548–52, 557–60).

more as the real engineers. Durkheim was able to influence the students of the Ecole Normale Supérieure directly, since he gave his course of lectures on the history of secondary education in France at the rue d'Ulm, a course given each year from 1904 to 1913 (Mauss 1925 : 19; Lukes 1972 : 619–20). As for Mauss and Hubert, they were still operating within the Ecole Pratique des Hautes Etudes. Twelve of the new collaborators, seven of them former students of the Ecole Normale Supérieure, had been registered students of the EPHE, most of them in the fifth section (i.e. history of religions, etc., the section to which Mauss and Hubert were attached).[40]

We should give some weight, too, to a network for recruiting Durkheimians which was not of the university, and which was one of the factors of mutual acquaintance and of integration for a large part of the group: the commitment to socialism.

A first opportunity for reinforcing the unity of the initial team had been given by the Dreyfus affair, linking, for example, Durkheim and Bouglé more tightly together.[41] All the collaborators were actively pro-Dreyfus, except for Muffang, who did not wish 'at any price to associate [himself] with the protest movement for revision [i.e. of the case]' (letter to Bouglé dated 26 January 1898).[42] But most important, a considerable fraction of the Durkheimians gathered, round Lucien Herr, in the Group for Socialist Unity founded in December 1899.

This group was the militant off-shoot of the 'Société Nouvelle de Librairie et d'Edition' (New Society for Bookselling and Publishing) which had just been founded by Herr and other intellectuals close to socialism, with the purpose of preventing the bankruptcy of the Bellais press. (Bellais was a friend of Péguy, and had allowed Péguy to use his name for the press.)[43] Among the stock-holders of this society are found no less than thirteen of the collaborators current or future of the *Année* (first series), and these not minor figures: G. and H. Bourgin, Demangeon, Fauconnet, Gernet,

[40] Apart from the three already named, they are G. Bourgin, David, Davy, Gernet, Jeanmaire, Marx, Reynier and Roussel. Note too that Doutté was, it is certain, recruited by Mauss (cf. Mauss's autobiographical text in this volume, p. 142; and Mauss 1969 : 520).

[41] On the Dreyfus Affair and its consequences for the commitment of university teachers (people's universities, Ligue des Droits de l'Homme etc.), Bouglé wrote, 'Moral and political sympathies did, no doubt, serve the cause of the social sciences: they spread a soft carpet beneath its feet' (Bouglé 1907 : 348). Right-wing critics of Durkheimianism drew on this 'confession' of Bouglé's, which they took as explaining the change in attitude of socialist intellectuals like Lucien Herr towards Durkheimian sociology, to which they had at first been opposed. See, for example, the book by Lasserre (1913), the polemicist of Action française.

[42] Muffang's attitude can be explained, no doubt, by his need to maintain good relations with the military authorities, for his anthropometrical research. See Foubert's letter to Bouglé, dated 25 January 1898 (GED).

[43] On the Society and its various activities, see Bourgin 1938 : 259–65; Andler 1932 : 181–96; Lindenberg and Meyer 1977 : 170–7. On the role played by socialism in integrating the Durkheimian group, see also Clark 1973 : 186–8.

Halbwachs, Hertz, Hubert, E. Lévy, Mauss, Roussel, Simiand and Vacher.[44] Simiand and H. Bourgin were members of the board of directors alongside Lucien Herr, Léon Blum and Mario Roques. These university teachers met not only at the stock-holders' meetings, which were fairly frequent, but also in common activities: thus, the Socialist School (1899–1902), which, unlike the people's universities, delivered formal lectures to students; in these, E. Lévy, Simiand, Mauss and Fauconnet took part.

This society published, among other things, the *Bibliothèque socialiste* and the review *Notes critiques – Sciences sociales* (1900–6), in which Simiand was the driving force. Now, as Lapie noted in his letter dated 18 February 1900 (below), almost all of the *Année*'s collaborators, including Durkheim, reviewed works for *Notes critiques*. In 1900, the only ones, apart from Bouglé and his friends Lapie and Parodi, not to participate were Richard, I. Lévy and Muffang (who was about to leave the *Année*). The interpenetration of the two publications was to continue: some were to be recruited to the *Année* after reviewing for *Notes critiques* (Maître, Vacher, Gelly, and Gernet), whereas, in the case of others, their collaboration was fixed at about the same date (H. Bourgin, Chaillié, Halbwachs, Beuchat, Reynier and Stickney).

The New Society for Bookselling and Publishing and the commitment of several Durkheimians to socialism were, in all likelihood, major factors in the integration of the more active collaborators of the *Année*; there were, however, three exceptions: Richard, then teacher at the *lycée* of Le Havre, who showed little sympathy for socialism; Bouglé, who was to lean towards the radical-socialist party; and, of course, Durkheim himself, despite his participation in *Notes critiques*.

As Andler noted, 'the friendship formed in this group proved still active long after' (1932 : 196). It is not, then, surprising that some of them came together again during the war in the Ministry of Armaments which had been entrusted to Albert Thomas: among the Durkheimians, let us mention especially Simiand, but also H. Bourgin, Halbwachs, Hubert and Maître.[45]

Fractions and stratification

Neither the existence of solid links of friendship between certain collaborators of the *Année* (not to mention kinship – Durkheim and Mauss, and the brothers Bourgin) nor the progressive homogenisation of the recruitment exclude a certain lack of integration in the group as a whole. G. Davy remarked, 'There were no councils, no meetings, no watchwords.' And, in his words, 'The little community gathered in its entirety around the master only once, and then only as an expression of affection' and to present him with a

[44] See Vogt 1976 : 118.
[45] This information from Bourgin 1938 : 382–3, 442–7; Andler 1932 : 196–7.

bust of himself to commemorate his twenty-five years in higher education.[46] Davy does not mention another occasion on which the group met, i.e. the dinner, at which Jaurès was guest of honour, which took place at Durkheim's house on the occasion of the tenth anniversary of the *Année*, probably in 1907 (Bourgin 1938 : 192). This, no doubt, was the 'collective banquet' to which Fauconnet alluded in his letter published below. The same letter reveals the existence of a project for a *Festschrift* for Durkheim's fiftieth birthday.

The fact that such a project was never realised and that meetings of all the collaborators at once were extremely rare suggests that the integration of the Durkheimian group was much weaker than is generally imagined. To quote, haphazardly, some other indications of the low level of interaction and even of mutual acquaintance: when, in 1912, subscriptions were being sought for the bust of Durkheim, Simiand wrote, in error, not to R. Hourticq, Durkheim's former student in Bordeaux and collaborator of the *Année* for ten years, but to his brother, former student of the Ecole Normale Supérieure.[47] In his book on the Ecole Normale, H. Bourgin did not even mention Parodi's name, though he had been a student there and had been a regular collaborator of the *Année*; and, speaking of Hubert, Bourgin regretted that he 'had not known him better' (1938 : 382). Bouglé, who lived in Montpellier and then in Toulouse until 1907, pursued a close correspondence with Durkheim, Lapie and Parodi, but received letters only infrequently from Fauconnet, Halbwachs, Simiand and Mauss, and apparently none from other Durkheimians.

The *Année*'s team of collaborators thus did not constitute a group whose members were personally known to each other. There were close relationships only within fractions of the whole. A sociogram of the group tentatively showing links of friendship, of collaboration, intellectual affinities and the various occasions for interaction would certainly display Durkheim in the central position (see diagram). But it would also reveal the existence of 'sociometric cliques', relatively autonomous and each one grouped around a leader at the centre of communications. The two most easily identifiable sub-groups of this type are the one which assembles around Simiand, Halbwachs and the Bourgin brothers, and the one constituted by Bouglé, Lapie and Parodi.[48] As for the pair Mauss–Hubert, it is attached directly to

---

[46] Davy 1919 : 195. Simiand assumed responsibility for the collection of subscriptions for this bust; early in 1912 he had letters on this subject (Institut Français d'Histoire Sociale) from Aubin, Bianconi, David, Davy, Foucault, Hourticq and Charmont (cf. n. 32). The meeting took place, in fact, on 8 May 1913 at Durkheim's house (cf. Durkheim's letter to Davy, dated 17 April 1913, in Davy 1973 : 303).

[47] See R. Hourticq's letter to Simiand dated 6 April 1913 (Institut Français d'Histoire Sociale).

[48] Bouglé's central position in this group derives in part from the fact that Lapie and Parodi were not very close to one another.

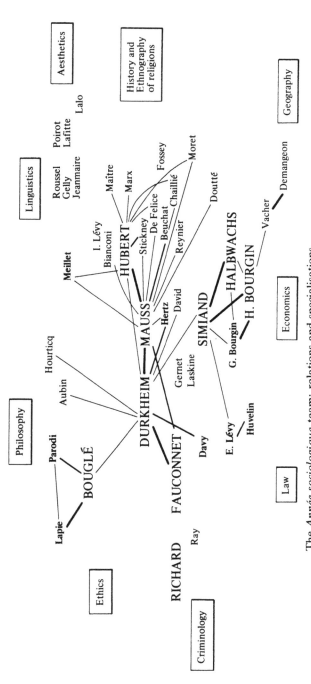

The *Année sociologique* team: relations and specialisations

The lines between individuals symbolise relations (of collaborators, teacher–pupil, friends, etc.) known to be of a certain importance. They vary in thickness according to the intensity of these relations. Likewise, the names of the *Année* collaborators are printed in varying sizes of type according to the size of their contribution.

27

Philippe Besnard

Durkheim and gathers round itself most of the *Année*'s younger collaborators, who had been pupils of Mauss, of Hubert and/or of Durkheim. Among the closest to Mauss were Bianconi, Beuchat, De Felice and Reynier; David and Hertz had been in direct contact with Durkheim, while Stickney the American, Chaillié and Marx were chiefly linked with Hubert.[49] Fauconnet, very close to Durkheim, also gravitates about this central kernel. Otherwise there are the dyads of the jurists of Lyons, E. Lévy and Huvelin, and of the geographers, Demangeon and Vacher; and, finally, there are completely isolated individuals having only episodic relations with the central figure, Richard being the perfect example.

About Richard, Lapie wrote to Bouglé in 1903 that he did not know that, inside the *Année*, 'he was on our side' (letter dated 4 March 1903, below). It might be an exaggeration to say that Durkheim had a strategy aimed at the prevention of the formation of coalitions, some of which (like the alliance of Richard with the Bouglé group) might have imperilled the doctrinal orientation he intended to impress on the *Année*.[50] Nevertheless, the increasing homogeneity of the *Année*, along with the progressive concentration of power in Durkheim's hands, are difficult to understand except as the result of a deliberate choice.

We have already noted the concentration of the networks of recruitment: Simiand enrolled no new collaborators from 1905 onwards, and Bouglé, after the first volume, recruited only his friend Charmont, author of one article. Another indication of the increasing centralisation may be found in the evolution of the designation of responsibilities in the *Année*'s table of contents: from volume 4 on (1902), Bouglé, Richard and Simiand are no longer designated as responsible for a section. Durkheim's preponderant role, attested in his correspondence, in the distribution of tasks and books is known. In addition, it was he who often acted as intermediary between the different collaborators.[51] Another means deliberately employed by Durkheim to reduce the expression of discord was to insist on impersonality. This can clearly be seen in a letter he wrote to X. Léon on 21 September 1902, in which he complained of the aggressiveness of the *Revue de métaphysique et de morale* towards the *Année*: what he deplored most of all was that '*my sociologism*', '*my method* ... [should be] presented as impedimenta which

[49] See Mauss 1925, Hubert 1979 and various biographical sources (obituaries etc.).
[50] Richard's isolation sprang also from his age and his post as teacher in the *lycée* of Le Havre until 1902. Lapie was to meet Richard at the University of Bordeaux in November 1903. He gave an appreciative review of Richard's *Notions élémentaires de sociologie* in vol. 8 of the *Année sociologique*, 1905, pp. 171–5. In the preceding volume, Parodi had expressed major reservations about another of Richard's books, *Année sociologique*, vol. 7, 1904, pp. 161–6.
[51] See, for example, the letter to Bouglé dated 6 July 1900 (below), in which Durkheim does a 'job' on Richard's behalf. Likewise, Bouglé and Mauss related *via* Durkheim.

28

my collaborators are invited to discard', when the *Année* was 'essentially a collective and impersonal work'.[52]

Durkheim's efforts were crowned with success, for there was no dramatic break-up – and in particular no schism by any sub-group – within the team. It is true that the contribution of the Bouglé group decreased constantly.[53] But such exclusions and breaches as there were concerned only collaborators who had been marginal (Muffang) or isolated (Richard).[54]

Despite the centralisation which characterised the functioning of the *Année*, Durkheim did not hold absolute sway. When there were important decisions to be taken concerning the future of the review, he did not fail to consult the team's council of officers, as it were, consisting of Bouglé, Fauconnet, Hubert, Mauss and Simiand. Such was the case in February 1902, when Durkheim contemplated dividing the *Année* into two, which would have meant separating the articles and the reviews. But as Bouglé and Simiand were in favour of the *status quo*, while 'Fauconnet, Hubert and Mauss, though accepting the idea of a change, do not agree on the ways and means', Durkheim came over to the support of the 'present system'. 'To change it would have required a device favoured by all, not a disputed arrangement' (letters from Durkheim to Simiand dated 15 and 18 February 1902, below). In the first of these letters, Durkheim brought the inner group of the *Année* likely to supply articles down in number to five or six persons, himself included.[55] The names are those found in the letter Fauconnet wrote to Bouglé five years later (below); in connection with the *Festschrift* envisaged as a homage to Durkheim, Fauconnet distinguished a central kernel (comprising Simiand, Mauss, Hubert, Bouglé and himself, to whom he added two other collaborators likely to provide sociological contributions of quality, viz. Hertz and Huvelin) from other

---

[52] Durkheim 1975 : 465. The anonymous author of this review of the *Année* in the *Revue de métaphysique et de morale* was none other than Elie Halévy (see letters from Halévy to Bouglé).

[53] Lapie and Parodi contributed nothing to the last volume (1913), contrary to the information given on the title-page, where Parodi's name still figured. It is true that Lapie had entered on an administrative career two years earlier by becoming rector of the Academy of Toulouse (i.e. director of education in the Toulouse area) in 1911.

[54] The case of Richard is obviously the more serious of the two, when one considers the size of his contribution to the *Année*. For the intellectual reasons for his departure, see Pickering 1979. It may be noted too that he left shortly after his establishment as permanent professor of social science at Bordeaux in November 1906, this being the post left vacant by Durkheim. Before this, Richard from 1902 to 1905 was employed only as lecturer in social science, and was made professor of philosophy in 1905. Note also that Richard's departure coincides with the 1907 crisis and reorganisation of the *Année*.

[55] The possible sixth is either Fauconnet, because he had not written an article for the *Année*, or else Bouglé, because of his heterodoxy. The articles had to come 'from *ourselves* or from people who agree with us wholeheartedly'.

friends, among whom he named Aubin, Hourticq, Lapie and Richard.[56]

These distinctions are not surprising: the distribution of power within the *Année* was, in large measure, the reflection of the considerable disparity between the various contributions, never to be lost sight of when speaking of the *Année sociologique* team. This will be seen more clearly in Table 1, which classes the collaborators by order of the decreasing importance of their contribution (see the notes to Table 1). A large number of people took part in the *Année* only in an episodic way and the core of the work was done by a fairly small group. Durkheim, Mauss and Hubert were, between the three of them, responsible for nine out of the eighteen articles written by collaborators of the *Année*, for 44 per cent of the reviews of one page or more, for 50 per cent of the short notes, and for 58 per cent of the notices (for definitions, see the notes to Table I). The nine principal collaborators of the *Année* wrote 78 per cent of the full reviews, 84 per cent of the short notes and almost all the notices. It is then to be stressed, for it does not always so happen in this kind of enterprise, that those who played a role in deciding on the *Année*'s policy all made a major contribution to the collective task. But the converse is not altogether true: Table I shows, intercalated between 'officers' of the *Année*, Gaston Richard and Hubert Bourgin (whose proportional contribution is all the more striking since they did not participate in all twelve volumes). Interestingly, these two collaborators, whose active role was not commensurate with their contribution, were the two who, at different dates and by different means, withdrew from the Durkheimian group.

Finally, it should be noted that these indications of the distribution of power within the *Année* point in fact to an 'emergency council'; the indications relate to moments when important transformations were contemplated. Three crises show through the correspondence: the first in 1900 (see Lapie's letters dated 18 February and 11 July 1900, below), probably linked to the appearance of *Notes critiques*; the second, as we have seen, in early 1902 when a division into two of the *Année* was mooted; the third in 1907 when this arrangement finally prevailed – the articles were detached from the *Année* which thenceforward appeared only every third year (1910 and 1913), so that the articles 'become the matter of a discrete library', the collection *Travaux de l'Année sociologique* (Durkheim 1910: i).[57]

Bouglé's letters to Halévy bear witness to the 1907 crisis which seems to

[56] Hertz and Huvelin had just published articles in the *Année*. But that was also the case with Richard, whom Fauconnet seems not to have suspected, at this date, of being about to leave the *Année*.

[57] There is also a practical reason for these moments of self-questioning in 1902 and 1907: every five years, Durkheim had to establish a fresh contract with the Alcan publishing house.

have been very serious. Bouglé wrote, notably, 'Basically, apart from the librarian, what is the personnel of the *Année* now? A male-nurse, a fanatic and a maniac (the maniac is myself).'[58] That last remark dulls the edge of Bouglé's comment, in which one must allow, as so often in his letters, for his taste for raillery, which he aims against himself as well as others. Then again, this was the period when Bouglé was having some trouble, over his book *Essais sur le régime des castes* (1908), with what he called the 'taboo-totem clan' or 'the United Sociological Party': 'I shall be well and truly hauled over the coals when *Castes* appears in print, by the taboo-totem clan. For, between ourselves, having, at Durkheim's bidding, sought Mauss's comments, I took not the least notice of them! And then, when it is proved that I can contribute nothing useful to philosophy, nor even to sociology, I shall have to go back to politics.'[59]

There is nothing surprising about these crises. What is astonishing is that they were not more frequent and more serious and that it was possible to perform for so long the colossal task the *Année* required. The letters are filled with the collaborators' lamentations when the books for review rain down on them in tens. Yet there were hardly any defectors among the 'workers' Durkheim had gathered round himself. To be sure, after 1907 the enterprise lost steam somewhat, when everyone was wanting to devote more time to his own work.[60] But the differences of doctrine, the low level of integration of the team as a whole and the crises – in short, all the facts I have insisted on so as to correct the image generally given of the Durkheimian group – should not conceal the fact that the *Année sociologique* was a formidable achievement for Durkheim, and that, without the *Année*, there would probably have been no reason to speak of a 'French school of sociology' and even less to speak of 'the Durkheimian school'.

[58] Letter to Halévy, undated (GED). The librarian to whom Bouglé alludes is obviously Simiand, librarian to the Ministry of Trade. The 'male-nurse' may be Fauconnet (because of his wife's poor health); and, in that case, the 'fanatic' would probably be Mauss. It is of interest to confront Bouglé's private complaints with the public vision he gave of the *Année* at the same time: 'It is generally agreed that the *Année* is a well-run ship: the fact is the crew likes the ship and its captain' (Bouglé 1907 : 349).

[59] Undated letter to Halévy (GED). The letter in question is obviously the one Mauss wrote to Bouglé on the 23 July 1907 (Mauss 1979). In the end, Bouglé did, up to a certain point, take account of Mauss's remarks: 'I have begun the task of correcting, or at least attenuating, *Castes*, so that Mauss shall not have pronounced his oracle in vain' (letter to Halévy, undated). His book was the first in the collection *Travaux de l'Année sociologique*. It was reviewed in the *Année* by Reynier, a pupil of Mauss, who gave it a rather short and unsympathetic analysis: *Année sociologique*, vol. 11, 1910, pp. 384–7.

[60] See, for example, Fauconnet's letter below, and Durkheim's preface to vol. 11 of the *Année* (Durkheim 1910 : i).

Philippe Besnard

Table 1 *Contributions to the* Année sociologique *1st series*

	Volumes	Articles	Full Reviews	Short Notes	Notices	Introductions
E. Durkheim	1–12	6	282	216	154	15
M. Mauss	1–12	4	270	194	444	10
H. Hubert	1–12	2	231	165	298	9
F. Simiand	1–12	1	139	115	338	15
H. Bourgin	4–12	1	99	91	112	11
G. Richard	1–10	1	101	63	11	2
P. Fauconnet	1–12	—	116	60	24	3
C. Bouglé	1–12	3	79	60	18	3
M. Halbwachs	8–12	—	70	10	52	—
P. Lapie	1–11	—	45	21	5	—
P. Huvelin	6–12	1	41	2	—	—
D. Parodi	1–11	—	33	26	3	—
G. Bourgin	8, 10–12	—	24	12	2	1
A. Meillet	5–12	1	19	2	5	3
R. Hertz	8–12	1	19	3	3	—
E. Lévy	1–12	—	17	17	2	—
G. Davy	11–12	—	19	4	—	—
A. Aubin	4–12	—	19	14	—	—
R. Hourticq	5–12	—	18	8	—	—
J. Ray	11–12	—	12	7	2	—
P. De Felice	9–12	—	11	8	3	—
H. Muffang	1–3	—	8	8	4	—
I. Lévy	2, 3, 6–8	—	8	8	—	—
A. Bianconi	8, 10–12	—	10	2	—	—
L. Gernet	11–12	—	9	1	1	—
J. Marx	12	—	7	6	—	—
E. Laskine	12	—	9	—	—	—
A. Milhaud	1	—	8	2	—	—
J. Reynier	8, 11, 12	—	6	2	2	—
M. David	11, 12	—	5	2	1	—
H. Beuchat	8, 10, 12	1 (coll.)	3	3	1	—
J. Poirot	9, 10	—	4	1	—	—
G. Gelly	9, 12	—	2	4	—	—
R. Chaillié	6, 9, 10	—	1	6	—	—
J. T. Stickney	3, 5, 6	—	4	—	—	—
A. Vacher	8, 9	—	4	—	—	—
E. Doutté	12	—	2	2	—	—
H. Jeanmaire	12	—	3	—	—	—
C. Fossey	6, 7	—	1	3	—	—
F. Sigel	3	—	1	2	1	—
P. Roussel	12	—	1	2	—	—
M. Foucault	2, 7	—	2	—	—	—
A. Demangeon	12	—	2	—	—	—
J.-P. Lafitte	11	—	1	—	—	—
C. Lalo	6	—	1	—	—	—
C. Maître	7	—	1	—	—	—
A. Moret	5	—	—	1	—	—
Unknown or uncertain	–	–	1	9	68	—
Totals		18	1,767	1,162	1,553	72

Note to Table 1

This table classes the collaborators of the *Année sociologique* 1st series according to the relative importance of their overall participation in the journal. The numerical distribution of the reviews has been established on the basis of an inventory compiled by Howard Andrews (University of Toronto), using a computer. I contributed to this inventory by revising all the doubtful attributions and attributing to one author or another the unsigned reviews (unsigned short reviews being very numerous). In addition, I added to the inventory the 'original memoirs' (articles) written by the *Année*'s collaborators, along with the introductions to individual volumes, to sections, sub-sections or groups of books.

Three types of review have been distinguished by the criterion of length: full reviews (a page or more), short notes (between six lines and a page) and notices (any commentary of less than six lines). No account has been taken of mere bibliographic references.

Articles written by two co-authors have been counted twice (whence a disparity with the total). By contrast a ½ point has been allowed for the few reviews by two co-authors (8 full reviews, 1 short note, 1 notice) and for those reviews which might be attributed to either of two authors (7 full reviews, 61 short notes, 432 notices). The case arises particularly frequently with Hubert and Mauss and with Simiand and H. Bourgin. The same procedure has been adopted for the introductions. The category 'unknown or uncertain' designates cases where the author might be any one of three or more.

This statistical table relates to the number of reviews and not to the number of books or articles reviewed, which is somewhat greater, as reviews may bear on a group of books or articles. In the table, only the first count has been kept, so as to avoid undue complication. But some overall information may be given here on the second count: in the twelve volumes of the *Année sociologique* 1st series, 1,767 full reviews took account of 2,003 books or articles, 1,162 short notes took account of 1,215 books or articles, and 1,553 notices took account of 1,581 books or articles; 4,203 books or articles were mentioned without further comment. Thus the total of all books and articles reviewed and mentioned in the twelve volumes is 9,002. The order of the collaborators by size of contribution remains unchanged even on the calculation of works each reviewed. The only difference to be noted is that Mauss reviewed a greater number of works in the full reviews than Durkheim did.

This table gives a fairly precise idea of the contribution of each collaborator of the *Année sociologique*. However the average length of the full reviews varies according to author. Simiand, for example, often wrote very long reviews, so that if the number of pages were to be counted he would come close to the leading three. Finally, it is to be noted that this table gives only an imperfect expression of the relative importance of the collaborators at any one time, since many of them did not participate in all twelve volumes: Halbwachs, for instance, contributed only to the last five volumes.

Table 2 *Dates of publication of the 12 volumes of the* Année sociologique *1st series*

Volumes	Years of publication	Volumes	Years of publication
1 (1896–1897)	1898	7 (1902–1903)	1904
2 (1897–1898)	1899	8 (1903–1904)	1905
3 (1898–1899)	1900	9 (1904–1905)	1906
4 (1899–1900)	1901	10 (1905–1906)	1907
5 (1900–1901)	1902	11 (1906–1909)	1910
6 (1901–1902)	1903	12 (1909–1912)	1913

The *Année sociologique* supposedly covered literature published between 1 July and 30 June in the two years mentioned on the cover; the last two volumes each covered three years.

Table 3 *University career of the collaborators of the Année sociologique 1st series (see note on following page)*

No.	Name	Participation in volumes of the Année	Matriculation Ecole Normale Supérieure	Degrees – Letters Agrégation	Degrees – Letters Doctorate	Degrees – Law Doctorate	Degrees – Law Agrégation	Ecole des Chartes Diploma	EPHE	Faculty of Letters: Maître de conférence or chargé de cours	Faculty of Letters: Professeur	Sorbonne	Faculty of Law: Chargé de cours	Faculty of Law: Professeur	EPHE: Maître de conférence or chargé de cours	EPHE: Directeur d'études	Collège de France
1	Durkheim, Emile (1858–1917)	1–12	1879	Philo. 1882	1893					1887	1896	1902					
2	Richard, Gaston (1860–1945)	1–10	1880	Philo. 1885	1891					1902	1905						
3	Muffang, Henri (1864–?)	1–3		Gram. 1890													
4	Foucault, Marcel (1865–?)	2, 7		Philo. 1891	1901					1906	1909						
5	Meillet, Antoine (1866–1936)	5–12		Gram. 1889	1897				1887						1889	1896	1906
6	Doutté, Edmond (1867–1926)	12								1901	1908						
7	Moret, Alexandre (1868–1938)	5		Hist. 1893	1903				1894	1897		1920			1899	1905	1923
8	Fossey, Charles (1869–1946)	6, 7	1891	Lett. 1894	1902				1894						1899		1906
9	Lapie, Paul (1869–1927)	1–11		Philo. 1893	1902					1898	1907						
10	Bouglé, Célestin (1870–1940)	1–12	1890	Philo. 1893	1899					1893	1901	1907					
11	Parodi, Dominique (1870–1955)	1–11	1890	Philo. 1893													
12	Aubin, Abel (1870–?)	4–12		Philo. 1898													
13	Chaillié, René (1870–1923)	6, 9, 10							1902								
14	Lévy, Emmanuel (1871–1943)	1–12				1896	1901						1896	1901			
15	Lévy, Isidore (1871–1959)	2, 3, 6–8		Hist. 1894	1926				1896	1919		1924			1899	1905	1932

No.	Name	Courses	Entry	Degree					
16	Milhaud, Albert (1871–?)	1		Hist. 1894		1889			
17	Demangeon, Albert (1872–1940)	12	*1892	Hist. 1895	1905	1896			
18	Hubert, Henri (1872–1927)	1–12	1892	Hist. 1895		1896	1905 1908 1911	1901 1908	
19	Mauss, Marcel (1872–1950)	1–12		Philo. 1895					1901 1907 1931
20	Hourticq, Robert (1873–?)	5–12		Philo. 1899					
21	Huvelin, Paul (1873–1924)	6–12		1897 1899		1898	1898 1899		
22	Poirot, Jean (1873–1924)	9, 10	*1894	Germ. 1902	1913		1920 1920	1911	1932
23	Simiand, François (1873–1935)	1–12	*1893	Philo. 1896	1904		1920		
24	Vacher, Antoine (1873–1920)	8, 9	*1895	Hist. 1900	1908		1905 1909		
25	Bourgin, Hubert (1874–1955)	4–12	*1895	Lett. 1898	1905 1906				
26	Fauconnet, Paul (1874–1938)	1–12		Philo. 1895	1920				
27	Stickney, Joseph (1874–1904)	3, 5, 6			1903				
28	Maître, Claude (1876–1925)	7	1895	Philo. 1898			1907 1921		
29	Halbwachs, Maurice (1877–1945)	8–12	1898	Philo. 1901	1913 1909		1918 1919 1935		1944
30	Lalo, Charles (1877–1953)	6		Philo. 1901	1908		1933 193? 1933		
31	Beuchat, Henri (1878–1914)	8, 10, 12				1902			
32	Bourgin, Georges (1879–1958)	8, 10–12				1903		1924	
33	De Felice, Philippe (1880–1964)	9–12				1903			
34	Lafitte, Jean-Paul (1881–?)	11				1907			
35	Hertz, Robert (1881–1915)	8–12	*1901	Philo. 1904					
36	Reynier, Jean (1881–1915)	8, 11, 12	*1903	Philo. 1908		1905			
37	Roussel, Pierre (1881–1945)	12	1901	Lett. 1905	1916	1906	1919 1935		
38	Bianconi, Antoine (1882–1915)	8, 10–12	*1903	Philo. 1906					
39	Gernet, Louis (1882–1964)	11, 12	1902	Gram. 1905	1917	1907	1921 1923	1948	
40	Davy, Georges (1883–1976)	11, 12	1905	Philo. 1908	1922	1910	1919 1922 1944		
41	Gelly, Georges (1883–1917)	9, 12	1903	Gram. 1912		1905			
42	Jeanmaire, Henri (1884–1960)	12	1905	Hist. 1909	1939	1907	1921		
43	Marx, Jean (1884–1974)	12				1912 1907			
44	Ray, Jean (1884–1943)	11, 12	1904	Philo. 1907	1926 1914			1947	
45	David, Maxime (1885–1914)	11, 12	*1904	Philo. 1907		1907		1924 1927	
46	Laskine, Edmond (1890–1943)	12	1908	Philo. 1911					

Note to Table 3

The collaborators of the *Année sociologique* 1st series (1898–1913) are presented in this table in the order of their dates of birth, which allows some of them to be seen in relation to each other (e.g. Hubert–Mauss or Lapie–Bouglé–Parodi) and permits the display of certain evolutions within the typical career (thus the younger collaborators are almost all ex-students of the Ecole Normale Supérieure). To find particular names, consult the alphabetical index below which refers to line-numbers of the table.

– F. Sigel, teacher at the University of Warsaw, who contributed two reviews and a note to volume 3, does not figure in the list.

– For the Ecole Normale Supérieure, the dates given are the dates of matriculation. The asterisk signifies that the candidate had been accepted for admission the previous year (matriculation delayed by military service).

– For the Ecole Pratique des Hautes Etudes (EPHE), the dates are those of the first registration as *élève titulaire* (full student) in the fourth or fifth sections, or in both at the same time.

– Simiand was librarian in the Ministry of Trade from 1900 on and professor at the Conservatoire National des Arts et Métiers in 1919.

Sources: Victor Karady kindly allowed me to consult his valuable sets of card-files. The information thereby obtained was filled out from the most various sources: the Directory of *L'Instruction publique*, the Administrative Bulletin of *L'Instruction publique*, the Directory of the Association of Friends of the Ecole Normale Supérieure, individual files in the Archives Nationales, various sets of bibliographical card-files etc. The more detailed biographic information on the Durkheimians so gathered may be consulted at the Maison des Sciences de l'Homme, Paris.

Alphabetical index to Table 3

Philippe Besnard

References

Andler, C. 1896. 'Sociologie et démocratie', *Revue de métaphysique et de morale*, vol. 4, pp. 243–56. 'Réponse aux objections', *ibid.*, pp. 371–3.
    1932. *La Vie de Lucien Herr* (new edition. Paris: Maspero, 1977).
Bouglé, C. 1896a. *Les Sciences sociales en Allemagne. Les Méthodes actuelles*. Paris: Alcan.
    1896b. 'Sociologie, psychologie et histoire', *Revue de métaphysique et de morale*, vol. 4, pp. 362–70.
    1904. '"L'Année sociologique" et le progrès de la sociologie', *Revue scientifique*, no. 21, 21 May, pp. 653–8.
    1907. 'L'Année sociologique', *Pages libres*, no. 353, 5 Oct., pp. 337–51.
Bourgin, H. 1938. *De Jaurès à Léon Blum. L'Ecole normale et la politique*. Paris: Fayard (reprint Gordon and Breach, 1970).
Brunschvicg, L., and Halévy, E. 1894. 'L'Année philosophique 1893', *Revue de métaphysique et de morale*, vol. 2, pp. 563–90.
Clark, T.N. 1968. 'The Structure and Functions of a Research Institute: *The Année sociologique*', *Archives européennes de sociologie*, vol. 9, no. 1, pp. 72–91.
    1973. *Prophets and Patrons : The French University and the Emergence of Social Sciences*. Cambridge, Mass.: Harvard University Press.
Davy, G. 1919. 'Emile Durkheim : l'homme', *Revue de métaphysique et de morale*, vol. 26, pp. 181–98.
    1973. *L'Homme, le fait social et le fait politique*. Paris: Mouton.
Durkheim, E. 1886. 'Les Etudes de science sociale', *Revue philosophique*, vol. 22, pp. 61–80 (republished pp. 184–214 in Durkheim 1970).
    1893. *De la division du travail social*. Paris: Alcan (*The Division of Labor in Society*. New York: Macmillan, 1933).
    1898. Préface, *Année sociologique*, vol. 1, pp. i–vii.
    1910. Préface, *Année sociologique*, vol. 11, pp. i–iii.
    1970. *La Science sociale et l'action*. Paris: Presses Universitaires de France.
    1975. 'Lettres d'Emile Durkheim', pp. 389–487, in E. Durkheim *Textes 2. Religion, morale, anomie*. Paris: Editions de Minuit.
    1976. 'Textes inédits ou inconnus d'Emile Durkheim', *Revue française de sociologie*, vol. 17, no. 2, pp. 165–96.
Fauconnet, P. 1898. Review of *Le Suicide; Revue philosophique*, vol. 45, pp. 422–31.
Hubert, H. 1979. 'Texte autobiographique de Henri Hubert', *Revue française de sociologie*, vol. 20, no. 1, pp. 205–7.
Lapie, P. 1895. 'L'Année sociologique 1894', *Revue de métaphysique et de morale*, vol. 3, pp. 563–90.
    1896. 'L'Année sociologique 1895. La morale sociale', *Revue de métaphysique et de morale*, vol. 4, pp. 338–61.
Lasserre, P. 1913. *La Doctrine officielle de l'Université*. Paris: Mercure de France.
Lindenberg, D., and Meyer, P.A. 1977. *Lucien Herr, le socialisme et son destin*. Paris: Calmann-Lévy.
Lukes, S. 1972. *Emile Durkheim : His Life and Work, a Historical and Critical Study*. New York: Harper and Row.
Mauss, M. 1925. 'In Memoriam, l'oeuvre inédite de Durkheim et de ses collaborateurs', *Année sociologique*, new series, vol. 1, pp. 7–29.
    1927. 'Divisions et proportions des divisions de la sociologie', *Année sociologique* new series, vol. 2, pp. 94–176.

1969. *Oeuvres*, vol. 3. Paris: Editions de Minuit.

1979. 'Lettre de Mauss à Bouglé sur les castes', *Revue française de sociologie*, vol. 20, no. 1, pp. 45–8.

Pickering, W. S. F. 1979. 'Gaston Richard : collaborateur et adversaire', *Revue française de sociologie*, vol. 20, no. 1, pp. 163–82.

Richard, G. 1898. Review of *Le Suicide*, *Année sociologique*, vol. 1, pp. 397–406.

Simiand, F. 1897. 'L'Année sociologique française 1896', *Revue de métaphysique et de morale*, vol. 5, pp. 489–519.

1898. 'L'Année sociologique 1897', *Revue de métaphysique et de morale*, vol. 6, pp. 608–53.

Vogt, W.P. 1976. 'The Politics of Academic Sociological Theory in France, 1890–1914'. Doctoral dissertation (Ph. D.) Indiana University.

Documents: correspondence concerning the 'Année sociologique'

The letters presented here have been chosen to document and illustrate the majority of the points touched upon in the preceding article: the birth of a sociological vocation in young philosophy professors (Lapie and Bouglé); doctrinal discussions with Durkheim; the beginnings and the functioning of the journal, the *Année sociologique*. The majority of these letters have been published in French in the *Revue française de sociologie* (vol. 17, no. 2, 1976 and vol. 20, no. 1, 1979) and others in E. Durkheim *Textes* (vol. 2, Paris, Editions de Minuit, 1975). For the latter we have reviewed the transcription, corrected some errors, and added certain passages that had not been reproduced there.

Letters from Emile Durkheim to Célestin Bouglé

Bordeaux, 179 boulevard de Talence,
14 December 1895

Dear Sir and Colleague,
I thank you very much for your kind thought in sending me your book. I have read it with keen interest, or rather reread it, for I followed your articles in the *Revue de métaphysique*. I have, in fact, noticed that it was unanimously well received, deservedly so. It is a work which cannot fail to do us great credit on the other side of the Rhine; and, by showing the Germans how carefully and sympathetically we study them, it will perhaps lead them to be less uninterested in what we are doing. For it seems to me, though I might be wrong, that Germany is now making the same mistake we made before 1870, and is shutting itself off from the outside world.

I also thank you for the attention you have given to my own works and for the great courtesy you paid me with your most interesting discussion. It is difficult for me to answer you by letter; however much I may wish to lessen the distance which separates us or seems to separate us, and, though I believe it quite possible to do so, I don't wish to dog you with arguments under the

40

pretext of thanking you – I feel I must, however, indicate to you one or two points on which I have failed to gain your understanding of my thinking.

(1) I have never said that sociology shares nothing with psychology and I wholly accept your statement on page 151, namely that it is a psychology *but distinct from individual psychology*. I have never thought otherwise. I have defined the social facts as actions and representations, but *sui generis*; I have said that the social being is a psychic individuality but of a new kind (p. 127). However, that being said, I draw the conclusion that one is not allowed to treat collective psychology as a prolongation, an enlargement, a new illustration of individual psychology. Would that be where you cease to follow me? It seems to me, however, that once the principle is laid down the consequence necessarily follows.

(2) What realism is there in saying that *inside the facts* (and not outside them) there exists a category with specific characteristics, which consequently must be abstracted from the real and so studied separately? In what way is this to hypostatise them? Perhaps I could refer you to what I say on the subject in the note on page 127. Besides, you seem yourself to have very lively sense of the specificity of social facts. So, how can we not agree on the two essential points mentioned above and which, basically, are but one. Now, they are the ones I feel most strongly about.

(3) I never meant to say that tendencies, needs etc. are not factors of development (see p. 119); but, to explain the changes which originate thus, the tendencies themselves must have changed and, to explain that, one must look outside them for the causes which have so determined them.

Forgive me these explanations. By showing you how much I wish to be understood by you, they only prove how much value I attach to your work. See nothing else in them.

Please accept, my dear colleague, my best and most distinguished greetings.

Bordeaux, 179 boulevard de Talence,
24 March 1896

My dear Sir,
       I thank you for your thoughtfulness in writing to me about Andler's article, and I beg your pardon for not having replied immediately. Yesterday I was finishing off my first-term course, and, as a final lecture is always a little harder than the others, during the last days of that week I was extremely busy.

I had read the article before receiving your letter, and I too thought it useful to give a reply. As it would hardly be possible for me to do it myself, because of lack of available time, I was thinking of giving the job to one of my former students who is now an *agrégé* in philosophy and to whom the *Revue de métaphysique* has opened its pages. I had him in mind all the more naturally because he is something of an *alter ego* to me, and what is more I had already pointed out to him your article in the January number, with the suggestion he might answer the question you were posing. But it is clear that if, as your letter seems to indicate, you are yourself ready to intervene, you are more qualified in the matter than he. The fact that we may differ on certain points should be no reason for you to abstain; for it is sociology which has been attacked through me and it is sociology which must be defended above all. It seems to me, moreover, as you say yourself, that on the major question raised, and so miserably, by Andler's article, i.e. heterogeneity of psychic and sociological facts (whatever their relations may be), we are in agreement. That is the important thing; indeed it is on that point, I think, that the practical solution to the problem you raise is to be found. A collective intelligence alone is fit to judge collective phenomena. Especially when one says of the former that it is more-or-less mediocre, one must be very careful to compare it only with intelligences of the same kind, viz. collective intelligences, whereas it is being compared, by a real sophism, to individual intelligences. But leaving aside my own explanation, since we are close to agreement on the basic issue, I cannot see that it can be other than advantageous that you should speak. This specificity of social facts, of which you have the sense, seems to me to be one of the points upon which agreement is very close to being reached. Maybe it would be useful to have a direct statement made – and by someone other than myself, who may seem too directly concerned in the question.

In any case, I think it profitable not to stay silent. Sociology has been compromised lately by charlatans who have exploited its premature fashionableness. It will result in sociology falling into disfavour which will benefit those who are disturbed by it. And it disturbs the little churches which have their faith, their priests and their congregation. It is important to separate ourselves from those who are a discredit to sociology, so as to shield it from well-founded arguments in the attacks it will undergo. That is why I should be grateful if you in turn would let me know if you are carrying through your plan to reply. If not, I shall give it further thought. I am to leave Bordeaux on the 29th or 30th. Could you let me know by then the line you are finally taking?

Do you no longer travel via Paris? I should like to talk over all this with you. I shall be there for a few days during the next holidays.

Please accept, my dear Sir, my best and most sincere wishes.

[PS] I will say nothing of the error concerning the historical method of Comte. It betrays a very great superficiality.

Bordeaux, 179 boulevard de Talence,
16 May 1896

My dear Sir,

Just as I received your letter, I was myself planning to write to you to tell you what pleasure it gave me to read your article and to thank you for your care in defending me personally on certain essential points as well as in defending sociology. I am most grateful to you. When I saw, in Andler's additional note, that he contests the manner in which you interpret some of my propositions, I thought momentarily of intervening very briefly. But when I reread your piece, I decided I could add nothing to what you said and that this discussion had reached its natural conclusion.

I have not written to you earlier about the results of the interview I had with Alcan, because there is nothing definite. In principle, Alcan is ill-disposed towards *Années*. The *Année philosophique* lives on only with the help of ministerial subsidies. *The Année psychologique* is Binet's property; Alcan is merely the depository. However, he has not given me a definite *no*. There is one arrangement that would please him, which would be to divide the *Année philosophique* into two, which would then become an *Année philosophique et sociologique*. The two parts would be distinct, though united *provisionally* in the same volume. I doubt if Pillon would accept. In any case, the arrangement has no charm for me. I am seeing Alcan in the near future and, as soon as a solution is reached, I will let you know.

I hope that reading the economists is more useful to you than it has been to me. I thought too, when I began 15 years ago, that I should find the answer to the questions which preoccupied me. I spent several years doing so and gained nothing, except what may be taught by a negative experience. It is true that, in that very respect, there is a virgin territory to explore. With statistics and history, one could make some fine discoveries.

I have cancelled my lectures since the end of April so as to be able to devote myself wholeheartedly to the book I am preparing on *Suicide*. I hope that when it appears, the *reality* of the social fact, about which my view is contested, will be better understood; for what I study in the book is the social current of suicide, the tendency of social groups towards suicide, isolated from its individual manifestations (by abstraction, of course, but no science isolates its object in any other way).

I am most cordially yours, with, again, all my thanks.

Documents

Bordeaux, 218 boulevard de Talence,
[April 1897]

My dear Sir,

I was prevented from replying earlier to your letter by the worries of moving house, proofs to correct, the closure of my winter course of lectures.

There is, I think, no need to dwell on the doctrinal scruple you raise: the letter I addressed to Mr Lapie at the very moment you were writing to me contains my response to it, and he has doubtless communicated its content to you. First, I have never clearly seen the difference between the formulation you have accepted and the one I stated. To repeat, I have never meant to say that sociology could be practised without some psychological culture, nor that sociology was anything other than a psychology; but only that collective psychology cannot be deduced directly from individual psychology, because a new factor intervenes which transforms the psychic material, a factor which is the source of every difference and every novelty, the factor of association. A phenomenon of individual psychology has as its substratum an individual consciousness, a phenomenon of collective psychology, a group of individual consciousnesses. Anyway, my next book will return to the question and I shall be able to clear up any ambiguity. In any case, although we might most usefully underline what we have in common, if, in this connection, the publication of the *Année* is to be an event of interest – for this is the first time that a group of sociologists will be seen to be devoting themselves to the same task and working together towards the same goal – it is neither necessary nor desirable that everyone voice the same formulations. And so you can rest assured the preface will offend no one.

I have written to Simmel who has replied to me and has accepted. He will send me an article of 40 or 50 pages entitled *Die Selbsterhaltung der Gesellschaft*. For the years after we shall see. Perhaps we could arrange something with jurists like Esmein or Girard. And I shall have a look at Grosse's book; I intend to analyse it.

As to the distribution of work between yourself and Mr Lapie, take it as settled. One section will be entitled *Legal and Moral Sociology* and he will be entrusted with the moral part. I already have several books to send him. I have sent the Giddings on to you; I think you must have received it. I shall get you the others shortly; tell me which ones you would like; I am keeping an eye open here ...

Of course, with the studies of general sociology, which date quickly, we should take nothing earlier than 1896. Even in the other sections, it would be good to follow the same rule, though with more moderation.

Everyone is beginning to set to work. I am beginning to see the trend of each one's different articles taking shape. Let us hope it will all work.

I am writing to you on the eve of a departure and in a state of extreme fatigue. I think, however, that I have replied to all your questions ... I am very sorry that we will not be able to see each other but I have a meeting on the 24th with Mr Lapie whom you will undoubtedly have seen before me. We shall be able to chat, with him as intermediary.

Yours ever.

Bordeaux, 218 boulevard de Talence,
6 July 1897

My dear Sir,

I find your second plan far preferable to the first; the opposition between books on 'principles' and those which treat 'particular questions' seems to me somewhat artificial, given that the questions treated are of such a general character.

What will help you find a title [for your rubric] is that my *Suicide* comes under another heading than yours; we have a special one, and a very full one, for criminal sociology, comprising criminology and moral statistics, which are inseparable. Richard holds that post. I sent you my book as a memento and a token of friendship, not as a piece of work for you. Set your mind at ease.

Now then, does the title *Psychological Sociology* wholly render Simmel's idea. He has, I think, a sense of the specificity of social facts but he does not pursue his thought to its conclusion and so lingers on generalities. Perhaps you could take 'Psychological and Specific Sociology' as a heading. But you alone are competent to judge this point.

Another scruple. Is the Vignes well-placed among the philosopher–sociologists? In Le Play there is another tendency, as far as I know it. But that again is only a question I am putting to you. Perhaps, if you do adopt the rubric *Psychological and Specific Sociology* you could put it in the third group. But if it really is a philosophical work, class it in the first.

As to the Lazarus, I am going to ask Mr Lapie to deal with it and I think he will accept, as he is not too overburdened; he only has 6 or 7 books to analyse so far. If you do not want to part with your copy, would you be kind enough to ask Lazarus for another for the *Année sociol.* It would be one letter less for me to write and I am overwhelmed by them. Consider that we get 80 to a 100 books and that, as for many of them more than one letter is needed, in these, past two and a half months I have done something like 150 letters. – Lazarus could send me a copy direct to avoid the cost of postage from you to me.

I should like the *Année* to appear in March; for that [to be possible], I must have manuscripts by the end of November or beginning of December, so that printing can start in January.

To come to what you say about my *Suicide*. There is a great deal of truth in your remarks. Perhaps it would have been more expedient not to present things in that form. But first of all, like it or not, it is my nature to present my ideas with the point of the sword rather than with the hilt. Moreover, it seems impossible to me, if you pursue your thought to its conclusion, not to reach a formulation more or less like mine. If the social is something other than the individual, it has another substratum, although it could not exist without the individual. That strikes me as a truism. Society is not in any individual, but in all the individuals associated in some determinate form. Thus it is not with the analysis of individual consciousness that sociology can be done. Now, shouldn't one, above all, pursue one's thought to its conclusion? Apart from the fact that one must, there is benefit in doing so, because the method is more solidly based. The social fact must be considered from the outside not only in consequence of a necessary artifice and so as to preclude replacing things by one's own views, but because [the social fact] actually transcends the individual. And then is there not some interest in showing that morality is partly external to individuals? Many things are thereby explained. As you say, however simple the proposition, fundamentally, it is natural to shy away at first. Since Hobbes, at least, the idea is latent in every attempt at sociology; one can see it emerging with enormous slowness and difficulties, even as one notices how necessary the thinkers find it!

Although you will not have to review my *Suicide* in the *Année*, it is possible that Ribot will ask you to discuss it in the *Revue philosophique*. I was anxious to let you know so that I would know how to conduct myself in consequence and so that nothing is done which you might not like. As long ago as last April Ribot suggested to me you should take charge of my book. Knowing you were going to be very busy with the *Année sociologique*, I dodged the issue so as to spare you the additional work. I told him he should see for himself, that perhaps you would not have the time, etc. But, according to a letter he has just written you, he has not yet chosen anyone. Richard is out of the question, first of all because he is reviewing it in the *Année* and also because, as I presented his two books in the *Revue*, it would look like a repayment . . . of two loans. Tarde is equally out of the question, for other reasons. That is why Ribot feels hampered, and he would like to reach an agreement with me on the subject . . . Would you like me to exclude you categorically on some pretext or other? Would you be willing to take on the task? Answer only according to your own inclinations.

I have just this moment received a letter from Lapie, from which it transpires that the agreement between us on the great controversy is as complete as may be and I am most pleased. I fancy that, apart from some questions of form, we two have come to something similar, have we not?

Most cordially yours.

[PS] We have no special compartment for aesthetic sociology. Ouvré, who was to take charge of it, has definitely turned to novels. When something of the kind appears, we should analyse it, and for all the works which will not be numerous enough to warrant a particular heading, there will be a rubric *Miscellaneous*.

Forgive my disorganisation, I am extrₑmely tired.

I am resuming this letter to add a few words about your section-title. By now you must be well aware that the whole issue is concerned not with whether there is an extra-psychological sociology, but with whether collective psychology has its own laws. The word psychology has an ambiguity which prevents agreement between authors who are nearly of one mind. Someone who has the sense of the specificity of social facts, such as Simmel, I think, does not follow through with his idea, because he thinks the psychic is the ultimate form of reality and he does not see there are two sorts of psychic realities. That is why he describes his sociology as psychological. But his psychological sociology is very different from Tarde's, which dissociates the social from the generalised individual. This confusion is one that especially needs to be ended. You are well-placed to do so, and in this respect the term specific psychology as it would be explained by you in the course of your analysis would be useful. I think on that point you would perform a real service. Not only would you facilitate a certain mutual understanding, you would also perhaps help some thinkers to achieve greater awareness of their own thought.

Bordeaux, 14 May 1900

My dear friend,

I am sending you a parcel by post containing some more books destined for the *Année*, the books you need for your work. I cannot any longer recall whether it is Leist's *Jus Civile* or *Jus Gentium* that you want; uncertain and without looking for your letter, I am sending you the first, which is my own copy. If you want the second, it is in the Bordeaux law library; you can easily get it via the administration.

To answer the questions you put to me in your letter this morning.

(1) No, the clan is not to be defined by the totem. I did so in my article because that narrow definition made for an easier exposition. But if one held to that [definition], one would have to refuse the name of clan to all the survivals and derived forms, like the gens, the γένος. The rectification necessary so as to have a broader definition is actually easy and fairly minor. The name clan applies to a group of individuals who consider one another as kin (i.e. as descending from the same origin) and who recognise their kinship by this sign and this alone, that they all bear the same name which is the name

47

of the group, and this is the *nomen gentilicium*. Between *gentiles* there is no genealogical tree, no defined relations of consanguinity. All those who bear the same *nomen* are *gentiles*. You see the analogies with the fact of bearing the same totem.

(2) It was in a work by Conrady that I saw the fact in question. I have also come across it in a book by Buhl on the Hebrews. The two are analysed in our volume 3 (about to appear). I am sending you the first. You shall have the second when you want.

(3) It was Smith who drew attention to the importance of the communal feast. I am sending you the book.

(4) There are works by Brentano and, I think, Schmoller on the question of the corporations. But would you not be interested, in fact, by the primitive form of the corporation, when it first appears in Rome, in Greece? Those are the cases where you could best grasp its peculiar characteristics, perhaps, what distinguishes it from family groups and from castes. If so, you have Waltzing (I have a copy), Potier (you have one, Bibliothèque d'Athènes).

If you really need to be better informed on the sociology of the family – and I am not surprised, I told you you would – I could, if you could read them, let you have my courses of lectures on the question. They are fully written up and if you can read my letters without too much difficulty, you could read those still more easily. They are still quite crude (the first dates from 1888–9!); but they might inform you quickly. In any event, you decide; they are entirely yours to use. At the moment Fauconnet has them. But Fauconnet wrote to me yesterday that he has finished the first, which comprises 25 lectures. He could therefore pass it on to you without delay.

My nephew lives at 22 avenue des Gobelins. While on the subject, I am letting you know that Hubert is to return to Paris today.

The article I mentioned to you, about or rather against 'formal sociology' appeared in this month's number of the *Rivista italiana di sociologia*. They undertook a kind of enquiry on various sociological conceptions; and that was the viewpoint I spoke from. If you want to discuss it, instead of sending you an offprint I could let you have the manuscript; that would be better, anyhow, than a translation I have revised only [hastily?].

I return to the question that preoccupies you, and since you have reached a phase of groping for ideas, I am going to submit to you my inklings (oh, very hypothetical too). If these too summary views can be of any use to you, I should be very happy. If they are of no use to you, which indeed would not surprise me (as I have never reflected on the matter, except casually), well no harm will be done.

I too have always had the impression that the caste had some relationship to the clan. The link which unites the members of a caste is a blood-link. By that feature the clan is distinguished from the corporation which has never had that characteristic. And here is how I view the difference between these two organs. In some cases, professional life has been organised inside the framework of the family (caste); in other cases, it has been organised outside the framework of the family (corporation). Basically, moreover, the family framework is the prototype of the one as of the other. The corporation, originally, is modelled on the family group, and has its own cult, tombs, meals in common (see Waltzing), but is nonetheless something external, something else. In the case of the caste, there ought to be a relation of derivation properly termed.

Now, how is it that the development takes place in one way in one case, and in another in the other case? Both the phenomena are linked to the phenomenon of the constitution of aristocracies and of 'lower' classes. That is obvious for castes; it is true too, I think, for corporations which are at first humble artisans' societies, much despised, and which only assumed importance when industrial life itself assumed importance. In principle they sheltered the humblest forms of social life. Now this is what I notice. Aristocracies seem to have been formed in two very different ways. In certain cases, the aristocratic clans absorb within themselves, but as subordinates and more or less enslaved, the *humiles* of the plebs. In that case, the society is formed only of clans, *gentes*, γένη, comprising (1) subjects who have full rights, patricians etc., who are the proper elements of these clans (2) subjects who have lesser rights, and that is true at every degree (clients). That was the case at Rome, until the plebs itself achieved self-organisation into *gentes* (*gentes minores*). And so no castes. The only social frameworks are the clans of the rich. But, as the *humiles* begin to lead a life of their own, they seek to organise themselves. Would that not be the source of the first corporations??? In other cases, the inferior elements keep their own family frameworks, remain clans, and a hierarchy is established between these clans of unequal social dignity.

To summarise: when the clans that are subordinated because of their economic or other inferiority keep their integrity as clans, professional life divides upon the basis of the existing family frameworks. And so there are castes. When the subordinate subjects are led to be assimilated into the richer clans as integral, but lesser, elements, there is something else. The higher functions (political, religious) have frameworks that are ready-made: viz, those formed by the privileged clans (patricians). The lower functions have none, but [invent?], in [the image?] of the only ones that exist (the corporations).

I am ashamed to seem to tackle a question with which I am so unacquainted. Decide if, out of the views hazarded here, there is something which might provisionally be kept. At all events, I have unburdened myself.

Yours.

Bordeaux, 13 June 1900

Dear friend,

I was waiting to get together some new points before replying to your previous letter. But if I had delayed any longer, my letter would have been too long.

You are – and you appear – less harsh than I am on this year's papers. Richard's is indeed the best. As to Steinmetz's, I thought momentarily of refusing it, but that would have meant making an enemy for the *Année* and I had not the time to fill the gap [that would have been left] if he had refused the major alterations I thought necessary (he sent me his work piece by piece from the 15th of January to the 29th and I had to put it into French piecemeal); so I carried on and contented myself with cutting twenty pages or so. It has been a decisive test. I shall not easily find sociologists more significant than Ratzel and Steinmetz; the latter has done some good pieces of work. And yet you see what the result is. Consequently we shall not be satisfied with the papers unless we ourselves are their authors. That is what we must aim at.

That is why I was most pleased to see you undertake something. Simiand will follow your example next year and Hubert is preparing something on Magic. I might add that, in some respects, I am not sorry to learn that you are progressing laboriously in your work. It is inevitable and it proves that your work is being done properly. Nevertheless I hope that your awareness of the difficulties will not make you afraid of not finishing and make you want to be discharged from the responsibilities you speak of. I did, however, ask myself the question as I read your letter. Reassure me sometime, if you can.

Do not pity me because of the small amount of time I give to the *Année*. Ever since I have seen that everyone was attached to the *Année* and that the group so formed was not without homogeneity nor without solidarity, I find that the best I can do is to give it all the time that professional tasks leave free. Consider indeed that it is the first group of the kind to be organised, in which there is a real division of labour and cooperation. And so, if we can last, it will be a good example. It is also the best way to prepare for sociological activity and to stimulate it. If each of us gradually sets to, we shall have some result. Moreover, there is no doubt that, imperceptibly, the intellectual context of sociology will change in France; that a distinction will be drawn in public opinion between the good workers and the others, and we shall have played some part, a large part, in bringing that about.

I now reply to your previous letter.

As to the Powell (not good) agreed. As to the Dahlman and the Baden-Powell, will you take on the reviews? *Give a reply on this matter, please.*

As to the anthropo-sociology, I have written to Muffang to tell him I was cancelling the rubric. I shall not ask for any more books on the subject; but a few books of anthropology have come which I cannot refuse.

We shall create a short *Anthropology* rubric at the end, the constituents of which I am sharing out. The Lapouge is in Hubert's hands and he has already taken care of it.

-I have asked for the Bergson.

As to the quantity of books to be sent to Aubin, ask him about it. Send him first the books needing a serious analysis. You can move on to the short notes afterwards depending on his speed. For the moment, in any case, he has some administrative difficulties. He has been made the object of a report by his [academic] inspector, over the tendencies of his ethics teaching: now, the ideas he develops are the ones I taught him. I have written to Rabier about the incident, which threatens our freedom to teach. He has been reproached with having said that the old social frameworks destroyed by the Revolution can no longer be restored, and reproached, I am told, because this sort of formulation is a condemnation of the reactionary right.

Yours.

6 July 1900

My dear friend,

Today I am sending you a new batch comprising, besides a few books, several numbers of journals containing articles which we cannot ignore. I have underlined these articles in ink; many, I think, need only to be mentioned. I have pointed them out, but of course it is for you to judge.

I [should like?] to discuss with you a small question of doctrine which has to do with our classification.

You have a certain number of works concerning the psychology of groups. Are they well-placed in general sociology? The arrangement is suitable while it is a question of groups in general, but, as soon as it is a question of specific, determined groups, the inappropriateness of the expression shows. I already felt this when I sent you the work on the Mystics and Sectarians. It has nothing to do with general sociology. The incorrectness of this classification has become even more apparent to me lately. I received a book entitled *Psychologie der Naturvoelker*, far from brilliant actually, in which the civilisation of the primitive is explained by the character peculiar to these groups of peoples. Every detail of their ethics and religion is reviewed. With this work we are even further from general sociology and yet this book is difficult to separate from the others.

From another angle, wherever these works are placed, what rubric do we count them under? The expression *collective psychology* or *psychology of groups* or *psychology of peoples* which is often used as a sub-title to them seems to me to be as inappropriate as can be. Everything is collective psychology or group psychology in sociology. In what way, when myths or moral beliefs and practices are studied, is it less a collective psychology, less a study of social mentality than when crowds or one sect or another are taken as the subject? This is an inappropriateness of expression that covers a confusion of ideas, one which we might profitably react against. In reality, the characteristic of these works is that they treat not one or another kind of mental manifestation in particular, but constitutional ways of thinking and acting peculiar to a certain, determined group. That is to say that they study temperaments, collective characters, the characters of primitive society, the characters of sects, of mystic groups, etc. Would it not be suitable to adopt the expression *Collective Ethology*. There indeed is a social ethology as there is an individual ethology, and the issue can usefully be raised. Already in volume 2 I employed the expression but without insisting. If you share the above views, we could take up the rubric and place it among the *Miscellaneous* (with Aesthetic Sociology) and put before the analyses an introduction in which we should raise the issue, show the disadvantages of the term *Social Psychology*, and broadly indicate what this branch of sociology could be. As the rubric would be begun, because I am analysing that book on the *Naturvoelker* I spoke to you of above, what I offer you is to draft the introduction which you would revise so that we could reach agreement.

These issues of classification are important; for it is sociology which is thereby organised. It is of some importance to bring a little order to this shapeless mass. Maybe it will be one of the things that will be a lasting achievement of the *Année*. Gradually, we are reaching towards a rational classification. This year we shall take, on this other point, another step forward.

Richard has given me the job of asking you if you would let him have a copy of your thesis. I am glad to perform the task. Richard, as you know, teaches in Le Havre.

Yours ever.

[1901?]

My dear friend,

I have no knowledge of Espinas's intentions. He says nothing of them in the letter in which he expressed his astonishment about that part of your article concerning the *Année*; and it was not addressed to me, but to a mutual friend with a request to communicate it to me.

And he has not replied to my reply.

Quite certainly, I should prefer to see you undertake some personal research rather than a popularising book. But that consideration apart, I am convinced your publication will serve in more ways than getting the money to buy a bicycle. There is just one point to which I would draw your attention. If you defend sociology against materialist metaphysics, and against that alone, you will be accused of wanting a metaphysical sociology of spiritualist tendency. Now, the latter is no less of an obstacle than the former, in fact if not in principle. Just as materialism inclines towards solutions of an anthropo-sociological or other kind[1] (without being formally obliged to, but by a natural disposition of the minds professing the doctrine), in a similar way the current spiritualist metaphysics, especially the classic and amorphous spiritualism, the one that has become and has remained current in France since the middle of the century, tends, by a natural inclination, not perhaps to monopolise sociology, but to declare it impossible, in short to oppose it. There is no doubt in my mind that people like Darlu, for example, accept the word but deny the thing itself. All of them, in fact, are prone to isolate representations from the rest of reality, to make of them a separate world; consequently they cannot admit that there can be a *science* thereof, in the proper sense of the word. Being heirs to religious thinking, they set themselves as defenders of this last bastion, and, without realising it, labour to remove it from the reach of profane thinking. It is said here are things too subtle, too complex to be taken over by the crude procedures of science; that all is a matter of nuances, of uncategorisable qualities, which sentiment, intuition alone can appreciate. Ah! Nuances! That is the slogan of men who will not think.

If you share these ideas to some degree, and I find it hard to believe we could be seriously at odds on this matter, you might usefully say so; you are known to be a moderate, without doctrinal violence, unprejudiced against metaphysics or even spiritualism, and you would have some chance of being heard. All my bridges are burned. I could claim to be hyper-spiritualist as much as I like, I should be mistrusted.

You don't mistake my meaning, I hope. I think sociology can be of use to metaphysics without using it or above all depending on it, of whatever tendency it may be. But, as is natural, each type of metaphysics tends to mark [sociology] with its own impress; and it would be useful to signal its position in relation to all the schools [of metaphysics]. I think it could even help this amorphous, literary spiritualism to become more substantial. I did not answer your question earlier, because I wanted to write all this to you.

I have no need of my article; keep it. If the Mazel interests you, you may keep that too; you would free me a little library space. It is not worth the cost of return by post – the author is an employee of the Navy Ministry who was compromised in last year's scandals.

[1] Anthropo-sociology refers to physical anthropology.

Documents

The journals you talk of have reviewed the *Année* except for . . . Marillier's *Revue*. Explain that as you will or can.

We have just made some conquests in the law faculty in Lyons. I have had offers of collaboration.

Yours.

Plombières, Villa des Marroniers (Vosges),
13 August 1901

My dear friend,

Your article in the *Revue philosophique* gave me great pleasure in several ways.

I am, first of all, very grateful for that act of solidarity, the moral effect of which will, I hope, be considerable. Of all the services we can render the most valuable is to show that there are in sociology workers who are more concerned with joining their efforts in order to cooperate, than with differentiating themselves in order to show their originality. Also I was very pleased with the terms in which you spoke of Espinas. They are unjust to him in Paris, where they are calling him an old fogey. He made the mistake of accepting a teaching post for which he was unprepared; but that is no reason to forget what he has done and turn him into a new incarnation of Waddington-Kastus. You were quite right not to confuse him with that amateur Novicow. But at the same time it was very easy to point out to him that what he calls for is being done, and, after what he wrote to me, I fail to understand why he did not differentiate us more from the others. It is true that had he done so his article would no longer have been justified. For fear of seeming unduly personal, I said nothing to him, but the remark needed to be made.

I would have said all this to you earlier if I had not had all my time taken up since my arrival by the treatment and also by an indisposition, attributed, in the [. . . ?] words, to the effect of the waters. Anyway, I am over it and I am beginning to hope my stay will do me some good. It is a pity you never come [this way?]. Pine woods and a little altitude are excellent for excitable people; I feel myself alive again here and take pleasure in strolling about. It would do you good, I think. It is true that the reasons for my being so attached to these parts are the same as the ones that make an impenitent Breton of you, no doubt. And I notice that one becomes more attached to one's native soil the older one gets . . .

Letters from Emile Durkheim to François Simiand

[February 1902] Sunday

My dear friend,

Since I was very busy yesterday, I could not acknowledge your proofs; they have indeed reached me. Don't worry about the cost of corrections. As long as the *Année*'s bank is not broken, it should cover such expenses.

You know that the time has come to [renew?] with Alcan for 5 years. I have sent Hubert the proposals that were made to me along with my observations, and have requested him to send both to you and get your advice. In sum, Alcan wishes the *Année* not to exceed 35 sheets (560 pages). This is possible on the condition that the papers and the reviews be separated. I wonder whether that separation is not a good thing in itself. On the other hand, those papers are written in abnormal circumstances, since they are required to be ready on fixed dates. You must have made an enormous effort this year. Moreover, there is always the danger of subordinating the fate of the *Année* to all the accidents that may prevent a work from being ready on time. What would have become of us had you fallen ill in Oct.? Last year I had to hurriedly do what I could to fill a gap. As for vols. 2 and 3, we have got by with [studies?] from the same people. Would you therefore think about the following arrangement: (1) The *Année* reduced to reviews along with the development of review essays; (2) Separated from the *Année*, volumes of studies which would appear when the material was ready (let us say, one large volume each year). The fees gained from these volumes could be put into the *Année*'s account, which would make us rich. We could pay foreign contributors.

Give me your advice as soon as possible so as to have [talked with a . . . ?]

Yours.

Should you agree, could you indicate a subject that you could handle from now into an indeterminate future, say 2 or 3 years?

Bordeaux, 218 boulevard de Talence,
15 February 1902

My dear friend,

I am sending you the second proofs of printer's sheets 1 and 2 of your paper. I think, in effect, that you want to correct them yourself. This is in all ways preferable. When you have finished, I would ask that you return the first proofs to me along with the copy of the second that is not for the printer.

Fauconnet spoke to me about your meeting on Monday. He told me that you personally would be inclined to keep the existing system. I should point out that there seems a contradiction between that opinion and another that Fauconnet says is shared by you all, that is, that the Collection of Papers, either in the *Année* or outside of the *Année* must be *our* work or the work of people completely in accord with us.

That last principle appears to me in all ways excellent. I don't need to tell you how much it cost me to publish certain things. I did it at first because, in the beginning, I dared not hope for the intellectual homogeneity that has been established among us and because I thought only of making the *Année* a collection where, to enter, it would suffice to be scientifically honest. I did it also because there was no means of doing otherwise. But it is clear that that eclecticism, even as limited as it has been, spoils the impression of the whole. I would add, of that which has been published, only that which has come from us has value.

But if one establishes that principle (as I would be very happy to do so), how could one maintain the present system? We five or six could not commit ourselves to providing every year the two works which at minimum would be necessary. Look at what could happen with volume 6. Hubert and Mauss cannot put their work on Magic into adequate condition by the end of the year. I might therefore have to go begging among outsiders since, among us, I see no one who could do something for us.

Furthermore, and it is an important consideration, in the present state of the *Année*, the papers are overwhelmed by the book reviews which draw all the attention to themselves.

The original reasons for keeping the papers in the *Année* no longer exist. One could have believed that, by furnishing material for reviews, they could have made us known. But now we are known to the public that we wish to reach. Besides, that very public has often expressed the opinion that the papers were out of place.

Weigh all that. Join to it the concern there is for being able to do those works at leisure and for not exposing the *Année* to some mishap that could prevent the author of an important paper from being ready, and consider if you should not modify your first impression. Ask yourself if, for all these reasons, the dogmatic effect will not be augmented thanks to the bipartition.

The disadvantage could be that one might feel less necessity to produce. But we could get around it easily by fixing some dates, except that they would no longer be as imperative as in the past, and by my having the right to remind you of the agreements. That is why I insisted on a programme being settled in advance.

But, of course, if you have any objections to the above, let me know. I will not do anything we have not agreed on among ourselves.

Yours.

Bordeaux, 18 February 1902

My dear friend,

I am sending you the second proofs of the end of your paper. You will find only one copy of the last sheet, which I must keep to correct my own paper, as it takes up nearly all of that sheet.

You should now let me know how many copies of your off-prints you want. I need to indicate that on each sheet along with the printing order.

I received a letter yesterday evening from Bouglé who shares your views on the question of the schemes concerning the *Année*. In these circumstances, if your opinion is not appreciably modified, given that Fauconnet, Hubert and Mauss, however much they accept the idea of a change, are not in agreement on the ways and means, I would strongly favour maintaining the present system. It has proved itself and appears viable; modifying it would have required a scheme that would have had everyone's support, not a contested arrangement. There is besides a serious objection to that arrangement: it is the difficulty of grouping the papers in fascicles that are homogeneous with regard to the subjects treated.

Please tell me then if, upon reflection, you continue to find the present system preferable. That will enable me to make up my mind. I will then make some proposals to Alcan. But it appears to me impossible for the *Année* to include less than 38 or 39 sheets. On the other hand, if the two present type-faces are retained, I think that one could go ahead with 608 pages. That would oblige us perhaps to do a less purely bibliographical, less scattered work, to focus ourselves better. But I think we have everything to gain in doing this.

On the other hand, what I said on the subject of the papers will still apply to some extent. It must not happen that each year I have to search here and there. But, because this time we should have an existence assured for five years, we had better be sure to establish a programme for those five years. Given that the year is advanced, volume 6 could be something of a transition volume. Volume 7 could be taken up by the paper on Magic. For the eighth and ninth, could you with Bourgin, furnish an article of about 90 pages and a more extensive paper? In this way, one could make a start on these various works right away and no longer live from year to year. In this way also, the papers, prepared in advance, will not get in the way of the preparation of the book reviews.

Yours affectionately.

Even if a letter from you is on its way from Paris today, Tuesday, would you please reply to this one because of the new elements to be evaluated that it contains?

Documents

Letters from Paul Lapie to Célestin Bouglé

Tunis, 5 rue de Marseille,
13 December 1893

My dear Bouglé,
... In short, I have been unable to make up my mind about the subject of the work which should occupy my entire existence, at least the coming years; therefore I can work on nothing. Being used to having a defined goal, an examination to prepare, makes all capricious work unbearable: and I have no other. Sometimes I study sciences with some colleagues; Fredo the experiments in physics or chemistry, which one must remember in order to have a smattering of science, in the hope of acquiring the general ideas of scientific methods that are now necessary for the construction of any metaphysics. They are necessary even to psychology; sometimes, in fact, I apply myself to that science; I read the English and I gather some observations; I particularly study affective facts, desire, and I ask myself if the impulsion that pushes us towards an object is absolutely reducible to a mechanical force: I see some effects that seem to me particular to conscious forces; this one, for example: the being who desires has as an end the state *contrary* to the one that it is experiencing at the moment: are there mechanical forces that thus tend toward their own destruction? Again, in order to know, one must occupy oneself with the sciences of nature. Or sometimes, I read the sociologists (besides, desire is the very object of sociology); I read in particular the disciples of de Mun, the papal encyclical, etc., then the advocates of the cooperative movement, of profit-sharing, of which I was unaware until now; I do some practical sociology by observing what is happening around me; but, here again, it would require more concentrated attention and very lengthy observations, and observations that would also be very difficult, for all, Arabs or Colonists, hide their feelings, their hopes, even their situation: and we are victims, when we arrive here, of the prejudices that we import from Europe or that we find already established ...

Tunis, 2 rue de l'Obscurité,
11 November 1894

... Great projects is one way to put it: ambitious projects would be better: I had expected to gather some precise observations on the mores, the institutions, the laws of the Israelites and the Muslims. I have some, and I even have a great many of them. I spent my month interviewing the chief rabbi, the professors of the Muslim University, etc. But all that did not give me the results I had resolved to obtain. Yet, it adds up to a little collection of social facts which could be used later, if indeed I do sociology. And I indeed believe that I will do it ...

Tunis, 2 rue de l'Obscurité,
30 January 1895

... I first read the sociology works Halévy swamped me with. There are some interesting ones. Here is what I decided to do for the article I just sent. Instead of a separate analysis of each work, I dealt successively with the object and the method of sociology. What definitions are given of societies? (repetition of the discussion of the formula, society is an organism). What definitions are given of social facts? (discussion of the definitions of Durkheim, Tarde, Lacombe, etc. – conclusion: a social fact is a psychological fact, a desire transmitted by suggestion). In that part is found the idea that you have already expressed several times about Germany: the sociologists tend to refer sociology back to psychology. Actually, that is the central idea of my work; I believe we are in agreement on that point. The second part is devoted to method: some explain social facts by the laws of evolution; I try to show that this is to begin with the end, that one can find laws of evolution only after having found universal and eternal laws – others look for those laws and believe they have found them in the human mind, but in general they explain social facts by the laws of sentiment, of need, by that which in the human mind is, if one can so put it, less mental, less conscious: such are Lacombe's explanations: everything is explained by desire. I believe that desire itself, when it is expressed and transmitted by suggestion, is the social fact: the problem of sociology is thus to explain it by something other than itself; and since I believe that all desire is born of the opposition of two ideas, it is by that logical opposition that social facts, sociological laws, and logical laws are explained. That is Tarde's view: I raise for discussion in Tarde's book certain logical changes of what are rather egregious logical errors. But I do not see why I am summarising all that for you since you will be able to read it. Perhaps it is because I should like your views on the plan itself. I admit that I am not very satisfied with my work: it is too long, and I fear that its length will lead Halévy to ask me for modifications: that would annoy me very much, for I have already devoted too much time to that task, and I would not take it up again with pleasure. And length is not its only shortcoming, but it is useless to enumerate the others, you will certainly see them. I was rather embarrassed; I had to be severe (Halévy asked me to), and I did not have the right to be so; besides, I could not concentrate at length on any point. But at last it's finished, and I hope it's completely finished. We will doubtless not agree on the conclusion, and I fear that it will not raise any new objection for you; I have tried to exclude teleology from sociology so as to make of it a rigorous science, expressing necessary relations. Without denying that men act with an end in view, pleasure for example, I tried to show that this problem is not sociology's problem, but that of ethics; the sociological problem would be: how does man conceive of his ends? or, rather, how does man transmit his ends to others? or accept the ends of others? It is not a question of knowing with what end in mind social facts are produced, but by what series of reflections men propose those ends to themselves ...

Tunis, 2 rue de l'Obscurité,
18 February 1895

My dear Bouglé,

We are very much closer to agreeing than we imagine. Your teleology frightened me; but since you would begin by distinguishing 'consequence, result, goal, tendency, etc.' so as to clearly define the end, I believe that after these rigorous definitions, we could be in complete agreement. What in fact do you ask of 'teleology'? A classification of social ends and social forms, the second subordinated to the first, since the forms depend upon the ends. Now, I admit that one must in fact classify social ends. To deny it would be to affirm that one must not take psychological facts into account in sociology, and I agree completely with you on that point: exterior facts become social causes only if they pass through consciousnesses and are interpreted by them. Since social facts have psychological causes, since they are desires, it is important to classify those desires: that is the first step in science. You are àgain right to say that this classification is in itself explanatory; a classification that was not explanatory would be completely artificial, would be joining heterogeneous things, would have no grounding in reality: now, that is not the case with a classification of social desires, of social ends, since we have just seen that they are social reality itself. The only point for discussion that could separate us is the following: is the science concluded when the social forms are classified according to their ends? What type of explanation gives us knowledge of those ends? In my view, that knowledge is not the explanation for which social science must look. Should you know the end sought by a financial association, or by an army, you would have the definition of those two societies, you would not know how they exist; you would have the definition of their essence, not the explanation of their existence. Beginning by defining is excellent; without that definition one would not know where one was going, one would be proceeding blindly; but definition is only the beginning of research. How is the end conceived? That, then, is the question that seems to me most important; and, here again, I realise that we are not far from agreeing since you say that 'social facts are determined not only by the ends of societies, but also and *perhaps above all* by the way in which social units conceive of their ends'. At bottom, perhaps, there is nothing between us but a difference of terminology. The term 'teleology', which you like to use, made me fear that you were concluding the explanation of social facts with their ends; since you say that, on the contrary, the explanation must not stop there but must seek the cause of the ends themselves, we are of the same opinion. Social science has for its object: (1) the classification of social facts (and those facts are desires, that is to say, ends) – and that classification is already the beginning of explanation; (2) the search for the causes of those ends: how are they conceived and pursued? But to look for the cause of an end is not to do teleology, it is on the contrary to give to the science of ends itself the form of the mechanistic sciences ...

Pau, 20 November 1896

... Do you have some project in mind for the *Année sociologique*? Have you received any books? – if you are still contemplating the classification of social facts, here is an idea that was suggested to me by my *Tunis*. One generally classifies human families according to the number of their members: polyandry, polygamy, monogamy. That appears to me as artificial as classifying books according to their size. Two polygamous families can in fact be as different from one another as two octavo volumes one dealing with psychology and the other with ethics. The Tunisian Jews and Arabs are equally polygamous *by law*, but for one of them the plurality of wives is a sort of economic necessity: it is aimed at facilitating the division of labour in the family, which is faced with providing clothing, food, and shelter for its members. For the other, polygamy is aimed at assuring the propagation of the species. It is all but obligatory if the first marriage is without issue. The rules of divorce, very different for the two peoples, stem from this: these two equally polygamous families must not therefore be put in the same class. To classify institutions one must thus look for their psychological principle, and not observe their exterior differences. You get the gist? and do you think you could get some use out of it?

Your letter gave me another idea. You say that the Kabyles, the Dahomeans, and others do not conform to the laws of sociology. I am convinced that they do conform to them and that your book is inaccurate. You know my view of books about savages. It would be better were the *Année sociologique*, instead of summarising all the errors made about the [F ...?], [D ...?], and the Boshimans by Spencer, to begin studies of the social facts that surround us, of French society, where the laws are perhaps easier to know, although they are less known than those of some primitive societies. Why, for example, doesn't one do a precise study of the forms of

61

religious sentiment in France? Statistics on *ex-votos* would perhaps be interesting; not that I have much taste for statistics: it matters little whether a fact be frequent or rare, it is enough that it exists for it to be interesting; but intelligent statistical studies, classifying facts according to the sentiments that provoked them, according to the aim that the agent had in mind, would not be unimportant for the advancement of social science. There must be, on this point, some facts that escape current observation and that would permit one to establish some laws. But I am unaware whether your intention is to make the *Année sociologique* a research tool or an inventory of discoveries ...

Pau, 14 March 1897

My dear Bouglé,

I received, a few days before yours, a letter from Durkheim explaining the goal of the *Année sociologique* to me and asking me if I was still inclined to collaborate on it. I should indicate to you the general lines of my reply, for I would like your advice on two points. First, Durkheim appears to me to be hesitating on the meaning of the term 'social psychology', which marks out the works that we are supposed to review. He writes to me that 'Mr Bouglé told me that you and he would take in hand general sociology and the sociology of mores as well. He doubtless meant by that the history and the ethnography of mores and the sociological works relating to them. Have I understood properly'? I'll admit that I understand that thing less than our term 'social psychology'. I replied: *Yes*, just in case, but must one understand by that customs relative to clothing, to nutrition, etc.? Rather, that belongs either in Aesthetics (Ouvré) or in Political Economy (Simiand).[2] Must one mean by that moral customs, obligations, practices, or finally, domestic institutions? When we talked about it together, I understood that term to mean works done according to a psychological method. But I see that the division of labour among the collaborators has not been made on that principle: each has his 'department' and must examine the books that fall into his domain, regardless of the method that inspired the author. Are we thus having books on the history of morals reserved for us? Since I noted that none of the collaborators had asked to do the bibliography on domestic institutions, I asked Durkheim to add that chapter to our task; that could be interesting for me, but I want to know if that combination suits you. Perhaps it was implied in the general title: '*History and Ethnography of Mores*'.

A second point on which I want to get your advice is the question of the

---

[2] Lapie writes 'Simian' here. One will note that aesthetics was a rubric envisaged in the *Année* from its creation. Doubtless because of Ouvré's withdrawal, it appeared, as a sub-section, only from volume 3.

programme. It is necessary, Durkheim tells me, that the collaborators be in agreement on the 'necessity to do *sociology sociologically*, that is to say, without referring that science back to something other than itself'. I replied to him by saying that among the sciences of the mind I granted to sociology an independence analogous to that of physics or biology among the sciences of nature, but that, in my view, that independence did not go so far as to make sociology a self-sufficient science, its ties to psychology have to be affirmed. Is that profession of faith all right with you? Or do you believe I was wrong to make it? Do you yourself have news of the *Année sociologique*? When are we going to start working on that job, and how will we proceed in establishing our bibliography, procuring books, and sharing the work? If you come to Paris at Easter we could come to an agreement on that subject ...

Pau, 24 March 1897

... I have read your letter to Durkheim and am sending it to him this morning. You insist at length on the relationships between psychology and sociology, but are right to believe that he himself does not want to separate the two things absolutely. He wrote to me in fact: 'I see in sociology nothing more than a *psychology, but a psychology sui generis*' (underlined in the text). He cares only – and he is right – that one insist on the *sui generis*. I replied that in this we are in agreement.

I also replied to him that I accept the division of labour that you propose. No, I do not care for *general sociology*, for my current preoccupations are now pulling me more towards pure ethics or pure psychology. And, conversely, it is necessary for you to stay up-to-date with purely sociological trends. Thus I accept the department that you have named *sociology of morality*. But I do not see its limits clearly, despite the examples that you have chosen. I do not see how it can be separated from sociology of law: why should not Marillier's *L'idée de justice chez les sauvages* or even Spencer's *Justice* go into sociology of law? And if the studies I would deal with are to be limited to books that try to discover relations between systems of morality and social facts, it is so rare to find a scientific and methodical book on the subject that I shall play a very insignificant role in the *Année*.[3] Anyway, I am not complaining about it, for if I indeed want to concentrate on my thesis, I will not be able to give myself entirely to the *Année sociologique*. But I call your attention, as I did Durkheim's, to that point, because it seems to me that the bibliographical divisions of the future *Année* are not systematically established. Its morsels have been carved according to the taste of each individual. Would it not be better to make the divisions according to the

[3] The text reads: 'I will play the role of Marlborough's fourth officer', an allusion to a French popular song.

63

natural divisions of the science? Even for the reader, but above all for the research worker who will look for some documentation, it will be much more convenient if he is to find himself faced with a systematic classification rather than a somewhat artificial and very unstable division such as the one that is proposed. According to Durkheim, the study of the family will go into the chapter on *Law*. Why? Similarly with the study of *Punishment*: what will remain then for criminology? I hinted to him that we could perhaps try something more systematic by making two large divisions (that would follow general sociology): the study of *social facts*, the study of *social rules*. The first would be divided into: economic sociology, domestic, political, religious and aesthetic sociology; the second into law (with criminology as an appendix) and into morality. But I do not know what that division is worth in itself, and above all, one would have to distinguish with precision, law, which would contain the rules with political sanctions and, morality, to which would be reserved rules with subjective sanctions. I should add that I did not specify that classification in my letter to Durkheim; I simply called his attention to the fact that the present classification has gaps and obscure parts, and I asked him to define my department himself. Since he asked me to specify a project that I had submitted to him, as I had before to you (I asked him if the *Année* would undertake to do some surveys), I have given as an example of a possible survey the one I had spoken of to you on the exterior manifestations of religious sentiment and the survivals of old customs in the midst of Christian practices. But, once again, I do not know if that really fits into the programme of the *Année* ...

Pau, 7 May 1897

... My visit to Durkheim was long and rather confused. He is less clearly a psychologist in speech than in writing. What I came away with most clearly from that meeting was that, according to him, one must do sociological sociology, and only then see if the facts thus observed can be reduced to psychological or other laws. And, he still leaves that second part of the research in extreme darkness. Basically, he explains everything, *at this moment*, by religion; the prohibition of marriage between relatives is a religious matter; punishment is a phenomenon of religious origin; everything is religious. I protested but gently against a certain number of assertions that appeared doubtful to me; but I do not have the requisite competence to dispute a gentleman who is so well informed and so sure of his *current* assertions. – Apart from that, he is charming, and I have begun to work for him by reading a book that in different ways I find as insignificant as that of Ehrenfels, of disagreeable memory: it is the book by Bernès: *Sociologie et morale*. It is only a course outline that you may have already seen in Worms's *Revue*, and one can hardly judge it without further elaboration – or one could be tempted to judge it very harshly, since that outline lacks concision, clarity, and structure.

My other call was on Alcan. It was short. Mr Vidal Lablache had spoken to him about my manuscript: he accepted it then and there, and promised me 350 francs for my royalties. Our contract is signed. The book will doubtless appear in October, since the season is bad now, or so it would seem. Alcan suggested that I change the title; I think that he finds *Tunis* too short and not serious enough, more appropriate for a travelogue than for a book which is to appear in the Library of Contemporary History. He suggests: The Three Civilisations of Tunis (Muslim, Israelite, European) – and I do believe that I shall accept that title which is long but rather specific. I would like to add further: *A Study in Social Psychology* – which he would accept – but I truly worry about lengthening it beyond measure. Tell me what you think about it ...

Pau, 10 June 1897

... Can you work? and what are you doing? You should read, at least, the *Revue philosophique*. There is a little article in it by our collaborator Richard that seems to me to be about you: the young sociologists given to abstraction who embrace sociology in order to 'suffocate' it and who are moreover 'just out of the school of the German Universities' appears to me to resemble the authors of a review of the book by the same Richard on socialism and social science. It's harsh ...

Pau, 28 June 1897

... I am not as burdened as you by the *Année sociologique*, up to the present only two books, the one by Bernès about which I understand nothing, the other by an Italian who, under the pretext of speaking about the idea of law, constructs an entire philosophy. Nothing 'fruitful'. I do not even see how I could write four lines about those two volumes. Luckily, Durkheim promises some more inspiring ones. But, in any case, I cannot be too taken up with that side of things. I will be very pleased to see your reviews; I will begin mine only later, and it will be good for us to send our works to one another so as to give some unity to the volume ...

Pau, 9 July 1897

... Durkheim has just thrown three or four fat books at me; I'll doubtless drag them along to Val André, for they are in German and they are long. I had hoped to get by with two or three books, but an avalanche threatens.

65

I read Durkheim's book with great pleasure. What do you call scientific 'narrow-mindedness'? I find in it a great deal of conscientiousness and much ability in the interpretation of facts. Basically, it is not so distant from social psychology; there are some pages evidently inspired by our correspondence and by the desire to make concessions to us. Besides, his assimilation of social forces to physical forces shows we are right: in the same way that physical forces are nothing without moving molecules, social forces are nothing without conscious individuals. I know, of course, that he insists that the motives driving social man are unconscious; but whether his egoism, altruism, or anomie are more or less conscious, they are nonetheless psychological causes. That is what I have just written to him.

And I added several remarks about his own point of view: the proof did not always seem complete to me, above all in the criticism of opposing hypotheses: he refutes them in turn without noticing that the same procedure applied to each of the parts of his theory, taken singly, would permit a refutation analogous to that with which he contents himself for his adversaries. It nonetheless remains that the book makes one think, and that it proves one can express rather interesting general ideas all the while confining oneself to meticulous observations. The greatest reproach that I could perhaps make of it (I have not told its author) would be that it presents as new a rather old statistical method: Is there anything to it, if one disregards the interpretations suggested by the very use of that method? ...

Pau, 31 rue Porte Neuve,
20 October 1897

... Finally, I am finishing, full steam ahead, the reviews of the sociology books, for I must admit that I had given up dedicating my September to that monotonous work. Some books on Darwinism that I had run across had tempted me to study that question, and Lazarus has suffered for it: I have not yet opened it. For some days now I have worked on a review around the clock: it's poorly thrown together and contains nothing either sociological or personal. Too bad: the deadline approaches. Simmel's 156 pages make me fear for the *Année sociologique*: will it be interesting? On that condition alone will the *Année* succeed. Apart from Durkheim's article and your reviews, it will be the only thing sociological in the collection, for several collaborators (Lévy, Milhaud) who I ran into in Paris were as struck as I was to find nothing truly sociological in the works that they have to review. And if Simmel's article puts readers off, will the utility of the *Année* be keenly felt by the public despite the interesting things you and Durkheim will say? ...

Pau, 16 March 1898

... Has Durkheim sent you the statutes of the *league for the defence of the rights of the citizen*? If not, I have a copy for you in case you should like to join. It is an attempt to consolidate and conserve the group that was formed in January – and to forestall some acts analogous to those which the January group could not prevent. I hesitated before enrolling because I thought that the law on associations could be applied to that league; but since the society has as its goal the defence of the principles of '89, I do not believe that it could be treated as a subversive society ...

Rennes, 18 February 1900

... I was unaware of the crisis of the *Année sociologique*. It certainly occupies Durkheim completely. But, aren't the *Notes critiques* of Bellais[4] going to supplant the *Année*? Except for Parodi, you and I, the collaborators are nearly the same, with the addition of more severe judges such as Herr and Andler. The *Notes* have the drawback of being as much political as scientific, but they have the advantage of being short and of appearing more frequently than the *Année*. I worry greatly about the additional work that the *Année* could inflict upon you; I am very conscious that my collaboration will not be of great service to you. I know too few foreign languages to be useful, and I do not have sufficient bibliographic competence. Also, the solution that would appear to me to be preferable would be merger with Bellais ...

Rennes, 11 July 1900

... I have received some volumes from Durkheim, which proves to me that the *Année sociologique* will at least have a fourth volume and that it will undergo no modification. Perhaps, however, since the *Notes critiques*, its bibliographical utility is lessened. I wonder if we should not henceforth force ourselves to classify our book reviews more in such a way as to present the current state of research for each sociological problem: we could continue to draw up as completely as possible the inventory of publications, but we would do fewer isolated reviews and more review essays; does not the *Année psychologique* proceed thus? What preoccupies me is the necessity of giving our *Année* an original character distinct from some similar publications. Besides, I have not yet opened volume 3, but I am going to do so, for, as usual, the *Revue générale des Sciences* asked me for a review of it ...

---

[4] Bellais was Péguy's figure-head. See above, p. 24.

Documents

Aix, 4 March 1903

... I have just read Richard (Evolution) for the *Revue des Sciences*. I found it to be very contingentist and to interpret evolutionism very narrowly. On the other hand, often in confused form, he says some sociologically interesting things: 'Sociology is a social psychology, or it is nothing.' I did not know that he was on our side in the *Année* ...

30 October 1904

... Have I told you of my visit to Durkheim on Saturday, 4 October? He urged me then to do sociology and declared that 'on the basis of what he knows of me, I am altogether capable of doing it according to the positive method'. Translation: let Richard become professor of philosophy and wait to take my chair at Bordeaux, should it become vacant. But I am waiting before I take the smallest step until we know where the affair of the Collège de France stands. Likewise, Durkheim was very impressed by the rumour that we circulated about the chances of Jullian's candidacy. He went so far as to say: 'were I sure that Jullian had such a good chance, I would not bother myself further and would withdraw my candidacy'. But, at bottom, he believes in his own chances and that precedent would not permit divesting an Academy of a chair by converting the chair into a chair of national antiquities and moving it out of the domain of the Academy of Moral Sciences to that of Inscriptions. It is true that precedent does not allow the alteration of a chair founded by François I, and this is the case of the chair of ancient philosophy, the chair of Ramus. However, Durkheim considers that the maintenance of that chair will be voted only if it is impossible to reach agreement about converting it. But you perhaps are more in the know....[5]

Letters from Dominique Parodi to Célestin Bouglé

no date [1897]

My dear Bouglé,
		I have read *Suicide* with much interest. Here, at last, is a true sociology book and one that goes beyond the eternal questions of method. And, in addition, on the whole, sound doctrines are applied in it: it is deductive nearly all the time. All the explanations of the statistical data did not, however, seem to me equally satisfactory: for example, I do not really see why, if the growth of suicides from January to July is explained by the greater intensity of social and economic life, that intensity does not

[5] On that affair, see the article by George Weisz in this volume.

68

produce as regular a growth in murders or other abnormal acts which presuppose the same relations between men and the same conflicts of interest. And still other points remain rather strange: I should have, I admit, the greatest curiosity to know why, if marriage in France favours and protects the husband more than the wife, things are exactly the converse in the Grand Duchy of Oldenbourg. But, despite all that, there are many striking things and some truly extraordinary regularities in those statistics: indeed, I believe more and more in sociology. And so, forward with Equality;[6] forward sociologists: to work on a new science and almost to establish it, good gracious! There's a savoury prospect. – The bittersweet polemic, more bitter than sweet, with Tarde pleased me; I nonetheless find that Durkheim has not yet succeeded in specifying sufficiently the relations between the psychological and the social; it is obvious what he means and that he is right; but from a theoretical point of view, it did not seem to me to have as yet all the desirable clarity ...

no date [May 1899]

... I too congratulate myself on having collaborated on the *Année*, the second volume of which appears to me excellent and very superior to the first. Do you not sometimes find, in Durkheim and Mauss, a bit of a tendency to set up the so-called sociological explanation as a *thing in itself*, to insert a degree of defiance [...?] toward research of a psychological [origin?]. For example, doesn't his definition of the religious phenomenon seem to you a little materialist and exterior? And can the 'obligatory beliefs connected to practices' define religion apart from the sentiment that accompanies them or the need to which they respond? But that matters little; in fact, it seems to me that the notion of sociology is being better and better defined and specified by these works, and I am very happy to see my name there, above all closely joined with yours.

Letter from Paul Fauconnet to Célestin Bouglé

Cherbourg, 26 February 1907

My dear Bouglé,

Your letter pleased me greatly. Since you give your unqualified adherence to the project about which I have spoken to you, and which is Durkheim's, we can expect that it will be carried out. Mauss will be won over. Thus, it remains only to convince Simiand; and Durkheim, who saw him, thinks that we will succeed. – Since Durkheim knows that I have

[6] This is an allusion to the subject of the doctoral thesis Bouglé was preparing.

written to you and has asked me to make your opinion known to him, it is to him that I am first sending your letter, erasing the sentence about the *'collective banquet'*.

The title that you propose, *Mouvement sociologique*, is worth considering; it is better than those which have already come to my mind. What you say about the papers stands to reason.

Of course, Durkheim must keep the upper hand; and in the new circumstances, he can retain the editorship and collaborate without inconvenience. I nonetheless think that it will be very important for him to be relieved of a part of the work, and now that you no longer stand for a conception of the *Année* that was not mine, it would seem to me very reasonable if you were to be, for the time being at least, Durkheim's auxiliary, since Simiand has the urgent duty of finishing his thesis – and me too – while you can presently take on some new burdens.

If you have brought back from Paris the impression that the *Année* has cost us all much time, I congratulate myself for having contributed to [diminishing it for us?]. You say that it is necessary for Durkheim to produce. That is not enough: we have to also. That is why I resisted your proposals; they could not resolve the problem, since they would maintain the *Année* only by overburdening us or by causing it to lose, through an excessive eclecticism, what appears to me to be its *raison d'être*.

If upon reflection you think it would be advisable to undertake a *Festschrift* for Durkheim's fiftieth birthday (1908), write to me about it. Simiand, Mauss and Hubert, you and I could certainly contribute papers. Hertz and Huvelin also. – Would you think it better to ask Lévy-Bruhl for one, or not to go outside the *Année*? And how do you believe we ought to proceed vis-à-vis some other friends, Aubin, Hourticq, Lapie, Richard, etc.? Ask something of all of them? at the risk of it being less sociological and too large? Choose? There is a problem here. The book must be worthy of the master – and yet it must offend no one. Think about it.

Most cordially yours.

Of course, Durkheim is unaware of the proposed 'Banquet'.

2. The Durkheimians in Academe.
A reconsideration

VICTOR KARADY

Durkheim's intellectual originality has been widely recognised as equal to that of other founders of sociology, Marx, Tocqueville, Max Weber, and Pareto. However, Durkheim's work is unique among these in as much as it was a group venture. The collective nature of the achievements of the Durkheimian school is part of the anecdotal lore of sociology. So legendary is the Durkheimian group, as a group, that we might be blinded to the individual accomplishments of its members. In the future, we would surely be justified to dedicate selective attention to the work of individual scholars in the Durkheimian cluster, studying their separate, important contributions to certified scholarship. However, in my judgement, the prior step ought to be one that explicitly examines the social facts which underlie the widespread, if often poorly understood, interest in the group's collective nature. The following essay contributes to this latter project by outlining the issues pertinent to a reconstruction of the ways and means the group functioned, the external constraints it faced, and the strategic actions it embarked upon. Such an attempt at a sociological interpretation of the Durkheimian school does not aim at or result in a diminution of the debt we owe to the uncontested head of the group. On the contrary, it seeks to impose an objectivist appreciation of what has proved to be one of his major achievements, unique (if only partly successful) in the European intellectual market-place of his time: the academic institutionalisation of a synthetic science of society. This study of the intellectual implications of the early French sociologists' academic affiliations will draw upon findings and data I have previously published (but which I will not repeat here).[1] My purpose is to outline comprehensively the network of causal or probabilist determinations that both limited and gave social meaning to their accomplishments. Such an approach can help to illuminate the often forgotten revolutionary aspects of the French school as well as the social conditions of its appearance as representative of a fully legitimate discipline.

[1] This essay, deliberately published without detailed references, rests entirely upon the evidence produced in my previous studies relevant to the academic institutionalisation of French sociology. These are, in chronological order, the following:

71

Victor Karady

The pre-conditions: sociology as response to social demand

When in 1887 Durkheim was appointed a lecturer in 'education and social science' at the Bordeaux faculty of letters, there was no working institutional provision in France to foster scholarship in matters Auguste Comte had defined two generations earlier as the object of sociology. This remarkable fact holds true even if one allows for the then active, but private, Le Playist groups dedicated to empirical social research. For reasons related to their operating conditions – non-academic recruitment of staff members, short-range ideological objectives, pragmatic techniques of investigation lacking any acknowledged scientific legitimacy, etc. – the Le Playists appeared to be entirely isolated in the intellectual field proper, if not on the political scene where their impact was far from negligible. The Le Playists were more of a social movement than an intellectual undertaking.

Thus, we can say that the idea of a comprehensive science of society survived as an ideal in the late 1880s deriving from Comtean theoretical precepts as well as from Spencer's work, widely translated into French. But in France, before Durkheim's initial courses and books, there had been no systematic attempt to lay the paradigmatic foundations of sociology. Hence, the importance of his attempts to draw up a general theory of social order and of its historical types (as outlined in the *Division of Labour in Society*, 1893), elaborate a set of methodological principles (*Rules of Sociological Method*, 1895), and apply the method (as offered in the *Suicide*, 1897). Accordingly, the span of time between Durkheim's appointment to his yet marginal academic position in the provinces and the first issue of the *Année sociologique* (1898), published by the best contemporary Parisian editor of modern humanities (Alcan), must be regarded as the formative years of the sociological discipline in France for reasons different from, if not independent of, Durkheim's personal accomplishments.

Karady, V. 1968. 'Présentation de l'édition', pp. 1–53 in M. Mauss, *Oeuvres*, vol. 1, Paris: Editions de Minuit.

Karady, V. 1972a. 'La naissance de l'ethnologie universitaire', *L'Arc*, no. 48, pp. 33–44.

Karady, V. 1972b. 'Biographie de Maurice Halbwachs', pp. 9–22 in M. Halbwachs, *Classes sociales et morphologie*. Paris : Editions de Minuit.

Karady, V. 1972c. 'Note sur les thèses de doctorat consacrées à l'Afrique dans les universités françaises de 1884 à 1961', *Social Science Information*, vol. 11, no. 1, pp. 65–80.

Karady, V. 1974. 'Stratification intellectuelle, rapports sociaux et institutionalisation. Enquête socio-historique sur la naissance de la discipline sociologique en France.' Paris: report for le Centre National de la Recherche Scientifique (typewritten).

Karady, V. 1976. 'Durkheim, les sciences sociales et l'Université : bilan d'un semi-échec', *Revue française de sociologie*, vol. 17, no. 2, pp. 267–311.

Karady, V. 1979a. 'Stratégies de réussite et modes de faire-valoir de la sociologie chez les durkheimiens', *Revue française de sociologie*, vol. 20, no. 1, pp. 49–82.

Karady, V. 1979b. 'Forces of Innovation and Inertia in the French University System in the Late Nineteenth Century (with special reference to the social sciences)', *Westminster Studies of Education*, pp. 75–97.

At this time a number of external social events produced a strong public demand for sociological expertise. First, there was an exacerbation of tensions in industrial relations both factual (strikes) and symbolic (growth of the unions and of the socialist party), which the French ruling classes feared more than ever since the *Commune* of 1871. On top of this, there was the internal disruption in the ruling class itself as manifested in cases of political bribery (the Panama affair, 1891), in discord between Church and State (over lay public education in particular), in the rise of political anti-semitism (formulated popularly in Edouard Drumond's *Jewish France* in 1886), and ultimately in the Dreyfus affair (1894–9) that brought France to the brink of civil war. The ideological destabilisation of the ruling classes became such that their members increasingly tended to act, in all major national issues, as agents of competitive establishments (e.g. clerical versus lay, royalist versus republican). In this situation the search for a discourse on society invested with the authority of objective science gained a strategic importance for the French power elites, regardless of allegiance. For example, although they had different intellectual ambitions and catered for very different social clientèles, the Action française of the anti-republican Right (masterminded by such prominent authors as Charles Maurras or Maurice Barrès) and, on the opposite side, the Solidarist movement (initiated by the radical politician Léon Bourgeois) tried to fill the ideological vacuum and at the same time mobilise large proportions of sympathetic opinion in the interest of their contrasting political objectives. Sociological thought, its scientific pretences notwithstanding, was appealed to by both sides. Response to such a public demand actually came in various disguises and from various poles in the intellectual field. Responses to this demand took a number of forms: the split of the Le Playists (1886) and the birth of the *Science sociale* journal (inspired by Abbé de Tourville), the foundation by René Worms of the Institut International de Sociologie with a corresponding scholarly periodical (1893) as well as the Société Sociologique de Paris (1895), the introduction of *le mouvement sociologique* as a regular topic in the leading academic bi-monthly *Revue de métaphysique et de morale*, the systematic review of social studies in the authoritative *Revue philosophique*, and the setting up of several more-or-less academically oriented private schools of sociological training like the Collège des Sciences Sociales (1895), the Ecole des Hautes Etudes Sociales (1900), and the Ecole Russe des Hautes Etudes Sociales.

The organisation of the Durkheimian cluster took place within this large intellectual reaction to the crisis in French Society. It is worth noting, for example, that its philosophical references to scientism and positivism and, for that matter, to authors like the historian Fustel de Coulanges, were not basically different from those of the most sophisticated *idéologues* of the reactionary Action française. Durkheimian social theory was also from its

73

inception explicitly influenced by the need to explore the conditions necessary for the restoration of the consensual unity of French society under the auspices of the republican ideal. The Durkheimians pursued this goal by means of research – a truly scientific detour – incomparably more exacting than their potential rivals were capable of. Nonetheless, Durkheimians, like their rivals, found their ultimate social legitimation in the same source.

Some of their major subjects of study – lay morality, types of social cohesion, the social functions of religion, law and social order – and, as well, some of the essential concepts they had developed – anomie, collective consciousness, the sacred and the profane, normality and pathology in society – appear to be closely related to the public demand they faced for well-established scientific guidelines able to lead the contemporary State out of the ideological disorientation of the republican establishment. It is well known that most of the group took an active part in at least some of the political activities that marked the coming to power of the radical Left; namely, the fight for Captain Dreyfus (for which Durkheim himself collected petition signatures), street action in Paris during the trial of Emile Zola (with Simiand as a commando leader), the foundation of the socialist daily *L'Humanité* (with Mauss and Hubert as regular contributors), the *université populaire* movement (with Hubert Bourgin as an activist), and the creation of a socialist press (with Hertz and Halbwachs). This did not imply, however, any sort of direct interplay between the Durkheimians' political and scientific practices. On the contrary. In spite of their generally much closer entanglements with the republican Left (Durkheim was a friend of Jaurès, leader of the Socialist Party; Simiand, Bourgin, Mauss and others belonged to the circle of Lucien Herr who acted as the *éminence grise* of the socialists; Bouglé was a recognised member of the radical establishment), they were extremely cautious in keeping their intellectual production separate from their political or other public activities. A content analysis of the French sociological literature around 1900 (based on evidence from reviews and articles published in the *Année sociologique*, the *Revue internationale de sociologie, La Science sociale, La Réforme sociale*, and *Notes critiques – Sciences sociales*) reveals that, among the groups of authors active in this field, the Durkheimians were far less inclined to deal with current 'social problems'. Even the short-lived *Notes critiques* (intended by its founder François Simiand to fill the gaps of the *Année* by covering publications on social and political issues of the day) actually reserved less space for these than the non-Durkheimian journals. Thus the Durkheimians' exploitation of their acquired social legitimacy hardly meant that the cluster's work would rest on political commentary. They feared that a lapse into political journalism would threaten the basis of their academic and intellectual legitimation. This caution proved to be, as we shall see, a vital asset which contributed to their success in the other than social–ideological market.

Institutional legitimation of sociology: a conquest of limited scope

Durkheim's nomination for a social-science faculty position is understandable only as an administrative innovation due to the personal initiative of Louis Liard, then head of the higher education department of the Ministry of Public Instruction. Though at that time the future leader of the French school of sociology scarcely possessed any professional merit (he had published only trend reports and book reviews), Durkheim's appointment was in keeping with several aspects of the prevailing reforms in educational policy. This policy included a general attempt to widen the disciplinary range of courses given in the university, specifically in the arts and sciences faculties which were relatively free from the constraints of professional training (unlike the medical and law schools). This policy of curricular broadening moved especially toward branches of knowledge possessing, in France and abroad, some kind of academic foothold. Descriptive geography, experimental psychology, and educational science (*science de l'éducation*) were among the first disciplines that took advantage of such administrative promotion. Sociology merely followed suit. Appointments were made usually to junior positions (Durkheim was at the start only *chargé de cours*) and, for a long while, the courses offered in the new disciplines led nowhere on the academic career ladder. Nor was provision made to perpetuate or to spread these innovations in the university system. Some disciplines satisfied such strong needs, both social and properly academic, that their teaching was quickly generalised to every faculty of letters (fifteen in all). Human geography, as developed under Vidal de la Blache and his disciples, is a case in point. Others, like educational science, scarcely survived the upsurge of enthusiasm for school reforms at the turn of the century. After the official steps leading to its establishment as a university course, the fate of academic sociology lay in the hands of its practitioners. Its maintenance in the faculties had to be regarded as a victory largely ascribable to the Durkheimians' accomplishments and strategies. Not only did their scholarly pursuits conform to academic expectations, but the disciplinary alliances and associations they entered into and the effective lobbying they performed in various academic consultative and decision-making bodies (Ministry of Public Instruction, Comité des Travaux Historiques et Scientifiques) stabilised, even improved their positions in the universities and the more specialised schools of scholarship.

The academic legitimacy of the Durkheimians was based almost exclusively on the prestigious academic backgrounds of its sponsors and members. Most of them held the *agrégation* and a substantial number were educated in the Ecole Normale Supérieure's liberal-arts section, the most prestigious training the French university system could provide. These basic academic assets were the result of the elementary recruitment patterns of Durkheim's disciples and fellow-contributors to the *Année sociologique* (wherein *normalien* bonds, togetherness in the Dreyfusard battles, and various personal connections with teaching colleagues played a major role). The alliances and strategies set the group aside from their professional antagonists, who drew more heavily upon the staff of law schools (the 'Internationalist' sociologists) or were simply academic outsiders (Le Playists). At the same time these assets virtually guaranteed job security within the State secondary – or higher-education systems and, consequently, created rather high career prospects. As they achieved the degree of intellectual liberty associated with high-level teaching positions (a liberty further enhanced by affiliation with the politically dominant establishment), the same high academic placement also determined the limits of their disciplinary orientations. *Agrégés* and *normaliens*, they were mostly trained as philosophers or, less often, historians, hence the Durkheimians' bias for philosophy and history. These academic assets operated as general factors objectively determining the essential options open to the group in its search for recognition as legitimate representatives of a new academic profession.

To attain their collective goals the Durkheimians did their utmost to capitalise on their initial investments in Academe and to maximise the value of the institutional capital at their disposal. As section leaders in or regular contributors to the *Année*, each member belonging to the inner cluster followed the university-career track by completing a *doctorat*. Those who did not (Mauss, Hubert and Simiand) were involved in equivalent career patterns. Some of them (Simiand, Hubert, Bourgin, Halbwachs, Davy) held a *doctorat* or other degree from a law school in addition to the full training obtained at the Paris liberal-arts faculty. Their career strategies normally included the following elements: an early as possible entry into the staff of a provincial faculty or of a Parisian *lycée* with a teaching position in their *agrégation* speciality (philosophy, history or even letters proper); one or more years of leave abroad (Germany, England, or Holland) on travel grants; the use of post-graduate scholarships in order to complete theses or acquire specific professional skills; research and publications in one of the specialised sectors of the emerging social sciences but preferably in a non-specialised academic journal (like *Revue philosophique*, *Revue de synthèse historique*); the teaching of special courses (*cours libres* or *cours complémentaires*) at a liberal-arts faculty or at the Ecole Pratique des Hautes Etudes; and attempts to transform their teaching areas into permanent specialised chairs. The 'conversion' from a classical to a sociological disciplinary pursuit and a move to make it recognised as a new academic speciality were the crucial elements of their strategies. Their success depended largely on the exceptional intellectual performance of assigned scholarly tasks, no less than on direct pressure on ministerial decision-makers and, above all, on the confirmation of the discipline's identity, autonomy and utility as they were defined by Durkheim.

Sociology was created at first in the form of free lectures outside any regular curriculum. Since it did not lead to one of the useful teaching degrees (*licence, agrégation*), sociology emerged first as an auxiliary discipline at best, a superfluous academic luxury at worst. From the beginning Durkheimians benefited from their multi-disciplinary associations with academic philosophy as trained philosophers (which all of those engaged in classical university careers actually were: Durkheim, Fauconnet, Richard, Bouglé, Halbwachs, Lapie, Davy). As self-proclaimed heirs to Comtean positivism, they stressed the indispensable character of their contribution to the teaching of philosophy. Later they endeavoured with some success to make the new social sciences (sociology, pedagogy, psychology) parts of academic programs leading to a *licence*. This happened first when, beginning in 1905, Durkheim's own socio-pedagogical course (the famous 'Pedagogical Evolution in France' lectures) became obligatory for all candidates for a higher teaching degree. Then the 1920 reform of the liberal-arts faculties coupled sociology to ethics as part of the four comprehensive thematic examinations composing a *licence de philosophie*. At the same time a special examination in sociology (*certificat*) was recognised as a possible option for a 'free' (that is non-teaching and non-specialised) *licence*. Thus, apparently, sociology achieved its complete academic recognition, but on conditions that effectively deprived the discipline of its independence and made it, institutionally, a minor *ancilla philosophiae*. Ironically, the Durkheimians' success in this respect turned into a semi-failure. Its institutional dependence was counter-productive for the autonomous development of scientific sociology even if, for most members of the cluster (with Hubert Bourgin as a notable exception), this meant a secure teaching position in the faculties attained at a reasonably young age and, for some others (Mauss, Hubert, Hertz, Simiand), a more marginal but more research-oriented position at the Ecole Pratique or, later, at the Collège de France.

Though significant for the personal career of group members, the Durkheimians' collective academic success was in fact less than conspicuous and compares rather unfavourably with that of other social sciences such as human geography, psychology or even, before World War I, educational science. In 1914, for example, there were only four courses in sociology in the faculties of letters supplemented by six para-sociological courses in other institutions of higher education. But most of the latter (like all those in the Collège de France at that time) and some of the former (like the Bordeaux chair conferred on Richard who, by that time, had broken with Durkheim) were in the hands of non-Durkheimian scholars.

The philosophical training of most of the Durkheimians is only partly responsible for the enduring philosophical bondage of early sociology. The ever-worsening critical state of academic philosophy in France at the end of the nineteenth century left it unarmed in the combat with the new sociologists. Without intending to be a new philosophy, Durkheimian sociology, nonetheless, offered scientific solutions to a number of basic problems (the categories of thought, religion, morality) with which philosophy had grappled for ages in a purely speculative manner. Thus, Durkheimian social theory unwittingly came to take an important place in the field of academic philosophy.

There were at least three reasons for this turn of events. First sociology, by its internal cohesion, its scope and its ambition, was the most powerful discourse in an intellectual field marked in France by the epigones of Kantianism, at least before Bergson's appearance. (Let us remember that Bergsonian institutionism was kept outside the faculties, its academic foothold being in the Collège de France. Bergsonianism was exploited by fractions of the anti-republican Right, just as Durkheimian positivist sociology was exploited by the republican establishment.) Secondly, philosophy was by far the most prestigious disciplinary association accessible to the new sociology because it was at the top of the traditional disciplinary hierarchy in the French university system. This is why some of the outstanding theoretical statements and research findings elaborated in the Durkheimian workshop (like Durkheim's theory of religion, Simiand's discussion of the relationship between history and sociology) were made public at meetings of the Société Française de Philosophie or published in one of the major philosophical journals. This was in contrast to the group's relatively meagre contributions to academic scholarly societies or to specialised journals akin to their own specialities. Thirdly, the quasi-exclusiveness of the Durkheimians' association with philosophy in the faculties reflected to a large extent their failure to be received as equal partners by other dominant disciplines – historians, jurists, economists, human geographers. Enjoying a well-established disciplinary autonomy, in the form of faculty chairs catering for students in specialised curricula, these disciplines were reluctant to share their monopoly over professional teaching in the faculties. Their reluctance remained even when they happened to sympathise with or actually use – as did the human geographers and social historians – the work of the Durkheimians. This undoubtedly was due, in part, to the fact that the academic market at the turn of the century – in terms of job opportunities and career chances in the faculty letters – was far more favourable to historians and geographers than to philosophers. The latter could hope to improve their professional expectations by disciplinary conversion to sociology, while the others could not. These circumstances, among others, determined the disciplinary pattern of recruitment in the

Durkheimian cluster, and explain its limited attraction for others than those trained in philosophy.

Sociology's entrenchment in philosophy turned, by its own operative logic, into a self-perpetuating process. Because the Durkheimians recruited scholars from among young *agrégés de philosophie*, they failed to achieve the group's original ideal, which was to become the meeting point of all the social scientific disciplines. Without adequate institutional prospects, the Durkheimians' synthetic ambition was soon reduced, for all intents and purposes, to a career pattern that excluded students of the social sciences proper (historians, geographers). More importantly these institutional constraints tended in the long run to disadvantage those who closely pursued the major Durkheimian breakthrough in which the emerging sociology extended its thematic scope to include such rarely examined academic topics as the demographic behaviour, archaic societies, survivals of popular culture, traditional law. Even while Durkheim lived, there was an apparent contradiction between the aggregation of disciplinary subject-matters, upon which rested the intellectual legitimacy of the new science, and its rather narrow academic base.

Intellectual legitimation of sociology: an unprecedented success

We have already noted that much of the Durkheimians' initial success was due to the excellence and ambition of their work. This 'intellectual over-performance' could well be empirically demonstrated. But, let us dispense with such a demonstration here and content ourselves with the compelling observation that Durkheimian sociology emerged from virtual non-existence before the foundation of the *Année sociologique* (1897) to become, within a few years, a dominant force in the French intellectual field. To be sure, the legitimacy acquired by the group had themes in common with legitimation strategies of related disciplines (especially human geography and psychology), namely, reliance upon the existing or supposed legitimacy of the discipline abroad (most notably in Germany) and the strict observance of academic practices (that is legitimate practices proper) typical of established classical scholarly pursuits. But, it is striking that many aspects of this process derive also from radical innovations. The Durkheimians aimed less at the imposition of a new scientific paradigm upon an old one than at the construction of a new paradigm which stood out against the shadowy background of the vague and conflicting statements, beliefs, and hypotheses of competing groups. The very non-paradigmatic nature of pre- or extra-Durkheimian sociological initiatives sharpened the doctrinaire edge of Durkheimian theory and practice. Extremism in this respect (as, for example, in the group's cognitive and religious sociology) was a working

strategy to illustrate a consistent and distinctively Durkheimian interpretation of social order. By dramatising its distinctive features the Durkheimians
sought to establish theirs as the only plausible paradigm. In reality this hardly
meant that Durkheimian sociology (including its social or moral implications) went uncontested. It did mean, however, that during roughly the first
half of the twentieth century in France it was able to define the terms of all
debate on matters concerning global society and also, to some extent, on the
technical details (terminology, privileged subjects, statistical indicators) of
social research itself.

One aspect of the Durkheimians' scientific extremism, often denounced by
contemporaries (whether social scientists or not) as disciplinary 'imperialism', seems to be particularly difficult to explain if one does not take into
account the Durkheimians' legitimation strategy. 'Sociological imperialism'
had indeed far-ranging implications for, at least, the following aspects of
their enterprise: the disciplinary identity of sociology (as the science of social
facts which are *sui generis*, that is, irreducible to those studied by
psychologists, biologists); its methods (using objective indices like the
natural sciences); its thematic scope (comprising all social phenomena,
including mental states and acts – like faith, art, technical inventions –
hitherto commonly ascribed to the individual); and, by inference, sociology's
relationship to other established disciplines in the humanities. The generic
idea of a synthetic social science, as put forth by the Durkheimians, implied
an extension of sociology's competence to the point where it infringed upon
the territorial suzerainty of virtually every branch of the liberal arts, from
philosophy (which the Durkheimians proposed to supplant to some degree)
to history (to which they denied any form of epistemological specificity). Of
course such universalistic ambitions were not alien to other disciplines.
Experimental biology and psychology and comparative history, all formulated their scientific paradigm during the era of positivism in the nineteenth
century. Their subject matter was by no means limited to a narrow aspect of
human experience. To a certain extent, this universalising urge was typical of
the times. But the 'laws' of biological or historical evolution and the
regularities observed in individual psychology did not challenge the classic
representation of man as autonomous master of his destiny and works,
except for the universal determinations to which everybody is subject, and,
consequently, did not encroach on the vested interests of scholars specialis-
ing in the humanities or in social studies. Sociological 'reductionism' (that is,
the explanation of individual behaviour with reference to the state of society,
its institutional arrangements, the survival of earlier social forms, the force of
group specific collective consciousness or representations and social 'functions') did offer such a challenge. Durkheimian social relativism was
promptly considered 'imperialistic' because it tended to picture the various

disciplines as mere purveyors of facts, while reserving for itself the noble tasks of interpretation and explanation. Whatever long-lasting impact this imperialism had made on several social sciences (as represented in the *Annales* school of social history, in the birth of French collective psychology or in the reshuffling of field ethnology along Maussian lines), and disregarding the prominent territorial disputes (with positivist historians, Kantian philosophers, historians of religion or of art), one must realise that the underlying precepts were indispensable to the assertion that an autonomous science of society was possible and legitimate. The forceful imposition of such claims, often regarded as downright dogmatic, was a vital compensation for the fact that sociology was as yet poorly endowed with those intellectual assets – a stock of certified knowledge with a public 'visibility' and a particular methodology – that can result only from many years of work.

More often than not such a primitive accumulation of symbolic capital precedes, as precondition, academic establishment. To a large extent this was the case in France for regional and human geography and for experimental psychology (introduced into the faculties by Théodule Ribot's disciples). For sociology a measure of academic recognition actually came before full intellectual legitimation was achieved. In due course, however, the Durkheimians were able to achieve legitimacy as well as recognition. Their teaching effort in Academe helped to produce a basic stock of generally acknowledged research results as well as to test the technical implications of their research. But the essential instrument of sociology's intellectual legitimisation was the *Année sociologique* itself, an uncontestedly collective creation of the cluster.

In some respects the idea of an annual bibliographical survey of the relevant professional publications lacked originality. Most of the established disciplines in the liberal arts had journals of this type. The unique and revolutionary character of the *Année* was that it catered to a callow, newly born discipline whose very constitution was the ultimate objective of its editorial work. Thus the imperial design underlying the intricacies of the *Année*'s thematic divisions partook of a strategy. Through the *Année*, the Durkheimians sought to present an overall view of a *potential* science of society, its internal organisation, its auxiliary disciplines, its place in the system of sciences, its method. The critical nature of the journal offered the Durkheimians an important public forum by which they gained entry to every major contemporary debate related to the social sciences, whether technical (e.g. the problem of totemism) or theoretical (e.g. the religious origin of social institutions). All this without necessarily drawing upon personal research accomplishments which of course did not exist at the beginning. Precisely because the *Année* published, at first primarily later (after 1909) exclusively, review articles, discussion of virtually unlimited scope (often reaching the size of lengthy studies) was possible on all basic issues whatever their connection with the works under review. Even more, since the admitted aim of the *Année* was to build up the framework of the new social science, the Durkheimians readily resorted to the relevant historical, geographical, ethnological, statistical, demographic literature, while often ignoring the self-proclaimed sociological works of their contemporaries. Indeed, among the French they tended actively to disregard the latter as a means of disassociating themselves from the competing groups. Hence a two-fold advantage: by ignoring them, the Durkheimians deprecated their rival's competence; by acknowledging their counterparts abroad (especially of German *Sozialwissenschäftler* or Anglo-American social anthropologists) the Durkheimians elevated their own status by association with highbrow international companionship. A scant quarter only of the *Année* was dedicated to French literature, while they lavished attention on foreign work and promptly, if critically, integrated it into their own scholarly production. Of course, this strategy had been used before, with success. In the new Sorbonne, the positivist school of history (around Gabriel Monod's *Revue historique*) and Vidal de la Blache's new regional geography (around the *Annales géographiques*) used just this tactic to emerge from nineteenth-century provincialism into scholarly prestige.

The *Année* was not only a tactical but also an epistemological device for the legitimation of sociology. It fixed, in practical terms, the thematic outline of the discipline, thereby channelling research efforts toward the essentials of the Durkheimian theoretical program. Accordingly, the critical reading of contemporary literature was highly selective, determined largely by wider theoretical considerations. Thus the social functions of religion or the collective foundations of cognitive structures – problem areas neglected elsewhere – were central to the scientific pursuits in the *Année*. This was in contrast to their fellow sociologists' preference for 'social problems'. The Durkheimians' epistemological high-road strategy entailed a constant effort to examine the scientific constitution of research objects on the basis of theoretical and research-generated principles. Thus they were unwilling to accept the topics usually studied by their contemporaries: 'poverty', 'prostitution', 'hygiene' and the like. The Durkheimians defined research objectives in terms of problem-solving in sociology instead of social-problems commentaries. This approach was instrumental in creating the framework of a new disciplinary macrocosm within which oppositions then considered 'natural' were effectively abolished. Among the oppositions thus overcome were: diachronic and synchronic approaches (history versus sociology proper), the study of 'primitive' versus Western societies (ethnography versus sociology), or between techniques of fact-finding and fact-description (like the statistical or quantitative versus the qualitative). The intellectual division of labour practised by the Durkheimian cluster conformed more to realms of intelligibility than to headlines in the daily press.

A visible consequence was an unprecedented revaluation of the ethnological literature and its full integration into sociology's quest for the laws of social evolution in terms of the performance of 'social functions' (like religion, law, political and domestic organisation). For the first time in the annals of the academic disciplines, archaic societies became a major scientific concern (as against the exclusive attention given to the 'great' Western or Oriental cultures). This was, obviously, a breakthrough with regard to the outright ethnocentric value system implicit in every classical branch of study. Just as ethnology's dedication to far-away civilisations (especially Australian) was reassessed in the *Année*, so also were Western folklore, criminal statistics, demography, and the history of techniques reconsidered. The elimination of all epistemological differentiation between lofty or noble subjects and base or ignoble ones represents another significant breakthrough. Moreover, the gradual shift of attention from industrial societies to archaic ones (with important contributions by Mauss, Hubert, Hertz, Beuchat and Durkheim's own crowning work on the *Elementary Forms of Religious Life* in 1912) relieved the classical social disciplines from the thematic pressure of sociology. Sociology appeared to have at last a private thematic domain, even when its pretensions led to an emerging, new universal science, capable of encompassing in its analytical schemes facts identified in contemporary civilisations whether literate or illiterate as well as in ancient cultures whether 'high' or 'low'.

The Durkheimians and the changing academic value system

The Durkheimians' epistemological concerns jarred traditional scholarly practices in most of the established disciplines in Academe. Nonetheless, in other respects, they corresponded to contemporary developments in the new Sorbonne. To understand fully the meaning of the Durkheimian miracle one must keep in mind at least the basic aspects of the dominant academic value system and the changes it was undergoing at the time. This is all the more important since the Durkheimians never recognised as their own any reference group other than the academicians. So important was their identification with the academic world that their participation in other than explicitly academic societies or gatherings was always kept to a minimum. In particular, they avoided meetings organised by would-be fellow sociologists (for example they abstained from the Institut International de Sociologie and disregarded enterprises like the Collège des Sciences Sociales and its later variants). Their refusal to form a specific professional institution outside the university probably came from strategic considerations. The French faculty system, then in the midst of a process of thorough modernisation, appeared to be the only institution able to guarantee the future development of a new discipline. In order for their scientific merit to be duly acknowledged and stable provisions made for their full integration into the system, the Durkheimians could not ignore the dominant values in the academic market-place.

Knowledgeable later observers of the academic scene at the turn of the century must still be filled with amazement at the prodigious ambition and accomplishment of that group of *agrégés de philosophie*. These chosen ones, called to fulfil the noblest tasks in Academe, undertook, instead, the concerted study of savage societies (Durkheim, Mauss, Hertz), working-class budgets (Halbwachs), historical price trends (Simiand), and changes in the legal system (Fauconnet, Davy). In so doing they violated several fundamental rules that implicitly governed intellectual production in the nineteenth-century university. They ignored the traditional separation of the humanities and law, failed to respect disciplinary specialisation, refused to give preference to the culturally established subjects, attacked the ethnocentrism inherent in the choice of scholarly activities and in value-judgements, scorned the exclusiveness of individual (as against collective) work, and gave little credence to the thematic unity of teaching and research. Some of these transgressions derived from the logic of particular activities, and thereby could not be regarded as mere strategies or even as deliberate intellectual behaviour. Nonetheless it is important to realise that, whatever prompted them, these transgressions proved to be strategic in the Durkheimians' long-term struggle for the legitimation of sociology in Academe. We should not forget that their success depended upon the extent to which the university system was able to change and accept hitherto unacceptable elements.

The disciplinary specialisation of academic scholars, though widespread, had never been a strict dogmatic arrangement. Double disciplinary training within one faculty was possible either in complementary form (*agrégation de grammaire* taken before the more demanding *agrégation des lettres*) or, more rarely, in the form of transfer from one discipline to another. Disciplinary conversions of this sort, especially at an advanced stage of the career, were exceptional and usually penalised through belated professional promotion. The similarity of subject matters or research methods or even of traditional scientific taxonomies between two disciplines often made such conversions easier. The establishment of chairs of human and regional geography in every faculty of letters (at first reserved for trained historians) and the gradual (if partial) introduction of experimental psychology and educational science into the same faculties are cases in point. More radical conversions rarely occurred, though one example does come to mind. Aulard, who formerly taught French literature, did transfer to the first Sorbonne chair dedicated to the history of the French Revolution. Double training in a law school and in a liberal arts faculty usually entailed an exclusive choice between the two professional tracks. Moreover, the principle of unitary pursuits in teaching and research, if it had never been formally laid down or explicitly enforced, was a tacit precondition of a normal career in the faculties and even more so in the schools of specialised learning (Ecole des Chartes, Ecole Pratique des Hautes Etudes). Up to the late 1950s the liberal-arts sector of the French university system had not experienced the far-reaching disciplinary overlap and interchange as brought about by the *Année* team. Sociological teaching, as it was first instituted via Durkheim's post at the Bordeaux faculty of letters, was immediately laid claim to by the law faculties. Indeed the Durkheimians did their utmost to maintain an ambiguous place for their discipline in the structural taxonomy of the *Université*. The often crass hiatus between their research and teaching (the latter being regulated always by academic demand, as for example by *agrégation* programs in the liberal-arts faculties) was in fact a working mechanism to revolutionise the disciplinary stratification of the French academy. Their multi-disciplinary scientific approach foreshadowed a mutation so organic that the French university system needed more than half a century to bring it about operationally. This transformation was first truly institutionalised as late as 1947 in the form of the sixth section of the Ecole Pratique des Hautes Etudes (the first graduate school exclusively devoted to multi-disciplinary teaching and research in the field) and later, in 1968, by the creation of social-science faculties. Though late in taking its current form, the idea had not ceased to haunt French academics since the first foundation of the Ecole Pratique a century earlier (1868).

The implementation of a collective plan of action to build the new sociology could well be seen as a major deviation from the individualism of the old *Université*. There were, however, other disciplinary clusters, based mostly on the functional interdependence between a group of disciples and their charismatic, often intellectually inventive and academically powerful master. In this form the group served as an intellectual clientèle and as potential heirs to positions retained by the head of the cluster. Victor Cousin's spiritualist school of philosophy which achieved a high degree of dominance in Academe during the first half of the nineteenth century is an illustration of this. But the academic and intellectual design of such groups was conceived and fully executed by the master. Members of the cluster could only add complementary nuances to a work whose scholarly identity, though publicly present d as if it were collective, was wholly defined by the master. Such a group arrangement neither supposed nor admitted a thematic division of tasks within the cluster. As a result there was little or no specialisation of skills. Its focus was more on the operative reproduction of existing certified knowledge than the development of new ways and realms of thinking. Outside the university system, and especially in the second half of the century, another model of cumulative and acquisitive scholarly clusters emerged, often under the banner of positivism (although Comte's own positivist school can hardly be considered as one of them). Their implicit aim was to follow patterns of discovery set down by the natural sciences. Such was the case of the Ecole Anthropologique around Broca and Quatrefages, a group that revolutionalised physical anthropology with its far-fetched ambitions to become a global science of man. This model was also operative in the school of regional and social geography headed in the *Université* by Vidal de la Blache or, for that matter, in other scholarly gatherings around masters of the new Sorbonne defined as those of the 'positivist generation' (namely: Théodule Ribot, the father of French experimental psychology, himself, atypically, a non Sorbonnard; Gustave Lanson, the literary critic; and Charles Seignobos, the historian).

All these, concretely and spiritually related to the Durkheimians, usually fell short of developing a completely integrated group based on a strict division of labour related to problem areas and epistemologically specialised competences. This goal was sought and to some extent achieved by the sociologists only by means of the strategy of offering a comprehensive image of a yet embryonic discipline, which covered all potential fields of research and incorporated them into a coherent theoretical framework. The *Année* was once again instrumental in this enterprise, as is illustrated by the frequency of joint or unstated authorships of review articles (which practice, by the way, makes it very difficult to study the paternity of *Année* articles), and, more importantly, by the pattern of exchange of scientific principles among the Durkheimians that constituted the basis of their intellectual communion. Though not unprecedented in the new Sorbonne, the Durkheimian model of heuristically oriented collective scholarship represents the most accomplished discipline-building device attempted in the academic establishment of the time.

The Durkheimians could not have become a working institution without a radical redefinition of practical scholarly priorities resulting in preference given to problem-solving studies or focused research reports over books or, more specifically, to critical monographs. Some Durkheimians among the most central figures of the cluster (Mauss, Hubert, Hertz) never published books as such. Durkheim himself stopped publishing anything but articles and reviews during most of the *Année*'s actual existence, from 1897 till 1912. Clearly the need for empirical scientific breakthroughs in problem areas regarded as epistemologically essential for the consolidation of the new social science (such as the major 'functions' of social cohesion, law, morals, religion, education) were assumed to be less compatible with full-length books than with research articles. As for critical reviews, they fulfilled the capital task of affirming the Durkheimian theoretical precepts – its 'sociological view' – in all fields of relevant scholarship, especially in those that were then beyond the reach of direct exploration by members of the cluster. So heavy an epistemological charge had probably never before in the social sciences been laid on review articles, not even in the contemporary journals (like the *Revue historique*) of the positivist generation. Like the Durkheimians, the positivists made painstaking efforts to keep up with foreign research via comprehensive reviews. But they lacked the theoretical ambitions of the Durkheimians.

The scope of Durkheimian inventiveness can be best appreciated if one keeps it in mind that, in this respect, none of the contemporary sociological journals were the equal of the *Année*. Some, like *La Science sociale*, abstained altogether from publishing book reviews, while, for certain leading members of the *Année* team, reviews became a major vehicle of scientific expression (with approximately 50 review articles, notes and notices annually from 1897 to 1912 by Mauss, 41 by Durkheim, 37 by Hubert, and 35 by Simiand). This effort did not boil down to a simple and irrepressible desire to keep informed and to inform. Reviews were used as privileged means to intervene directly (without waiting for occasions offered by topical studies only) in significant technical debates in the social sciences at large. Indeed it was a way to shift attention to the major technical problems so as to make scientific debate in the social, as the natural, sciences part of a cumulative process leading to the establishment of falsifiable statements about specific subjects consistent with evidence and with broader theoretical principles. As such the Durkheimian cult of reviews became a practical condition for the theoretical breakthrough the group had masterminded. Their model of action in this respect was to be used later by such prominent innovators in the social sciences as Lucien Febvre and Marc Bloch in the *Annales* group but, before the Durkheimians, it was unprecedented in academic scholarship.

Concluding remarks: the aftermath of the Durkheimian breakthrough

It is relatively easy to summarise, as I have just attempted to do, the extent of social, intellectual, and academic legitimacy achieved by the Durkheimians. It is not much more difficult to assess the reasons why this did not open the way to the enlarged reproduction of the sociological cluster or the creation of more positions for sociologists in the faculties. In the interwar years research work fell to a low ebb and the number of specialised positions hardly exceeded that of Durkheim's era. The *Année* ceased publication after two postwar issues (of which the latter appeared incomplete) and the succeeding

Victor Karady

Annales sociologiques appeared irregularly afterwards. The intellectual resources of the other sociological journals petered out altogether.

Such a feeble institutional foothold (if not in scholarly performance, still maintained in highly specialised research by a Marcel Mauss or a Maurice Halbwachs) characterised the aftermath of the most prestigious scholarly gathering that had appeared at the turn of the century. The institutional weakness was, to some extent, the direct consequence of the Great War. Durkheim's promising only son (the would-be socio-linguist of the *Année*) and Robert Hertz (one of its most gifted talents) were among the many (such as one third of the prewar classes at the Ecole Normale Supérieure) who died in the war. But this does not account for the virtual standstill in new recruitments that lasted till the late 1930s when a new generation of sociologists came to productive age. These men (Raymond Aron, Georges Gurvitch, Marcel Griaule, Georges Friedmann, Jean Stoetzel, Claude Lévi-Strauss, among others) proved to be mostly alien and sometimes hostile to Durkheimianism if not devoid of personal or institutional links with some of the surviving members of the cluster. Mauss (whose spirited teaching at the Institut d'Ethnologie gave rise to French academic social anthropology), Halbwachs (heading the socio-morphological section of the *Annales sociologiques* and bridging the gap between social history and sociological theory), and Bouglé (with his Centre de Documentation Sociale at the Ecole Normale, a prototypical sociological workshop) were active in attenuating the generational conflict that threatened the very maintenance of a research tradition (versus essayism and political philosophising) in French sociology. But the new start in research, followed by continuous institutional growth, occurred only in the 1950s according to largely exogenous models and under scholars who paid little more than lip service to their Durkheimian forebears.

Obviously, the causes of such an intellectual discontinuity must be traced to the institutional field proper. There is no break whatsoever in social anthropology, where the Durkheimians' heritage, reinterpreted and developed by Mauss, has kept its operative force in the work of Lévi-Strauss, Louis Dumont and others. This discipline's strongholds are still today the same institutions as in Mauss's, Hubert's and even Hertz's times: the Ecole des Hautes Etudes and, later, the Collège de France. However, no other Durkheimian speciality appeared to be as firmly embodied by a surviving ancestor or represented in an institution as was social anthropology. Without research-minded heirs who could take over the few available university chairs in sociology, these other Durkheimian lineages could hardly generate new research effort. They carried on by managing a symbolic capital in the manner of *rentiers*, trying to conserve it unchanged, without any intellectual entrepreneurship. Integration into the professional training of philosophers tended to make sociology a purely theoretical (that is, rhetorical) pursuit and crippled its heuristic potential. Thus no pressure could be applied for the expansion of the academic teaching of the discipline and indeed no new positions were created before the mid-1950s. Intellectual conservatism could further no institutional dynamics which, in its turn, for lack of career chances, discouraged new recruitments under the sociological banner. Indeed any faculty-centred development of a research-oriented discipline (which, unlike the classical disciplines, disposed of only a limited amount of certified knowledge worthy of reproduction) was precluded until the liberal-arts faculties were to undergo a profound change of function; that is, until their teaching was to cease to focus almost exclusively on the training of secondary teachers. This actually did not happen before the late 1950s, when the *agrégation* program in faculty curricula started to lose their overwhelming importance.

3. The republican ideology and the social sciences; the Durkheimians and the history of social economy at the Sorbonne

GEORGE WEISZ

Between 1880 and 1900, French higher education was reformed to the conditions which persisted with only minor modifications until the 1960s (Weisz 1977a). The desire of the academic profession to raise its status and gain autonomy from the central administration was an important factor in this transformation. But the ultimate success or failure of this movement rested on support by the successive governments of the Third Republic. The almost unconditional patronage of major politicians like Jules Ferry, Paul Bert and Léon Bourgeois derived essentially from their faith in the moral potentialities of a reformed university system. They believed that higher education, properly directed, could promote consensus in a society divided by bitter social, political and religious conflicts. They hoped that professors would apply scientific procedures to the study of social problems in order to elaborate the theories and ideas which in turn would promote political moderation and social integration. These 'scientific' notions would then be diffused, first to students gathered in large university centres and then throughout society. Only the 'scientific spirit', argued Jules Ferry (1883: 429), the patron of republican educational reform,

can temper and soften the penchant for the absolute, for chimeras, which is the snare of sovereign democracies. The scientific spirit, gradually descending from higher education into the two other levels of education, is really the only barrier against the spirit of utopia and error which, left to itself and not regulated and enlightened by science, readily becomes disorder and anarchy.

Such rhetoric notwithstanding, it was exceedingly difficult for institutions devoted primarily to professional training and certification to fulfil these rather excessive aspirations. Emile Durkheim, for one, announced in 1900 that universities had failed to discharge their social mission (Durkheim 1901). But if this political task was often overshadowed by more pressing needs, it was never abandoned. Failure or not, it exerted a profound influence over the development of the university system.

Representatives of many disciplines in search of financial resources or more elevated status invoked criteria of ideological efficacy.[1] More rarely, some applied themselves to the task of developing the social and political implications of their work. Of those in the latter category, social scientists – practising an amorphous collection of disciplines linked together only by the reference to a common title – unquestionably staked their institutional destiny most directly on the ideological needs of the republic. Some of those who called themselves social scientists, like the historian Henri Hauser, sought to provide practical recipes for social and political action. Others, notably Durkheim, argued that their subjects could offer an accurate vision of social life which, fully understood, would permit individuals and groups to coexist pacifically. Durkheim's opening lecture in Bordeaux in 1887 ended with a definition of the social role of sociology. The social problem, in his view, was largely the consequence of a weakening of the collective spirit; it was therefore imperative to regain a sense of the organic unity of society:

... sociology, better than any other science, is capable of restoring these ideas. It will make the individual understand what society is, how it completes him and that he is unimportant when reduced to his own powers. It will teach him that he is not an empire within an empire but an organ within an organism and will show him the beauty of conscientiously fulfilling his role as an organ. (Durkheim 1888: 47–8)

In the pages that follow, we shall describe the ideological and institutional milieu within which sociology arose by following the evolution of a single course established at the Sorbonne in 1893. The history of social economy was the first recognised 'sociological' subject introduced at the Paris Faculty of Letters; it thus played a significant role in the development of the Durkheimian school. In the first part, we shall examine the situation of the various social sciences in the faculties of letters and those of law just prior to 1893. We shall then go on to describe the creation of a course in the history of social economy, emphasising its character as a reaction to and weapon against socialism. In a final section, we shall examine the Durkheimian takeover of this course in 1907; the process gave Durkheim an opportunity to exercise his considerable skills in the art of academic politics.

The social sciences in the faculty system

Despite a growing public interest in the 'social question', state institutions of higher education were in the early 1890s just beginning to offer courses in the social sciences. These disciplines were best represented in the Collège de France, which traditionally welcomed new and untested subjects. In 1892, at least six of its chairs were devoted to fields that could be considered social or

[1] See especially the articles that appear regularly in the *Revue internationale de l'enseignement* to plead the cause of various disciplines.

George Weisz

human sciences.[2] But chairs at the Collège were not ordinarily permanent; their titles changed regularly to conform with the expertise of scholars deemed worthy of a professorship. Furthermore, since the Collège granted no degrees, scholars could not train successors, which made disciplinary continuity impossible. No subject could be fully institutionalised in France until it secured a place in the faculty system.[3]

The social sciences were only modestly represented in the faculties of letters. Geography was the first subject of this sort to be introduced, after the defeat of 1870 at the hands of Germany underscored the military need for accurate knowledge of European terrain. But enterprising professors of geography soon began to claim another role for their discipline: serving France's colonial and commercial interests. Throughout the 1870s, scholars and businessmen joined together in establishing geographical societies in the major commercial cities. Those in Bordeaux and Paris were immediately constituted as societies of commercial geography. Those in Lyons and Marseille aimed initially at applying geography to all branches of human activity; but they too soon came to focus almost exclusively on commercial matters, particularly on the discovery of new markets and sources of raw materials. By 1880, an entire institutional structure of societies, journals, and national as well as international congresses had come into existence. It functioned as a powerful pressure group on behalf of geography, so that by 1892 the discipline was represented in thirteen out of fifteen faculties of letters.[4]

Pedagogy was the next social-science discipline to be introduced. Courses in the science of education began to spring up in the faculties of letters in 1882 and 1883 in conjunction with republican efforts to establish a state system of compulsory primary education. Many of the early courses in the provincial faculties were municipally supported and were mainly for the training of future primary teachers. Soon, however, a separate system of *école normales* was established to train these *instituteurs* although special courses for their benefit continued to be offered in the faculties. The focus of university courses in pedagogy shifted to the preparation of teachers for secondary schools, who, as a result of reforms in the later 1870s and 1880s, were to have their training in the faculties. By 1892, a chair in the science of education existed at the Sorbonne, and six other courses in pedagogy were being

[2] These were experimental psychology (T. Ribot); comparative legislation (J. Flach); political economy (Paul Leroy Beaulieu); geography, history and statistics (E. Levasseur); history of religion (A. Reville); general history of science (P. Lafitte).
[3] By faculty system, I refer to the 60-odd faculties of letters, law, medicine, science and theology (as well as the schools of pharmacy) under the jurisdiction of the Ministry of Public Instruction and whose main function was training for the liberal and teaching professions. These were dispersed and largely unconnected until 1896 when they were organised into universities.
[4] On the geographical societies see George Weisz 1976: 231–35, and Donald MacKay 1943.

offered in the larger faculties in the provinces. Before 1903 these courses were not obligatory, although in Paris students for the *agrégation* (which was the highest degree for a career in teaching – the *licence* being the first diploma) were, in the words of the dean, 'expressly invited' to take part. For those already teaching in secondary schools, the ministry provided travel grants to encourage attendance at lectures in the faculties. Courses in pedagogy were, in fact, only one part of a more extensive effort to improve the quality of teaching. At the Sorbonne and at the Ecole Normale Supérieure, special lectures on methods of teaching history and philosophy were also organised. The examinations for the *licence* and *agrégation* were revised on several occasions and a special effort was made to provide prospective teachers with a practical apprenticeship in the classroom.

The sudden interest in pedagogy undoubtedly reflected a desire to improve the quality of teaching in secondary education, where standards were believed to be low. But there was a great deal more involved. Republicans believed that social conflicts were essentially a result of the failure to achieve consensus; such consensus, they thought, could only be produced through a proper education. It was therefore necessary, in their view, to provide teachers with a special training to qualify them for their new social responsibilities. Since the ultimate goal was to promote unity in French society, it was first imperative to establish some measure of consensus about goals and methods among those destined to teach the nation's youth. The courses of pedagogy were expected to fulfil this immense task, while raising the quality of teaching. Georges Dumesnil of Toulouse insisted that his course would serve as 'a natural point of contact for the three levels of education and as a means of advancing the unity of theories which might perhaps lead to the unity of [human] wills in the country' (1888: 551). It is a well-known fact that sociology entered the university in 1887 when Durkheim took over a course in the science of education at Bordeaux, and the words 'social science' were added to his title.

In the thirteen faculties of law, the development of the social sciences was far more extensive. Between 1865 and 1914, the number of chairs in these institutions more than doubled, from 85 to 198. This growth was due, for the most part, to the expansion of a new sector of studies devoted to politics, economics and society. The fields represented included political economy, comparative legislation, constitutional law, international law, financial science, industrial legislation and colonial economy. Many of these subjects, in fact, had a strong legal orientation; but the men who taught them insisted that their primary foci were the social realities upon which judicial systems were based. Hence, they had no compunction about calling themselves social scientists.

A number of factors account for the development of these new fields.

George Weisz

Above all, legal thought shifted dramatically towards the end of the nineteenth century. Jurists were no longer content to interpret legal texts. Instead they sought to examine law as a social phenomenon intimately linked to other institutions. Consequently, the study of social 'facts' became a basic element in the work of the most eminent jurists like Léon Duguit, Raymond Saleille and Maurice Hauriou and, on a more pedestrian level, in the training of lawyers.[5] Furthermore, professors of law shared the general anti-professional sentiment that swept through the entire faculty system during the early years of the Third Republic (Weisz 1977a: 227–31). Rather than restricting themselves to the often banal task of educating lawyers, legal academics wished to become 'scientists' studying society in all of its complexities and ramifications. In speeches and articles, academics usually associated these new subjects with 'disinterested' science as opposed to utilitarian professional training. But, in actual fact, there were two very practical aspects to the development of the legal social sciences.

Firstly, the introduction of these new disciplines was expected to have significant political benefits; the lawyers, administrators and politicians trained in law schools would enter their new careers with correct views about major social issues. This was certainly true in the case of political economy, the earliest subject of this sort to be introduced. Since 1843, when they grouped together in the Société d'Economie Politique, economists had campaigned for the introduction of their subject into the education system on the grounds that it was a vital weapon in combating revolutionary ideas (Weisz 1976: 125; Levasseur 1883: 20–7; Lutfallia 1972: 512–13). During the Second Empire, the Minister of Public Instruction, Victor Duruy, accepted this reasoning and included political economy in the program of the newly established modern section of secondary education. He also created a chair in the discipline at the Paris faculty of law in 1864, explaining in his report that England had been spared a bloody revolution in 1848 because of the widespread understanding of the principles of political economy (Duruy, n.d.: 826). Duruy, however, lacked the funds to establish courses in the provincial faculties. It was not until the Paris Commune had thoroughly alarmed the ruling classes that politicians proved willing to invest public funds in the subject. A reform commission convened in 1871–2 recommended the introduction of political economy into the schools of law on the grounds that false economic doctrines were dangerous and that the future leaders of society needed to be capable of popularising the true principles of science.[6] In 1876, the administration found a place for the discipline in the second-year examination leading to the *licence*, and its future was assured.

[5] On the history of legal thought see Julien Bonnecasse 1928, and Albert Brimo 1967.
[6] See the commission's report in the *Revue critique de législation et de jurisprudence*, 1871–2, p. 604.

By 1892, chairs of political economy existed in eleven out of thirteen faculties and courses were being offered in the two others.

Such political considerations extended to most of the legal social sciences. In 1894 the Minister of Public Instruction, Emile Spuller, made the government's expectations abundantly clear to law professors:

Families are placing in your trust the young men who will be called upon one day to live in a democratic society. It is necessary that when these young men leave your hands and the schools [of higher education], they possess ideas that are just and verified about the most crucial social problems ... if only to be in a position to refute errors, dissipate prejudices and rectify opinions falsified by utopians and soap-box orators. When so many members of our working classes are attracted to and captivated by the study of social questions, can these questions be ignored by those who will one day become lawyers, magistrates, businessmen and public administrators? (Spuller 1894: 560)

A second factor which made it imperative to develop the legal social sciences was the problem of training in administration. Throughout the nineteenth century, law faculties had monopolised the education of middle- and upper-rank civil servants;[7] or, more correctly, those individuals with the personal connections necessary for a successful administrative career usually completed their education with a *licence* of law. During the 1840s, the Minister of Public Instruction, Salvandy, attempted to develop specific courses of study for future administrators, and established chairs of administrative law in five faculties. But he got no further, at least partly because law professors opposed his plans. Most were willing to accept some form of administrative training within existing programs, but few supported the organisation of autonomous studies and diplomas in administration. Parisian professors proved even more intransigent, arguing that civil law should remain the basis of training for administrators (Laboulaye 1845: 78–82).

During the short-lived Second Republic, a state school of administration was finally established; it was supposed to recruit students on the basis of merit rather than patronage and then train them to be loyal servants of the republic (Wright 1976). The school was suppressed by the legislature in 1849, less than a year after it opened. But in 1871 law faculties were presented with a more formidable challenge when Emile Boutmy and a group of bankers and politicians associated with the Centre Left created the Ecole Libre des Sciences Politiques. The new institution quickly developed an informal monopoly over a number of prestigious administrative corps including the Council of State, the Inspection of Finances, and the Ministry of Foreign Affairs (Osborne 1974: 94–6; Weisz 1976: 247–9). During the early years of the republic, politicians opposed to the conservative and elitist character of

---

[7] For instances see V. Wright 1972: 65; V. Wright and B. Leclerc 1973: 189.

the school again proposed the creation of a state school or at least the transfer of the Ecole Libre to the jurisdiction of the government. But a majority of senators and deputies preferred the far cheaper alternative of developing administrative studies within the law faculties.

Consequently, the legislature during the next decade invested considerable sums of money in developing the social and economic sciences that seemed necessary to train future civil servants. Law professors put up little resistance because they recognised the need to compete effectively against the Ecole Libre and because a serious stagnation of student enrolment during the 1870s and 1880s made imperative the development of new professional courses of study.[8] Nevertheless, a majority was opposed to the establishment of autonomous administrative programs which threatened to depopulate traditional law courses and to destroy the unity of faculty studies.[9] As a result, the administration was forced to introduce new disciplines to existing examination programs. Only in the case of the doctorate was it possible in 1894 to divide the old degree in two: a doctorate of law and another devoted to political and economic studies.

The development of the legal social sciences provoked considerable tension between law schools and the Ecole Libre des Sciences Politiques. Emile Boutmy campaigned incessantly against efforts to establish programs of administrative training in law schools, fearing that they would lead to a faculty monopoly over recruitment to the state services.[10] On a lesser scale, the development of the social sciences in the faculties of letters brought these into conflict with the schools of law. Sociology was viewed with an especially jaundiced eye and Durkheim's appointment to a course of social science in 1887 provoked intense protests (Espinas 1889). Academic jurists recognised that the development of sociology in other institutions threatened their monopoly over the social sciences; but they were not especially eager to introduce the discipline to the schools of law. Essentially, they wished that it would go away.

There were some exceptions. In 1883, for instance, the dean of the Toulouse faculty of law suggested to the ministry that courses of sociology be established to provide a general introduction to law studies.[11] The Bordeaux faculty of law counted two fervent supporters of sociology on its staff: Léon Duguit and Ferdinand Faure. The former, destined to become one of the

---

[8] Enrolment in law schools was 4,326 in 1851, 4,913 in 1865 and 4,976 in 1878. It did not start rising significantly until the late 1880s.

[9] See the responses to a ministerial enquiry in 1878 found in F 17 12560. The archival series F 17, A.P. and AJ 16 cited here are all located in the Archives Nationales in Paris.

[10] See Boutmy's brochures (1876, 1889). Also see his letters to Jules Simon in A.P. 87 and to Ferry in F 17 12560.

[11] In *Enquêtes et documents relatifs à l'enseignement supérieur*, 124 vols., 1880–1914, Paris: Imprimerie Nationale, see vol. 16, p. 593. Also see Despagnet 1891: 11–12.

great names of French public law, offered public lectures (*cours libres*) in sociology during the early 1890s in addition to his regular courses of public law. In response to Durkheim's appointment, Duguit (1889) published an article in which he advocated the introduction of sociology to the faculties of law where all the social sciences belonged. Faure was a republican politician and professor of political economy at Bordeaux whose growing interest in statistics led to his appointment in 1892 to a chair in that subject at the Paris faculty of law. A year later he sponsored a motion in the Faculty Council of Professors (Conseil de la Faculté) requesting that a chair of social science be established.[12] The rejection of his proposal on the grounds that sociology was insufficiently developed incited Faure to produce a pamphlet in defence of the discipline. Starting from the Comtean premise that sociology was a body of ideas uniting all the specialised sciences of society, Faure reasoned that the many disciplines introduced into law programs over the past decade

need to be based on a certain number of fundamental notions that are common to them all and which no one of them can elaborate directly. Their conclusions must be reconciled and each must supplement the others. This involves an immense work of assemblage and coordination, which is necessarily the highest task of a general science. This general science is sociology. (Faure 1893: 10)

Although he didn't mention it, Faure – a prominent radical–socialist politician – undoubtedly expected the body of coordinating ideas which made up sociology to have a very definite political cast. This probably accounts for the hostility of most law professors – traditionally more conservative than those of letters – towards the new discipline. It certainly explains the attitude of Maurice Hauriou, another future giant of public law. Then professor of administrative law at the Toulouse faculty of law, Hauriou also taught a course of public lectures in sociology. But his variant of sociology was deeply conservative and heavily influenced by the work of Gabriel Tarde.[13]

In response to Faure's pamphlet, Hauriou in 1893 published an article criticising sociologists for attempting to direct other disciplines. Such pretensions were unjustified, he argued, since sociology consisted of little more than philosophical speculation of a particularly dangerous kind. Sociology would be accepted by law professors, he declared, only when it became a true science.

But so long as you remain at the level of philosophy, and at philosophical systems so exclusive that they are irreconcilable with our education system, we do not want to let ourselves be directed by you; we intend to remain independent in philosophical matters. (Hauriou 1893: 4)

[12] See his letter to Ernest Lavisse dated 12 January 1894 in the Fonds Lavisse no. 25167 at the Bibliothèque Nationale. This series will be cited as BNFL with the appropriate volume number added.
[13] He dedicated his early sociological work (Hauriou 1896) to Tarde and Georges Dumesnil. On his later legal thought see Broderick (ed.) 1970.

Hauriou's article provoked an anonymous defence of sociology in the *Revue internationale de sociologie*[14] (probably written by its editor René Worms who was to be appointed in 1897 to teach the history of economic doctrines at the Caen faculty of law). This prompted Hauriou to respond in that journal with yet another article developing his critique of sociology. Science, he declared, is dangerous because it poses serious problems of social conduct. Of all the sciences, sociology is the most dangerous because it takes society as its subject matter. Its practical consequences, he continued, are 'social reforms, if not insurrections or criminal acts. Well then, it is this science, that can so easily be murderous, that you wish to teach to large audiences and to insert into programs of study.' Before teaching sociology officially, it was necessary to obtain results 'that are not contrary to old moral and religious traditions'. This was possible, Hauriou suggested, if sociologists followed the lead of Gabriel Tarde and emphasised individual psychology. Social structure was only of secondary importance; by making it paramount, sociology led inevitably to socialism because improvement required the reorganisation of society. Hauriou, in contrast, re-affirmed his belief in progress through 'the improvement of the individual' (Hauriou 1894: 393–5).

Hauriou was probably unusual among jurists both in the depth of his conservatism and in his perceptive understanding of sociological theory. But the mistrust he expressed was fairly widespread and posed serious difficulties for the supporters of sociology in the law schools. An article by René Worms (1894), defending sociology against the charge that it was socially dangerous, had little impact. Professors of law continued to be suspicious of a discipline that had yet to prove its worth and that seemed to have reformist, if not outright collectivist, implications. Still, supporters of sociology had one thing in their favour; even the most vigorous opponents of the discipline preferred to accept it rather than allow it to be appropriated by the neighbouring faculties of letters. For, if sociology became established elsewhere, the virtual monopoly enjoyed by law schools over the social sciences would be seriously challenged.

The history of social economy

In 1893, sociology began finally to emerge as an autonomous discipline in France. That year, Durkheim defended his doctoral thesis, and René Worms created the *Revue internationale de sociologie* and the Institut International de Sociologie. The Catholic Faculty of Lille opened up a special section of social and political science and the municipal council of Lyons founded a

[14] Un docteur en droit, 'La sociologie et les facultés de droit', *Revue internationale de l'enseignement*, 2, 1894, pp. 63–7.

public course of sociology at the faculty of letters (taught by A. Bertrand).
Throughout the spring of that year the General Council of Parisian Faculties
(Conseil Général des Facultés de Paris) discussed the possibility of creating a
new program of economic and administrative studies. This was in fact to be
little more than an administrative reorganisation of existing courses in the
faculties of law and letters to enable the former to compete more effectively
against the Ecole Libre des Sciences Politiques.[15] The project, moreover, was
soon abandoned in favour of a plan to reform the doctorate of law; but it
served to focus attention on the need to develop studies in the social sciences.
Simultaneously, political events lent a new urgency to the 'social question'.
In the elections of 1893 held amidst intensifying labour violence and
anarchist terrorism, the various socialist groups won a combined total of
forty-eight seats in the Chamber of Deputies.

In November 1893, the daily press announced that a group of
revolutionary-socialist students (Le Groupe des Etudiants Socialistes Révo-
lutionnaires) intended to organise regular lectures in the Latin Quarter.[16]
Among the advertised speakers were leading socialist politicians like Jean
Jaurès, Jules Guesde, Jean Allemane, Paul Brousse and E. M. Vaillant.
Several days later, the historian Ernest Lavisse – one of the most influential
professors at the University of Paris – reacted to the news with an article that
appeared on the front page of the prestigious daily, *Journal des débats*.[17]
Lavisse admitted that there existed no coherent program in the social
sciences despite the great interest shown by students in these matters. In
Germany and Belgium, he claimed, the social sciences were being developed
on a large scale. In France, however, these subjects were taught in a
fragmented and incomplete manner. It was necessary to create new courses
and to arrange those in existence into a coordinated program of studies.
Lavisse reassured those who feared that such a program would establish 'a
state doctrine of social science and something like an official dogma'.
Teaching in the faculties would centre on the concrete realities of social life,
and theory would be constantly modified by experience. And certainly, there
would be far more 'impartiality, independence and liberty' in the state
faculties than in the recently announced socialist school.

A major difficulty, Lavisse suggested, was the lack of courses in the social
sciences. Although the state was unable to furnish necessary funds, the
faculties since 1885 had been authorised to receive private donations.
Recently, the University of Montpellier had even become the proprietor of a
vineyard. 'Let people give us money, land, grape-vines, anything they like,

---

[15] See the minutes of the General Council of Faculties for 24 April 1893 and 24 July 1893, in AJ
16 2569, pp. 314–6, 325–7.
[16] *Journal des débats*, 14 November 1893.
[17] 17 November 1893. All the quotations that follow are taken from this article.

on condition that we provide the University of Paris with a program in the social sciences.' Was there any need more pressing, Lavisse asked, than that of instructing young men in the problems of society and in proposed solutions? It was necessary to teach them methods of study and reflection and 'to put them on their guard against temptation, but also against indifference, ignorance, inertia, more dangerous than blind passion because it provokes this passion and then does nothing about it'.

Lavisse's appeal soon had an effect. Five days later, at the regular meeting of the Council of Professors at the Paris faculty of letters, the philosopher Paul Janet introduced a motion calling on the minister to establish a course in experimental psychology. (It is worth noting that his nephew, Pierre Janet, was the man most likely to be appointed to teach this course.) Another well-known philosopher, Emile Boutroux, reminded everyone present that there existéd an equally glaring lacuna that needed to be filled: sociology 'that branch of studies that occupies such a large place in discussions going on in political and scholarly circles'.[18] On both social and scientific grounds, Boutroux insisted, it deserved a place at the faculty.

In the debate that ensued, there was some disagreement about the demonstrated scientific character of sociology. Eventually the real level of interest in both psychology and sociology became apparent when the council voted unanimously to request, before anything else, a second conference of Latin. Only then did it pass motions calling for the creation of courses in experimental psychology and sociology. These requests were then sent on to the General Council of Parisian Faculties for approval before going to the Ministry of Public Instruction.

Soon after this meeting, Lavisse received a letter from Dick May (the pen-name used by Miss Jeanne Weil), a woman who was soon to become closely associated with a number of private institutions devoted to the teaching of social science. She was writing, she explained, on behalf of the Count Aldebert de Chambrun, who had been favourably impressed by Lavisse's recent appeal in the *Journal des débats*. He would therefore like to found a chair at the Sorbonne in the field of social economy[19] (a term popularised by Le Play and used by Chambrun interchangeably with sociology).

Chambrun was by this time a blind old man nearing the end of an eventful life. Married to the heiress of the Crystal Works of Baccarat which he managed, he also served as a prefect and legislator under the Second Empire. After the Paris Commune, he was elected as representative from the Lozère, first to the National Assembly and then to the Senate where he sat with the Orleanist Right. In 1879, he renounced politics in order to devote himself to

[18] Meeting of 22 November 1893, in AJ 16 4748, p. 186.
[19] Letter dated 21 November 1893, in BNFL 25169, fols. 371–2.

writing and good works. At the Exposition of 1889, the social-economy section awarded his factory a prize in the category of institutions established by employers for the welfare of workers; the honour and his wife's death two years later seem to have inspired him to dedicate himself to 'sociology', as he referred to all studies of the social question. He wrote a number of largely incomprehensible books inspired loosely by the Catholic social reformism of Le Play and by the associationism of men like Charles Robert, Léon Say and Jules Siegfried. He was also a generous philanthropist, donating money to Le Play's Société d'Economie Sociale and Siegfried's Société Française des Habitations à Bon Marché. A few months before Dick May's letter to Lavisse, he donated money to the Ecole Libre des Sciences Politiques for the foundation of a chair in social economy, to which the Le Playist writer Emile Cheysson was appointed.[20]

By the time Lavisse announced the donation to the General Council of Parisian Faculties,[21] Chambrun had agreed to provide an annuity of 5,000 francs for a period of twenty-three years. (Somewhere along the line the subject matter of the new course had become the *history* of social economy.) The donation was too small to finance a chair and a supplement had to be found to get even a course started; but the gift was unanimously accepted. At another meeting of the council a month later, a representative of the law faculty expressed his unease about the introduction of social science to the faculties of letters. He pointedly asked just what the term social economy actually signified. 'Until now the moral and political sciences had a sense that no one could mistake. Sociology's invasion of the faculties appears very dangerous to him.'[22]

Representatives of the faculty of law could hardly suggest that a private donation be refused. But they were plainly worried by the recent turn of events. The original request for a course of sociology submitted by the faculty of letters was, just at that moment, being reviewed by a special commission of the General Council of Faculties. If the response proved favourable, sociology would be firmly entrenched in the faculties of letters. Consequently, when the Council of Professors of the Paris faculty of law met in January of 1894, the dean, Colmet de Santerre, strongly advised that they too request a course of sociology. The response of most of his colleagues was lukewarm. The professor of Roman law, Cauwès, expressed fear that the subject matter of sociology was 'indeterminate', i.e. ideologically objectionable. Ferdinand Faure reassured him that, since sociology lacked any fixed doctrine, there was nothing to fear. But the professors grudgingly supported the dean and

[20] On Chambrun's life see the collection of speeches in *Obsèques du Comte de Chambrun*, Paris, 1899, and the obituary in *Réforme sociale*, 16 February 1899. For his sociological ideas see Chambrun 1892.
[21] Meeting of 27 November 1893, AJ 16 2569, p. 410.
[22] Meeting of 23 December 1893, AJ 16 2569, p. 436.

passed his motion unanimously. Their attitude was summed up by one professor of administrative law who declared that he would under normal circumstances have advocated a long delay to permit careful consideration of the question. But in the present case, haste was imperative. 'It is vital that we do not leave it to the faculty of letters to realise this conquest. We cannot maintain an expectative attitude and we must intervene so that sociological teaching is given in the faculty of law to which everything links it.'[23]

Soon after, the dean sent the request to the vice-rector of Paris. He argued that the faculty was already teaching the basic elements of sociology in such courses as the history of law and constitutional law. He also emphasised that professors in the law faculties could be counted on to treat the subject in a moderate and politically reliable manner, implying that philosophers in the faculties of letters could not. The social importance of such a course, he stated,

appears manifest when one contemplates the tendencies of the most reputed sociologists. In general, they teach doctrines that can be considered dangerous from the societal perspective. Their books are in the hands of French youth who are unaware that refutations are possible. It would thus be extremely useful to have a prudent instruction that demonstrates that the ideas expressed in these books are not dogmas and that they can be seriously and scientifically contested. The professors in our faculties present the most certain guarantees with respect to the scientific character of the courses they teach.[24]

The sudden enthusiasm for sociology in the law faculty did not run very deep, of course. In January 1894, Ferdinand Faure wrote to Lavisse to warn of the developing opposition to sociology in the faculty and to request his support.[25] Sure enough, at the next meeting of the Council of Professors held a few days later, two senior professors of civil law who had not attended the previous meeting severely criticised the dean for over-stepping the bounds of his authority.[26] As members of the General Council of Faculties they assured their colleagues that a special commission of that body would probably have adjourned the request for a course of sociology by the faculty of letters had the law faculty not intervened. Now the Sorbonne's claim would almost certainly be approved unless both requests were adjourned. Since most professors had voted for sociology only under duress, the council quickly rallied behind the proposal and voted the following rather obtuse resolution:

The Faculty, without going back on the vote adopted at the meeting of 10 January 1894, considers that there is only need for its representatives to insist on the creation

[23] AJ 16 2560, p. 477.
[24] *Ibid.*, pp. 478–9.
[25] Letter dated 12 January 1894, BN94, BNFL, 25267, fols. 157c–157d.
[26] Meeting of 18 January 1894, AJ 16 1795, p. 439.

of a course of sociology at the faculty of law so long as the request of the faculty of letters has not been adjourned.[27]

Soon after, in fact, the faculty of letters abandoned its request for a course of sociology, presumably satisfied with the one in the history of social economy. The faculty of law followed suit, and also withdrew its bid.[28] Aside from an occasional course of public lectures, sociology was thus not introduced officially in law schools, despite the fact that Chambrun founded a course of social economy for Charles Gide at the Paris faculty of law in 1898.

Chambrun had some fairly definite views about the qualities necessary to teach the history of social economy; they needed to find a scholar somewhere between the two extremes of revolutionary socialism and economic liberalism, he told Lavisse.[29] But, although he suggested several names drawn from Le Playist and Associationist circles, he was quickly made to understand that the faculty had its own recruitment procedures and criteria.[30] In this case, the decision appears to have been left to Lavisse and to his friend, the philosopher Henri Marion. Even before Chambrun's gift was officially accepted, the two were busy deciding on a candidate. Everything depended on defining the subject matter. If the history of social economy was understood as theoretical sociology, then Emile Durkheim was unquestionably the most qualified man for the position.[31] If, on the other hand, the history of social thought was to be emphasised, then the ideal candidate was Alfred Espinas who had published a history of economic doctrines in 1891. Espinas was more senior than Durkheim and had the good fortune to study at the Ecole Normale Supérieure during the 1860s at roughly the same time as Lavisse and Marion. (From their correspondence he appears to have been a good friend of Marion.) An early and militant republican, he defended a doctoral thesis in 1871 that is generally considered to be the first serious academic work of social science. He went on to help Théodule Ribot popularise psychology and, as professor of philosophy at Bordeaux, offered one of the first courses of pedagogy in France. He had even served as dean of the Bordeaux faculty of letters. His only drawbacks, in fact, were poor health and difficulties as a public speaker.[32]

Facing such stiff opposition, Durkheim applied for the job while making it clear that he would willingly defer to Espinas and be satisfied with the vacant

---

[27] *Ibid.*, p. 430. One professor aptly expressed the reasoning behind this motion: 'It is in fact only the fear of seeing courses of sociology organised in the faculty of letters that moved it [the faculty] to approve the project immediately. If this fear does not exist, it is preferable to adjourn examination of the question.'
[28] AJ 16 2570, p. 15.
[29] Letter of 23 November 1893, BNFL 25169, fols. 333–4.
[30] See Chambrun's letter to Lavisse dated 8 January 1894, BNFL 25169, fol. 337.
[31] See Espinas's letter to Lavisse dated 1 December 1893, BNFL 25167, fol. 140.
[32] See Espinas's dossier in F 17 22193.

chair of philosophy at Nancy.[33] Leaving nothing to chance, he went to see Lavisse during a visit to Paris.[34] Such persistence was rewarded a year later when Durkheim was promoted to the chair of social science at Bordeaux.

Espinas, meanwhile, was informed by Marion only a few days after Lavisse's first meeting with Chambrun that his appointment was likely. Throughout December of 1893, he and Lavisse exchanged letters in order to work out the details of his move to Paris.[35] Financial conditions had to be set but, above all, the subject matter of the new course required clarification. Much to Espinas's dismay, Lavisse pressed for a course of contemporary (starting from the French Revolution) social and economic history. Espinas preferred to begin much earlier with subjects that did not excite political passions. After having gradually acquired the necessary authority, he reasoned, he could take on subjects of topical interest. More important, he could not agree to teach economic and social history which was in the domain of 'historians properly speaking'. Instead he proposed to concentrate on social doctrines and, eventually, on theoretical sociology.

Lavisse, however, was persistent, driving Espinas almost to distraction. The latter begged Lavisse to remember that he had never taught history. 'You must', he wrote, 'accept me as I am, that is as a fifty-year-old philosopher.' In the end, a compromise was reached. Espinas would examine neither doctrines nor economic facts. Instead, he wrote to Lavisse, he proposed to go beyond social economy and to examine 'the general principles of practical social activity, that is to attempt to found a school of theoretical politics'. He would thus attempt to do for politics what Henri Marion was doing for education. By analysing the 'responsibilities and means of action of government and the citizen', he hoped eventually to produce 'a philosophy of action'.

'Philosophy of action', as it turned out, came dangerously close to being political propaganda. In the spring of 1894 Espinas was elected unanimously by the Council of Professors to teach the course. (He was, in fact, the only candidate.) A few weeks later he gave his opening lecture which was subsequently published in the *Revue internationale de sociologie*. Espinas began by outlining his theory of action. Utilising the notion of biological differentiation, he arrived rather circuitously at the conclusion that human action is, in large measure, based on irrational beliefs and desires 'formulated in the obscure parts of the collective consciousness' (Espinas 1894: 327). The second part of the lecture developed the political consequences of this analysis; according to Dick May who was there on behalf of

[33] See his letter of 5 December 1893 (Durkheim 1979: 113–14).
[34] See Durkheim's letter to Lavisse dated 8 January 1894 (Durkheim 1975: 486).
[35] In BNFL 25167, fols. 140–50.

Chambrun, this section provoked considerable consternation among his listeners.[36]

If human action is irrational, Espinas argued, then the scope of social reform must necessarily be limited. With this established, Espinas went on to attack socialist theorists for basing their thinking on an abstract universal morality that led inevitably to radical individualism. Instead, political ideas should be the expression of an organic and national morality which demanded subordination and voluntary obedience. What could do more for the progress of civilisation? Espinas asked: 'the collectivist state, the creation of abstract reason, the deification of the individual or the historical state as we know it?' In serving the *patrie*, he concluded, we serve humanity. 'That is the solution to the current crisis. Bitter and arrogant demands, class hatreds, civil war, do not augur well for the regime of harmony that is being proclaimed' (Espinas 1894: 349–50).

Espinas's lecture was not well received by Dick May,[37] whose dissatisfaction intensified during the succeeding months. In May, she insisted on an immediate audience with Lavisse to discuss the course which 'embarrasses me a good deal. It seems to me that it is developing in a manner contrary to what you desired and Monsieur Chambrun hoped for.'[38] She apparently was not the only one unhappy with Espinas. In August she reported to Lavisse that socialist student groups were planning to disrupt the course and to demand *en tumulte* that Durkheim be assigned to teach it.[39] (There is no indication that any disruption took place.) Administrators were critical of Espinas's inability to attract auditors. One inspector reporting on the poor attendance, suggested that 'the young Israelite Durkheim, so unhappy to have been passed over in favour of Monsieur Espinas', could almost certainly have drawn larger crowds.[40]

The issue soon disappeared from the correspondence between Dick May and Lavisse, overshadowed by the developing project to establish the Musée Social. By the end of May, the dean of the faculty of letters could reassure the General Council of Faculties that Espinas's course was being conducted in 'an elevated philosophical language'; and Lavisse added with some understatement: 'One need not fear adventures with Monsieur Espinas; rather one might consider his doctrines too moderate.'[41] Although Beudant of the faculty of law registered a token protest against the ideas developed in

[36] Letter dated 3 April 1894, BNFL 25169, fols. 349–50.
[37] See her letter of 3 April 1894, BNFL 25169, fol. 380.
[38] Letter dated 2 May 1894, *ibid.*, fol. 384.
[39] Letter dated 22 August 1894, *ibid.*, fol. 386.
[40] In F 17 13224. For most of the lectures, the report stated, there were only about a dozen people in the audience. I am grateful to Roger Geiger for sending me this citation.
[41] Meeting of 28 May 1894, AJ 16 2569, p. 487.

George Weisz

Espinas's last book, no one criticised the course. Espinas did little after 1894 to advance either the social sciences or political thought, but he did his work conscientiously.[42] He was routinely promoted to a professorship in 1904 when the ministry provided the supplementary funds necessary to transform his course into a full chair.

The Durkheimians and the history of social economy

In the years that followed, the need for courses and institutions capable of combating socialism had a major impact on the intellectual life of the Latin Quarter. Most of this ideological activity took place outside the Sorbonne, which continued to be rigidly defined by professional programmes and examinations. Dick May played a singular role in organising the most important institutions of social science (May 1896–7; Clark 1973: 155–7). First, she helped Chambrun establish the Musée Social in 1894. But, recognising that the Le Playists and liberals at the Ecole Libre des Sciences Politiques were exercising a growing influence over the old count, she was prominent in founding the Collège Libre des Sciences Sociales in 1895. Five years later, in disagreement with the Collège's educational philosophy, based on the premise that the confrontation of opposing doctrines led inevitably to the discovery of truth, she was a leading member of the group that created the Ecole des Hautes Etudes Sociales. These latter two schools were private; but both enjoyed a semi-official status that enabled them to obtain small government subsidies and to utilise the services of numerous university professors. The Durkheimians, like everyone else, participated occasionally in the activities organised by Dick May despite Durkheim's own antipathy for the woman.[43]

Although the Sorbonne was not capable of devoting itself completely to ideological tasks, neither was it able to ignore political pressures. In 1896, the legislative assembly granted funds for a new course in the history of political doctrines (for the philosopher Henry Michel); it was supposed to combat socialism and all 'false political doctrines'.[44] A year later, the council of professors of the faculty of letters requested a course in the history of scholastic philosophy, made necessary by the intense polemics then surrounding the theories of Aquinas and the doctors of the Middle Ages.[45] Pressure came from the Left as well. In 1898, Jean Jaurès, leader of the Socialist Party, provoked a passionate debate in the faculty by requesting authorisation to teach a course of public lectures on the history of socialism.

[42] For Durkheim's opinion of Espinas see his letter of 13 August 1901 to Bouglé (Durkheim 1976: 178).
[43] See his letter to Bouglé of 21 July 1900 (Durkheim 1976: 178).
[44] *Journal officiel, débats Sénat*, 10 July 1897, p. 1221.
[45] Meeting of 30 October 1897, AJ 16 4748, p. 349.

106

Some professors argued that granting permission would lead to political disorders in the faculty and would, at the very least, contribute to the spread of dangerous ideas. Others, however, including Lavisse, Espinas, and Ferdinand Buisson, adopted a more liberal stance. Although he found most of Jaurès's ideas utopian, Lavisse argued, there existed no society without either the capacity or need for reform; 'in consequence, every project for the transformation of society needs to be a subject of study in a university, if that university wishes to be involved in general social life'. Nevertheless, 21 out of 37 professors rejected the liberal position, agreeing with Dean Alfred Croiset, that: 'in granting authorisation to Monsieur Jaurès, the faculty will appear to have approved, to have sponsored a vehicle of political propaganda, of which it shall be, to a certain extent, the accomplice and dupe'.PY

Owing to its tradition of innovation and the flexibility of its institutional arrangements, the Collège de France was once again the best place to introduce chairs with political content. Consequently, the government in 1897 requested legislative appropriations for a chair of social philosophy at the Collège. The financial commission of the Chamber of Deputies denied the funds, provoking the ire of several moderate republicans. The issue was brought up in the Senate where one member insisted that, at a time when certain professors at the Sorbonne were expounding 'socialist doctrines', it was absolutely necessary to teach questions of social economy from the correct point of view. This new course of 'sociology', added the Minister of Public Instruction, Alfred Rambaud, was just as necessary as the one in the history of political doctrines created the year before at the Sorbonne. False social theories needed to be combated with the same zeal as false political doctrines: 'The more one studies the social doctrines that have played some role in our history, and the more one is forced to examine them critically, the greater the possibility that certain doctrines will cease to be dangerous for the social order.'PΘ

A few days later, Rambaud somehow succeeded in obtaining a small subsidy. The minister who had complete freedom to appoint the professor for any newly established chair, settled inexplicably on Jacques Izoulet, a philosopher of doubtful reputation whose views were sufficiently amorphous to be condemned by both conservatives and reformers.PI The nomination was a blow to Durkheim who had been declared a candidate; in a letter of candidacy to the minister he had argued that since he was the first professor of sociology in France, the appointment of anyone else would be interpreted as a sign that he had failed in his task (Durkheim 1979: 114–15).

Durkheim finally got to Paris in 1902 when he was appointed *chargé de*

PY Meeting of 16 July 1898, AJ 16 4748, pp. 376–8.
PΘ *Journal officiel, débats Sénat*, 16 July 1897, p. 1221.
PI See *Le Siècle*, 14 August 1897, concerning Izoulet's nomination.

George Weisz

cours in the science of education at the Sorbonne. It took him only two years to make himself a serious contender for a professorial chair. In 1904, Henri Bergson, then professor of Greek and Latin philosophy at the Collège de France, decided to move over to the chair of modern philosophy left vacant by the death of Gabriel Tarde. The assembly of the Collège decided to transform Bergson's old chair so that it could be filled by a distinguished scholar in another field of knowledge. At this point, however, professors divided up along disciplinary lines. Historians wanted it transformed into a chair of general history (for Gabriel Monod), while classicists campaigned for one of national antiquities (to be filled by Camille Julian); philosophers rallied behind a proposal to establish a chair of sociology for Durkheim. In addition to the proven qualities of their candidate, Paul Janet argued, the creation of a chair in sociology would maintain the existing equilibrium between philosophy and history at the Collège.[49] Because of the deadlock, discussion was postponed until a later meeting at which Henri Bergson acted as spokesman for Durkheim's supporters. Bergson's intervention on behalf of the founder of sociology, rather surprising in view of the philosophical disagreements between the two men, testified to the predominance of disciplinary divisions in such matters. But the philosopher's efforts were unsuccessful because historians and classicists banded together to vote in favour of a chair in the history of national antiquities.[50] Durkheim had to wait two more years before his routine promotion to a chair at the Sorbonne.

Durkheim, we can see, was brilliantly successful in his career. But he failed to translate the growing public interest in social issues into new chairs of sociology. His only real victory during this period was the establishment of a chair of social philosophy at the letters faculty of Toulouse, to which Célestin Bouglé was appointed. This lack of success largely explains the importance which the history of social economy assumed for the Durkheimians. Unlike the chair of education at the Sorbonne, linked with sociology only because Durkheim was the incumbent, the history of social economy – along with the chairs of Bouglé in Toulouse and Gaston Richard in Bordeaux – had a recognised 'sociological' character. It was thus imperative for the Durkheimians to take control of it as soon as it became vacant.

Among the Durkheimians, Bouglé was in the strongest position to succeed Espinas, having taught in the chair of social philosophy since 1901. His career, moreover, had been brilliant; his scientific credentials were impeccable and he had proven himself to be a gifted orator and teacher. His work as a political polemicist of solidarism was viewed favourably by the radical republicans in power and his books stimulated wide popular interest.[51]

[49] Meeting of 28 November 1904 in F 17 13551.
[50] Letter to the minister dated 16 January 1905 in F 17 13557.
[51] See the numerous reports in his dossier F 17 23569.

When, in 1906, the Council of Professors at the Sorbonne prepared a list of two candidates to fill the chair of education, Bouglé was named second to Durkheim. (For any established chair, the faculty presented a list of two candidates, as did the Conseil Supérieur de l'Instruction Publique. The minister could then choose someone from either list.)

But by the time poor health forced Espinas to request a leave of absence in the fall of 1906, Bouglé's position was far from secure. Certain historians at the Sorbonne – including Ernest Lavisse – had decided that Henri Hauser should be named in place of Espinas and that the chair should be devoted to economic history rather than social thought.

Historians, it should be emphasised, benefited handsomely from the reform of higher education undertaken by the Third Republic. In 1865, there had existed only sixteen chairs of history in all faculties of letters; by 1914 there were forty-one. This expansion resulted from the gradual breaking up of the chairs of general history into more specialised chairs of ancient, mediaeval, modern or even contemporary history. The study of the modern and contemporary eras was particularly relevant politically, because Left and Right in France were traditionally divided by their diverging views of the Revolution of 1789. Consequently, by 1914 there were ten chairs throughout France devoted to modern and contemporary history. Even the *Revue historique*, founded by mediaevalists, devoted more and more space to the modern era (Gérard 1976: 353). In 1899 a younger generation of historians founded the *Revue d'histoire moderne et contemporaine*.

Most of this work, however, was devoted to traditional political and diplomatic history. The developing new field of economic–social history was largely neglected, despite the increasing recognition of its importance by younger academics (Rhodes 1974: 182–6). With the exception of a handful of first-rate scholars like Henri Hauser, Camille Bloch and Gustave Glotz, few individuals produced significant work in this domain before World War I. Unlike local history and, to a lesser degree, history of religion, economic–social history failed to become a distinct sub-speciality. In all of France before 1914, there existed only one chair with the words 'economic history' included in the title (at the Collège de France), and the man who taught it, Emile Levasseur, considered himself an economist. Nor did professors of history apply very much energy to changing this state of affairs.

On the rare occasions when the issue was raised by historians, the conclusions were not necessarily favourable to this new sub-discipline. In his book, *La Méthode historique appliquée aux sciences sociales* (1901), Charles Seignobos argued that all the social sciences needed to be based on history (implying that only historians were capable of producing anything worthwhile in this field). But he also insisted that social history could never be anything more than an auxiliary science for other types of history because social and economic factors were only the 'conditions' of other phenomena rather than their cause. Since the influence of social phenomena was slight, 'their history has only limited usefulness for the understanding of other phenomena' (Seignobos 1901: 314). It is worth noting that the few writers who bothered to respond to Seignobos were all linked to the Durkheimian school;[52] academic historians ignored it as they did a book published two years later by Henri Hauser[53] which defended the claims of social history against those of sociology and political economy.

Seignobos's insistence on the secondary status of social and economic factors was not without political significance. The contrary emphasis on the primacy of these phenomena brought one dangerously close to Marxism, as Maurice Hauriou had recognised in 1893. So it is not surprising that most of the support for economic–social history came from the moderate Left. The subject described the exploitation of workers in the capitalist system and explained why the working classes sometimes rebelled against exploitation. Consequently, it demonstrated the urgency of resolving current class tensions through social reform.

With enthusiastic support from leading members of the Socialist Party and the moderate labour movement, economic–social history gained some ground. In 1900, the Municipal Council of Paris founded a chair in the history of labour (for George Renard) at the Conservatoire des Arts et Métiers. (The chair was to be transferred to the Collège de France eight years later.) In 1903, the Chamber of Deputies established a special commission headed by the historian Alphonse Aulard, and the socialist leader Jean Jaurès; its purpose was to arrange for the publication of documents pertaining to the economic history of the French Revolution.[54] Three years later a group of socialist intellectuals, including Eugène Fournière, editor of the *Revue socialiste*, approached Gabriel Monod about the possibility of introducing two courses, in the history of economic theory and in the history of social theory, at the Ecole Pratique des Hautes Etudes. They were rebuffed by Monod but seem to have had better luck when they approached Ernest Lavisse. Fournière wrote to his friend Aristide Briand, then Minister of

---

[52] Notably François Simiand (1903) and Hubert Bourgin in the *Revue d'histoire moderne et contemporaine*, 3 (1901–1902).

[53] H. Hauser 1903. The *Revue historique* never reviewed this book. The *Revue de synthèse historique* chose a known Durkheimian, Hubert Bourgin (1903), to review the book; predictably, Bourgin devastated it. Bourgin also did a six-line review of the book in the *Revue d'histoire moderne et contemporaine*.

[54] The link between economic history and a Marxist vision of historical development emerges clearly from the argument made by Jaurès when he proposed the establishment of this commission to the Chamber of Deputies. 'The essence of history does not consist of the exterior development of political forms. It is very certain that it is the play of economic interests and social forces which determines the movement of history and gives it its meaning' (*Journal officiel, débats Chambre des Députés*, 27 November 1903, p. 2956).

Public Instruction, that Lavisse had agreed to the creation of a course in economic–social history at the Sorbonne. Believing that a job would soon be available, Fournière warmly recommended a young professor of history named Henri Hauser, then teaching at the Dijon faculty of letters. Hauser, Fournière wrote, was 'the promoter and creator of this branch of studies. Personally, I owe a great deal to his work, especially his book *Ouvriers du temps passé* [published in 1899] which destroyed the myth that workers of yesteryear enjoyed security and well-being.'[55]

Hauser, as it turned out, had other supporters on the moderate Left. Throughout July 1906, the ministry received letters on his behalf, including five from deputies or senators. (The best-known was Durkheim's predecessor in the chair of education, Ferdinand Buisson.) Two leaders of the Chambre Syndicale des Employés (representing white-collar workers), also wrote to emphasise the importance of the new chair for 'reformist' trade unions and to endorse Hauser who had made himself known through public lecturing; his appointment, their letter stated, 'would arouse strong sympathies in our circles'.[56]

At about the same time, the matter came up, in somewhat different form, at a meeting of the Council of Professors at the Sorbonne devoted to possible new courses.[57] Alphonse Aulard, who occupied the chair of the history of the French Revolution, proposed the establishment of a new course focusing on the economic history of the French Revolution. (Labour history was not mentioned and Hauser was not one of the two candidates that Aulard suggested.) Most historians who expressed themselves at the meeting reacted with marked hostility, arguing that more pressing needs in the teaching of history should be given priority. Nevertheless, by a vote of 13 to 10, the Council placed the economic history first on a list of new courses to be requested.

Despite these pressures, the minister refused to establish a new course in this field.[58] But in the autumn of 1906, historians received another opportunity when Espinas requested a temporary leave of absence for reasons of health. The title of his chair was sufficiently ambiguous to cover the sort of social history practised by Hauser. Almost overnight, Bouglé's undeclared candidacy was in serious trouble. Lavisse, probably the most powerful man at the Sorbonne, committed himself to Hauser. Even more damaging was Espinas's decision to support the historians; as the current chair-holder, his opinion about the choice of a successor was likely to have considerable weight. In a letter to Bouglé, Espinas justified his decision on

[55] Letter dated 17 July 1906 in Hauser's dossier, F 17 24507.
[56] Letter dated 24 July 1906, *ibid.*
[57] Meeting of 28 June 1906, AJ 16 4749, pp. 200–3.
[58] See his letter of 7 January 1907 sent out to the deputies and senators supporting Hauser in F 17 24507.

the grounds that he had endorsed Hauser before Bouglé had even announced his candidacy.[59] But his explanation was less than convincing. Espinas certainly remembered that Bouglé had been indiscreet enough in 1901 to publish an article in the *Revue philosophique* criticising theories of social organicism (Bouglé 1900). Although he had been exceedingly gentle with Espinas, one of the fathers of 'biological sociology', the old philosopher had responded immediately with an article defending organicism and, in passing, dismissing Bouglé's own work as an *'a priori* psychology'.[60]

Consequently, when the question of a successor came up before the Council of Professors in January 1907, Durkheim decided to stall. He argued that it was not necessary to appoint a successor because Espinas would only be gone for a year; during that time, Durkheim himself would take over Espinas's course preparing candidates for the *agrégation*. Historians at the meeting countered by emphasising both the 'scientific' necessity of continuing to offer the subject and the harmful effects on the budget and on the morale of provincial professors that would result if a vacancy were not filled. But what was really at stake – as everyone knew – was the essential character of the chair. Only once did professors permit themselves to bring up the central issue, and this in an exceedingly guarded manner. According to the minutes of the meeting:

Monsieur Boutroux is of the opinion that Monsieur Espinas's chair *must keep the character it now has*, and that it is perhaps useless to look for someone who will not, properly speaking, substitute for Monsieur Espinas. Responding to this observation, Monsieur Lavisse declares that *one must not endlessly maintain the same character in a course of studies*.[61] (italics mine)

Despite such opposition, the Council decided by a vote of 13 to 8 against replacing Espinas.

During the next year, Bouglé campaigned actively for the position, presenting himself as the representative of philosophers against the claims of historians. He even sought Espinas's support and was rewarded with a vague promise that the latter might still abandon Hauser.[62] Espinas did not, in fact, change his mind; but, as it turned out, his backing proved unnecessary. A meeting of the Council of Professors in November 1907 was a personal triumph for Durkheim.[63] First, Lucien Lévy-Bruhl was chosen as the faculty's candidate for the chair of modern philosophy. Lévy-Bruhl had taught the course for several years as an adjunct-professor; the nomination was thus due to a normal process of advancement rather than to Durkheim's

[59] Letter dated 29 October 1907, in the archives of the Groupe d'Etudes Durkheimiennes (GED) at the Maison des Sciences de l'Homme, Paris.
[60] Espinas 1901. For Bouglé's response, see Bouglé 1901.
[61] Meeting of 19 January 1907, AJ 16 4750, 3.
[62] See Espinas's letter to Bouglé dated 29 October 1907 in the archives of the GED.
[63] 23 November 1907, AJ 16 4705, 71–5.

influence. Still, it meant that a philosopher close to the Durkheimians had obtained a chair. Next, Georges Rodier, Durkheim's former colleague and friend at Bordeaux, was elected as the faculty's candidate to teach the course of ancient philosophy. Durkheim played an active role in this affair, reading a letter of support from the current holder of the chair, Victor Brochard, who was absent due to serious illness. Rodier's majority was so overwhelming that it seems likely that Durkheim simply supported a winner. But, in the final vote over the history of social economy, Durkheim's prestige was clearly on the line. Espinas came down emphatically on the side of Hauser who was a real economic historian; whereas Bouglé 'is a logician, a sociologist, and a politician served by a rare talent for oratory'. In response, Durkheim read another letter signed by Victor Brochard, but bearing all the marks of Durkheim's own style. It argued that Chambrun in founding the chair had deliberately linked it to sociology and to pedagogy; the appointment of Bouglé would ensure that this connection continued to be maintained. Surprisingly, most historians at the meeting accepted his reasoning. Ernest Denis declared that it was not necessary to examine the credentials of the two historians who were candidates because 'it is the opinion of most historians that the vacant course of studies has a philosophical character'.[64] Consequently, Bouglé was elected by 25 out of 31 votes cast.

What had happened in less than a year to make historians abandon their campaign? In the absence of documentation one can only speculate. The use of Brochard's name was a wise tactic because it served notice that philosophers were united behind Durkheim's effort to maintain the character of the chair. Durkheim undoubtedly exhibited considerable political skill in campaigning for Bouglé, but it is difficult to imagine what he could have offered historians in exchange for their backing. At the deepest level, his success probably reflected the firmness of his commitment to Bouglé in contrast to the tepid support historians gave Hauser. Few historians at the Sorbonne really cared very much about economic history or about Hauser, for that matter. It was, moreover, difficult to claim that history courses were needed because the Sorbonne had obtained six new chairs of history since 1904.[65] For Durkheim, in contrast, the chair was vital and he could appeal to the elementary sense of fairness that usually prevailed in these matters. As a result, Bouglé came to Paris while Hauser remained in Dijon until 1919 when he was appointed *chargé de cours* of modern economic history at the Sorbonne.

Bouglé's appointment left vacant his old chair of social philosophy at

---

[64] *Ibid.* This part of the minutes is also reproduced in Clark 1973: 75–6.
[65] The chairs obtained in 1904 were: Greek history, Roman history, civilisation and institutions of the Middle Ages, political and diplomatic history of modern times. Those of 1906 were: auxiliary sciences of history, history of modern Christianity.

Toulouse. Durkheim set to work to secure the position for a collaborator of the *Année sociologique*. The ministry received strong letters of support in favour of Paul Fauconnet from Durkheim (1979: 115–16), Lévy-Bruhl, Bouglé and the rector of the Academy of Toulouse. Consequently, Fauconnet was appointed *chargé de cours* in spite of the fact that he had not yet completed his doctoral thesis. It is worth noting that Durkheim's prestige and good relations with leading administrators were effective in this case because social philosophy was considered a branch of sociology over which Durkheim's competence was unquestioned. This emerges clearly in the recommendation which the director of higher education, Charles Bayet, sent to the minister:

Monsieur Fauconnet is not yet a doctor of letters while other candidates are. But the previous work of these other candidates does not appear to the Comité Consultatif to make them obvious choices for teaching social philosophy. Monsieur Fauconnet has, for several years, been the active collaborator of Monsieur Durkheim in publishing the *Année sociologique*. Messieurs Durkheim and Lévy-Bruhl report him to be totally qualified to teach social philosophy.[66]

To put it another way, Durkheim was in every respect an influential *grand universitaire*. But in the narrow institutional sphere of sociology, he reigned supreme precisely because his domain was so tiny.

Another paper in this volume discusses Bouglé's career in Paris after 1907; therefore, I will conclude with a brief account of the subsequent history of his chair, which continued to be closely bound up with the fortunes of the Durkheimian school.[67]

Bouglé remained *chargé de cours* until 1915 when Chambrun's foundation expired and the chair disappeared. After his military discharge in 1918, he became *chargé de cours* in Durkheim's old chair of sociology and education. Since he had no experience teaching sociology, it was decided to fit the chair to his qualifications; the Council of Professors thus transformed Durkheim's old chair into one of history of social economy and appointed Bouglé full professor. The fact that a famous chair could be disposed of in this manner demonstrates the fragility of sociology's place in the university system, despite the brilliant success of individual sociologists. But the subject did not disappear from the curriculum; in 1921, Paul Fauconnet who had finally completed his thesis the year before was appointed *chargé de cours* of sociology and education. Fauconnet became a full professor in 1932 when the chair of English language and literature was, in turn, transformed into a chair of sociology. When Bouglé became director of the Ecole Normale Supérieure in 1935, Maurice Halbwachs substituted for him in teaching the history of social economy.

[66] In Fauconnet's dossier at the Archives Nationales.
[67] The information that follows is based on the dossiers of Bouglé and Halbwachs at the Archives Nationales and on the minutes of the Paris faculty of letters.

Two years later, Halbwachs became the third Durkheimian holding a chair at the Sorbonne when he was appointed professor of scientific methodology and logic. He stayed in this post until 1939 when he replaced the deceased Fauconnet in the chair of sociology. The history of social economy was apparently not taught from 1937 until 1940, when Bouglé died and the peripatetic Halbwachs returned to the chair of history of social economy as a full professor. Since the chairs he had just occupied were never filled, Halbwachs spent the war as the only Durkheimian occupying a chair at the Sorbonne. In 1944, just before his death, he moved yet again, this time to the Collège de France. All the chairs of sociology disappeared temporarily from the Sorbonne's course catalogue, reappearing one by one a few years after the war.

Conclusion

The specificity of this case study demands that general conclusions about higher education and the social sciences in France be approached with modesty and caution. Two remarks, however, are in order.

First, the rise of academic social science in France was closely related to the ideological needs of the moderate republic; the new disciplines were perceived as a weapon of combat against socialism. It is true that Durkheim's case was somewhat more ambiguous for he was considered a socialist in certain right-wing circles. But in emphasising the evolutionary, pragmatic and sometimes conservative aspects of his thought, Durkheim successfully reassured leading academics and politicians. The political character of the social sciences, one must emphasise, did not produce ideological uniformity among its practitioners. A variety of philosophies and political doctrines were expounded. Each faculty – especially, but not only, those in Paris – enjoyed considerable autonomy in appointing professors. Aside from the fact that the political atmosphere in different institutions could vary significantly (the Sorbonne, for instance, was markedly more 'progressive' politically than the Paris faculty of law), faculty councils seeking to fill a position considered many factors; a man's publication record or seniority were often more important than his political views. For these reasons, sociologists as far apart on the political spectrum as Durkheim and Tarde could be appointed to Parisian posts within the same two-year span; that is also why Bergson could serve as spokesman for an attempt to bring Durkheim to the Collège de France. There was, moreover, not a great deal that could be done to 'heretics', beyond minor harassment in career advancement. The expulsion of Ferdinand Brunetière from the Ecole Normale Supérieure was an isolated exception explained by the fact that he had vigorously attacked the idea of 'science' and hence that foundation of the republican education system.

Ministerial appointments were, of course, nearly always political. But each minister (and men did not remain long in power) acted on the basis of very personal prejudices, illustrated most dramatically by the back-to-back nominations of men as different as Henry Michel and Jacques Izoulet (in 1896–7). The diversity of political views within the university in fact expressed the diversity of views and class interests within republicanism itself; and this defined its outer limits. One could function comfortably within a political area bounded by conservative republicanism on one hand, and the moderate socialism of Jaurès on the other. This excluded those Catholics who were too vociferous in opposing the secularisation of the education system and, of course, revolutionary socialists along with the few unrepentant monarchists.

A second conclusion that emerges from this case study, is that there is little evidence to corroborate the theory of 'clusters' elaborated by Terry Clark (1973: 66–92) several years ago. As I argued in an earlier review (Weisz 1977b), Clark's analysis is problematic on several counts. It is difficult, for instance, to find evidence of 'clusters' in the faculties of letters (with which Clark deals) during much of the nineteenth century. (The notion of 'clusters', I would suggest, is more applicable to the faculties of medicine.) Furthermore, he fails to distinguish between an amorphous and disorganised system of patronage and influence, which unquestionably existed, and a structured network of 'clusters' whose existence is never demonstrated. The present study suggests that Clark's analysis needs revision on a number of other points as well. With respect to academic appointments, for instance, it is impossible to reduce the variety of institutional conditions and individual strategies that we have encountered to a simple play of 'clusters'. Certain professors were appointed by a minister on the basis of their social and political ideas (Izoulet). Others were logical choices for colleagues because of their seniority and past record of scholarship (Espinas). The brilliant careers of Henri Marion and Durkheim reflected the exceptional quality of their work, recognised even by those who disagreed profoundly with what they taught. Henri Hauser could count on the backing of influential figures on the moderate Left and Célestin Bouglé enjoyed numerous advantages, not the least of which was Durkheim's firm support. In every case, factors like the influence of classmates, evaluations made by teachers and administrators, the scholarly value of work accomplished, seniority and the quality of patronage came together in a unique combination.

Furthermore, key institutional questions were often fought out at the level of faculties and disciplines rather than 'clusters'. The introduction of the social sciences, we saw, was shaped largely by the rivalry between the faculties of law, those of letters, and the Ecole Libre des Sciences Politiques. Durkheim was considered for a chair at the Collège de France as a representative of philosophy against the candidates of other disciplines; the same rivalry resurfaced three years later when Bouglé was elected to the Sorbonne. What emerges most forcefully from this study is the extraordinary complexity of the French system of higher education; beneath the centralised and rigid structures there seems to have persisted great diversity and even disorder. The connection between the centralisation and rigidity of institutions on one hand, and the elasticity and multiformity of behaviour on the other is essential for any analysis of French education and deserves more detailed investigation.

References

Bonnecasse, J. 1928. *Sciences du droit et romantisme; le conflit des conceptions juridiques en France de 1880 à l'heure actuelle.* Paris: Sirey.

Bouglé, C. 1900. 'La Sociologie biologique et le régime des castes', *Revue philosophique*, vol. 49, pp. 337–52.

   1901. 'Le Procès de la sociologie biologique', *Revue philosophique*, vol. 52, pp. 121–46.

Bourgin, H. 1903. (Review of Hauser 1903) *Revue de synthèse historique*, vol. 6, pp. 241–5.

Boutmy, E. 1876. *Observations sur l'enseignement des sciences politiques et administratives.* Paris: Martinet.

   1889. *Des rapports et des limites des études juridiques et des études politiques.* Paris: Colin.

Brimo, A. 1967. *Les Grands Courants de la philosophie du droit et de l'Etat.* Paris: A. Pedone.

Broderick, A. (ed.). 1970. *The French Institutionalists: Maurice Hauriou, Georges Renard and Joseph T. Delos.* Cambridge, Mass.: Harvard University Press.

Chambrun, A. de. 1892. *Aux montagnes d'Auvergne; mes conclusions sociologiques.* Paris: C. Lévy.

Clark, T. N. 1973. *Prophets and Patrons: The French University and the Emergence of the Social Sciences.* Cambridge, Mass.: Harvard University Press.

Despagnet, F. 1891. 'La Fonction sociale des facultés de droit', *Revue internationale de l'enseignement*, vol. 22, pp. 1–24.

Duguit, L. 1889. 'Le Droit constitutionnel et la sociologie', *Revue internationale de l'enseignement*, vol. 18, pp. 484–505.

Dumesnil, G. 1888. 'Les Cours de science de l'éducation', *Revue internationale de l'enseignement*, vol. 16, pp. 537–55.

Durkheim, E. 1888. 'Cours de science sociale: leçon d'ouverture', *Revue internationale de l'enseignement*, vol. 15, pp. 23–48.

   1901. 'Rôle des universités dans l'éducation sociale du pays', *Congrès international de l'éducation sociale, 26–30 sept. 1900*, pp. 128–38. Paris: Alcan (Republished in *Revue française de sociologie*, vol. 17, no. 2, 1976, pp. 181–9. English translation in *Minerva*, vol. 14, 1976, pp. 377–88).

   1975. *Textes*, vol. 2. Paris: Editions de Minuit.

   1976. 'Textes inédits ou inconnus d'Emile Durkheim', *Revue française de sociologie*, vol. 17, no. 2, pp. 165–96.

   1979. 'Lettres de Durkheim', *Revue française de sociologie*, vol. 20, no. 1, pp. 113–21.

George Weisz

Duruy, V. n.d. *L'Administration de l'instruction publique de 1863 à 1869*. Paris: J. Delalain.

Espinas, A. 1889. (Speech appearing in) *Revue internationale de l'enseignement*, vol. 17, pp. 67–71.

 1894. 'Leçon d'ouverture d'un cours d'histoire de l'économie sociale', *Revue internationale de sociologie*, vol. 2, pp. 321–51.

 1901. 'Etre ou ne pas être ou du postulat de la sociologie', *Revue philosophique*, vol. 51, pp. 449–80.

Faure, F. 1893. *La Sociologie dans les facultés de droit de France*. Paris: Giard et Brière.

Ferry, J. 1883. (Speech appearing in) *Revue internationale de l'enseignement*, vol. 5, pp. 425–30.

Gérard, A. 1976. 'Histoire et politique; La *Revue historique* face à l'histoire contemporaine (1885–1898)', *Revue historique*, no. 518, pp. 353–405.

Hariou, M. 1893. *Les Facultés de droit et la sociologie*. Paris: E. Thorin.

 1894. 'Réponse à "un docteur en droit" sur la sociologie', *Revue internationale de sociologie*, vol. 2, pp. 390–5.

 1896. *La Science sociale traditionnelle*. Paris: L. Larose.

Hauser, H. 1903. *L'enseignement des sciences sociales; état actuel de cet enseignement dans les divers pays du monde*. Paris: Chevalier-Maresq.

Laboulaye, E. 1845. *Quelques réflexions sur l'enseignement du droit en France*. Batignolles: Hennuyer et Turpin.

Levasseur, E. 1883. *Résumé historique de l'enseignement de l'économie politique et de la statistique en France*. Paris: Ed. Journal des Economistes.

Lutfallia, M. 1972. 'Aux origines du libéralisme économique en France', *Revue d'histoire économique et sociale*, vol. 41, pp. 494–517.

MacKay, D. 1943. Colonialism in the French Geographical Movement, *The Geographical Review*, vol. 33, pp. 214–32.

May, Dick. 1896–97. 'L'Enseignement social à Paris', *Revue internationale de l'enseignement*, vol. 32, pp. 1–29; vol. 34, pp. 28–45.

Osborne, T. 1974. 'The recruitment of the Administrative Elite in the Third French Republic, 1870–1905; The System of the Ecole Libre des Sciences Politiques'. Doctoral dissertation, University of Connecticut.

Rhodes, R. 1974. 'The Revolution in French Historical Thought: Durkheim's Sociologism as a Major Factor in the Transition from Historicist Historiography to the Annales School: 1868–1945'. Doctoral dissertation, Los Angeles, University of California.

Seignobos, C. 1901. *La Méthode historique appliquée aux sciences sociales*. Paris: Alcan.

Simiand, F. 1903. 'Méthode historique et science sociale', *Revue de synthèse historique*, vol. 6, pp. 1–22; 129–57.

Spuller, E. 1894. (Speech appearing in) *Revue internationale de l'enseignement*, vol. 27, pp. 559–68.

Weisz, G. 1976. 'The Academic Elite and the Movement to Reform French Higher Education, 1850–1885'. Doctoral dissertation, Stony Brook, State University of New York.

 1977a. 'Le Corps professoral de l'enseignement supérieur et l'idéologie de la réforme universitaire en France, 1860–1885', *Revue française de sociologie*, vol. 18, no. 2, pp. 201–32.

1977b. (Review of Clark 1973) *British Journal for the History of Science*, vol. 10, pp. 151–5.

Worms, R. 1894. 'Observations critiques', *Revue internationale de sociologie*, vol. 2, pp. 395–9.

Wright, V. 1972. *Le Conseil d'Etat sous le Second Empire*. Paris: Fondation Nationale des Sciences Politiques.

1976. 'L'Ecole Nationale d'Administration de 1848–1849; un échec révélateur', *Revue historique*, no. 255, pp. 21–42.

Wright, V., and Leclerc, B. 1973. *Les Préfets du Second Empire*. Paris: A. Colin.

4. Durkheimian sociology under attack: the controversy over sociology in the Ecoles Normales Primaires[*]

ROGER GEIGER

The controversy that provides the occasion for this study has little to do with the intellectual growth of the discipline of sociology. It nevertheless constitutes a revealing episode in the history of the sociological movement in France. Briefly stated, in 1920 Paul Lapie, director of primary education, created as part of a new program for the Ecoles Normales Primaires a course entitled 'sociology applied to morality and education', to be given for one hour per week during the second year of study. The subsequent attempt by Léon Bérard, Minister of Public Instruction, to remove sociology from this program resulted in, first, Lapie almost being removed from his position, and then a sustained attack upon the course and upon sociology. This offensive failed to gain its objective, but it brought forth the old antagonists of Durkheimian sociology, and it called into question the public role of the discipline. In reaction, the Durkheimians were prompted to re-evaluate not only the course, but also the contribution that their science could make to French society.

The introduction of sociology into the Ecoles Normales was part of a larger plan to upgrade these institutions. It was Lapie's ambition to elevate the future *instituteurs* 'from the level of the third year of upper primary school, to that of good pupils of the philosophy class or first-year students in the faculties'. To do this meant transcending the standardised and simplified primary curriculum, while at the same time preparing the pupils to teach it. Lapie expected to accomplish this by approaching the familiar materials from fresh, more sophisticated perspectives. This was the justification for introducing sociology and for applying it to the most sensitive subject in the primary program, *la morale*: 'to renew the study of moral problems for our *normaliens*', Lapie wrote, 'it is necessary to make the pupils see from a new perspective questions that they have already heard treated *ad infinitum*'.[1]

[*] This article owes its existence to the efforts of Philippe Besnard, who first encouraged me to write about this episode, and then unearthed the material necessary to complete the story. The original research was conducted with support from the Yale Higher Education Research Group and the Yale University Institution for Social and Policy Studies.
[1] Lapie 1920: 1460, 1474. For the course program, see pp. 769–70.

The connection that Lapie made between sociology and *la morale* is highly relevant to the most fundamental issue of this controversy. While defenders of the course preferred to minimise its Durkheimian content, critics identified it totally with the doctrines of Durkheim (cf. below the letters of Bérard and Bergson). Lapie's justification of the course reveals its essentially Durkheimian inspiration:

[sociology] has its law like other sciences; they show that customs do not evolve by individual caprice and that, although everything can be explained, everything is not equally good. The objective study of social facts suggests an appreciation of their value, and consequently, far from leading to a form of indifference, it ends by solidly justifying our moral practices. (Lapie 1920: 1475)

The Durkheimians were directly involved in the organisation of the course. For the first four years (1921–5) they conducted instructional weeks at the Sorbonne before the beginning of the school year in order to acquaint the directors with the subject they were charged to teach. Bouglé collaborated with Lapie in writing the actual program, and later taught sociology directly to the future directors of Saint-Cloud and Fontenay.

A look at the widely used manual by Hesse and Gleyze provides a direct means of judging the true content of the course.[2] In the two longest of the five sections – economic sociology and political sociology – a sociological perspective is merely superimposed upon the familiar materials of political economy and civics. The section on domestic sociology was drawn largely from Lapie's own work, *La Femme dans la famille*, just as the short section on criminology was beholden to Fauconnet's *La Responsabilité*: but both incorporated non-Durkheimian literature as well. The last section, however, centring on religious sociology, was the most purely Durkheimian, and also the most inflammatory to those who did not share its assumptions.[3] It consequently became the chief focus of the attacks upon the course.

The campaign against sociology in the Ecoles Normales began in the ministry of the rue de Grenelle and only gradually expanded into the public arena. Bérard's ministry was devoted above all else to restoring Latin and Greek to obligatory status in the secondary schools (Bérard 1923). This crusade, which had strong support in the *lycées* and among the *haute bourgeoisie*, was quite indicative of Bérard's conservatism in all educational matters – curriculum, pedagogy and social recruitment. In fact, his social philosophy was just the opposite of Lapie's. By eliminating the *section*

[2] André Hesse and A. Gleyze, *Notions de sociologie appliquée à la morale et à l'éducation*, 1922. Other texts failed to match the popularity of this manual, which appeared in its 7th edition in 1935: they were Michel Souriau, *Notions de sociologie*; Georges Davy, *Eléments de sociologie*; René Hubert, *Eléments de sociologie*; and C. Bouglé and J. Raffault (eds.), *Eléments de sociologie*.

[3] For example 'Let us study, following Durkheim, the most primitive of known religions, totemism, and we will have the opportunity to discover the true origin of religion' (Hesse and Gleyze 1922: 242).

moderne from the secondary programs he intended to put greater distance between secondary education, reserved for the nation's elite, and the entire primary system, including the Ecoles Normales, serving the remainder of the country.[4] It was not until July 1923 that he succeeded in getting the approval of the Chamber for his plan. Bérard was then free to turn his attention toward primary education about which he was less informed and with which till now less concerned. Coincidentally, Lapie's sociology course was brought into public view at just this time by a lengthy article in *La Grande Revue*.

The author, René Hubert, was a *maître de conférence* at the faculté des lettres de Lille who taught, among other things, 'introduction to social science'. He combined a positive view of the legitimacy of sociology with an eclectic approach to the subject. However, the question he posed in his piece was whether the *normaliens* had sufficient intellectual preparation, enough critical sense to profit from this rather special science. Specifically, Hubert raised the fear that sociology, by bringing a false certitude to complex social phenomena, might induce a harmful dogmatism in immature minds; or conversely, by emphasising the relativity of beliefs and institutions, it might undermine the idealism of future *instituteurs* with debilitating scepticism. After making a great deal of these dangers, Hubert concluded that with prudence they might be avoided: taught in the proper spirit, entrusted to the mature discretion of the directors, the introduction of the teaching of sociology in the Ecoles Normales Primaires would be an opportunity for new progress toward intellectual liberalism. Perhaps. But the minister of education had no such confidence in the subject, the teachers, nor the intellectual capabilities of the pupils.

Despite their differing views on the social function of education, relations between Lapie and Bérard had apparently been quite proper (cf. Bérard to Lefas below). Moreover, Lapie's position at the summit of the bureaucratic hierarchy of Public Instruction was outside the play of partisan politics. All this changed abruptly on 12 October 1923 when Bérard asked Lapie to remove sociology from the programs of the Ecoles Normales Primaires. The minister's motives certainly included a deeply felt animosity toward Durkheimian sociology, as well as condescending distaste for the intellectual pretensions that the program seemed to imply (cf. Bérard to Lefas below). But more was involved. In the arena of national politics the *instituteurs* were among the most vocal opponents of the clerical proclivities of the governing majority (Bloc National). Removing Lapie and his program would be an

[4] In preparation for a reform of primary education (see below), one of the things Bérard asked French educators was, 'Does not the very function of [primary education] imply that it be clearly distinguished from...[secondary and higher education] and, consequently, that there would be some danger in trying to make the former follow the methods and aims of the latter?' (*Revue universitaire* 1924, no. 1, p. 136).

unmistakable and ominous act of political vindictiveness.[5] And there was probably an element of office politics as well. It soon became known that Lapie's successor would be Paul Crouzet, then acting director of secondary education, who had been responsible for Bérard's reform of the secondary curriculum.[6] The request to expunge sociology, then, was not made with any expectation that Lapie would, or could, comply.[7]

By refusing to repudiate his own work, Lapie became a lame-duck director on frigid terms with his minister. He resisted outright resignation to prevent the pious Bérard from taking complete control over appointments and programs in lay primary education.[8] Also, given his long and distinguished university career, Lapie was entitled by custom to an equivalent position. Bérard soon settled that issue by creating a chair in the science of education at the Sorbonne.[9] However, even as these arrangements were being made, opposition to Bérard's coup began to make its presence felt.

Paul Lapie, from all indications, was widely respected personally throughout primary education despite the existence of divisive policy issues such as unionisation. Those who rose to defend him, nevertheless, perceived his impending dismissal as a veiled attack upon the principle of *laïcité*. Indignation ran highest among the personnel of primary education, for the campaign against Lapie was in large measure aimed at them as well. In response, the several associations representing 'the 130,000 functionaries belonging to the directorate of primary education' all joined in a declaration protesting the politically motivated campaign against Lapie and the threat that it constituted to the 'entire scholarly work of the Third Republic'.[10] Bérard seized upon this as a pretext to force the director out. He asked Lapie to prepare disciplinary action against the signers of the declaration supporting him – a demand he would naturally refuse. His insubordination was then referred to the prime minister for final judgement. But at this point Bérard's scheme collapsed. Poincaré, although conservative on most issues, remained a staunch supporter of *laïcité*. Moreover, with an election likely in the near future, he hardly wanted to provoke a confrontation with the

---

[5] Lapie 1937. Bérard seems to have been supported in this policy by the president of the Republic, Millerand, who favoured a more forceful governmental policy against the Left.

[6] Lapie 1937; Glay 1923.

[7] Lapie's response to Bérard was that he was fully ready to prepare 'slight reductions or retouches to the 1920 course programs. But if it was a question of undoing what I have done, and what I consider as the best of my works, I could not.' Quoted from a manuscript memorandum of the conversation in P.O. Lapie 1937: 178–9.

[8] Glay 1923. Bérard was a devout Catholic who was later named French ambassador to the Vatican. His education had been entirely in Catholic schools.

[9] The Paris faculty of letters was willing to accept Lapie, but was sharply critical of the apparent creation of a faculty chair for reasons of 'political convenience': P.O. Lapie 1937: 192–4. This chair, however, was created and filled by Thamin.

[10] See P.O. Lapie 1937: 197ff for the text of the declaration and the subsequent controversy it provoked.

Roger Geiger

nation's *instituteurs*. The prime minister decided that Lapie would remain in his post; and as for the sociology course, the ostensible source of the 'Lapie affair', the programs of the Ecoles Normales Primaires would be reconsidered in due course as a matter of government policy.

Bérard, despite this setback, remained determined to eliminate sociology, and consequently brought the issue before the next meeting of the Permanent Section of the Conseil Supérieur de l'Instruction Publique.[11] As a pretext it was argued that the sociology course had never been properly debated by the Conseil in 1920 prior to its promulgation. The argument raised against it now was that it would be dangerous to found moral and civic education upon so immature and so conjectural a science. Those charged with teaching it did not understand it, and the manuals were inadequate for the purpose. It was consequently suggested that the program of 1905 be restored in its place.[12] Lapie, now that he was personally vindicated, was able vigorously to defend his creation. Primary students, he argued, receive the same instruction in *la morale* for ten straight years. Approaching this subject from a sociological perspective did not change the fundamentals of *la morale*, but presented them in a refreshingly different manner. Three years of experience had fully justified these expectations: students showed a great interest, the teachers were pleased with the course, and the instructional weeks had been a success.

Henri Bergson was the first to answer Lapie, even though he claimed that the controversy was new to him (see Bergson to Bouglé below). After some faint praise for the Durkheim school, he cut to the heart of the issue. The real problem, Bergson felt, was with the section on religion. This was the truly sociological part of the program and also the most dangerous. The complicated questions posed surpassed the level of culture of the *normaliens*, and that of their teachers as well. Without the necessary level of cultivation and philosophical neutrality the sociological presentation of these matters would be inescapably biased; it would give students a facile certitude about difficult and uncertain topics. Bergson consequently advocated suppressing the religious section altogether, and reverting basically to the previous program for *la morale*.

Lapie countered that the directors of the Ecoles Normales were well aware of their obligations of neutrality, and that the members of the Permanent Section could be confident of their impartiality and tact. As for the charge of inducing dogmatism, Lapie pointed out that the purpose of the sociology course was precisely the opposite – to develop a critical sense and an appreciation of the scientific method.[13] But Lapie had clearly failed to gain

[11] Archives Nationales F 17 13668. Section permanente, Conseil Supérieur de l'Instruction Publique: 18 January 1924.
[12] Bérard's suggested changes are given in Albert-Petit 1925: 134–5.
[13] Lapie at this point denied the implied identification of his own conception of *la morale* with that of the sociologists (see Bérard to Lefas below).

the sympathies of his listeners. Like Bergson, the other members had only a minimal tolerance for sociology – one disdainfully announced that 'for linguistic reasons he did not accept even the word "sociology"'. Their confidence in the intellectual abilities of the pupils and teachers of the Ecoles Normales was similarly low. They thus approved, for consideration by the full Conseil the following week, a proposal that would have effectively removed sociology from these schools (Bergson to Bouglé below).

In a Conseil discussion described as 'concentrated, tense and passionate', Bergson and Lapie re-enacted their previous confrontation.[14] Bergson was more adamantly opposed than before: sociology was no more than the philosophy of Durkheim, he now charged, and it could not help but have a harmful effect upon minds with only hasty and incomplete philosophical preparation. Crouzet contributed to the prosecution with numerous selections chosen from Durkheim and the manuals of sociology, through which he intended to show the inconsistency and obscurity of this 'science', and hence its unsuitability as a foundation for *la morale*. Against this offensive Lapie again offered his familiar justification, stressing that it was simply a matter of using sociological material to revitalise a stale and hackneyed course. On this occasion, however, Lapie did not stand alone. The representative from the Ecoles Normales gave a strong endorsement of the course. Despite some initial confusion, he reported, sociology was now popular with both pupils and teachers; furthermore, no explicit complaints had been made against it.

For the majority of the Conseil members, who had little knowledge of and little stake in this issue, both the intensity of the debate and the contradictory claims finally became disquieting. They came to feel that they were being stampeded into a hasty decision on a matter that was not at all urgent. In fact, Bérard had just announced an enquiry into all of primary education for the purpose of drafting future reforms (Beaulavon 1924). It was therefore suggested that consideration of the sociology course be deferred until the June meetings when it could be taken up in the light of these results. The Conseil then approved the resolution that 'it was impossible usefully to examine the proposed decree before having studied the entire question' and that 'there are grounds for leaving things in their present state'. An effort by Crouzet to revive the issue was ruled out of order. The reprieve of Lapie's sociology course, it would seem, was as narrow as his own.

During the early months of 1924 the fate of sociology in the Ecoles Normales remained in suspension. However, it was obvious that the approaching elections would play a larger role in any determination than the merits of the issue. The victory of the Cartel des Gauches in May virtually precluded any further action against sociology. The new minister of public

---

[14] AN F 17 13648: 25 January 1924. Beaulavon 1924. N.B. The accounts of this meeting in Mosse-Bastide 1955: 267 and in Clark 1973: 222 are erroneous.

Roger Geiger

instruction, François Albert, was above all determined to reverse Bérard's classical reform. The whole problem of reforming primary education was consequently displaced from the next agenda of the Conseil Supérieur. An ill-advised attempt by Crouzet to reintroduce the topic of the sociology course resulted in a withering response by Lapie and an ignominious withdrawal.[15] No longer able to control the rue de Grenelle, the opponents of sociology now had to conduct their campaign through other means.

Such would seem to be the inspiration for Albert-Petit (1924) to make an eloquent case against sociology to the Académie des Sciences Morales et Politiques. The author skilfully developed his case around the standard arguments of the inadequacy of sociology as a basis for *la morale* and its unsuitability for *normaliens*. Sociology, Albert-Petit insisted, was a science 'more nascent than existing'; 'it opens magnificent, but vaporous, horizons'. He supported this contention with quotations from the course manuals attesting that sociology was not yet a fully constituted science. Its proper place was therefore 'in higher education, and only on the condition of being considered more as an object of research than as a matter for teaching'. To offer such material to 16- and 17-year-old *normaliens* was, for Albert-Petit, 'the invasion of higher education into primary'. Not only did the pupils lack the background to comprehend the subject, but the directors, especially women directors, were totally unprepared to teach 'what they had never learned'. Albert-Petit therefore concluded with a plea to the public to demand the restoration of the program of 1905, as Bérard had proposed.

The sentiments of Albert-Petit found considerable support among his auditors, but they were squarely contested by Célestin Bouglé (1925), the perennial 'bulldog' of Durkheimian sociology. Using familiar themes, he argued that sociology schooled the pupils in social reality, not conjectural theories; and that the awareness of the nature of society was an antidote to one of the worst moral dangers, egoism. Bouglé then shifted to a defence of Durkheimian sociology, even though Albert-Petit's remarks concerned it only by implication. He first tried to disassociate the course from the Durkheimian school by stressing, somewhat disingenuously, the pluralism of French sociology; and then argued that it was not dangerous in any case. Through studying it a pupil 'is warned and virtually immunised against the materialist conception of the world'.

In this exchange it is once again quite apparent that the adversaries, speaking from their respective ideological positions, are merely uttering contradictory assertions: '*normaliens* lack the critical faculties for under-

[15] AN F 17 13658. Voeux présentés au Conseil Supérieur de l'Instruction Publique: Voeu no. 315; F 17 13668: 20 June 1924. Lapie attacked Crouzet for reopening in the Section Permanente a discussion formally concluded in the Conseil Supérieur, and also for publishing a tendentious account of that discussion in the *Bulletin administratif*.

standing sociology' versus 'sociology will form in them those critical faculties'; or, 'sociology produces dangerous intellectual tendencies' versus 'sociology counteracts dangerous tendencies'. There was consequently good reason to refocus the debate upon the modest dimensions of the issue – one part of one weekly course during one year of the *normalien* program.

This was the virtue of G. Hébert's reply to the critics of sociology.[16] As directeur of the Ecole Normale de Saint-Brieuc, Hébert had given this course since its inception. He emphasised that 'sociology applied to morality' should be seen as part of the progressive teaching of *la morale* through the primary grades. And 'which sociology is that?' he asked: 'certainly not the sociology taught at the Sorbonne or in the faculties of letters'. It is not a question at this level of choosing between competing sociological theories, but merely of bringing out the most basic truths about social relations. Using the example of domestic sociology, Hébert demonstrated that the application of sociology does not give rise to a new and different *morale*, but rather gives the pupils 'new motives for following their civic and professional duties'. The course had its imperfections; the manuals in particular were poorly suited to the pupils. But it had fulfilled its purpose by stimulating the interest of the students. Therefore, asked Hébert, 'can one not have more confidence in us, just as the reformer of 1920 had perhaps because he best understood the needs of the school and the devotion of its teachers?'

It seems only fitting that Hébert would conclude with a tribute to Paul Lapie. In his defence of sociology Lapie had put his career on the line in order to prevent the primary program from being manipulated for what were largely external considerations. He soon received a further vindication when he was named the following year to the highest administrative post in the University – vice-rector of the Academy of Paris (1925) – where he served with distinction until his untimely death (1927).

Unfortunately, Hébert's piece was not the last word on sociology in the Ecoles Normales. The course continued to irritate opponents of the discipline and to provoke intermittent attacks.[17] The standard arguments about the *normaliens'* insufficient preparation, the hypothetical character of sociology and the tendentious writings of Durkheim and Lévy-Bruhl, for example, were presented to the Chamber of Deputies in 1927 by the Abbé Gaston Louis. The minister of public instruction on this occasion, Edouard Herriot, reminded the abbé that the social theories of Bossuet were presented to the *normaliens* as well as those of Durkheim, and assured him

---

[16] Hébert (1924) was answering the criticisms of Albert-Petit (1925) and Olivier Le Roy (*Revue de l'école*, 1, 8 and 22 June 1924).

[17] The criticisms of Gaston Richard (1928) should not be included with these hostile attacks. He defended the sociology course in general, but strongly urged that Durkheimian sociology of religion be excluded from it.

that there was no official sociology at the rue de Grenelle.[18] Another such attack several years later in the Senate seemed to presage a new assault against the course.[19] The threat on this occasion stimulated the Durkheimians to undertake a re-evaluation of the sociology course. The result is interesting not only for what it reveals about sociology in the Ecoles Normales, but for what it reveals about them as well.

The Durkheimians themselves were well aware of the imperfections of Lapie's course. They understood better than anyone the relative immaturity of their science, and they knew from direct experience how ill-equipped the directors were to give this specialised type of instruction. Yet, as involuntary partisans in this controversy, they were in no position to offer criticism. With the sociology course under constant attack from the Right, an absence of support on their part could irreparably undermine its defence. The Institut Français de Sociologie, interwar gathering point for the Durkheimian cluster, had taken up this issue in the wake of the Lapie affair, but had not agreed upon a formal position.[20] In 1931 they began a drawn-out and somewhat convoluted reconsideration of the subject. First, Paul Fauconnet was given the responsibility of presenting an 'ideal' introduction to sociology, actually more appropriate for the university (9 December 1931). The subsequent discussion explored different conceptions of teaching sociology, and also drew nearer to the problem in the Ecoles Normales (18 June 1932). A final session then focused directly upon the problem, and eventually brought a Durkheimian program into contrast with the prevailing practice (8 February 1933).[21]

The details of Fauconnet's program need not concern us here. Using the basic divisions of sociology utilised in the *Année sociologique*, he compressed the material into an unwieldy 'minimum' of 120 lessons. Fauconnet pursued sociology into all its specialities and special applications, but the identity of a central, unifying sociological enterprise seems to be absent, or at best merely implied. The discussion which followed Fauconnet's presentation gradually concentrated on this essential point. Bouglé likened the plan to an 'encyclopedia of the social sciences', and suggested that the vital element, the sociological point of view, could be conveyed without all that detail. Granet expressed a strong dissent to both Bouglé and Fauconnet. He advocated emphasising sociology's independent existence through a paradigmatic

---

[18] *Journal officiel, Chambre des Députés*, 25 November 1927, pp. 3224–7 and 3233–4. For other attacks see *Le Temps*, 23 and 26 August, and 1 September 1927: here too the villain is Durkheimian sociology.

[19] Cf. the reaction in *Bulletin de l'Institut Français de Sociologie*, vol. 1, no. 2 (1930–1), p. 69; vol. 2, no. 1 (1931–2), p. 5.

[20] *Bulletin de l'Institut Français de Sociologie*, vol. 2, no. 3 (1931–2), p. 95.

[21] *Bulletin...*, vol. 2, nos. 1 and 3; vol. 3, no. 1. The following account draws upon these three sessions.

approach – one that would concentrate on specific topics that sociology had treated in an exemplary manner, such as suicide. This would best develop 'critical sense, positive spirit and a scientific feeling for social facts', all of which constituted the real aim of sociology in the Ecoles Normales. Other speakers felt that this kind of result could only be achieved by returning to the original Durkheimian source of inspiration. They consequently suggested a presentation of the history of the discipline as a means of impressing upon pupils Durkheim's commitment to the scientific study of social facts.

The consensus on this last point would seem to explain why this ostensibly tightly-knit cluster disagreed so markedly, not only about the manner of teaching sociology, but about the essential nature of the subject. What bound together the diverse specialists who assembled in the Institut Français de Sociologie was above all the personal and intellectual example provided by Durkheim. They were aware how this example had fertilised and guided their own research, but they were no longer confident of its significance for French society, of its relevance in the Ecoles Normales Primaires. Hence, the appeal of *une recherche du temps perdu*.

At the conclusion of the discussion, Fauconnet agreed to attempt to synthesise the different views expressed into a program specifically intended for the Ecoles Normales. This was to be supplemented, at Bouglé's suggestion, by an enquiry among the directors into the actual results of the existing course. This produced two contrasting perspectives on sociology in the Ecoles Normales after more than a decade of experience.

Changing from a principle of inclusion to one of exclusion, Fauconnet's second presentation removed all practical questions from the course, all the 'applications' of sociology to politics, to *la morale*, or even to pedagogy. Much of this material could be placed in a separate civics course where the political implications would not embarrass sociology. There would consequently no longer be a section on political sociology because 'there are no important *sociological* works on these matters in French'.[22] The principal addition would be an extensive introduction portraying the evolution of what can best be called 'Durkheimian rationalism'. Although this could provide the foundation for moral education, Fauconnet insisted that they had no right as sociologists to propose such a doctrine. The rest of the course would be divided between economic sociology, as taught by Simiand, and studies of the family and religion. On the latter subject, still the most controversial of the program, Fauconnet offered no concession: 'it provides particularly good ground', for demonstrating the possibility of a completely objective and truly scientific study of social facts. In sum, Fauconnet proposed a course that would be more narrowly an introduction to sociology than Lapie's original

---

[22] *Bulletin...*, vol. 3, no. 1, p. 18. This was directed against Bouglé, who had previously advocated the inclusion of political sociology, and whose own writings clearly belonged to this genre.

creation. However, that would make it even further removed from the way the course was actually being presented.

The small enquiry proposed by Bouglé and conducted by his colleague J. Raffault showed the directors to be strongly opposed to any formal change.[23] This was partly because the course seemed to be working well: students were quite interested and seemed to be benefiting from it, and after considerable effort a competent corps of instructors now existed to teach it. But it was also because the hostile attacks upon the course had made it a symbol – 'a flag for which one fights'. It was true that the course was heavily overloaded, and that the theoretical content was above the level of the pupils; but in their classrooms the teachers had enough freedom to adjust to these difficulties. They would concentrate on only a few of the topics, and render the material as practical and concrete as possible by focusing on contemporary issues and aspects of everyday life. 'Strictly speaking', Raffault therefore concluded, 'there is no sociology course, but rather *des leçons de choses* ... bringing forth the careful, impartial, objective study of facts that the pupils can directly observe.'

The notions of the Durkheimians and the realities of sociology in the classroom diverge radically from the initial conception of sociology and *la morale*. For Durkheim the most fundamental purpose of sociology was to establish upon a scientific foundation *la morale* appropriate to a modern secular society. This implied that the fruits of this science would eventually contribute to the moral formation of French youth.[24] The creation of a sociology course for future *instituteurs* seemed to be an important step toward the fulfilment of this vision. To the opponents of this world-view, on the other hand, the idea of Durkheimian sociology being taught in 200 Ecoles Normales 'would constitute a frightening social and national danger' (Izoulet 1928: 247). But, in fact, both this dream and this nightmare turned out to be equally insubstantial. Not only was sociology diluted in practice to 'des leçons de choses', but the ideology of Durkheimian sociology had by 1930 become outmoded. No longer eager to impose their ideas upon the political questions of the day, the Durkheimians now wished above all to avoid them. Their commitments were now to their own specialised branches of social science; and they had more to lose than to gain from too close an involvement with public affairs. This may have been a natural consequence of the maturation of the discipline, and perhaps it was a fortuitous one as well, but it was

[23] 'Note de M. Raffault sur l'enseignement de la sociologie dans les écoles normales', *ibid.*, pp. 35–46.

[24] Besides Durkheim's course, 'L'Education morale à l'école primaire', subsequently published as *L'Education morale* (1925), Fauconnet describes another course entitled 'L'Enseignement de la morale à l'école primaire' : 'it is the popularisation of the scientific study of morality, to which he has consecrated the major part of his works and his courses' (Fauconnet 1922: 21).

nevertheless reinforced by the confrontation between sociology and its adversaries over the course in the Ecoles Normales Primaires. When they were forced actually to defend 'sociology applied to morality and education', the Durkheimians found their position to be tenuous and uncomfortable. In the end they expressed no regret at seeing this form of sociology absorbed by the same *esprit primaire* it had originally been designed to combat.

References

Albert-Petit, A. 1925. 'La Déviation de l'enseignement primaire: la sociologie dans les écoles normales', *Séances et travaux de l'Académie des Sciences Morales et Politiques*, 21 June 1924, no. 1, pp. 114–42 (also in *Revue de Paris*, 15 July 1924).

Beaulavon, G. 1924. 'La Session du Conseil Supérieur de l'Instruction Publique', 22–26 January 1924, *Revue universitaire*, no. 1, pp. 131–3.

Bérard, L. 1923. *Pour la réforme classique de l'enseignement secondaire*. Paris: Colin.

Bouglé, C. 1925. 'La Sociologie enseignée dans les écoles normales', *Séances et travaux de l'Académie des Sciences Morales et Politiques*, 5 July 1924, no. 1, pp. 143–7.

Clark, T.N. 1973. *Prophets and Patrons: The French University and the Emergence of Social Sciences*. Cambridge, Mass.: Harvard University Press.

Fauconnet, P. 1922. 'L'Oeuvre pédagogique de Durkheim', pp. 1–33 in E. Durkheim, *Education et sociologie*. Paris: Alcan.

Glay, E. 1923. 'L'affaire Lapie', *Revue de l'enseignement primaire*, 18 November.

Hébert, G. 1924. 'La Sociologie dans les écoles normales', *Revue pédagogique*, vol. 85, no. 11, pp. 325–40.

Hesse, A. and Gleyse, A. 1922. *Notions de sociologie appliquée à la morale et à l'éducation*. Paris: Alcan.

Hubert, R. 1923. 'L'Etat présent de la sociologie et son enseignement dans les écoles normales', *La Grande Revue*, vol. 3, pp. 287–324.

Izoulet, J. 1928. *La Métamorphose de l'Eglise*. Paris: A. Michel.

Lapie, P. 1920. 'Ecoles normales', *Bulletin administratif de l'Instruction Publique*, new series, no. 108, pp. 1460–75.

Lapie, P.O. 1937. *Paul Lapie: une vie, une oeuvre*. Paris: Société Universitaire d'Editions et de Librairie.

Mosse-Bastide, R.M. 1955. *Bergson éducateur*. Paris: Presses Universitaires de France.

Richard, G. 1928. 'L'Enseignement de la sociologie à l'école normale primaire', *L'Educateur protestant*, vol. 7, pp. 198–209; 233–43; 295–307.

Documents on the 'Lapie affair'[1]

The correspondence presented here comes from two of the principal protagonists in the debate recounted by Roger Geiger. In a letter sent to Bouglé two days after the meeting of the Conseil Supérieur de l'Instruction Publique (see p. 124), Bergson explains the reasons for his reservations about the teaching of sociology (in particular Durkheimian sociology) in the Ecoles Normales Primaires. In the excerpt that we are publishing from a letter sent in 1941 to Alexandre Lefas,[2] Léon Bérard, at the time French ambassador to the Vatican, explains his role in that affair by insisting on the power of the Durkheimian 'church' in the university and on the political dangers that the teaching of 'sociological morality' represented in the Ecoles Normales. He also puts forward his view of the functioning of the Ministry of Public Instruction.

Letter from Bergson to Bouglé

Paris, 32 rue Vital,
20 January 1924

My dear friend,

Your amiable letter reached me at the very moment I was on my way to the session of the Permanent Section. The question of the teaching of sociology was discussed there. You know that the minister's proposal as it was presented to us called for the abolition pure and simple of the sociology program of 1920 and a return to the system of 1905. The new draft that the Permanent Section decided to propose introduces social psychology: above all, we asked that the program of 'general, theoretical and practical morality' be composed of all the questions of the current sociology program that appear possible to join to it. (The Conseil Supérieur, or a commission named by it, would establish that program.) You could thus have a certain degree of satisfaction, a degree that could be rather large. Was it possible

[1] These documents were graciously made available by, respectively, Mlle Jeanne Bouglé and M. Pierre-Olivier Lapie.
[2] A. Lefas, senator from Ille-et-Villaine from 1933 to 1941, had been elected vice-president of the Senate's education commission in 1940.

for us to go further? I do not believe so. Here is my personal opinion on the whole affair.

The program of 1920 appears to me to be made up of two distinct parts. The first is constituted by chapters I, II, and III, the second by chapter IV. The first is composed of questions the greater part of which, I believe, already figured in previous programs, but in a less ample and less lively form: one ordinarily classified them under rubrics such as 'practical morality', 'civic instruction', and 'political economy'. But the second has a different character. One finds there problems which relate both to sociological science and to a sociological *philosophy*. No matter how precise the research of a Durkheim might be, for example, I consider his conception of the relations between religion, on the one hand, and society and morality on the other to be a matter for philosophy as much as and more than for science.

It is above all the teaching of this last part that appears to me to present drawbacks, when it is addressed to students of the Ecoles Normales Primaires. I would find it completely natural that one taught Durkheim's philosophy, for example (I cite that one because it is the philosophy of many of our sociologists), to young people who had followed a complete course of philosophy in our *lycées*: they have witnessed, for an entire year, the conflict of systems, they know what a philosophical theory is; even if they accept one of them, they will not make a dogma of it. It is quite otherwise for students who have not received that special training. What aggravates the danger here is that one moves imperceptibly from certain sociological research findings, which are precise, positive, and truly scientific, to a particular conception of social reality which, for example, is far from having the same scientific character and far from presenting the same degree or the same type of certainty. Only minds practised in the manipulation of philosophical ideas can make that distinction.

I would add that, if sociology can on many points enliven the materials contained in chapters I, II, and III of the program, there are, even here (above all for the questions in chapter III), great precautions to be taken. From the fact that an institution began by being this or that, one can draw no decisive argument for justifying it or for combating it in its present form; historical origins are one thing, rational foundations are another. I am sure that no true philosopher would confound the two things; but I am no less sure that one must already be a philosopher, and very much a philosopher, in order not to make that confusion. All this without considering that one must equally be a bit of a historian, and not simply 'know some history', to see that which is hypothetical reconstruction in a history which goes back to origins.

Besides, whether it is a question of one or the other part of the program, I well recognise what would be done here by a professor who was truly a philosopher and truly a sociologist, even if his auditors had not been trained in historical and philosophical research. He would highlight the hypothetical character of many of the findings; he would indicate their degree of probability; finally, he would show sociology to be a nascent science: he would not limit himself to saying it, he would at all times give one a concrete feeling for it. But for that we would require as many Bouglés as there are Ecoles Normales in France.

There, my dear friend, are the difficulties that I perceive. I indicated as much, the day before yesterday, at the Permanent Section. Having to speak right after Lapie, who had just defended (with much talent) the program of 1920, I naturally stressed the reservations to be made to it. If I had spoken last – and I should have preferred to – I would have perhaps appeared, on the contrary, as the one who sought to conserve the greatest possible amount of the program of 1920, for I was able to observe before the session, by chatting with one or two of the members of the Permanent Section, that the minister was far from being the only one a little frightened by the sociology program. The program had passed unnoticed three years ago – drowned in the ensemble of the programs of the Ecoles Normales Primaires (on which, as I remember it, we voted very quickly and as a whole at the end of the session). But, now that attention is drawn to this quarter, I am sure that many will have doubts and scruples at least as strong as mine.

Yours sincerely.

Letter from Léon Bérard to Alexandre Lefas (excerpt)

Vatican City,
3 April 1941

My dear friend and colleague,

When it is a question of 'laicism' and of the deviations from neutrality, one finds the same abdications, the same responsibilities, and they are of the same origin. Here, my dear Lefas, is a rather forgotten episode, hardly amusing, but full of meaning and which, in my opinion, explains and clarifies many things in the history of the dying Third Republic. The year was 1920. The Bloc National and the Arago group reigned, though they did not govern. M. Honorat was Minister of Public Instruction, and, Lord knows, he did not mean badly. M. Lapie, director of primary education, renovated the program of studies of the Ecoles Normales from top to bottom. That reform – of major import – went by completely unnoticed. No one knew anything of it in the Chambres and, if my memory is good, the press was equally unaware of it. Elsewhere at the same moment, at the instigation of M. Brunot, dean of the Sorbonne, another pedagogical revolution was taking place, in the same silence and the same secrecy, in the midst of the same academic indifference: they invented a *licence ès lettres* with neither Latin nor Greek. That was perhaps the hardest blow struck against classical studies. The hidden influences and the obscure powers who lead Public Instruction never stopped. Changes of political direction and the overturning of majorities mattered little to them. They pursued their course patiently, silently; and, taking advantage of the agitation or the difficulties that kept the attention of parliamentary circles on other things, they planned to and succeeded at perpetrating, under the guise of *technical* reforms, their most audacious and most controversial schemes.

Let us return to the program of the Ecoles Normales of 1920. These were encyclopaedic programs, such that someone who could possess all the knowledge catalogued therein could rival a Sorbonne professor. The avowed goal of Lapie and his collaborators or inspirers was to make the student-teacher the *equal* of a first-year student in the faculties. The goal was to 'outflank' secondary education by exalting primary and by fortifying its autonomy. But there was in that program of studies a novelty well worthy of notice: to these normal school students who came from the Higher Primary Schools, who had not done one hour of philosophy, they were going to teach not philosophy, but, among the hundreds or thousands of diverse systems, one fixed system of philosophy: Durkheim's sociology. I must tell you that for several years the teachings of that rabbinical ideologue had become a sort of official and practically obligatory academic doctrine. The sociologists were in possession of magisterial chairs at the Sorbonne. Among them, there was a man of great worth, only one: Lévy-Bruhl. From them emanated the decisive and directing influences: any philosopher who would not at all take the sociological vows of obedience would have to content himself with teaching at Grenoble or Clermont-Ferrand. Jacques Chevalier, for example. It was a masterly and premeditated blow to annex future teachers to the Durkheimian chapel, now become a very powerful church. Of course, the professors in the Ecoles Normales Primaires generally knew not a word of that sociology. They had hardly heard of Durkheim, nor of the 'totem' in vogue among the Polynesian tribes, nor of the origin of the prohibition of incest, nor of the evolution of humanity explained by the religious beliefs observed by savages. Overnight, they began to prepare manuals of sociology with the aid of which the Ecoles Normales professors could learn while teaching and could teach while learning. I have no need to tell you the degree to which and the way in which the moral teachings of these sociologists were contrary to those of Jules Ferry and Ferdinand Buisson. The reform of 1920 can be summarised and characterised simply in the following way: to the future teacher, they were going to teach an interpretation of human and social facts such that in his future class he would not know how to allude to them without thereby lacking in neutrality merely by doing so. To the extent that he retains something of that materialistic and naturalistic theology (for it is nothing other than that), the teacher will no longer think of scholarly neutrality other than as an outdated expedient. The sociological morality of the Ecoles Normales will exist truly in harmony, in its eyes, only with one doctrine, which it is destined to multiply the propulsive and explosive force of: Marxist materialism. One could not have done better if one had wanted to make of the teacher a natural auxiliary of the communist revolution. More than the first two years of my ministry (1921–4) were absorbed by the reform of classical studies and the interminable but fine debate of which it was the object in the Chambre. Once that question was settled, I was led to occupy myself with primary education, and it was only then, I confess, that I truly discovered the programs of 1920. Perhaps you remember the conflict that broke out between Lapie and myself with respect to this – a conflict of ideas and doctrine and not at all a personal conflict. I have always held Lapie to be a very honest man, of great rectitude and dignity of life and character – with all sorts of chimerical ideas about life and man. I asked Lapie if, in collaboration with me, he would consent to revise and remould the program of studies of the Ecoles Normales. He answered that he could not disavow his work of 1920. In other respects, I could not discern why he had introduced sociology. I am reminded of the curious declaration he made to me then: 'I am not at all a disciple of Durkheim; personally, I am a Cartesian.' In the face of that disagreement, the Council of Ministers decided, at my suggestion, that M. Lapie would end his functions at the ministry and that he be entrusted with a chair at the Sorbonne. There was an uproar about this in the left-wing press and in all the (illegal) teachers' unions. I was accused of wanting to destroy the work of Jules Ferry. Threats of an interpellation in the Senate. A veritable political crisis which meant that the Cabinet had to go back on its decision. I was constrained to continue a wholly nominal collaboration with Lapie. In the midst of the difficulties coming from the occupation of the Ruhr and the monetary and financial situation, could I, an old collaborator of Poincaré, add to all those predicaments? I had to submit.

I left the rue de Grenelle, after an experience of three and a half years, with some rather disabused views of the 'free play' of our institutions. All the good that I could have done was much confounded with the evil I could have prevented. I left there with the conviction that any serious change in matters of education was possible only if it was preceded by profound political changes ...

Part II. The Durkheimians and the scope of sociology

5. An intellectual self-portrait

MARCEL MAUSS

This unpublished manuscript by Mauss[1] was presented to Charles Andler and Sylvain Lévi as a confidential 'memoir'. It was almost certainly written in 1930 when he was competing for a position in the Collège de France. This text is of crucial importance, for in it Mauss gives an overview of his work, highlights his principal contributions, goes back over his scientific trajectory and recalls his joint work with Durkheim and Hubert as well as his participation in the *Année sociologique*.

I cannot divorce myself from the work of a school. If there is any individuality, it is immersed within voluntary anonymity. Perhaps what characterises my scientific career, even more today than formerly, is the feeling of working together as a team, and the conviction that collaborating with others is a drive against isolation and the pretentious search for originality.

There are two reasons for my position. The first is one of doctrine. As a positivist, I believe only in facts and even hold the superior certainty of the descriptive sciences over the theoretical sciences (in the cases of phenomena which are too complex). If I practise a theoretical science – and I may even do it well – I only think that it has an interest in so far as, extracted from facts, it can help perceive and record other facts, and classify facts in a different way; the interest of this theoretical science is preserved in so far as it goes into depth rather than generalising and materially asserts itself rather than rising to the lofty realms of historical hypotheses and metaphysical ideas. Now, it is only through the collaboration of many specialists that a broad knowledge of facts is possible. Deprived of laboratory conditions, sociology does not lack the means to control facts on condition that all historical social facts as understood by specialists of each branch of history can truly be compared. Such a task is impossible for one person. The only way of achieving solid results is through the mutual control and relentless criticism which comes out of opposing facts.

The second reason is one of fact. The progress made by sociology in France

[1] A copy of this text was held by G. Davy whose private library has been acquired by the Maison des Sciences de l'Homme.

in the twenty years between 1893 and 1914 was only possible because we were a group working together. We were not merely a school of blind disciples, gathered round a master or a philosopher. Of course, Durkheim was full of far-reaching ideas. What drew us to him, however, was that we knew that here was a scholar with a very sound method and whose knowledge was vast and scrupulously verified. The aspects of his mind which most seduced us, and me in particular, were his Cartesianism, his ever realist and rationalist search for facts, and his ability to know and grasp these facts. These are the qualities that I think I have consciously and conscientiously developed in myself, in my friends and in my students. Every science is the product of collective work. Carried out by individuals who are joined together through their common interest in reality, science emerges out of the facts and ideas brought by these individuals to a unique market place. An identical process occurred in the effort to create sociology. We required an enormous amount of data and a precise language to record them. All this presupposes a group and agreement. On the other hand, in exploring this social domain newly opened to science, we were perplexed wanderers who could find their way in the forest only by calling out to one another. Even the description of a fact or the mere assessment of problems raised unending difficulties which could be resolved only by an ongoing group. Alone in Bordeaux, Durkheim was painfully aware of the vastness of this task and his relative powerlessness. Regardless of his genius, he could have only a limited overview of the resources of history, of the past and of research into contemporary societies. I took the initiative and became Durkheim's recruiting agent between 1895 and 1902. This is how we came to form a group of competent and specialised scholars and confidently overcame the first major problems in our science.

Such a workshop atmosphere requires a great sense of self-sacrifice. A good laboratory depends not only on the person in charge but also on the existence of reliable participants, i.e. new and old friends with a lot of ideas, extensive knowledge and working hypotheses and who, most importantly, are ready to share these with one another, to join in the work of the longer-standing members and to launch the works of the newcomers. We were such a team. This team lives and has even been reborn. Neither Durkheim nor myself spared our efforts or our ideas. The accomplishments would have been impossible had we not devoted ourselves to the school in a spirit of sacrifice and if I did not continue to so devote myself to it.

From this involvement my life took on two features. First of all, I have perhaps worked too much in collaboration with others, and such activity takes up the major part of my time. I contributed to Durkheim's *Suicide* (quantitative method, classifying 26,000 suicides individually arranged on cards and distributed in 75 cases). I worked on everything he wrote as he also did with me; often he even rewrote entire pages of my work. I published two monographs with him, including *Primitive Classification* in which I provided all the data. With Hubert, I published a monograph on *Sacrifice* and another on *Magic*, and the preface to our *Mélanges*. Generally, I took part in everything which he did which was not strictly criticism or archaeology. He always read over everything I wrote. I had planned simply to collaborate with Beuchat, but then I had to completely take over the work on *Seasonal Variations of the Eskimos*. My collaboration in the work of my students and friends has also been considerable. If I feel somewhat overwhelmed at present, it is because I have taken upon myself the enormous task of publishing the numerous unpublished manuscripts left by Durkheim, Henri Hubert and Hertz. Through me, their works will become available to the public at a rate of one or two volumes a year.

My teaching and supervision of research at the Ecole des Hautes Etudes and at the Institut d'Ethnologie perhaps have been too demanding and have contributed to the delay of my own publications. But can I be reproached for being too exigent and professionally conscientious? The quality and quantity of my students all over the world demonstrate that this teaching has not been without value. The research which I have inspired and seen through to completion, the manuscripts and proofs which I have corrected and the guidance that I have provided, when taken together, demonstrate that this aspect of my work has not been negligible. If it were not for the war, this work would have stood out more brilliantly.

The greatest setback of my scientific life was not the work lost during the four-and-a-half years of war, nor from a year lost due to illness (1921–2), nor even my helplessness brought about by the premature deaths of Durkheim and Hubert, it was the loss of my best students and friends during these painful years. It could be said that it was a loss for this branch of French science; for me, everything had collapsed. Perhaps the best that I had been able to give of myself disappeared with them. The renewed success of my teaching after the war, the establishment and success of the Institut d'Ethnologie (surely due in great part to my efforts), again demonstrate what I can do in this area; but it can hardly take the place of what I have lost.

Finally, I would like to dispel certain misconceptions of my pedagogical activities. It has been suggested that I have slanted my teaching in favour of sociology; nothing could be further from the truth. My courses have never entirely overlapped with my personal research, no matter how fruitful they were nor how much free time they left for my research. In my chair of *History of the Religions of Non-Civilised Peoples*, I have been faithful to its baroque title and to the spirit of the Ecole des Hautes Etudes. In this position I have strictly limited my teaching to a non-comparative, critical and historical point of view, even when the facts that I was studying interested me only from a

Marcel Mauss

comparative perspective. In that context, I have never been a militant of sociology. I have been responsible for lecturing on ethnography at the Institut d'Ethnologie, the statutes of which I drew up, and where, along with Rivet and Lévy-Bruhl, I oversee the teaching, publications and the day-to-day activities; in this position I have always confined my teaching to the purely descriptive. Perhaps this sense of dedication and impartiality is worthy of scientific merit.

In any event, these factors account for why, at the end of my career, I wish to teach what I have always worked on: the comparative history of societies and of religions especially. At my age, it is quite legitimate to make use in my teaching of my research preparation and my completed work, whether published or unpublished and, in any case, previously untaught. I even integrate in my teaching the unpublished work left by my best friends; in this way, its publication will be facilitated, their memory will be better preserved and my general teaching will have a wider scope, being not only mine, but theirs as well. Not only would I be teaching my own work, but also the ideas and corroboration of the ideas elaborated by my friends, including Durkheim, Hubert, Doutté and Maurice Cahen.

Published work

My published work is somewhat discontinuous. I do not hold much with scientific systems and have never felt the need to express more than partial truths. In addition to a continuity in ideas, however, there has been a material continuity in my work. What unites these disparate contributions is the publication of the *Année sociologique* and the *Travaux de l'Année*. The continuity of my efforts is shown by the fact that I revived the publication of these two ventures after a hiatus of ten years and that I have seen the annual publication of two to four volumes in the *Collection des Travaux*. These efforts should be considered in this light and this is where their unity lies.

The 'Année sociologique'

Quantitatively, most of my – of our – work has been dedicated to the writing, editing and publishing of the *Année sociologique*. Out of the ten or eleven thousand pages of the fourteen volumes published or in press, I have written approximately two thousand five hundred in octavo (400 pages in volume 1 of the new series and 300 pages in volume 2 of the same series, if I include my bibliographic contributions to all the different sections). I shall not mention here the importance of this bibliography and the work of selection it presupposes, nor shall I go into my efforts of keeping up with current developments, personal relationships, correspondence, etc.

I would like to justify my personal efforts within the context of this collective enterprise, and stress the legitimacy of this joint endeavour as well as of my own contribution. Some may have thought that these efforts were exaggerated, disproportionate to their results, that they had an unattainable objective. Nothing could be more incorrect.

Durkheim founded the *Année* in order to enable us and himself to systematically put forward our point of view on a variety of sociological topics. Soon, however, in all our minds, it became neither a vehicle for propagating a method nor a platform to oppose the different schools of economists, historians of religion, theoreticians of jurisprudence, etc. Under Durkheim's direction, and I dare say my own drive, we all agreed to try to organise not merely ideas but above all facts. From volume 2 onwards, the *Année* became a kind of reasonably up-to-date repository for the different special sociologies. Naturally, the variety of our publications and of our work and taste and, even more, the magnitude of our ignorance sometimes led us astray. The correct balance of facts and the exact weight of ideas have not always been properly appreciated.

Theoretical developments, however, have always been carefully recorded. We have certainly been of use and, for the French-speaking world, perhaps even indispensable to those wishing to keep up with advances in theory. This has been so even for those in neighbouring disciplines (for example, philosophy and psychology of religion), for those in the special neighbouring sciences (law, economics, human geography, etc.) and all the more so for sociology.

We, and I especially, have above all dedicated ourselves to incorporating facts within a sociological framework, and simultaneously organising them and dissecting the raw data provided by the descriptive branches of our sciences. My own personal effort over ten years, the common effort of my students and myself, and finally my renewed, almost solitary effort over the last four years have precisely been to reveal and often to establish the facts taken from uncategorised civilisations.

Most of my reviews and some of my bibliographical notes have been theoretical. Some of them record not very easily accessible facts. Thus, it is still possible to read with profit my review of de Groot's *Religious System of China* (in seven volumes) and of Spencer and Gillen, of which, as a young man, I was the first to indicate the importance and even to elucidate the content. Other reviews contain theoretical discoveries, for instance, those of the books by Dietrich, Ossenbruggen and Elsdon Best in which I pointed out the significance of clan systems of first names. The set of reviews on North American Indians contains potentially all that we have since done on the potlatch and the juridical institutions of those tribes. In some other reviews, Durkheim and I resolved the problem of Polynesian and Micronesian

Marcel Mauss

kinship terminologies. Other reviews give shape to general problems like those of relationships between anthropology and the history of religions, and between the sociology and the psychology of religion, etc. Finally, other reviews show how geographical groups of facts, such as African religious systems, are constituted.

The basic point is that, while constantly remaining on factual grounds adequate to the ideas explored, we have been able to distribute notions logically and pragmatically within solid frameworks, which are now used everywhere and by nearly everyone, even our critics. Our system of classification has generally become that of the phenomenologies of the history of religions. The divisions established by the *Année sociologique* are so slavishly followed by everyone that I had to express Durkheim's and my own reservations on the value of this schema (see my paper on 'The Divisions of Sociology and their Relative Weight' and the series of general reviews which followed). Finally, although we never so intended, the *Année* provides a notable service to the French public. It is a sort of up-to-date handbook on one of the most recent and most important sciences; it is the ongoing expression of the work of what the entire world calls the French Sociological School (see Malinowski's article 'Social Anthropology' in the latest edition of the *Encyclopaedia Britannica*).

I shall not consider here the reviews by me which have appeared in other journals.

Theoretical work

There remains to be considered my theoretical work *per se* which might appear discontinuous. It is somewhat diverse, especially as of late when I have had to present sociology to quite varied audiences. These appearances are misleading, for my work has a logical unity. The overall scheme that Hubert and myself have followed can be found in our preface to the *Mélanges*. I have added only a few items since.

The order in which the questions have been posed, however, has followed that of our lives and science. Therefore it is not surprising that some biographical details which also concern Durkheim will enter this present account.

When I was a student, I vacillated between studies which would now be termed quantitative (in collaboration with Durkheim: suicide, history of towns, human spatial organisation – the last of which is echoed in my work *The Seasonal Variations*), the study of law (3 years) and the sociology of religion. Through a taste for philosophy and a consciously chosen aim (suggested by Durkheim), I specialised in the study of religious phenomena and I have almost entirely dedicated myself to this subject since that time. At

144

Bordeaux, Durkheim designed his course on the origins of religion (1894–5) for my benefit and for himself. Together we were looking for the best way to concentrate my energies in order to assist the nascent science to the best effect and to fill in its most serious gaps. We both felt that the study of institutions, the family and law, were sufficiently developed, and the study of ritual also seemed to us quite advanced except in one area. At that time, we were contented with the work of Frazer and, above all, Robertson-Smith. Only oral ritual and religious cognition appeared unexplored, so to speak. Even before my *agrégation*, I had prepared myself quite thoroughly through solid historical and philological studies in addition to my *agrégation* in philosophy, and through my familiarity with the works of foreign writers. At that time, I had already decided the topics of my theses. One was on the close relations between Spinoza and Léon L'Hébreu which I *discovered* in 1893, but which was a subject I wearied of in 1897 as a result of an act of indiscretion that enabled M. Couchoud to spoil and sabotage this topic. The other thesis was on prayer in all its aspects. The latter subject was indicative of the naivety and boldness with which we proceeded at that time. To deal with this subject, I embarked upon what I thought was to be a short period of philological studies: Vedic and Classical Sanskrit, Pali, Ancient Hebrew of the Talmud and of the liturgy, Christian liturgy, Zend. These studies, however, occupied me from 1902 to 1907. They quickly revealed to me a penetrating and subtle way, a more reliable means, to more general perspectives than by purely ideological procedures. A year of study in Holland and in England and my ethnographic and museum-keeping apprenticeship made me more exacting. The relationship that I established with Henri Hubert, who was to be my co-worker (*jumeau de travail*), also taught me to widen my perspective and to sharpen my analysis, despite the scantiness of ethnographic data at that time. To us, social phenomena appeared more and more complex and material on the one hand, and more and more spiritual and moral on the other. To us, the observations of the social realm and, within it, of the world of religion, appeared vast and more varied than we had expected. When we met, H.H. and I identified with each other and shared a period of intellectual exhilaration. Together we discovered the world of the prehistoric and the primitive and exotic, the Semitic and Indian universes along with the Ancient and Christian worlds which we had previously known. Having established a division of labour in our studies and specialised in order to know these worlds better, we felt somewhat mad. By sheer good sense and hard work, however, I believe we have accomplished our objective. Only with the death of Hubert did the project lapse. With the assistance of all our students and the support of the Musée de Saint-Germain, the Institut d'Ethnologie and the *Année socio-logique*, with our latest achievements matched with those of an ever-growing number of scholars in our sciences, mainly from abroad, we would have reaped the belated benefits of our efforts but for his death.

During this period we were filling the compartments of sociology with facts. We urged the investigation of new facts, we reclassified poorly classified facts and we re-analysed those which had been badly described. Discoveries and novelties were a source of constant delight for us. Leaving aside our work of criticism and the paying of our due to our predecessors, we have never published anything that could be considered repetitious or even loyal verification. When such a piece was produced, it never saw the light in a published form. I am not taking into account, then, all the work involved in circulating the ideas of other people that I might have done and my *curriculum*[2] does not even mention the essays of my youth on Andrew Lang, the Inca Empire, etc.

Institutions

My work as a whole can quite easily be divided into four fields to which I have contributed quite a number of ideas and new facts. In pursuing my studies in the sociology of religion, I have never lost sight of my early interest in institutions. Furthermore, one aspect of our method is precisely to relate institutional and structural phenomena to mental phenomena and vice-versa.

Before leaving this field of my early training, in the conclusion to a lengthy review article of Steinmetz's *Ethnologische Stüdien zur ersten Entwicklung der Sträfe*, which I entitled 'Religion and the Origins of Penal Law', I demonstrated what is now a classical hypothesis. I proved that it is our private civil law of responsibility and not our public criminal law which is based on feud, a phenomenon belonging to the politico-*cum*-domestic sphere of law. Public criminal law derives from the system of ritual prohibitions and ritual sanctions of the crimes so prohibited. The sort of indignation and public response against these crimes is identical to the reaction to crimes against religion.

Assisted by Beuchat, I furthermore showed that the Eskimo, and many similar societies (today known to be very many, including, for example, the Slavs) which had two social structures, one in the winter and another in the summer, equally had two systems of law and religion. This glaring case demonstrated that law and religion are closely connected to social mass and patterns of settlement. I have also suggested on several occasions, including in my forthcoming contribution for the Anesaki anthology, that the notion

[2] Mauss is referring to the bibliography prepared on the occasion of his candidacy for the Collège de France: *Notice sur les titres et travaux de M. Marcel Mauss*. Presses Universitaires de France, 1930, 16 pages.

of the soul and reincarnation is linked to the inheritance of first names within the clan and the family, and to the position of the individual as it is conveyed through titles, masques, dances, etc.

On other occasions, I have tried to explain the development of reciprocity and conflict in a society by looking at the place that men, women, and generations occupied in society. I thus identified certain important systems of moral phenomena such as the quite common institution of joking relationships (which raise a number of problems) and, above all, the phenomena associated with the potlatch, within which I prefer to distinguish between the systems of total prestations and the system of agonistic prestations or potlatch.

Guided by Boas's admirable descriptions of the American Northwest that Durkheim brought to my attention, I was able to bring out an entire system of facts that are very widespread throughout most ancient civilisations. I followed up traces of this system throughout North America, Melanesia, Polynesia and within practically the entire Indo-European, Semitic and Berber worlds. From these facts, I drew out the at once religious, mythical and contractual idea of the gift. I also brought out the idea of total prestation between clans, between generations (usually staggered), between the sexes and between descent groups (see Malinowski); I established the collective nature of archaic forms (see Davy) and, above all, this notion of 'total facts' which set the entire economic, moral, religious, aesthetic and mythical (see Granet) social whole in motion. Superimposed on reciprocity and conflict, a system of purely sumptuary, military, athletic etc. rivalries developed within these societies. On the basis of the evidence provided by North American and Melanesian phenomena, we considered the development of religious brotherhoods and politico-religious aristocracies in the same category (see Davy, Granet and Mauss). My personal contribution to these studies was to examine these phenomena in the Indo-European, Germanic and Roman worlds (for Greece, see Gernet).

In sum, my contribution has been to supplement the correct, but partial, classic views on the simple structure of clan society by drawing attention to the allocation of rights and duties between age, sex and generational groups that are both natural and social.

The idea of dual descent which Durkheim and I had elucidated in the Polynesian case, and that I had identified in the Nigritian world, will also result in a total re-orientation of the way we study the problem of the female and male lines.

In each of these areas, the previous ways of posing questions have been surpassed and displaced. And, furthermore, some solutions to general and even moral questions may be envisaged (see my conclusion to *The Gift*).

Marcel Mauss

Religion and ideation

The bulk of my work, however, deals with ritual and religious representations. My major work was a monograph on prayer, which I soon limited to the elementary forms of verbal rites in Australia. The initial project which I prepared envisaged two further volumes. One was to focus on the development of oral ritual in Melanesia, Polynesia and Vedic India; the other was to deal with the mystic sublimation in Brahmanic and Buddhist India, the Semitic and Christian individualisation of prayer and, finally, the regressions and automatic decline of prayer in India, Tibet and in Christianity.

I have given courses based on the material of the first volume, and two instalments of a provisional nature were privately printed in 1909 – these hardly represented a fourth of the planned book. Publication of this work was interrupted because in the meantime I came into contact with Strehlow's work on the Aranda and Loritja. Having received and copied the research notes, I corresponded with the author and assisted in the publication of his work. Just as I was plunging back into my work which Strehlow's material enabled me to bring up to date and to explore thoroughly, the outbreak of the war brought my studies to a halt.

But beforehand, from a sound methodological standpoint, I had to solve two problems. Furthermore, Hubert was also harbouring concerns similar to my own on both of these problems although we started from distinct perspectives. While Hubert's aim in his investigation of the Semitic origins of the Christian myth was to explain the sacrificial god, I wanted to see whether the ritual form of sacrifice was really so closely linked with it that the verbal rites were derived from the sacrifice. We also had to concentrate on magic, which was considered a primitive form or a pseudo-science having preceded religion.

In dealing with these two problems we became aware of others. Our work on sacrifice enabled us to conclude that sacrificial ritual was a very evolved form of religious life, and not fundamentally primitive. It was connected with a far more general system of consecration which I will not go into here. Nor shall I describe how we arrived at this conclusion, the developments preceding its emergence, nor its evolution towards the sacrificial god. In brief, following Robertson-Smith and Durkheim, what we did was to demonstrate a clear example of the way in which the idea of the sacred functions. Therefore, the problem of the sacred becomes fundamental, and we found this to be true again in the case of magic.

In this light, magic has a special place among religious phenomena. Like Max Muller, Frazer and Farnell, we had originally believed that it was a case of magical formulae. It had to be seen whether it was an exception, whether

148

it depended upon another sphere of mentality, and whether it had either generated religion or itself also derived from the idea of the sacred or from something similar. In our monograph on magic, we unravelled a great number of elements common to magic and religion; we proved that they set in motion the same mental mechanisms. In particular, at the foundation of both magic and religion we discovered a vast common notion which we called *mana*, borrowing the term from the Melanesian–Polynesian language. The idea of mana is perhaps more general than that of the sacred. Later, Durkheim tried to deduce it sociologically from the notion of the sacred. We were never sure that he was correct and I still continue to speak of the magico-religious basis. In any case, like the notion of the sacred, magic presents itself as a category; this led us to a new problem. But also everything took on a new light and emerged as a unique system.

Not all the notes to this monograph on magic were included in the text. The second section on magic and religion, in which we explain the relations between these two systems of phenomena, is finished and is to be published. It shows that the relationships between religion and magic are of a juridical rather than logical nature and that they have varied with different religions and societies.

Thus two new and extremely important questions weighed upon our work. One was the idea of the sacred, on which we have worked a long time; I hope to make known the results of our studies in the future. The second was the question of categories of thought. We had divided these problems between ourselves while at the same time drawing them together. Hubert was to study the sacred in time, which he did. I was to study the sacred in space, which I did partially, and our student Czarnowski is finally carrying the study to completion. In agreement with Durkheim, however, we soon focused on the problem of reason.

We approached the subject from many angles: the study of religious representations of a general nature and of natural beings in every volume of the *Année sociologique* from number 2 onwards. Included were studies of number and cause (in the monograph on *The Origin of Magical Powers*); space and time (in the monograph on *The Origin of the Notion of Time*); the soul (and not simply the notion of animism) and world (the notion of orientation). Durkheim and I dealt with the subject itself in our monograph on the notion of genus, entitled *Primitive Classification*. In particular the question of space and that of 'participation' and 'contrasts' are outlined. This was one of the most philosophical endeavours attempted by a school. Durkheim pursued the subject in greater theoretical depth in *The Elementary Forms of Religious Life*.

Together, Hubert and I prepared a series of studies converging on the notion of sustenance and its history from ancient times. I hope to publish

Marcel Mauss

this study in two or three volumes (Henri Hubert; *Vasen de Gundestrup*; M. Mauss, *The Archaic Form of the Notion of Nourishment: Ancient Greece and Vedic India Compared*). Perhaps a third volume will take this investigation into the domain of patristics. Hubert has published several sections of his study. I have published a rather difficult part of my studies in the collection dedicated to Sylvain Lévi.

Psychology and sociology

After Durkheim's death, I had to take his place to a certain extent. I have defended sociology on numerous occasions and from time to time I have even compromised to its benefit. On the other hand, psychologists (like McDougall, Dumas, etc.) began to address the problems of collective thought, action and sensibility. I even agreed to examine the problem in the third volume of Dumas's *Treatise on Psychology* (2nd edition); my discussions with Dumas on laughter, tears and the expression of feelings seen as signs required that I adopt a position on these matters which I did on several occasions. This year I shall complete these factual and methodological papers with some psycho-sociological considerations on what I term 'techniques of the body' (walking, running, jumping, gymnastics, swimming, rest, breathing, sleep, sexual intercourse, etc.). The long-standing and somewhat futile debate between psychologists and sociologists has thus shifted to a new level of understanding. In this way, for example, Mead's classic position on the symbolic activity of the mind agrees entirely with the theory of the importance of ritual, mythical, linguistic etc. symbol proposed jointly by Durkheim and myself.

In addition to these concerns, I have also worked on the nature of what I call total facts, the total human being, which is the only unit found by the sociologist. These reflections have met with quite general approval and I was particularly touched by that of Koelher. I also bring to your attention my work on Wundt's *Art and Myth*.

Methodology

The public is still too fond of sociological methodology and our students and colleagues are still too entrenched in philosophical reflections on the legitimacy of our studies. It would be better to know and to advance them rather than subjecting them to a transcendental critique. I have had to resign myself to taking part in them. In collaboration with Durkheim, Fauconnet and I wrote a small book on sociology, only two parts of which have appeared. The first part is the article 'Sociology' in the *Grande Encyclopédie* which, along with *The Rules of the Sociological Method*, is still regarded as a

150

manifesto of the school. The second part is the article by Durkheim and Fauconnet, in fact written by the three of us, which is entitled 'History of Sociology and the Social Sciences'. The third part has never been published. On several occasions I have revised, and I am presently still revising, this general question of methodology in volume 2 of the *Année sociologique*, new series, in the paper 'Divisions of Sociology and their Relative Weight'. An explanation was required of the extent to which we had to take account of recent research (Foy and Graebner) and new hypotheses (Koppers and Schmitt) on the history of civilisations. I have done this on several occasions (*Année sociologique*, volumes 8 to 12 inclusive and volumes 1 and 2 of the new series). I shall continue with a global study of the notion of civilisation in volume 3 of the new series. Part of this study has just been published in *Semaine de synthèse* (1929). My articles on 'Anthropology in France and Abroad', published in the *Revue de Paris* are proof that my research into this subject is of a long-standing nature.

Towards the end of this year I also plan to publish my Oslo lectures dealing with the use of the notion of primitive in sociology and in the history of civilisations. There one will find that, in agreement with Hubert, I relate the conditions of certain kinds of so-called lower societies to the great Neolithic and Eneolithic civilisations.

All things considered, I have never lost sight of the only goal of the discipline to which I have dedicated myself: to show and to specify the role played by social life in human life through the most precise and direct contact with facts.

I believe that I have contributed to heightening the sociological awareness of historians, philologists, etc. and the historical and statistical awareness of sociologists.

Throughout this present account of my works, I have not mentioned my written interventions in the normative sphere. I do not believe, however, that my incursions into this domain are without scientific and philosophical interest. They include my publications and even my scientific and didactic contributions on the cooperative movement (on statistics, Russian cooperatives, etc.), the extracts from a manuscript on Bolshevism (in *Monde slave*, and *Revue de métaphysique et de morale*) and my communications on the concept of nation and internationalism. Nearly all of these are part of a major work on *The Nation* (first principle of modern politics) which is nearly complete in manuscript form. This work will not be published in the *Travaux de l'Année sociologique* collection because I want to separate firmly even this totally disinterested theory from the pure science of sociology.

6. At the frontier of folklore and sociology: Hubert, Hertz and Czarnowski, founders of a sociology of folk religion

FRANÇOIS A. ISAMBERT

The relationship between sociologists and folklorists has always been somewhat strained. In the first series (1898–1913) of the *Année sociologique*, critics reviewing works on folklore recognised the erudition involved but were scornful of the method. The basic accusation against the folklorists was that they mixed facts of a very different order. 'The various facts related are not properly classified: some concern surviving customs, others disappearing customs, whilst yet others concern entirely primitive phenomena', writes Marcel Mauss (1898: 218), in the very first number of the *Année*, of a study of the folklore of India. It is a criticism which recurs frequently.[1]

It is not hard to see that the strain in the relationship springs from a much deeper source than mere divergence over method. What the editors of the *Année* have difficulty in grasping is the object itself of folklore studies. Not the least proof of this is the hesitation shown by the *Année sociologique* in classifying the facts and finding a general term to cover them. The initial classification, of course, is into the section on the sociology of religion, which not only reveals an interpretative bias, but also a choice: folklore is admitted only in so far as it collates, or at least can be linked to, religious facts. There still remains, however, the problem of the name to be given to these particular religious facts. The first volume speaks with fine assurance of 'folk cults in general, agrarian cults in particular' (Marcel Mauss). But works of a folkloric nature are also to be found in an earlier chapter on 'Beliefs and practices relating to death' and a later one on 'Myths'. The same dispersion is to be found in later volumes, but the general heading itself changes: 'Magic, sorcery and folk superstitions', 'Folk superstitions', 'Unorganised beliefs and folk practices'.

This last heading, which is used in several successive numbers of the *Année*,[2] deserves closer attention, since it brings us to the heart of the

[1] For example, Mauss's review (1910: 202) of Van Gennep, *Les Rites de passage*: 'We have often spoken of the disadvantages of these disorderly reviews.'
[2] Volumes 5 to 7. Then the problem is avoided by the use of the convenient phrase 'Beliefs and practices called popular'.

152

problem. Marcel Mauss (1903: 168) gives a clear indication of what he believes to be the fundamental obstacle to a treatment of folkloric facts by the sociologist (as well as by the ethnologist and the historian): 'folkloric data belong to the common people – they are unsystematic, they are relics of another time and in general no longer correspond to essential states and functions in society – whereas the institutions, techniques and regimes studied by history and ethnography are integrated, organic facts, characteristic of the societies in question'. The attempt to clarify the specific nature of the object of folklore studies by defining it as 'relics'[3] simultaneously emphasises how difficult it is for that object to be studied by a science for which to explain a phenomenon is basically to assign it a function in a society conceived of as an organised whole.

Consequently, we need to progress beyond this position. Henri Hubert believes that for one particular case at least the dispersion of folkloric facts is no more than an initial impression: 'no matter how heterogeneous and dislocated the folklore of a country like Macedonia may seem at first sight, we should not abandon the search for some rudiments of organisation which might enable it to become the object of sociological study as a unified entity and not merely in its separate parts' (Hubert 1905b: 311). However, the same Henri Hubert was also to develop a general theory of religion which did, in fact, transform folkloric phenomena into a proper object of study. Henceforth, Durkheimians would not only be able to evaluate the work of folklorists on the same level, but also contribute usefully to a sociology of folk religion (Isambert 1978). In addition to Henri Hubert, Stefan Czarnowski, who was his pupil, and Robert Hertz contributed to this development. However, for each of the authors individually, the work on folk religion fits into an opus of which it is not the main part. An intellectual biography of the three men is needed, then, if the works are to be put into context.

Henri Hubert and people's religions[4]

Born of a middle-class Parisian family (23 June 1872), Henri Hubert had already shown a special interest in history at the Lycée Louis-le-Grand where the school chaplain, Abbé Quentin,[5] was instrumental in developing his interest in the history of religions. After graduating from the Ecole Normale Supérieure and passing the *agrégation* in history, Henri Hubert's academic career began in the normal way, but he showed greater interest in

---

[3] See also Marcel Mauss's accusation (1900: 192–5) that the concept of *Volkskunde* is not restricted to surviving customs, which are the real object of folklore.
[4] For further details on Hubert's life, and his concept of social time, see Isambert 1979.
[5] Aurèle Quentin was the author of various Assyriological studies, as well as of a *Paroissien romain à l'usage des lycées, collèges et pensions*, 1885. After the 1914–18 war, he lectured in the fifth section of the Ecole Pratique des Hautes Etudes.

François A. Isambert

research than teaching and, instead of taking up a teaching post in 1895, began to specialise in the history of religions and philosophy at the Ecole Pratique des Hautes Etudes, in the fourth and fifth sections, where he attended the lectures of Carrière, V. Scheil, Joseph Halévy, Victor Bérard, Sylvain Lévy and Israël Lévi, and V. Derenbourg. At that time, he seemed to be equally interested in Celtic history and Oriental languages. Then he made the acquaintance of Marcel Mauss and the two collaborated on the first number (1898) of the *Année sociologique*. From the second number onwards, he had joint responsibility for most of the sub-sections in the chapter on 'sociology of religion' and contributed a score of book reviews. He was to contribute to the first two series of the journal.

In the meantime, he had been working since 1898 at the Musée des Antiquités Nationales of Saint-Germain-en-Laye, becoming assistant curator there in 1910. In 1901, he was appointed 'maître de conférences' in primitive European religions in the Department of Religious Sciences of the Ecole Pratique des Hautes Etudes, holding the post until his death, with only one interruption (between 1914–19) because of the war. Finally, from 1906 he also taught national archaeology at the Ecole du Louvre until the end of his life. His duties at both Saint-Germain and the Ecole du Louvre brought him into close contact with Salomon Reinach, whom he considered to be a man of great erudition but excessively sectarian.[6] Most of his works on archaeology seem to be related to his duties at the Musée de Saint-Germain, but his historical and sociological works bear the imprint of his teaching.

His first important publication (Hubert 1899a) was a historical work[7] based on the *Liber pontificalis* which had already been studied by Abbé Louis Duchesne (the future Monsignor Duchesne who was accused of modernism). In it, Hubert attempted to analyse the respective roles of politics and religion in the iconoclastic heresy which led to the formation of the Church Estates in the eighth century.

The best-known of Hubert's works are the ones written in collaboration with Mauss: 'Essai sur la nature et la fonction sociale du sacrifice' (1899c) and 'Esquisse d'une théorie générale de la magie' (1904b). An autobiographical note written by Hubert during World War I[8] clarifies one aspect of his own contribution. His thesis on the Syrian goddess[9] had led him to reflect

[6] S. Reinach mentions the disagreement between them when his *Orpheus* was published. See Hubert 1909b and Reinach 1927.
[7] The article appeared in 1899, but, as a note indicates, it was written before the publication of *Les Premiers Temps de l'Eglise pontificale* by Abbé Duchesne (1898).
[8] This note, left for the attention of his son, is an intellectual will, indicating what is to be done with the manuscripts and expounding the meaning of his works (Hubert 1979).
[9] The thesis was apparently never finished and we have no direct trace of it. However, besides the passage from the 'Essais sur la nature et la fonction sociale du sacrifice', there is a further hint of the work in the Preface to Czarnowski's *Le Culte des héros ... Saint Patrick, héros national de l'Irlande*. It is clear that Hubert was especially interested in a semi-divinity, associated at Hierapolis with the goddess, and who in the Lebanon today is given the names of

154

more especially on the sacrifice of the god (a theme which takes up the whole of the last part of 'Essai sur le sacrifice') and the way in which it typically relates ritual and myth. This biographical data can be supplemented by pointing to Hubert's dual competence in Greek and Roman history and in Semitic (Judaic and Assyro-Babylonian) studies – a competence demonstrated by his many reviews in these areas in the *Année sociologique* – whereas Mauss was more concerned with India on the one hand, and the so-called 'primitive' peoples (especially Australian) on the other. So their respective areas of expertise can be defined at least to some extent.

The collaboration on the 'Théorie de la magie' is to be interpreted in the same way. The wealth of facts relating to archaic cultures might suggest that Mauss was the principal contributor, but Hubert had published a long article entitled 'Magia' in the *Dictionnaire des antiquités*. It might be objected that this article is entirely documentary and highly unsystematic, that it contains hardly any sociological theory of magic, and that Hubert's contribution to the common work on magic is likely to be of the same kind. However, there is every reason to believe that Hubert had poured into the article a surplus of documentary material that he had been unable to use properly in the 'Théorie de la magie'.[10] Furthermore, it seems to be a characteristic of Hubert's work as a whole that he alternates theoretical works with works where the role of theory takes second place to erudition.

For this reason, it would be unfair to Henri Hubert's intellectual personality to separate his historical–archaeological works from his sociological works. His work as a historian of religions draws upon archaeology as well as upon a study of the texts, as we can see from a series of extended articles alternating between Celtic studies and studies of Near-Eastern antiquity: 'Kyréné' (1899d), 'Nantosuelta, déesse à la ruche' (1912a), his analysis of the 'Figure du dieu au maillet' (1915), and his last article 'De quelques objets de bronze trouvés à Byblos' (1925c). In its turn, the history of religions feeds into the sociology, as Mauss confirms when he describes him as one of the only two mythologists that sociology can boast of.[11] The unity of his thought took shape in a number of broad syntheses that were beginning to emerge from the multitude of minutely detailed studies. At the time of his death, he was

---

Eshmoun, or even Adonis. (A river with reddish water, to the north of Beirut, is said to be reddened by the blood of Adonis.) The 'Syrian goddess', sometimes anonymous and sometimes polynomous, celebrated by Lucian aroused the curiosity of quite a number of historians at the end of the nineteenth century. We can easily understand how this polymorphous divinity, linking different mythologies, would have interested Hubert the mythologist.

[10] The importance of Hubert's contribution to the 'Esquisse d'une théorie générale de la magie' is confirmed by Durkheim who, in a letter to Bouglé dated 12 June 1900, mentions only Hubert's name in relation to the projected work on magic (Durkheim 1976: 173).

[11] 'But we still have one mythologist, and that is Granet. There was one other, no less brilliant, and that was Hubert. I am trying to make up for the loss of Hubert and help Granet' (Mauss 1933: 112).

François A. Isambert

preparing an *Ethnographie préhistorique de l'Europe* (Berr 1932b). He left at Saint-Germain an exhibition which is by all accounts remarkable, tracing the technological history of mankind (Mauss 1930: 99–100).

This brings us to his death on 25 May 1927, apparently hastened by grief. In 1910 he married a German woman who bore him a first son in 1913. During the war he was mobilised but then recalled from the front and attached to the Ministry of Armaments with Albert Thomas. He was deeply affected by the death of Durkheim, but the worst blow was the death of his wife in childbirth in 1924. We do not know exactly what he himself died of, but we do know that he struggled for several years in a vain attempt to finish his work (Berr 1932a).

Hubert left several unfinished works: the thesis on the Syrian goddess, which he mentioned in his intellectual will in 1915 but which has vanished without trace; a half-finished work on *Les Celtes* based on his lectures on Celtic archaeology at the Ecole du Louvre; and another on *Les Germains* which was the text of his lectures at the Hautes Etudes. Both works had been promised to Henri Berr for his collection *Evolution de l'humanité*. *Les Celtes* was published in two volumes, in 1932 and 1933, as a result of the careful labours of his friends Marcel Mauss, Raymond Lantier and Jean Marx, who wrote up or summarised the parts left in note form. The text of *Les Germains* was in a more complete state. Hubert also left a series of lectures which were accurately edited, lesson by lesson, by Paul Chalus, but the book was not published until 1952, apparently through the carelessness of Mauss and one of his pupils. It is interesting to note that the lectures on the Germanic people had been compiled during the many years of teaching at the Hautes Etudes. The study of the Germanic calendar and feast days was the starting point for the study on 'La Représentation du temps', which is discussed below.

Returning to the theoretical aspect of Hubert's work, which played an essential part in the process of founding a theory of folk religion, Hubert describes as follows the direction of his collaboration with Mauss on this point:

The problems we had to solve were the following: the nature of religious phenomena, the conditions of religious phenomena, the nature and conditions of myth. These problems did not present themselves in an abstract manner: the particular way in which they were posed gave rise to our works on myth and magic ...

In the analysis of religious facts, the problem that demanded immediate attention was how to analyse the representations that preside over the development of these facts and regulate their logic. We isolated the concept of the sacred as a category of the mental operations involved in religious phenomena. (Hubert 1979: 206)

The themes of the collaborative work were to receive special emphasis in the two works published under Hubert's own name: the Introduction to his

1904 translation of the *Manuel d'histoire des religions* by Chantepie de la Saussaye, and the 'Etude sommaire de la représentation du temps dans la religion et la magie'.[12] Since the two works appeared at almost the same time, we shall ignore chronology in the following discussion of those sections which are of most interest to us.

The Introduction to Chantepie de la Saussaye is presented as a manifesto of the Durkheimian school and is of great value to us, because in it the author speaks collectively, giving us an account of what seems to him at that time to be the Durkheimian consensus in the sociology of religion (at least as far as the nucleus of Durkheim–Mauss–Hubert is concerned). More precisely, it defines the doctrine relating to the central role of the concept of the *sacred* (Isambert 1976).

A review of previous works on sacrifice and magic produces two results. On the one hand, the sacred, which can be taken as identical with the *mana*, is the ultimate referent in magic, as also in religion, since every magic or religious object or person is to be considered a modality of the sacred. On the other hand, it is a 'milieu', some idea of which could already be gleaned from the study on sacrifice, a milieu that 'one enters and leaves' (1904a: xlvi) and the nature of which regulates the operations that take place within it. From the point of view of the mind, it is a sort of 'category'. I shall return to this notion of 'category' in the discussion of sacred time, simply saying at this point that Hubert's aim is to show that the sacred acts 'by imposing conditions on experience and reasoning' (xlvii). In other words, the sacred, which in the physical world is the general form of the operational constraints upon ritual behaviour, becomes, in consciousness, the general form of the operational constraints upon religious thought.

This idea was to be developed in detail in the 'Etude sur le temps'. The starting point is that between the rite and the myth, which are to all appearances situated in different times, there is, in fact, a temporal connection. Now, although it is widely accepted that the time of the myth itself possesses mythic properties, it is less widely realised that the rite also, in order to function and take on meaning, presupposes a particular representation of time. More than that, it actually creates for itself a temporal *milieu*, so that those who envisage the rite as taking place in our time place themselves purely and simply in the time of the observation and not in the time which structures the rite itself. Now, in fact, this time-as-milieu possesses very special properties, common to all religious facts, from mythic representations right through to the ordering of rituals.

[12] Published under Hubert's name in *L'Annuaire de l'Ecole Pratique des Hautes Etudes, 5ᵉ section*, 1905. At the time of publication of *Mélanges d'histoire des religions* with Marcel Mauss, it was said to be a collaborative work, but in fact Marcel Mauss had no hesitation in disassociating himself from it in his review for *L'Année sociologique* (Mauss 1907).

François A. Isambert

These properties can be reduced to five:

(1) critical dates interrupt the continuity of time.
(2) the intervals between two associated critical dates are, each within itself, continuous and indivisible ...
(3) critical dates are equivalent to the intervals they delimit ...
(4) similar parts are equivalent.
(5) quantitatively unequal lengths of time are equalised and vice versa.[13]

Rather than examining these properties individually, which would assume their independence,[14] we shall try to bring out their systematic unity. Firstly, from a negative point of view these properties are opposed, term for term, to the properties of scientific time. Thus we have quality instead of quantity, discontinuity instead of continuity, indivisibility instead of infinite divisibility, compenetration instead of exteriority.

From the properties of this time-as-milieu, Hubert creates a framework structured by operational rules enabling the rite to function. It can be proved – and Hubert proves it by examples – that each of these properties structures the emergence of the myth as well as the unfolding of the rite and allows communication between them. The first three properties can be taken as rules of division, the last two as rules of equivalence, and it can be seen that the first set is matched against the second, since the rules of division can, in effect, be subsumed under a common perspective, that of compact temporal blocs where the critical date designates not only the moment but also what fills it. The most characteristic case in this respect is that of the feast days. Hence the obvious fact (obvious in one sense, that is) that the critical date interrupts the continuity of time, but also the less obvious fact that it sets up a different time. Hence also the indivisibility without which the moment would lose all significance, but which does not exclude a division into parts (the successive acts of the feast day). Hence, finally, the third property: 'when a phenomenon or a qualified act occurs at any given moment of the period conventionally assigned to it, it is considered to fill that period with its qualities, to contaminate it entirely' (1905a: 14).

The equivalences, if we confine ourselves to a mere listing, might seem to be simple rules of measurement. But, if we are to make any progress beyond this, we have to put aside our accepted temporal equalities and assume new equivalences based, this time, on similitude (in a sense of the word very close to the one it has in geometry). Now, from equivalence Hubert passes to identity, which is the basis for the repetitiveness of both myth and rite: 'every year, every seven years, every nine years, on the same date as that of the catastrophe, the town comes alive again, the bells ring, the lady of the manor

[13] According to the table of contents of *Mélanges d'histoire des religions* (1909a: 235–6).
[14] Mauss, in his review (1907: 304), reduces these properties to four, making the last one the corollary of the preceding one.

leaves her retreat, the treasures are opened, the guardians fall asleep' (p. 16). The same feast days recur on the same dates for the same reason: because, in religious time, and in a completely general way, 'the same dates bring back the same events'. The importance of all this can be seen if we now bring together the mythic phenomenon and the rite to which it is related. From identity we pass to reproduction. The Christian Easter 'perpetuates' the Jewish Easter on the one hand and the sacrifice and resurrection of Christ on the other, in the sense that it makes them happen again, it 'renews' them. And if Easter Sunday falls by tradition on the annual date of the Resurrection, 'the weekly Sunday commemorates, that is renews with less solemnity but just as efficiently as the annual Easter celebration, the sacrifice of Christ' (p. 17) through the equivalence of the relationship of Sunday to the week and Easter to the year.

These characteristics, whose operational value is clear, bring about the penetration into time of what Hubert calls the 'category of the sacred'. The essential point is that *time* itself becomes sacred and not just the beings who move within it. The 'sympathetic associations' (Lévy-Bruhl would say the 'participation') which exist between the moments of mythic and ritual time are of the same nature as those which link together sacred objects.

We must expect the intervention in some way of the idea of magic power, of *mana*, or of the sacred which provides the basis for the belief in magic and religion, in other associations of the same type. The associations which define the quality of the different kinds of time must be sacred in nature, as must also the terms which make them up, in other words, dates or their signs must have magico-religious power and the things signified, events or acts, must participate in the nature of that power. (1905a: 30)

The end of this passage is especially important. On the one hand, the word 'participation' is used. On the other, dates are presented as 'signs', but sacred signs, whose characteristic is precisely that they participate in the things they signify. The sacred dates, those of the feast days, attract one another, refer back to one another to the point of being interchangeable, like the feasts of Saint Martin, Saint Michael, Saint Nicholas, Christmas, Epiphany, Saint Anthony, etc. This veritable participation of the festive days with one another through their common sacred nature is the antinomy of the participation of a date with a precise fact, historical or mythical. So we are faced with a balance, forever in jeopardy, between the specificity of the feast days and their tendency to fuse into one another and to extend the area of fusion. 'They are invested with a kind of general qualification which is expressed in particular determinations' (p. 31).

Thus we see the gradual adumbration of the theoretical foundations which will permit a sociological approach to folk religion. For, by defining religion as 'obligatory beliefs', the first studies of religious sociology made by the

Durkheimian school directed research towards the orthodoxies, even though Durkheim strove to show the coexistence with these of individual beliefs (Durkheim 1899: 26–7). Such a frame of reference, provided it incorporates an array of micro-orthodoxies and micro-societies, is certainly not incompatible with the study of the many local variations of folk religion, but it is less suited than a much more flexible one which makes it possible to study the infinite variations of the sacred milieu which conditions both religious representations and practices, without the need to postulate some hypothetical authority from which the obligation to believe would come and which is difficult to find outside the organised religions.

But Hubert goes further. The 'Etude sommaire de la représentation du temps dans la religion et la magie' sketches out a theory of the feast day, at least in its temporal aspect. As a 'critical' moment of a 'time-as-milieu', the feast day is not restricted to any Church. Taking in the whole of a population at any given moment, it is of necessity *popular*. It is in relation to this that we should understand the great importance that Hubert seems to attach to defining the different types of religion – which brings us back to the Introduction to the *Manuel* of Chantepie de la Saussaye.

In all justice to Durkheim, it should first be said that he was the one who prepared the ground in his famous article 'De la définition des phénomènes religieux' where he states clearly from the outset:

We talk of religious *facts* and not *religion* because religion is a whole made up of religious phenomena, and the whole can only be defined after the parts. Moreover, there are very many religious manifestations which do not belong to anything that can properly be called a religion; in every society there are beliefs and practices which are diffuse, individual or local, and not integrated into any specific system. (Durkheim 1899: 1)

The issue is mainly one of methodology, but Hubert uses it to distinguish several kinds of religion which are virtually different meanings of the word 'religion'. 'We call religion the sum of religious manifestations in the life either of a people, or of a society specially formed for a religious purpose, in other words, a Church.' So there are people's religions and Church religions: 'We speak of Roman religion, Greek religion, or Assyrian religion; these are people's religions. Buddhism, Islam, Christianity are, or seem to be, Church religions' (1904a: xxi).

Church religions are, in fact, quite highly organised systems, comprising doctrine, cult and organisation. When a religion is defined by a people, it may be the case, as with the Jews, that 'the beliefs and practices of a people have become unified and codified like those of a Church'. But usually people's religions are 'very loose and very vague systems', as is the case with the Roman 'religion' or the Greek 'religion'. Finally, and of special interest to us, it may happen that we are dealing with unorganised phenomena.

There is a great mass of facts, individual practices or feast-day rituals, myths and various beliefs which apparently belong to no system, not even tribal or national: they are the *superstitions*,[15] the phenomena of folklore, which are themselves often the relics of ancient religions, and which have not always lost their religious character. (1904a: xxii)

The word 'religion' in the wide sense is to be understood as including all of this, and the first result of the analysis, as a continuation of the Durkheimian attempt to find a definable class to cover all religious facts, is to bring together in this way under the name of religion many phenomena that the folklorists dispersed under different headings.

But with the concept of 'people's religion' we have a framework capable of incorporating the narrower notion of 'folk religion', since the latter really is a 'people's religion', even if 'people' is taken in its most localised meaning. An exception must be made, of course, where Church and people coincide. On the other hand, however, there is no question of limiting folk religion to pure folklore. Finally, a somewhat hesitant line can be drawn between the total disorganisation of folklore and the organisation of the Church of a people or nation. As we shall see, Durkheimian studies of folk religion tend to shift back and forth between national cults and local folklore, but perhaps the unity comes from the decision, in both cases, to study that part of religion which is, at least at first sight, not organised. Two studies were carried out at almost the same time: one at the national level by Czarnowski, which Hubert himself was to build upon, and the other at the local level by Hertz.

Czarnowski and the cult of the hero

The intellectual career of Stefan Czarnowski[16] is very closely linked, in the area which concerns us, to that of Hubert, whose pupil he was at the Ecole Pratique des Hautes Etudes where he worked on Celtic legends.[17] In 1913, he completed a manuscript, parts of which had been the subject of discussion in Hubert's seminar[18] and which was first presented by Hubert in 1914 and 1915 in the *Revue de l'histoire des religions*. The work itself appeared in 1919, with

[15] Hubert makes no value judgement here. 'Superstition' is literally what 'remains over and above' religious systems, in short 'relic'.
[16] On Czarnowski, see Znaniecki 1937, Ossowski 1938, Assodobraj 1956, Lagneau 1978.
[17] The *Annuaire* of 1911 for the fifth section gives Czarnowski as 'titular pupil' of H. Hubert and mentions the lecture he gave on the Irish hero (p. 100).
[18] *Le Culte des héros*, Foreword, dated Warsaw 1 December 1913, p. ii. Czarnowski explains: 'M. Henri Hubert, whose pupil I was at the Ecole Pratique des Hautes Etudes, supervised all the stages of preparing and writing the book, showing concern for the details of composition, style and even the printing. M. Mauss, who was also my teacher, was the first to urge me to publish the results of my research, and spared me neither criticism nor advice. M. Vendryès had the kindness to read the proofs, and it is thanks to him that many philological errors have been avoided.'

François A. Isambert

a preface by Hubert which is a work in itself and in which the master defends, discusses and extends the thesis of his disciple.

But Czarnowski was more than just a disciple of Hubert, and his *Le Culte des héros et ses conditions sociales. Saint Patrick, héros national de l'Irlande* belongs to a highly individual intellectual career. Stefan Czarnowski was born at Kroczewo in Eastern Poland on 1 September 1879 to a family of landowners (judging by the appearance of the family house).[19] His early life reflected the situation in Poland at that time, which was divided up between Russia, Germany and Austria. After serving as a volunteer in the Russian army, he went to Leipzig in 1898 and then to Berlin, where he studied economics and philosophy and attended the lectures of Simmel. After taking part in student opposition movements in 1902, he was arrested and fled to Paris. It was at this time that he attended Durkheim's lectures at the Sorbonne and, then those of Mauss and Hubert at the Hautes Etudes and wrote his *Saint Patrick*. But in 1912 he returned to Warsaw where he took part in the publication of *Tygodnik Polski*, contributing articles on Celtic civilisation and also an important article on 'the sociological definition of the phenomenon of religion' (1912) which introduced the Polish public to Durkheimian thought on the subject.

His work was interrupted by the arrival of the German troops in 1915, when he found himself once more in prison. He then enlisted in the legions formed by Pilsudski in Austria to fight Russia.[20] After the war, he stayed on in the army, taking part in the 1920 military operations against Soviet Russia, and also carrying out geographical and strategic research for the General Staff. Throughout the whole of this time he shared the socialist and nationalist ideas of Pilsudski, but the latter evolved increasingly towards nationalism and away from socialism, whereas Czarnowski's position developed more towards Marxism. In 1923 he broke with Pilsudski, and in 1931 with the Socialist Party.[21]

The break with Pilsudski coincided with a revival of his work in sociology, and more especially in religion. He took part at that time in the Congress on the history of religions in Paris, where he gave an important paper on the 'division of space and its limitation in religion and magic', based on the work of Mauss and Hubert and attempting to do for space what Hubert had done for time. He returned to Paris for a few months in 1929 and, under the aegis of the Ecole Pratique des Hautes Etudes, gave a series of lectures on 'the concept of space in Italo-Celtic and Slav religion and folklore'.

He continued to work on the sociology and history of religion until his

[19] Cf. the photograph illustrating the biography of Czarnowski in vol. 5 of the *Works* (Czarnowski 1956).
[20] Pilsudski, of course, turned against Germany and Austria in 1917.
[21] See his resounding declaration at that time against the second International and in favour of the proletariat (in Lagneau 1978: 325).

death on 29 December 1937. During that time he produced the important paper on 'La Réaction catholique en Pologne à la fin du XVIe et au début du XVIIe siècle', in which he relates the religious policy of the nobility to the peasant forms of Catholicism. He also wrote his 'Argonautes dans la Baltique' which was published in the *Annales sociologiques*. However, he had not abandoned his political interests, but for the most part tended to give expression to them in a theoretical reflection on culture and society. The articles he published on this subject between 1932 and 1937 in the journal *Wiedza i Zycie* (Knowledge and Life) were later published in collected form by his friends under the title *Kultura* (1938).

In this eventful life, then, the work of the scholar and academic alternated with political action. But as Janina Lagneau (1978) demonstrates in her thesis, which ranks Czarnowski with the greatest of Polish sociologists, the fundamental unity of these two strands of activity is to be found in his preoccupation with national *consensus*. From this point of view, Saint Patrick is seen to be symbolic, and his struggle to unify an Ireland torn between rival clans is the image of what Czarnowski wanted for his native Poland. Czarnowski, then, approaches folk religion from the point of view of the collective consciousness at a national level. The frame of reference is still that of 'people's religion' as defined by Hubert, but at the level of the national cult and not of local folklore. Czarnowski gave greater attention to the latter aspect towards the end of his life when he no longer had any illusions about national consensus (Lagneau 1978: 333). His 1937 article on 'The religious culture of the Polish rural population' demonstrates the originality of the genuinely peasant religious productions. These, however, are not dispersed in a folklore, but brought together by the unifying principle of class.

It is the *Saint Patrick* (1919), however, which remains Czarnowski's most important contribution to a sociology of folk religion, and in this respect represents a significant advance, especially when it is taken together with Hubert's treatment of the subject. In *Saint Patrick*, Czarnowski was dealing with a particularly characteristic theme of folk hagiography. Saint Patrick, patron saint of Ireland, has a legend, a cult, and a place in the forefront of the national collective consciousness which is not to be contained within any purely ecclesiastical framework. The aim of Czarnowski's work is fourfold: to recreate the true historical role of Saint Patrick, to discover how the legend was formed, to describe the nature of his cult, and to propose a theory of the cult of the hero of which Saint Patrick is a remarkable example.

We shall not dwell upon the first point, except to say that Patrick's alliance with the *filid*, an intellectual class,[22] against the druids ensured the future

[22] And not 'noble warriors' as J. Lagneau writes (1978: 328), doubtless misled by the presentation in the obituary in *Annales sociologiques*.

creation and diffusion of the legend. Consequently, and this brings us to the second point, the legend was based in a class that was not split up into the clans which divided the warrior nobility, and led directly through conversion to the constitution of a national clergy which became a cornerstone of national unity. Thus depicted as the spiritual father of Irish unity, Patrick came to be looked upon as the founding ancestor, playing for the nation the part played for each clan by the traditional ancestor.

In his preface, Hubert for the most part accepts without discussion Czarnowski's particular analysis of the origin of the legend, and even emphasises its force and originality. His main intervention concerns the general theory of the hero as mythic character which Czarnowski derives from the particular case of Saint Patrick.

On several points, Hubert disagrees sharply. Firstly, there is the problem of Saint Patrick's dual nature as hero and saint. Czarnowski's position on this point is unclear. He refers us back to the general theory, but in the latter sometimes saints are seen as a kind of hero, and sometimes hero-saints are seen as forming a special class of saint (1919: 316–22). For Hubert, the qualities of the hero and saint are distinct, even if they can occur in the same person, as with Saint Patrick. In fact, the concept of hero requires a more careful definition than Czarnowski provides. For the latter, the cult of the hero is linked to the cult of the dead, from which it is just one step to the mythic ancestor. Hubert denies that this is the essence of the hero, even though the cult of the hero is generally created after his death. Similarly, Czarnowski tries to link the heroic death of the hero commemorated in the festival with the sacrifice of the god. Hubert, who was an expert on the matter, suggests that there is a difference between the commemoration of a death which may assume sacrificial aspects and the ritual renewal of the sacrifice of the god. Above all, Czarnowski makes the class of heroes rather wide, going from the exceptional man right through to the divinity. For Hubert, the characteristic of the hero, in opposition to the god and even the king, is his human nature. 'Further from the world, nearer to men, nearer to their age, such is the place of the hero in relation to the devils, the gods and the saints' (1919: xxxvi).

Whereas, therefore, the purpose of the cult of the god is to make him present ('Real presence is the characteristic of the gods'), the cult of the hero commemorates him through the feast. Thus, faithful to the method that goes from practice to legend rather than the opposite, Hubert aims to derive the hero from the feast. In this respect, he applauds Czarnowski for seeing the privileged link uniting the hero with the feast, in the case of Saint Patrick. In particular, Czarnowski had realised clearly that those heroes whose feast days are marked out in *time* rather than distributed over different *places* are the unifying principle for a national community (which is an application of

Hubert's theory of the feast day as sacred time). But Hubert wanted to advance beyond this position. The study of the feast presents us with an actual process of heroicisation. Far from the hero being the origin of the feast, it is the feast which establishes the hero through figurative *game* and *drama*, even when the object of this process is a historical person.

In this way, whilst bringing greater precision to Czarnowski's theory through the use of a more extensive and more rigorous comparative method, Hubert also brings the cult of the hero in a more topical way back into a sociology of folk religion. For Czarnowski, explaining the legend of Saint Patrick consisted in discovering its origin, which was to be found in the scholarly and 'mythopoetic' milieu of the *filid* (1919: 282). For Hubert, the origin is not essential to the sociologist, whose subject is the creation of the hero by the feast, hence by folk practice, even if the raw material on which this creation is based is itself of a scholarly nature. This dual origin of the folk cults was also stressed at the same time by Robert Hertz in the case of Saint Besse.

Robert Hertz and the study of an Alpine cult

Ultimately, the strongest commitment to a study of folk religion is to be found in Robert Hertz. Of all Durkheimian works, the study of the Alpine cult of Saint Besse is without doubt the one which is closest to ethnography in its fieldwork and its use of sources, but also the one which, taking the notion of folk religion in all its dimensions, goes furthest in the sociological treatment of the phenomenon. Is it the case, as Marcel Mauss wrote, that Robert Hertz wrote 'his delightful Saint Besse ... for amusement and pleasure, as a relief from the pressure of the greater work'?[23] Such was apparently not the opinion of Hertz's wife who relates how her husband, after witnessing the Saint Besse pilgrimage during a holiday in 1912, felt the need to return for a longer period the following year and to make a minutely detailed study of the cult (the fifty pages of 'Saint Besse', although picturesque, look far more than a mere intellectual pastime) extending into a theory of the genesis of myths, a point confirmed and taken very seriously by Durkheim himself (Durkheim 1916: 118).

Robert Hertz was born at Saint-Cloud on 22 June 1881. After studying mainly at the Lycée Janson de Sailly in Paris, he prepared for the Ecole Normale Supérieure at the Lycée Henri IV, and sat the entrance exam in 1900, coming second. It was then that he became acquainted with Durkheim

[23] Mauss (1922: 4). This underestimation of the importance of 'Saint Besse' seems to be connected with the unfavourable opinion held by Mauss, and no doubt some of his colleagues, of Hertz's attempt to integrate his views on folk religion into an overall theory of mythology. Hence, it would seem, the hesitation over the publication, and finally the non-publication, of the posthumous works of R. Hertz (Mauss 1922, 1925).

and published his first article on the rural populations of Germany. In 1904, he sat the *agrégation* in philosophy, coming first. He did not then take up a post, and Durkheim (1916) tells us that he had, in fact, a personal fortune from his family which freed him from the need to earn a living. After his marriage, he spent a year in London working on ethnographic documents at the British Museum, then returned to France and took up a post teaching philosophy in Douai, in spite, it would seem, of the objections of his friends who would have preferred him to devote himself entirely to research, as indeed he did a year later. It was then that he published his two major works on the collective representation of death and on the dominance of the right hand, and began his great work on expiation, of which only the introduction was to be published before his death.

Marcel Mauss (1925: 24) rightly points out that there is a fundamental unity to these works and stresses the thematic coherence: 'Hertz had chosen to study phenomena which are at one and the same time religious and moral, and had picked out the most difficult, the least studied part where everything had still to be done, that part concerning the dark side of mankind: crime and sin, punishment and pardon.' This evaluation does not apply only to the third of the studies, but obviously to the first, and even to some extent to the second, since the study of the dominance of the right hand is also to a large degree the study of the 'sinister' side of the left hand. Indeed, Hertz seems to have been obsessed by the idea of death, that death which he chose to some extent of his own free will in 1915,[24] and this might explain Mauss's tendency to place his folkloric works in the realm of recreation, not to say futility. In actual fact, his personality was many-sided, even contradictory: his taste for the sombre coexisted with perfect married happiness; he hesitated, as we have seen, between a sense of duty to teaching and a taste for studious leisure, to which must be added a strong militant streak; and, finally, his interests ranged from economics to mythology and folklore. Mauss himself (1922: 2) wrote, with a certain tone of aggression behind the admiration: 'Basically, in the whole of his brief but full life, he never once made a choice.'

Still considering the works that come under the heading of 'sociology of religion', we can find another kind of unity between the 'serious' works and the 'delightful Saint Besse'. This unity comes from the choice of a resolutely *anthropological* approach, understanding by that term the characteristic approach adopted by those belonging to what the Durkheimians called the 'anthropological school', an approach based on the idea that there is a profound, inter-cultural, unity in the meanings of human behaviour, an approach which enables us to trace through the different civilisations major

[24] Durkheim (1916) relates how Robert Hertz had himself transferred on his own request to a fighting unit so as not to be spared the risk, and was killed during a semi-suicidal attack, at the head of his section.

themes such as the representations of death, lateralisation, and expiation. On several occasions Durkheim and his colleagues acknowledged their debt to the English anthropological school whilst at the same time indicating in what ways they diverged from the latter's insufficiently differentiated comparativism. Nonetheless, the anthropological tendency remained strong in Mauss, Hubert, and Durkheim himself: had they not yielded to it, they would probably have been unable to give any *general* theory of sacrifice, of magic, or of religion itself. In the ensuing vacillation between relativism and universalism,[25] Hertz leant clearly to the latter. The penalty he paid was a certain loss of emphasis on social framework both for general social structures and for organisations (in this case, organised religions).

The advantage of the approach, however, was in Hertz's particular aptitude for grasping the disorganised in religion. The thematic elements he draws from the major religions, the primitive religions and folklore circulate freely in his work. That is why the *Mélanges de sociologie religieuse et de folklore* form an ultimately homogeneous whole: the *mélange* of the title occurs not only between works of different types, but also within each of the assembled works. What is more, the study of the cult of Saint Besse goes beyond a miscellany to provide us with a truly sociological synthesis of folkloric phenomena.

In one sense, 'Saint Besse, étude d'un culte alpestre'[26] represents the application of the Durkheimian method to folklore and local traditions. But it is, in fact, much more. The most attractive feature of the study is the way in which the author, whilst making full use of the resources of philology and comparative mythology, warms to his subject, observes it, gathers eye-witness accounts, adds to his observations by the use of historical documents and finally ventures to hypothesise a genetic explanation. In short, we are given a total anthropological analysis which attains the level of theory without ever losing contact with the facts.

Saint Besse is a place of pilgrimage on the border between the Val d'Aoste and Piedmont.[27] Every year, on 10 August, pilgrims come to the chapel of the same name, situated at an altitude of 2,647 metres above sea level, at the base of an enormous rock.

The celebration of the Mass, in the small, sumptuously decorated chapel, brilliant with light, renews and augments the holiness of the place. The priest's sermon extols

[25] Durkheim, in *Les Règles de la méthode sociologique* (1895: 94), contrasted 'the nominalism of the historians and the extreme realism of the philosophers'. He saw the concept of social species as an intermediary position between the two.
[26] First published in 1913 in the *Revue de l'histoire des religions*. Reproduced in Hertz (1928), new edition 1970, Presses Universitaires de France, Paris, pp. 110–59. Robert Hertz compiled his observations in 1912. He was to be killed in the Woëvre plain near Argonne in 1915.
[27] We reproduce overleaf the map included in the first two editions but omitted from the latest edition. It is necessary to an understanding of the phenomenon of Saint Besse.

167

François A. Isambert

the greatness of Saint Besse, his glory and his power, and at the same time summons his worshippers back to the paths of righteousness. But the centrepiece of the feast is the procession. The whole community of the faithful leaves the chapel in an orderly fashion, grouped according to sex, age and religious dignity; they return only after they have 'gone round the Mount', that is the rock, proceeding, of course, from left to right and saying the whole rosary. (Hertz 1928: 141)

The statue of Saint Besse, dressed as a Roman soldier, is borne, together with various trophies and banners, by eight young men, chosen each year for the honour from a different village.

The distribution of the cult of Saint Besse
(The map has been reproduced from that in the French original and therefore French forms of place-names have been retained. Names underlined are those of places where the saint is honoured.)

168

The cult brings together the inhabitants of five parishes, four of which belong to the Val Soana, in Piedmont, whilst the fifth is the small town of Cogne, belonging to the Val d'Aoste and separated from the others by a pass 2,900 metres above sea level which can only be crossed on foot. This curious Alpine community, cut in two by the high barrier of the Grées Alps, can be explained by the fact that in the past the narrowness of the ravines in the Val de Cogne long rendered communications with Aoste more difficult than with the Val Soana, in spite of the altitude of the pass. Nowadays,[28] the preservation of a common ceremony appears to be a kind of assertion of the collective identity of the mountain people against the inhabitants of the lowlands. But at the same time, the geographical division, which, as we shall see, has other dimensions, gives rise to keen rivalry between the pilgrims from the opposite slopes of the mountain. The village of Campiglia, which is nearest to the holy place, appoints itself the champion of the Val Soana in the attempt to deprive Cogne of its periodic right to carry the statue. This results in rioting and fighting in which knives express the desire to be first to honour the saint.

Now, Saint Besse has a legend, or rather several. According to the 'official legend of the diocese', he was a soldier of the Theban legion who took refuge in the Val Soana and was murdered by pagan soldiers on the spot where the chapel was erected. But another tale has been fitted into this framework: having taken refuge on the Mount (the rock overhanging the chapel), he was thrown off it by dishonest shepherds for refusing to share their meal of a stolen sheep and was found at the foot of the rock, still alive, by the soldiers of the emperor. In addition, Cogne, which does not belong to the same diocese (Ivrée), has preserved another legend. According to this, Saint Besse was a very pious and virtuous shepherd, 'a true man of God'. Consequently, his sheep were the finest of the region. Out of jealousy, two other shepherds threw him off the top of the mountain. At the end of the winter, his corpse was discovered at the foot of the rock, naturally still intact.

A comparison of the two versions brings out the composite nature of the first. Onto the tale of a pastoral – one might almost say Biblical – nature of the pious shepherd incarnating the folk virtues[29] and envied by the wicked is

---

[28] This refers to the time of Hertz. Does the pilgrimage still take place today? In 1929, Abbé Henry, a priest at one of the parishes of the Val d'Aoste, wrote: 'Cogne nominates procurators, called the procurators of Saint Bès, to collect the offerings and preside over the functions of the sanctuary when it is the turn of the people of Cogne. At present, there are five parishes which take turns in staging the celebration: Campiglia, Cogne, Ingria, Ronco and Valprato. In 1926, it was the turn of the parish of Cogne ... These five parishes vie for the honour of carrying the statue of Saint Bès in the procession: to avoid conflict, the honour is put up for auction, which brings in 200 to 300 lire for the chapel' (Henry 1929: 20).

[29] Compare this with what Hubert says about the cult of Saint Patrick (See above pp. 164–5) where the hero-saint is the incarnation of those values in which the community recognises itself.

superimposed the epic of a Roman martyr, which appeared with variants many times, if one compares the legend of Saint Besse with that of all the Thebans who underwent martyrdom in similar conditions. To the two versions, therefore, correspond two levels of elaboration and two origins. The Cogne version seems to be the oldest, springing directly from the Alpine environment. The diocesan version is the result of use (one might almost say 'recuperation') by the clergy of Ivrée who took up the original tale (a man cast from the top of a rock) and fitted it into the tale of the flight and death of the Christian martyr, modifying it to this end (Saint Besse no longer dies of the fall, amongst other details indicated by Hertz). We might add to this 'scholarly' version the critical interpretations, beginning with the *Acta sanctorum*, which try to separate the historical from the legendary, and going, with the most recent historians including the clergy, as far as describing the whole tale as legend.

But Hertz does not consider his task finished at this point. Although it is of less concern to us, mention should be made of the attempts, in the line of *Les Saints, successeurs des dieux* by Saintyves (1907),[30] to link the cult of Saint Besse with older cults. The difference is that Saintyves uses every means available to support his thesis, accumulating material of varying degrees of relevance, whereas Hertz proceeds with caution, discussing at length hypotheses to which in the end he refuses to give unequivocal support. It is claimed that the name of Saint Besse comes from the local word for *sheep*. In that case, we would be dealing with one of those innumerable saints whose name refers to the virtues or attributes which they incarnate.[31] But the name might first have designated the *place*, 'sheep mountain'. The cult with its procession round the rock would then have been originally a cult of the mountain and the stone, like many others that existed in the region.

Let us return, however, to our main theme. Hertz does not hide his preference for the primitive legend.

It is not surprising that the people of Cogne should be so stubbornly attached to the popular legend of Saint Besse; they feel at home with the mountain folk, whereas with the emperor Maximian, the Theban legionaries and the glorious martyr they feel out of place, ill at ease. They have respect but little feeling for a story where the best part goes to a foreigner who came from the plains to educate and moralise whilst the shepherds are portrayed as thieves and murderers. How much nicer is the other Saint Besse: a simple son of the land, the best shepherd with the finest flock ever seen in those mountains! (1928: 165–6)

[30] This book, whose title became the battle cry for all those looking for pagan origins to popular Christianity, was the cause of heated controversy. See Isambert 1978.

[31] Hertz, reporting an objection made by Meillet, admits that 'phonetic possibility is no proof' (1928: 185).

But Hertz rejects partiality, preferring to explain without judging.[32] Referring to the process whereby hagiography is produced, as analysed by Father Delehaye (1905), he demonstrates how these legends fulfil a need for edification, of one kind when the 'saint' has to extol local virtues, and of another kind when, in an ecclesiastical context, the nature of the values to be celebrated changes, as also the symbols used to express them. The most important element for us is the circuit, analysed along the way, which goes from the local tradition to its elaboration by the urban clergy, and back again to be reinvested in the local tradition where the new images feed into the popular feast.[33]

However, the last word is left to the primitive version which Hertz, in the manner of the period, prefers to consider in its relationship with its origins:

Up in the high valleys, beliefs and ritual action have been preserved for several millennia, not as relics or 'superstitions' but as a real religion, living a life of its own, and appearing in broad daylight under a transparent veil of Christianity. The main interest of the cult of Saint Besse is perhaps that it gives us an image, fragmentary and overlain, but still distinct and living, of prehistoric religion. (1928: 190–1)

Thus, for the first time, with absolute clarity, through the hypothesis of a link with prehistory, folk religion was presented as a coherent system whose reality could be discovered beneath the masks that the Church had imposed upon it over the ages. But we have seen that what we call 'folk religion' today, apart from the highly exceptional case of Cogne, consists of themes taken from the mountain tradition and modified by the 'scholars' before being restored to the 'people'.

Thus Hubert, Czarnowski and Hertz contributed, each in his own way, to making folk religion a proper subject for sociology. And since the result of this operation was to break down the isolation surrounding folkloric phenomena, it was of the utmost importance that for each of them the study of folk religion should be set in the context of a wider, but in each case different, approach to social facts.

For Hubert, the typology of the forms of religion, going from Church religions to people's religions, with folklore taking its place amongst the latter, provided the necessary flexibility for the conceptual framework. But, in addition, Hubert's particular perspective, which might be called the 'sociology of myths', including the part of sociology of knowledge implied by

---

[32] 'Are we to condemn them [the clergy of Ivrée] for doing violence to the local traditions they worked upon and for replacing the "true" image of the saint by a "fiction" more suited to their purposes? To do so would be a wrongful application of the rules of historical criticism' (1928: 168).

[33] This reinvestment has far-reaching effects, since, through this promotion, Saint Besse the legionary now becomes the patron saint for protecting men against the risks of conscription!

François A. Isambert

the analysis of mythic thought, furnishes, at the level of a folk cult such as that of a hero, the tools that enable us to understand the emergence of the figure celebrated in the practice of the feast day.

Although on this ground Czarnowski followed Hubert very closely, we have nonetheless seen how, on the other hand, his attempt to analyse the conditions in which national consciousness emerges led him to highlight, out of the possible meanings of 'people's religion', those folk cults which have a national dimension and significance. This brings us very close to the idea of collective consciousness formulated by Durkheim himself, with the hero functioning as totem.

With Hertz, we seem to be closer to the traditional perspective of the folklorists, since his studies on religious representations constitute a kind of extension of the folkloric approach to all religions. And yet, he gives us all the ammunition we need to answer Mauss's criticism of the folklorists. For Hertz, in the first stage of the process, analyses the successive strata to be found in folk cults, taking particular care to distinguish references to structures from the past (and even what can be surmised of very ancient phases of the phenomenon) from those produced by more recent, even contemporary, social organisations. But – and this is perhaps the main point – he does not stop with this classification. If a date can be put on the origin of certain practices, certain legendary elements, then they are reinserted, reinterpreted. On the one hand, the Church has, as it were, digested the folk legend and then given it back to the tradition. On the other hand, the cult and the prestige it generates have become the means by which the mountain communities can vie with one another whilst setting themselves apart, through their common characteristics, from the men of the plains. Thus, the term 'relic', for so long a methodological stumbling block in the attempts to use folklore in sociology, has been surpassed, or rather reincorporated, as a symbolic tool at the service of the collective identity.

References

Assodobraj, N. 1956. *Zycie i dzielo Stefana Czarnowskiego* [The Life and Work of S. Czarnowski], pp. 105–58 in S. Czarnowski (1956).
Berr, H. 1932a. Avant-propos, pp. v–xx in H. Hubert (1932a).
    1932b. Avant-propos, pp. vii–xvii in H. Hubert (1932b).
Czarnowski, S. See the following bibliography.
Delehaye, H. 1905. *Les Légendes hagiographiques*. Bruxelles: Société des Bollandistes.
Durkheim, E. 1895. *Les Règles de la méthode sociologique*. Paris: Alcan.
    1899. 'De la définition des phénomènes religieux', *Année sociologique*, vol. 2, pp. 1–28.
    1916. 'Robert Hertz (notice nécrologique)' *Annuaire de l'association amicale des anciens élèves de l'Ecole Normale Supérieure*, pp. 116–20.

1976. 'Textes inédits ou inconnus d'Emile Durkheim', *Revue française de sociologie*, vol. 17, no. 2, pp. 165–96.

Henry, A. 1929. *Histoire populaire, religieuse et civile de la vallée d'Aoste*. 3rd edition. Aosta: Marguerettaz, 1967.

Hertz, R. See the following bibliography.

Hubert, H. See the following bibliography.

Isambert, F. A. 1976. 'L'Elaboration de la notion de sacré dans l'école durkheimienne', *Archives de sciences sociales des religions*, vol. 21, pp. 33–56.

1978. 'Religion populaire, sociologie, histoire et folklore. De Saint Besse à Saint Rouin', *Archives de sciences sociales des religions*, vol. 23, pp. 111–34.

1979. 'Henri Hubert et la sociologie du temps', *Revue française de sociologie*, vol. 20, pp. 183–204.

Lagneau, J. 1978. 'Stefan Czarnowski ou l'engagement', pp. 319–43 in J. Lagneau, 'La Formation d'un système sociologique. Essai d'analyse des rapports entre société, science et sociologie chez les sociologues polonais entre les deux guerres mondiales'. Thesis Université de Paris V.

Mauss, M. 1898. Review of Crooke, *The Popular Religions and Folklore of Northern India*, *Année sociologique*, vol. 1, pp. 210–18.

1900. Review of Krauss, *Allgemeine methodik der Volkskunde*, *Année sociologique*, vol. 3, pp. 192–5.

1903. Review of Hoffmann-Krayer, *Die Volkskunde als Wissenschaft*, *Année sociologique*, vol. 6, pp. 167–70.

1907. Review of Hubert, *Etude sommaire de la représentation du temps dans la religion et la magie*, *Année sociologique*, vol. 10, pp. 302–5.

1910. Review of Van Gennep, *Les Rites de passage*, *Année sociologique*, vol. 11, pp. 200–2.

1922. Note de l'éditeur, *Revue de l'histoire des religions*, vol. 86, pp. 1–4.

1925. 'In Memoriam, Robert Hertz', *Année sociologique*, new series, vol. 1, pp. 23–5.

1930. 'La Civilisation. Eléments et formes', pp. 81–108 in *Civilisation. Le Mot et l'idée*. Paris: Renaissance du livre.

1933. 'Intervention à la suite d'une communication de M. Granet', *Bulletin de l'Institut français de sociologie*, vol. 3, pp. 108–13.

Ossowski, S. 1938. 'Stefan Czarnowski 1879–1937', *Przeglad filozoficzny*, vol. 3, pp. 7–19.

Quentin, A. 1885. *Paroissien romain à l'usage des lycées, collèges et pensions*. Paris: Oudin.

Reinach, S. 1927. 'Henri Hubert', *Revue archéologique*, 5th series, vol. 26, pp. 176–8.

Saintyves, P. 1907. *Les Saints, successeurs des dieux*. Paris: E. Nourry.

Znaniecki, F. 1937. 'Stefan Czarnowski (1879–1937)', *Przeglad socjologiczny*, vol. 5, pp. 521–36.

Bibliography: Henri Hubert, Stephan Czarnowski, Robert Hertz

This bibliography contains only the main works of the three authors. It omits bibliographical notes (except where these are quoted in the article) and texts outside the field of sociology of religion which are not easily accessible.

François A. Isambert

Henri Hubert[34]

1897 'Observation sur la chronologie de Théophane et de quelques lettres de papes', *Byzantinische Zeitschrift*, vol. 6, pp. 491–505.

1899a 'Etude sur la formation des Etats de l'Eglise. Les papes Grégoire II, Grégoire III, Zacharie, Etienne III et leurs relations avec les empereurs iconoclastes, *Revue historique*, vol. 69, pp. 1–40, 241–72.

1899b 'Fibules de Baslieux', *Revue archéologique*, 3rd series, vol. 34, pp. 363–81.

1899c (With M. Mauss) 'Essai sur la nature et la fonction sociale du sacrifice', *Année sociologique*, vol. 2, pp. 29–138 (reproduced in 1909a).

1899d 'Kyréné', pp. 873–6 in *Dictionnaire des antiquités grecques et romaines*, vol. 5, fasc. 27.

n.d. [1900 ?] 'Mithra', pp. 1134–8 in *La Grande Encyclopédie*, vol. 23.

1902a 'Magia', pp. 1494–521 in *Dictionnaire des antiquités grecques et romaines*, vol. 6, fasc. 31.

1902b 'La collection Moreau au musée de Saint-Germain', *Revue archéologique*, 3rd series, vol. 41, pp. 167–208.

1904a Introduction, pp. v–xlvii in Chantepie de la Saussaye, *Manuel d'histoire des religions*. Paris: Colin.

1904b (With M. Mauss) 'Esquisse d'une théorie générale de la magie', *Année sociologique*, vol. 7, pp. 1–46.

1905a 'Etude sommaire de la représentation du temps dans la religion et la magie', *Annuaire de l'Ecole Pratique des Hautes Etudes, section des sciences religieuses*, pp. 1–39 (reproduced in 1909a).

1905b Review of Abbott, 'Macedonian folklore', *Année sociologique*, vol. 8, pp. 310–14.

1906 'La Collection Moreau au musée de Saint-Germain', *Revue archéologique*, 4th series, vol. 8, pp. 337–71.

1908 (With M. Mauss) 'Introduction à l'analyse de quelques phénomènes religieux', *Revue de l'histoire des religions*, vol. 58, pp. 163–203 (reproduced in 1909a).

1909a (With M. Mauss) *Mélanges d'histoire des religions*. Paris: Alcan.

1909b Review of Reinach, 'Orpheus', *L'Anthropologie*, vol. 20, p. 596.

1910 'L'Origine des Aryens. A propos des fouilles américaines du Turkestan', *L'Anthropologie*, vol. 21, pp. 519–28.

1912a 'Nantosuelta, déesse à la ruche', pp. 281–96, in *Mélanges Cagnat*. Paris.

1912b 'Le Carnassier Androphage et la représentation de l'Océan chez les Celtes', pp. 220–30 in *Compte rendu de la XIVe session du Congrès international d'anthropologie et d'archéologie préhistoriques*. Genève.

1913 'Notes d'archéologie et de philologie celtiques', *Revue celtique*, vol. 34, pp. 1–13; 424–5.

1914 'Notes d'archéologie et de philologie celtiques', *Revue celtique*, vol. 35, pp. 14–43.

1915 'Une Nouvelle Figure du dieu au maillet', *Revue archéologique*, 5th series, vol. 1, pp. 26–39.

1919 *Le Culte des héros et ses conditions sociales*, Preface to Czarnowski, pp. i–xciv.

1925a 'Le Mythe d'Epona', pp. 187–211 in *Mélanges linguistiques offerts à J. Vendryès*. Paris: Champion.

[34] For more details concerning the bibliography of Hubert, see the one compiled by R. Lantier at the end of his 'Hommage à Henri Hubert', *Revue archéologique*, 5th series, vol. 28, pp. 289–307.

1925b 'Le Système des prestations totales dans les littératures celtiques', *Revue celtique*, vol. 42, pp. 330–5.

1925c 'De quelques objets de bronze trouvés à Byblos', *Syria*, pp. 16–29.

1927 'Les Premiers Celtes en Espagne', *Revue celtique*, vol. 44, pp. 78–89.

1932a *Les Celtes et l'expansion celtique jusqu'à l'époque de la Tène.* Corbeil: Renaissance du livre (avant-propos de Henri Berr, avertissement de Marcel Mauss) (3rd edition. Paris: Albin Michel, 1974 sans avant-propos).

1932b *Les Celtes depuis l'époque de la Tène et la civilisation celtique.* Corbeil: Renaissance du livre (avertissement de Henri Berr) (2nd edition. Paris: Albin Michel, 1974, sans avertissement).

1952 *Les Germains.* Paris: Albin Michel (avant-propos de Henri Berr, avertissement de Paul Chalus).

1979 'Texte autobiographique', *Revue française de sociologie*, vol. 20, no. 1, pp. 205–7.

Stefan Czarnowski

1904 'Filozofia spoleczna w Polsce w koncu XVIII i poczatk XIX wieku' [Social Philosophy in Poland at the End of the 18th Century and at the Beginning of the 19th Century], *Biblioteka Warszawska*, vol. 4, pp. 209–43.

1912 'Socjologiczne okreslenie faktu religijnego' [The Sociological Definition of Religious Fact], *Tygodnik Polski*, no. 2, pp. 22–3; no. 3, pp. 39–40.[35]

1919 *Le Culte des héros et ses conditions sociales. Saint Patrick, héros national de l'Irlande.* Paris: Alcan (préface de H. Hubert).

1925a 'Le Morcellement de l'étendue et sa limitation dans la religion et la magie', pp. 339–58 in *Actes du IVe Congrès international d'histoire des religions, Paris, octobre 1923.* Paris.

1925b 'L'Arbre d'Esus, le taureau aux trois grues et le culte des voies fluviales en Gaule', *Revue celtique*, vol. 42, pp. 1–57.

1925c 'Herkules Galijski' [Gallic Hercules], *Przeglad Historyczny*, vol. 5, pp. 238–60.

1927 *Nehalennia, la dame aux pommes.* Warsaw: Biblioteka Universitatis Liberae Poloniae.

1929 'Les Biens féminins en droit celtique', *Revue historique de droit français et étranger*, pp. 649–51 (summary of a communication, Journées d'histoire du droit, June 1929).

1930 'Le Dieu créateur des cosmogonies polynésiennes', pp. 104–5 in *Actes du Ve Congrès international d'histoire des religions, Lund, 1929.* Lund (summary).

1933 'La Réaction catholique en Pologne à la fin du XVIe et au début du XVIIe siècle', pp. 287–310 in *La Pologne au VIIe Congrès international des sciences historiques.* Warsaw: Société Polonaise d'Histoire.

1937 'Kultura religijna wieskiego ludu polskiego' [The Religious Culture of the Polish Rural Population], *Wiedza i Zycie*, pp. 271–82; 349–57.

1938 *Kultura.* Warsaw: Wiedza i Zycie (collection of articles).

1939 *Spoleczenstwo Kultura* [Society and Culture]. Warsaw: Biblioteka socjologiczna.

1940 'Les Argonautes dans la Baltique, convention et réalité dans la formation des idées géographiques grecques', *Annales sociologiques*, série B, no. 4, pp. 6–31.

1956 *Dziela* [Works], edited by Nina Assodobraj and Stanislas Ossowski, 5 vols. Warsaw: Panstwowe Wydawnictwo Naukowe.

[35] First of a series of articles in the same journal which includes a number of articles on the Celtic literatures.

François A. Isambert

Robert Hertz

1900 'Les Populations rurales en Allemagne', *Revue d'économie politique*, vol. 14, pp. 197–217.

1907 'Contribution à une étude sur la représentation collective de la mort', *Année sociologique*, vol. 10, pp. 48–137 (reproduced in Hertz 1928, pp. 1–98).

1909 'La Prééminence de la main droite, étude sur la polarité religieuse', *Revue philosophique*, vol. 68, pp. 553–80 (reproduced in Hertz 1928, pp. 99–129).

1910 *Socialisme et dépopulation*. Paris: Librairie Socialiste.

1913 'Saint Besse, étude d'un culte alpestre', *Revue de l'histoire des religions*, vol. 67, pp. 115–80 (reproduced in Hertz 1928, pp. 131–92).

1915 'Contes et dictons recueillis sur le front parmi les poilus de la Mayenne et d'ailleurs', *Revue des traditions populaires*, pp. 32–45; 74–91 (reproduced in Hertz 1928, pp. 195–228).

1922 'Le Péché et l'expiation dans les sociétés primitives', *Revue de l'histoire des religions*, vol. 86, pp. 5–60.

1928 *Mélanges de sociologie religieuse et de folklore*. Paris: Alcan (avant-propos de Marcel Mauss et préface d'Alice Robert Hertz) (new edition: *Sociologie religieuse et folklore*. Paris: Presses Universitaires de France, 1970, préface de G. Balandier).

7. Obligation and right: the Durkheimians and the sociology of law[1]

W. PAUL VOGT

Sociology of law was an important element in the Durkheimian disciplinary consensus, but it has rarely been studied systematically. Several factors have probably contributed to this gap in the history of the discipline. Since sociology of law is a comparatively small field in contemporary Academe, there has perhaps been less motive to search for 'roots' than there might be in sociological fields whose practitioners are more numerous today. Of course, the relative weight of sociology of law in today's division of academic labour is of no concern to serious historians of the discipline with the good sense to avoid anachronistic reasoning. More important, or legitimate as a reason, is the fact that of the three major problems of Durkheimian sociology – morality, religion, and law – law was the least important, if not in terms of numbers of students and studies of legal phenomena, at least in terms of the place of law in the usual Durkheimian explanatory hierarchy: phenomena of law were considered to be something rather like particular manifestations or types of moral and/or religious phenomena. Finally, because morality, religion, and law were so closely linked in the Durkheimians' works, the relatively more numerous studies of their sociology of religion and morality inevitably have 'covered' law, although generally in a rather indirect way. The purpose of this article is to assess more directly the importance of sociology of law to the Durkheimians as they mapped out a sociological terrain. By studying the features of their contributions to the sociology of law one can perhaps gain a deeper understanding of the general development of their sociology through an examination of one of its more important parts.

On the institutional plane there is ample evidence to indicate the centrality of phenomena of law to the Durkheimians. Several, and by no means the least important among them, pursued studies in faculties of law. Six held the

[1] Some of the research for this article was supported by a fellowship from the American Council of Learned Societies. I owe a great deal to M. Philippe Besnard who proposed the study and provided much encouragement and information. M. Jean Carbonnier helped me to understand more fully the relations between studies of law in the faculties of law and the faculties of letters.

doctorate in law; Hubert Bourgin, Maurice Halbwachs, Paul Huvelin, Emmanuel Lévy, Jean Ray, François Simiand (and Huvelin and Lévy were 'jurists' properly so called in that they also had passed the *agrégation* in law and were professors in law faculties). Three others, Georges Bourgin, Georges Davy, and Louis Gernet, held the *licence* in law; and Marcel Mauss was a bachelor of law. Thus ten of the forty-six who collaborated on the *Année sociologique*, first series, had formal training in a faculty of law.

Important though such indications might be, they are insufficient to establish a case for the significance of sociology of law in Durkheimian social science. Because disciplinary boundaries in the era in question were sometimes roughly drawn, knowing the institutions in which scholars studied and the degrees they obtained provides only a vague predictor of the sort of research they would do. For example, Gaston Richard and Paul Fauconnet, who specialised in the sociology of law, had no formal legal training. Hence, to assess fully the role of studies of phenomena of law in the Durkheimians' sociology, one must pay less attention to their institutional affiliations and background and more to the works they produced. Here the evidence for the importance of law is overwhelming.

The first three doctoral theses written by Durkheimians who had studied in faculties of letters were importantly concerned with legal phenomena. Gaston Richard (1892) wrote a study of the social origins of the idea of law. Durkheim (1893a) in his work on the division of labour used the evolution of legal sanctions to establish his thesis concerning the evolution of types of solidarity; and his supplementary thesis on Montesquieu examined the work of an undisputed forerunner of the sociological approach to the study of legal systems. Célestin Bouglé's doctoral thesis on egalitarian ideas (1899) surveyed the social conditions conducive to the rise of equality before the law; and he had earlier published an account of the works of the famous German legal scholar von Jhering.

Also significant in this regard is the division of labour amongst the Durkheimians as revealed by the structure of the *Année sociologique*. Two sections of that journal dealt by name with problems of law: the third on 'Legal and Moral Sociology' contained studies of the *origins* of legal and moral rules; the fourth on 'Criminal Sociology and Moral Statistics' contained studies of the *functioning* of legal and moral rules. These two sections of the *Année* (especially the third) occupied much of the collaborators' efforts. Just over half of them (twenty-four) wrote for one or both of the two sections. And Durkheimian interest in the subject did not pass with the passing of the *Année*. For example, in 1931 when a new annual publication called *Archives de philosophie du droit et de sociologie juridique* was established, six members of its editorial board had earlier collaborated on the *Année*.

One could adduce other examples of this sort, but the general point has been made: the majority of Durkheimians studied legal phenomena. Furthermore, given the Durkheimian notion of the nature of law as bound up with and rather closely determined by the nature of society, nearly everything they wrote was of at least indirect relevance to the study of law. In some respects, therefore, a study of Durkheimian sociology of law entails a study of all Durkheimian sociology from a particular perspective. Since that is clearly impossible here, I will examine only certain more-or-less representative works and authors concentrating primarily on their definition of the field and on the methods they used when working in it.

Definition of the field

How did the Durkheimians define law so as to study it? In trying to answer that question one is immediately confronted with some serious problems of terminology and translation. What I have been calling 'sociology of law' the Durkheimians referred to either as '*sociologie du droit*' or more frequently as '*sociologie juridique*'.[2] *Juridique* raises few difficulties. It means pertaining to courts of law *and* pertaining to *droit*. But, like the Italian *diritto* or the German *Recht*, the French noun *droit* is properly translated into English as either 'law' or 'right', while the adjective *droit*, in addition to referring to courts of law and legal codes, carries meanings such as just, equitable, correct, virtuous. Because of this, one not infrequently encounters statements the literal translation of which would be senseless, such as 'the law does not equal the law' ('la loi n'égale pas le droit'). To avoid such absurdities, I have, depending on the context, translated *droit* and *loi* in several ways, none of them fully satisfactory.[3] The importance of these considerations is much more than terminological, for the multiple meanings of the word *droit* (and therefore of *juridique*) facilitated the Durkheimians' theoretical linkings of legal and moral obligations and rights. That linking was the essence of their conception of law and, consequently, significantly shaped their definition of the field.

The Durkheimians' joining of morality and legality on the one hand and obligation and right on the other is more natural than it might at first seem. If one has a right, say to property or to a religious belief, this means that others have an obligation to respect the right and that they will encounter negative sanctions if they fail to do so. Right is thus the positive and law the negative side of a socially guaranteed practice. It is also clear that laws, especially

[2] According to H. Lévy-Bruhl (1961: 95), the term was coined in 1892 by the Italian scholar Anzilotti.

[3] Perhaps the best translation of *sociologie juridique* or *sociologie du droit* would be 'sociology of justice', since the English word justice carries similarly multiple connotations concerning both the administration of law as well as correctness, rightness, and equity.

penal laws, are implicitly moral injunctions, despite the fact that they are usually stated as simple definitions: the act of X constitutes the crime of Y, which is punishable by Z. This definitional language, however, is easily and often translated into normative language: the act of X constitutes the evil Y, which is evil to the Z degree. What was distinctive about the Durkheimians' definition of law was not therefore that they joined right and obligation or morality and law, but the ways they did so: (1) they focused on obligation much more than on right; (2) they claimed that the similarities between morality and law were vastly more important than the differences. These two characteristics are closely related. Their linking of law and morality combined with the fact that they saw morality as essentially a set of negative rules, of prohibitions, meant that the Durkheimians would pay greatest attention to the negative, obligatory, and prohibitive aspects of law as well.

In one of his earliest published works, Durkheim (1886) made the fundamental case. He and the other Durkheimians never departed from the notion that legal, moral, and religious phenomena constitute a system of rules and norms that form a unified 'regulatory function' at work in all societies. Law, morality, and religion all arose from the same social need for integration and constraint, the same need to 'assure the equilibrium of society' by exercising a regulatory influence; all three were thus expressions of the same collective conscience or consciousness. So convinced of the certainty of the connection were the Durkheimians that they often linked law and morality rather offhandedly, apparently believing that the bond between the two was so obvious that it did not need to be explained or demonstrated. Georges Davy was perhaps the Durkheimian most wont to do this. For example, in one of his works (1933: 28–33) he stated that 'social life always implies a very strict system of obligations', that these obligations are the 'condition of all morality and law', and that they impose on us an external pressure that is 'either moral or legal, it's all one'.

When the Durkheimians explained the nature of rather than merely asserted the existence of a tie between law, morality, and the collective conscience, they generally did so by referring to some sort of ineluctible necessity. Gaston Richard (1892: 261) said that legal solidarity is the 'indispensable complement' of social solidarity in modern civilisation. Davy (1922b: 27) concluded that the 'true source of law is one; it resides in collective opinion because law only represents and consecrates a value recognised' by collective opinion. And Marcel Mauss (1906: 104) affirmed that 'diverse legal and moral institutions only express to the collective conscience the conditions necessary to life in common'. This meant that, as those necessary conditions of social life varied, so too did legal and moral institutions. There was, in short, no doubt about the Durkheimians' answer to Davy's rhetorical question: 'Is the Law (*le Droit*) a formal logic or a living morality? Is it deduced *ne varietur* from the precepts of the Legal Code (*la Loi*), or does it adapt itself, while always referring to those precepts, to the living consciousness of society?' (Davy 1917: 283.)

As the above passages make abundantly clear, the Durkheimians held law to be inextricably bound up in a network of other normative facts. Well before Mauss (1925) coined the term and clarified the notion 'total social fact', the Durkheimians studied social phenomena as parts of a web, no strand of which could be understood without taking the others into account. Legal, moral, and religious facts, said Fauconnet (1920: 15), 'can be studied sociologically only if one perpetually sees them in the light of one another'. Thus, to explain law one had to refer to all that was social, and vice versa. Some have concluded from this that the Durkheimians were guilty of a sort of 'panjurism', others that by failing to define law sufficiently they over- or under-emphasised it, and still others that, in a sense, for the Durkheimians sociology of law is all of sociology (Carbonnier 1979: 16–20; Gurvitch 1947: 26–8; Bouglé 1935: 98).

Yet it is unquestionably true that the Durkheimians had at least some rough conceptions of differences between law and morality. They continued to use the two terms, sometimes even opposing them.[4] Likewise, the sections, and especially the sub-sections, of the *Année* certainly distinguished various elements of the sociology of law and morality. Of the distinctions between the two that the Durkheimians made, the most fundamental was that law comes second, historically, logically, and sociologically: law grows out of morality and not the other way around; one could imagine a society without law, but not one without morality; if there is a conflict between the two (and that will happen but rarely), it is law that ultimately will tend to yield. In short, because law is an expression of morality, and not, as some would have it, an expression of the balance of forces in a society's conflicts of interests, any differences between a society's legal and moral rules will be marginal, at least in the long run.

While this is an important set of assertions describing the relation between law and morality, it gives us but few operative criteria for distinguishing the two. And such criteria are necessary, for, as Richard (1906: 86) said, 'In historical reality law is mingled with other manifestations of social conscience, some more brutal, some less direct. But how is one to assess the relation and the difference between law and less advanced forms of constraint if one does not possess a definition of law?' Richard hinted and Gurvitch[5] insisted that sociology could get its definition of law only from philosophy, but in general Durkheimian sociologists of law were thoroughly

[4] At first, Davy contended, the potlatch has more a moral or social function than a legal function properly so called (Davy 1922a: 231).
[5] 'There is no sociology of law without a philosophy of law and vice versa' (Gurvitch 1946: 39).

unwilling overtly to borrow anything from other disciplines – except data.

Given that the Durkheimians were obliged, if they wished a definition, to concoct their own, one finds surprisingly few texts in which they did so. Mauss (1896: 689) stipulated that penal law must be characterised by a public or a general social reaction to an offence. Because of this, blood feuds were not an early manifestation of penal law; they were private or familial reactions of groups defending themselves. Richard (1892) pointed to a similar though more elaborate set of characteristics. Law, he said, is basically a social intervention regulating conflicts between individuals and groups. For there to be law, individuals must have the right to institute a procedure of obligatory arbitration. This brings into play rules that result in labelling certain acts as criminal and that can force restitution to the injured party and/or inflict a punishment on the guilty. Law, Richard continued, represents a progress of social solidarity because the right to institute a public criminal procedure eliminated recourse to private vengeance, the war of all against all. Criminal procedures of this sort, he also maintained, were the source of contract law. This meant that the contract was not the first type of law as many theorists had maintained.

The Durkheimians were predominantly, although not exclusively, interested in criminal law, because, as Durkheim (1893b: 293) pointed out in a review of the book by Richard just cited, criminal law was the germ from which *all* other forms of law grew (and, as we shall see below, the Durkheimians were especially interested in the genesis of forms of law). The sociology of criminal law on which the Durkheimians concentrated was of a particular sort. It was not, for the most part, criminology. Rather than study crime and criminals (i.e. the ways the rules are broken and those who break them), the Durkheimians focused on law and punishment (i.e. the rules themselves and the consequences of their being broken). Given this concentration, it is not surprising that one of their most explicit definitions of law as distinguished from morality rests heavily on a theory of types of inculpation and punishment. It occurs in Fauconnet's study of responsibility, although the ultimate source is Durkheim.[6]

Judgements of responsibility, said Fauconnet, play an essential and precise role in a system of moral and legal rules. Judgements of responsibility determine who must be and who must not be the object of a punishment or negative sanction. It is the manner in which questions of responsibility are decided and the way in which punishments are applied that provides a criterion for differentiating a moral from a legal rule. Judgements of moral responsibility and the sanctions they evoke are matters of collective opinion; they tend to be instantaneous and are applicable by anyone and everyone.

---

[6] These distinctions were first established in Durkheim (1893a), and Fauconnet said that he also used the manuscript of Durkheim's 1894 course on 'the theory of sanctions'.

They are, in a word, *diffuse*. Judgements of legal responsibility, on the other hand, are *organised*. They require the intervention of a specifically designated intermediary person or institution that makes the judgement after a process of deliberation and applies the sanction according to rules of procedure. Other than this essentially technical difference, however, moral and legal rules 'are at bottom the same', since laws are little other than an organisation of moral rules (Fauconnet 1920: 9–16).

What in sum then is the Durkheimian definition of law? Law, like morality, is a set of obligatory social rules designed to insure social equilibrium. Unlike morality, law requires the intervention of a third party or institution to render judgement and, when appropriate, to punish. Law, like morality, is dependent on the state of collective opinion, but law's dependence is less direct: if a moral rule is a representation of and an organising of an opinion implicit in a collective conscience, a legal rule is a representation of a representation, since it organises the implementation of a moral rule.

How adequate was the Durkheimians' definition of law? By pointing to law's 'organised' nature, to what has been called the criterion of 'adjudicability' (Carbonnier 1978: 186–95), the Durkheimians isolated what is clearly one of the primary traits of law as distinguished from morality. If, for example, someone steals my typewriter, and typewriter theft is punishable by six months of confinement, I personally can legally neither determine the thief's identity, nor can I lock him up in my attic for six months. Unlike moral offences, in other words, legal offences are adjudicated; recourse is had to a third party and to institutionalised rules. While this definition is quite workable, the Durkheimians made rather limited use of it. The criterion of adjudicability applies to much more than they typically studied under the rubric of law. Because they focused rather exclusively on punishment and on what is called 'objective law' (obligations), they tended to under-emphasise 'subjective law' (rights), certain aspects of civil law, and some forms of 'spontaneous law' only loosely backed by political authority. Much law, for example, is concerned with the rules of procedure that an individual or group may employ to do something (set up a limited liability corporation, apply for a government grant, register to vote, draw up a will, etc.), and these rules of procedure are quite distinct from the punishments and prohibitions of criminal law. Furthermore, there seems no good sociological reason to exclude from the category of law such phenomena as the rules of voluntary organisations. But the Durkheimians overlooked such instances of adjudicability and organised sanctions. Consequently, they had a (largely unwitting) tendency to be 'statist' in their definition of law.

The Durkheimians' conception of the relation between morality and law, while accurate to a point, was also somewhat insufficient. They were, as in the old formula, right in what they affirmed but wrong in what they denied. It is certainly true that in most societies at most times there is considerable overlap between moral sentiments and legal rules. The most grave moral violations (murder, assault, major theft, etc.) tend likewise to be grave legal violations. Or looking at it the other way around, violations of legal rules often occasion moral outrage. They are exceptions of course. The moral fault of spreading malicious gossip may give rise to no legal sanctions; avoiding customs payments may be a much more serious legal than moral infraction. But, in general, the connections between moral and legal offences are quite close; people ordinarily think that this is right, and they often contend that their moral beliefs should be backed by law ('there ought to be a law'). There is also a not infrequent tendency to think that one has a moral obligation to obey a law regardless of its content ('I don't like it, but it's the law after all'). Sometimes, as Emmanuel Lévy pointed out (1933: 60–1), moral considerations are even written into the law. Articles 1135 and 1136 of the French Civil Code, for example, stipulate that a contract 'must be interpreted according to usage, to equity, "rather than according to the literal sense of the terms"; it must not be contrary to good morals'. Finally, if in a given society there is an enormous difference between the laws, as enforced by political authorities, and general moral beliefs and customary practices, the inevitable result is a repressive political regime.

In short, the close tie between moral beliefs and laws has been stressed from Aristotle to H.L.A. Hart, and the Durkheimians were undoubtedly right in doing so as well. Yet the link between morality and law is never as close as the Durkheimians appear to have assumed. In general, they slighted the importance of conflict: between moral principles, between laws, and, most significant for our purposes, between legal and moral rules. Even if one fully accepts the notion that laws are *nothing but* formalised customs and moral beliefs, the distinctive characteristics of laws (as organised and adjudicable) entail more consequences than the Durkheimians generally studied. It is easy to think of examples. Laws can and do run counter to collective opinion, and not always in objectionable ways. In the case, for example, of laws prohibiting racial discrimination in a society where racist beliefs are the norm, one is confronted with a situation in which the moral beliefs of some powerful persons (legislators) clash with the collective conscience. Laws can also strengthen, and not merely reflect, moral or customary beliefs and practices by simply codifying those beliefs and practices. Legal guarantees of formerly traditional seniority rights might be a good example. Furthermore, laws, especially laws instituting rights, occasionally protect the moral or religious beliefs of minorities against the moral or religious beliefs of the common conscience. In some societies, for example, where conscientious objection to military service is allowed, the right of some persons to avoid the law is itself guaranteed by the law. Finally, because of the relative inflexibility of written laws, they can serve to defend individuals at times of nasty swings in public opinion.

The Durkheimians had to be aware of such facts of course. Many of them were Dreyfusards after all; and the major mechanism leading to legal evolution that they recognised was change in moral sentiments that forces change in laws. Put another way, divergences between a society's law and its morality constitute a category of normal social facts, much in the way that in the Durkheimians' analysis crime is a normal social fact. But, in general, they breezed over such considerations, more important for modern than primitive societies, and studied change only in the *very* long run. Second 'generation' Durkheimians did so as much as the group's original members. Thus one finds Henri Lévy-Bruhl (1961: 113) saying that 'for the sociologist, the true author of a legal rule' is much less the individual who writes it and much more the 'social group'. In formulating the law, the legislator merely 'translates the aspirations' of the social group. Such notions of immediate and unambiguous translatability evoke an image of judges and legislators divinely inspired by the collective conscience, when in fact one of the most important because most difficult problems in the sociology of law is explaining the quite intricate relation between legal and non-legal norms. The fact that the Durkheimians seldom considered the intricacies of that problem clarifies much about their sociology of law – about what they did and did not investigate, as well as about their methods of research.

Methodology and disciplinary context

Because the Durkheimians' sociology of law was well integrated into the rest of their sociology, their methods for the study of legal phenomena differed from their general methodology mostly in matters of emphasis, but these differences can nonetheless be quite instructive when studying their methodology and their relations with other disciplines. As is usual in the formulation of methodological precepts, when the Durkheimians argued for the methods they thought appropriate to the study of law, they did so largely in terms of why other methods, the methods of other disciplines, were inappropriate to the study of law. Such negativism in methodological pronouncements tends to be even more common than usual when, as was the case with Durkheimian sociology of law, a discipline is in a terrain already crowded with others studying the same phenomena. Hence, our discussion of Durkheimian methods will also be an account of the disciplinary context in which those methods were formulated.

The first point that must be made is that Durkheimian sociology of law grew up in an extremely rich and complex scholarly and political milieu.

Problems concerning the nature of crime, the value of punishment, the responsibility of the criminal for his acts, the legal status of groups such as trades unions, the need for legal reform, and the principled grounds for changing laws were all topics heatedly debated in the periodical press and political discourse as well as in scholarly meetings and publications – both within and outside of France. It is impossible to describe this context fully, since it is a bigger topic even than Durkheimian sociology of law, but one must say something about those elements of it important to the Durkheimians as they formulated their methodological precepts.

Among foreign sources, three are particularly worthy of mention. The German school of *Interessenjurisprudenz*, among whose members Rudolph von Jhering was one of the most significant for the Durkheimians, stressed the pre-eminent role of conflict of interest, or the clash of rights and wills in daily life, in the formation of laws and legal principles. Of perhaps greater import was the 'Italian school' of criminology, of whose representatives the most discussed by the Durkheimians was Enrico Ferri. Ferri was a sort of utilitarian socialist who held, for example, that the only legitimate function of punishment was the prevention of future crime, not the expiation of past crime, and that the best prevention was not punishment at all but social reform. Finally, some early English ethnographers searched for the origins of modern legal systems and concepts in their studies of primitive societies. Of these, Robertson Smith and Sumner Maine (e.g. 'Maine's law' concerning the passage from status to contract as one moved from primitive to modern societies) played a role in the formulation of the Durkheimians' ideas about method. Although these groups of scholars differed greatly from one another and while the Durkheimians' assessment of the value of their works varied considerably, they all had one trait in common. Like the Durkheimians, they were part of a very widespread movement in the direction of 'socialising' law and away from notions that law was based on certain inalienable and transhistorical rights and duties.

Within France the Durkheimians were not the only scholars to study law more-or-less sociologically, for the relations between sociology at its origins and law were particularly close – perhaps as close as those between philosophy and sociology (although, of course, sociology's early relations with philosophy and law were not especially amicable). There was, for example, a good deal of discussion in the faculties of law in the 1880s and 1890s about whether the proper place of sociology (like economics) was not in the law faculties rather than in the faculties of letters (Weisz article, this volume). And a goodly amount of French sociology was indeed in the faculties of law. We have already noted the legal training of several Durkheimians and the fact that at least two of them (Huvelin and Lévy) taught law. In addition, the (non-Durkheimian) sociologist René Worms taught in a law faculty while the jurists Hauriou and Duguit taught something approximating sociology courses. Finally, Gabriel Tarde was a magistrate by profession and director of the Crime Statistics Service at the Ministry of Justice. Tarde's views were important to the Durkheimians in several respects, although mostly in negative ways. In addition to the famous Durkheim–Tarde debate about the normalcy of crime, Tarde denied that the germ of modern legal institutions was to be found in primitive societies; and he affirmed that rapid social change was more characteristic in the realm of law than other social phenomena, because law was a highly conscious set of rules and therefore had a rather considerable independence from its base in morality (Tarde 1894).

Of all French legal scholars, the two most famous in France, especially after the turn of the century, were Maurice Hauriou (1856–1929) and Léon Duguit (1859–1928). Duguit, who taught at Bordeaux from 1886 until his death, has often been considered a disciple of Durkheim, but this is probably to simplify his thought. And Davy (1922b: 30) was partly accurate when he contended that Duguit was wrong if 'he believes that he builds upon sociological postulates and in particular on a conception of social solidarity that conforms with Durkheim's'. In any case, Duguit was one of those remarkable positivists who deny the existence of anything that does not hurt when dropped on one's foot. This led him to label 'metaphysical' all notions of subjective law, since, according to him, neither individuals, nor groups, nor states have rights. Rather, law had only two real forms: (1) positive law was composed of the legal statutes and institutions in fact in place in a society; (2) objective law was an organisation of the facts of association or social solidarity in a society and thus the expression of something approximating the 'collective conscience' (although he refused to use the term). For Duguit, in sum, laws (positive law) are or should be nothing other than the protection of objective law, i.e. the functions without which social life would be impossible (Duguit 1911).

Hauriou taught in the law faculty at Toulouse from 1882 until his death forty-six years later. He was best known for his extremely intricate theory of the 'institution', of which there were in fact several varieties. Simplifying greatly, one can say that Hauriou's institution is a concretised idea (or even Platonic ideal) embodying the will of the community. While this notion was also similar in certain respects to the idea of the collective conscience, Hauriou, like Duguit, rejected the term. Yet there were many parallels between Hauriou's work and that of the Durkheimians. He held, for example, that all 'social organisations have a real existence separable in part from the individuals in them', and that because such groups develop moral personalities they consequently have legal rights (Hauriou 1916: 54). Thus, like Duguit and the Durkheimians, Hauriou averred that one had no need for the theory of 'legal fiction' to cover groups with the principles of an individualistically based law. Groups were as real as individuals, and so were the rights and obligations pertaining to them.

The most striking feature of the scholarly context we have been surveying is its similarity to Durkheimian sociology of law. Thus, in their studies of law, one can conclude that the Durkheimians were moving with some important currents as much as they were digging new channels. While Hauriou and Duguit did battle with the Durkheimians (as well as with one another), the social component of their theories was vastly greater than that of major Durkheimian competitors studying the closely related field of morality. Neither Hauriou nor Duguit, nor von Jhering, Ferri, and Smith subscribed to the theses of 'natural law' legal doctrines, which were the equivalent in legal philosophy of neo-Kantian rationalism in moral philosophy. Perhaps because of this, one finds an unaccustomed gentleness and a conciliatory tone on the part of most Durkheimians (e.g. Bouglé 1935 and Davy 1922b) when they discussed the works of other scholars studying legal phenomena. Very often, other legal scholars were invited to join in a common enterprise rather than excoriated as being beyond scientific redemption. This is the case despite the fact that the Durkheimians had ample grounds for disagreement with their colleagues in the faculties of law. Most law professors were specialists in civil law (a field many Durkheimians considered to be among the least important), were importantly influenced by the doctrines of natural law, and had little respect for sociology. Yet, perhaps motivated by certain academic strategies, the Durkheimians chose not to stress their differences but rather emphasised points of agreement with well-known legal scholars.

Durkheimian relations were also quite good with practitioners of the highly developed (though rather marginal in the law faculties) field of legal history. Several times in his career, Durkheim suggested that in the absence of a well-developed discipline of sociology, history would be the best foundational study for university students, and he specifically recommended a reform of education in the law faculties requiring students to base their other studies on the history of Roman law (Durkheim 1975: 241–5). Historians such as Gustave Glotz were highly respected and frequently cited by several Durkheimians, at least two of whom (Louis Gernet and Paul Huvelin) were themselves historians of ancient law. Whence this importance of history to the Durkheimians, especially in their sociology of law? In the first place there were some fundamental similarities of scholarly outlook between the two. Historians of law could insist as much as sociologists that legal institutions were socially specific and changed over time. Thus, as late as the interwar period, one still finds sociologists such as Davy and Fauconnet referring to their method more often as the historical method than as the sociological method. In the second place, except for ethnography, history provided the Durkheimians with their largest source of data concerning legal phenomena. And they were heavily dependent on other disciplines for data since, with rare exceptions like Paul Lapie, who did empirical studies of the relations between juvenile crime, schooling, and family background (Cherkaoui article, this volume), they interpreted rather than established facts. Richard (1899: 615) described the situation thus: 'sociology in fact is much less a new science than the application of a new method ... to some old studies'. Or, as it was put in the introduction to one of the best-known Durkheimian works in the sociology of law: 'we are not looking for new facts; all those we will use are well known and, we believe, will not be contested'; however, 'in their interpretation we may separate ourselves from the historians who described them' (Fauconnet 1920: 22). Much of the Durkheimians' method, in other words, amounted to saying to their colleagues in other disciplines: Give us your facts and we will think about them better than you have done. Thus, Huvelin, a well-recognised historian of Roman law, stated in one article that among his purposes he hoped 'to encourage them [historians] to bring to sociologists a series of tested and verified results all ready for a synthesis' (Huvelin 1907: 5).

Put another way, Durkheimian method, perhaps more so in studies of law than in other fields, amounted to writing series of connected book reviews, to a sort of *explication de texte*. There is, of course, nothing inherently wrong with that. At least, before scoffing at scholars parasitic on the data of others, it should be remembered that only by using secondary sources could the Durkheimians conduct truly wide-ranging and comparative studies so as to arrive at sociological generalisations. Nonetheless, their reliance on this approach ought to have made them rather more reluctant than they sometimes were to denigrate non-factual, bookish, deductivist interpretations, when in reality their major contributions were bookish interpretations. At least, the Durkheimians' tendency to say they based themselves solely on the facts, while basing themselves mostly on good reasoning about facts, led now and again to some embarrassing slips.

Georges Davy's book on 'law, idealism, and experience' is a good example. Davy's aim was to show that law in fact has an ideal character. Since this ideal character stems from social facts that can be studied objectively, it is possible for a 'realist' basing himself on empirical data to retain an 'idealist' notion of law. To make his case, Davy adduced no facts. Rather, he studied the works of several theorists (principally Duguit, Gény, and Hauriou) 'from the point of view of the strict logic of the system'. Davy's own logic went as follows. If one can ground a realist ideal of law only by recourse to sociology and, if a particular author does not have recourse to sociology, then he cannot have a realist ideal. Therefore, we have 'proved' that one can only have a realist ideal by recourse to sociology; and (by finding some illogic in some

189

books), we have 'proved' something about the factual character of law in society, i.e. it has an ideal aspect! (Davy 1922b: 93, 106, 131.) While Davy's study, in sum, is in many respects an intelligent critical analysis of the works of some important legal philosophers on several questions of interest to sociology, it is a deductivist, if sociologistic, philosophy of law, and a rather question-begging one at that.

Durkheimian relations with philosophy of law were rather more complex and variable than they were with moral philosophy or epistemology as current in France at the time. Before the turn of the century, the Durkheimians were rather fundamentally hostile to philosophy of law. Gaston Richard's early works provide an instructive example. 'From the first day of its existence', he said in 1898, 'sociology came into conflict with philosophy of law.' While today philosophers of law are somewhat less hostile than they were twenty-five years ago, 'at bottom, the struggle is no less lively' between the two. In brief, 'no transaction, no conciliation whatever is possible between the old philosophy of law and sociology as applied to law' (Richard 1898: 645–6, 656). But, within a few years, Richard had softened his tone considerably. This change may have had something to do with his eventual break with the Durkheimians, although that is not necessarily the case.[7] At any rate, by 1901 he thought that there was a new philosophy of law, untainted with many of the problems of the old and consequently more amenable to reconciliation with sociology (Richard 1901: 173).

The 'old' philosophy of law was composed of what are usually referred to as 'natural law' theories, in which it is maintained that law (in the broad sense entailing right and justice) is an emanation of man's rational nature. The Durkheimians dealt with such theories quickly, by using one of their favourite 'methods' – the funeral oration. The formula is familiar since it is still widely in use: all would agree that the old ... (fill in the blank) is dead and discredited; in its place we can only put ... (fill in the blank), which, although it is still in its infancy (a mandatory disclaimer), holds great promise for solving problems heretofore beyond our ken. The usual response by followers of the thus interred doctrine is to write up birth or rebirth announcements. There were some of these in France at the time (e.g.

---

[7] Somewhat later, Richard (1906) was clearly looking for a means of alliance between philosophy and sociology of law. In 1909, in an article in which he cited Durkheim without any hostility, he went so far as to say that 'the domain of law must be divided between two provinces, the one properly sociological, the other axiological and ethical' (Richard 1909: 318). One may doubt that these views advocating a reconciliation with philosophy were fundamental in Richard's break with the Durkheimians (see Pickering 1979: 169–72 for a summary of his methodological differences with Durkheim). At least it was possible for other Durkheimians such as Bouglé to remain in the 'fold' while advocating similar ideas (Vogt article, this volume). In any case, Richard ceased contributing to the *Année sociologique* with the tenth volume (1907) after which one finds him, for example, using his objections to Duguit's syndicalism as an occasion to criticise Durkheim (Richard 1912).

Segond 1911) but few enough that one can conclude that neo-Kantian philosophy of law was seriously enfeebled if not quite dead. It is not easy to judge such matters, since there are few workable criteria, but it seems safe to say that the 'new' philosophy of law as represented by the likes of Hauriou and Duguit was dominant in French thought, if not necessarily in the law faculties, for the first few decades of the twentieth century. It may not have been strictly true that by the end of the nineteenth century everyone who studied law had been inculcated with 'the religion of fact' and that all had rejected the 'metaphysical idealism of traditional individualism' (Davy 1922b: 34, 37). But many had.

Yet the differences between the old and the new philosophy of law were perhaps not as significant as they might at first seem. In the last analysis, there remained in France a fundamental split between the sociological and philosophical approaches to the study of law. While most philosophers of law were willing to concede that legal institutions and even legal concepts were to *some* considerable extent relative to historical and social conditions, very few philosophers of law, even the 'new' ones, were willing to say that legal concepts were *totally* relative. Otherwise, they argued, there would be no way to account either for the ideal content of legal rules or for the fact that most basic legal–moral concepts were fundamentally the same in all human societies. To explain this unchanging and ideal character of law, one had, most philosophers continued to argue, to assume some common nature or reason was at work. To this Davy replied that 'it suffices . . . to believe in the reality of the collective conscience in order objectively to account for the ideal content of law' (Davy 1922b: 161).

What did the Durkheimians gain by saying that laws are not the more-or-less imperfect expression of an innate reason, but are rather the more-or-less perfect expression of a collective conscience? They gained the possibility of explaining legal change and variety by something other than the comparative ability of different societies to understand and to follow the principles of Reason. Their functionalism thus provided a way around a sort of rationalistic ethnocentrism. What did they lose? They lost the ability to have an independent standard for contending that a particular legal phenomenon was good or bad, just or unjust. As Fauconnet (1920: 222) expressed it, 'there are no aberrant facts. Nothing permits us to believe that the rules of responsibility that seem to us most disconcerting are the result of an error.' Yet they did not lose, so the Durkheimians contended, the ability to explain universal characteristics of legal and moral phenomena. Nor did they think that they lost the ability to make scientifically established proposals for legal reform. To see how this could be so, we must turn to their methods for studying ethnographic data. These were largely inspired by Marcel Mauss.

W. Paul Vogt

Ethnography, history, and the origins of law

The dominant characteristic of Durkheimian studies in the sociology of law was that they were 'genetic', that is to say, the main question to which the Durkheimians addressed themselves was that of the origins of legal institutions and concepts. They applied themselves much less to the problems of the functioning of legal rules in modern societies. Thus, while twenty-two Durkheimians contributed to the section of the *Année sociologique* dealing with the 'origins' of legal and moral rules, only eight (and for the most part only one, G. Richard) contributed to the section dealing with the 'functioning' of those rules. Despite the fact that the Durkheimians often referred to their method as historical, their primary data for scrutinising the question of origins was ethnographic, not historical; and this became increasingly the case after the turn of the century.

If any one individual should be given the credit (or blame) for the heavy Durkheimian reliance on ethnographic materials, that individual is surely Marcel Mauss. In an essay published when he was twenty-four years old, Mauss established the pattern for subsequent Durkheimian works in what one might call 'legal ethnography', which in turn was the most prominent part of Durkheimian sociology of law. In that essay Mauss contended that the only way scientifically to study the origins of law was through the use of ethnographic data; he examined some of that data in a painstaking review of another scholar's book; and he then went on to draw conclusions affirming the religious origins of penal law (Mauss 1896). Mauss's influence was undoubtedly also in no small part due to the fact that in his study of Eskimo societies he made one of the first truly convincing demonstrations, based on ethnographic findings, that law varies according to variations in the morphological structures of societies.[8] And Mauss was aware of the essential role he played in founding Durkheimian legal ethnography. In his autobiographical sketch (reprinted in this volume), he essentially took credit for the basic hypothesis, that had 'become classic', of Fauconnet's (1920) work on penal responsibility and for Davy's (1922a) study, via the potlatch, of the origins of contractual obligation (see also Mauss 1925: 149). Furthermore, Fauconnet and Davy frequently made strongly appreciative acknowledgements of their debt to Mauss, as did Huvelin (1907) and Lévy (1933).

Whence came this turn to the primitive in Durkheimian studies of law? The reasons for the shift from historical and contemporary data to ethnographic materials were many and complex. No one of them should be taken as sufficient to explain the phenomenon (Vogt 1976). The Durkheimians were probably motivated by the fact that ethnographic

---

[8] Of course, Durkheim had earlier (1893a, 1901) related legal evolution to evolution in social structure, but his evidence in those studies was primarily historical, not ethnographic.

studies were a relatively free terrain in comparison to the more crowded fields dealing with modern and historical legal problems. It is also probable that exotic societies carried something of a 'scientific' aura, free as they were from the heated political debates of the day in which Lévy and Jean Ray got ensnared by studying modern French legal issues. These were not of course explicitly avowed reasons for the Durkheimians' ethnographic penchant. They adduced more properly methodological and sociological reasons, and it is to these that we now turn.

The most obvious and one of the most important justifications for employing ethnographic data is quite simply that they are data. For sociologists who believed, as the Durkheimians did, that the major way to build scientific generalisations was the comparative study of societies, extra societies to compare would always be welcome. Yet the Durkheimians' proclivity for ethnographic evidence was stronger than that. Given the weight they placed on studies of primitive societies and their general avoidance of comparative studies of modern societies, it is clear that something besides a simple willingness to use additional data was at work.

As mentioned above, the Durkheimians often thought of their method in the sociology of law as historical – as the study of moral and legal regulations by 'trying to discover the real and successive causes of their appearance and of their transformation' (Davy 1922b: 47). In such an endeavour, Davy professed, a union of ethnographic and historical facts could be very fruitful indeed. In much the same way that history can serve as a sort of laboratory for the social sciences by providing a 'place' to test hypotheses, ethnographic findings can be something similar for users of the historical method. When, as often happens, historians lack the necessary data to confirm or confute a hypothesis, they can have recourse to ethnography to fill in the blanks. While ethnographic data are not perfectly suited to the purpose, they are infinitely better than the only other alternative, i.e. pure imagination (Davy 1922a: 12–14).

The Durkheimians also contended that their turn from the study of modern societies was one of the best ways to learn about modern societies, for, by analysing the widest range of social facts possible, one could begin to unearth universal social facts, features of social life common to all societies. Thus, the Durkheimians sometimes wanted to study the evolution of social facts and change over time and sometimes 'that which remains constant in the course of evolution' (Fauconnet 1920: 21–2); and it is not always obvious which of the two was being studied. With Mauss, however, the emphasis was clearly on the side of the constant aspects of all social life. One only has to look, he insisted, 'at what happens all around us, in our occidental societies, to find the same oscillations' present in Eskimo societies. From this he concluded that it is 'a law of probably very great generality' that all societies experience regular dispersions and concentrations of the intensity of social life (Mauss 1906: 127). Thus, in his work on Eskimos as well as in his more famous study of exchange and reciprocity (Mauss 1925), he sought to highlight features shared by all societies, from the most simple to the most complex.[9]

Of course, if through the interpretation of ethnographic evidence one could determine sociological laws applicable to all social groups, then it follows that one could apply such laws to modern societies, and even offer sociologically grounded suggestions for reform. And there is no question that virtually all Durkheimian sociologists of law were interested in the practical application of their studies, although no one among them produced scholarship designed to guide the decisions of judges, as was the case in the roughly contemporary work in American 'sociological jurisprudence'. There remained, however, several grounds on which one could contend that sociology of law had practical relevance. Most generally, by providing 'the most precise knowledge of the possible, it [science including sociology] makes us capable of attaining the possible' (Richard 1899: 641). This sort of point was frequently made, but it is very general. Emmanuel Lévy was much more specific. He studied law, especially civil law, with the avowed intention of finding the route to socialism. He wanted to demonstrate that a scientific study of civil-law institutions in fact in existence in modern France would lead inevitably to socialism. As he explained in one lecture, merely 'to describe institutions, to have the simplicity to observe them, to renounce legitimating them – there is the scientific method. And I will show that it is revolutionary' (Lévy 1933: 37). But this was too explicit, too direct for most Durkheimians who sometimes criticised Lévy for trying to be a prophet as well as a sociologist.

Yet it is hard to see how Mauss, while being less directly involved in the study of modern legal phenomena, was any less prophetic about them. Because he thought he had disclosed general laws of social relations, he believed he was scientifically justified in coming to the following sorts of conclusions: 'it does not suffice to observe the fact, one must deduce from it a practice, a moral precept'; it is not enough to say that a revolution in human relations is going on, 'one must say that revolution is good' (Mauss 1925: 165). The revolution in question was a return to the reciprocity and community feeling that once characterised social relations, including mercantile exchange and contracts. The peoples in the 'archaic' societies that Mauss studied were, he nostalgically opined, 'less sad, less serious, less greedy ... more generous' (Mauss 1925: 183). Thus, because Mauss thought

[9] This led Mauss to oppose, more firmly and frequently than any other Durkheimian, Lucien Lévy-Bruhl's theses maintaining a fundamental difference between primitive and modern mentalities.

he had discovered general laws, he believed he could make scientific statements about what was good and bad and therefore offer general recommendations for social policy. If human societies everywhere and at all times were characterised by a certain trait (in this case putting fellow-feeling above calculations of personal gain), and if modern societies had temporarily deviated from that norm, then one could conclude that any legal reforms reintroducing the trait, such as unemployment compensation, were good.

But even Mauss, who was most interested in constant features manifest in all societies, wanted also to study social evolution and large-scale change over time. From the very beginning of his career, Mauss insisted that 'there must be in the original types of jural reaction something that is the germ of our penal system' (Mauss 1896: 677). To talk of the origins of 'our system' in this way required basing himself on developmental and progressist hypotheses. Mauss did not draw back from that requirement. 'The evolution of criminal law', he averred, 'would appear to be absolutely continuous. From the legislation of the taboo to our codes, the march of progress was uninterrupted' (Mauss 1896: 698).

There are some serious difficulties with this mode of reasoning. Since the evidence about the 'legislation of the taboo' pertained to societies contemporaneous with those in which 'our codes' were in force, since in other words one did not precede the other, it is hard to see how one could be the origin of the other. These kinds of problems arose when the Durkheimians tried to combine three distinct sorts of research. First, especially in their sociology of law, they were interested in the origins of 'our system'. Second, they were concerned to define social types and the sorts of laws that correspond to them. Third, they sought to discover universals, qualities intrinsic to all social life. But, sometimes, in a rush of explanatory enthusiasm, they confused these separate problems, contending for example that the types were homologous with stages of evolution, with simple types coming 'earlier' and more complex types coming 'later'. In other words, they contended that if a particular 'primitive' practice was the functional equivalent of a particular 'modern' practice, the primitive practice was therefore the origin of the modern practice. Of course, it is difficult intelligibly to assert, as Mauss tried to do, that the twentieth-century peoples he described were 'from another time' (Mauss 1925: 260), since it is a dubious assumption that contemporary 'simple' societies have not evolved and are therefore the equivalent of societies of, say, ten thousand years ago.

Of all the Durkheimians, Georges Davy was most aware of the potential difficulties involved in mingling historical and ethnographic data. To have value, he affirmed, ethnographic data do not have to be thought of as distant in time, they do not have to be 'chronologically antecedent'. Therefore, in his use of ethnography, he would not try to establish a 'chronological filiation'.

Yet he was aiming nonetheless at 'sorting out the origins of the notion of contract' (Davy 1922a: 16–20). But how can one discuss origins if one 'does not pretend to fix a historical filiation'? It is worth quoting Davy's answer at some length.

> Between two groups of societies ... whether or not they are related, does one not have the right to say that the second is more advanced than the first if its social structure is less rudimentary, if its social frameworks are more stable, if in it power is more organised, classes are more distinct, and their relations more complex, and if in it institutions ... that are hardly born in the first are there clearly formed. (Davy 1922a: 26)

No, in fact one does not have the right to say 'more advanced', since bringing in the idea of advancement leads to two unacceptable notions: first, it is to introduce an evaluative standard, with 'more advanced' meaning 'more like us'; second, it is to introduce a temporal criterion, a 'historical filiation', i.e. the very thing Davy rightly said he did not want to claim to be doing.

None of this means that the Durkheimians were 'wrong' to use ethnographic evidence or even that historical sociologists studying actual origins (i.e. those having some connection with and occurring before the things to which they give rise) must dispense with ethnographic data. If, as Davy suggested, a certain twentieth-century community has several important traits in common with a community distant in time, one can reasonably use evidence pertaining to one of them to suggest hypotheses for research into the features of the other. Mauss pointed to a similar use of ethnographic data when he said that they 'can be used to explain historically our own societies'. If, for instance, in studying an ancient civilisation, one encounters in it what appear to be traces of practices similar to practices ethnographers have described, then one can use the ethnographers' descriptions to suggest ideas for research into the ancient civilisation · (Mauss 1925: 127). Finally, questions of time can be irrelevant to the task of establishing social typologies. If, on the basis of certain criteria, one can establish societal types, and if one discovers that societies of the same type date from different times, that does not invalidate the typology. But the Durkheimians sometimes, rather more frequently when they studied legal than other social · phenomena, went beyond such legitimate uses of historical and ethnographic data by employing non-historical typologies to establish historical generalisations. While this constitutes a problem for their sociology of law, it does not vitiate their positive contributions to the sociological study of ethnographic and historical evidence pertaining to legal phenomena.

Conclusion

The Durkheimians made several distinctive contributions to the sociology of law. They helped to extend the range of studies of law to non-Western societies, to societies that many scholars ethnocentrically assumed had no law. Through the comparative analysis of ethnographic and historical evidence, the Durkheimians formulated comprehensive generalisations concerning the social conditions that make legal institutions possible and explained the fundamental similarities and relations between legal rules and other social norms. Their studies of legal phenomena are a striking instance of the explanatory power of their sociology, of their ability to account for all social facts with the same model – a power sometimes gained at the price, it could be maintained, of insufficiently distinguishing between those facts.

A study of the Durkheimians' sociology of law also provides a useful perspective on their relations with other disciplines. In their studies of law they confronted a situation different from that in their work on morality and religion: here several important practitioners of competing disciplines were rather more in accord with their basic theses; and the Durkheimians chose to stress this accord. Because their differences with some jurists and historians of law were less severe than their differences with most moral philosophers and theologians, they were in a position more of having to find a sort of ecological niche for themselves and less of needing to fundamentally redirect studies of law. They saw themselves as having only to encourage developments well under way.

The Durkheimians found their niche in the ethnographic approach to the study of legal institutions and practices. Hence, one of the constitutive traits of their sociology was importantly shaped by considerations pertaining to their sociology of law. Furthermore, one of the fundamental characteristics of their ethnographic work – their tendency to combine social typologies and stages of evolution, to conflate functional equivalents and origins – was greatly encouraged by their concerns when doing the sociology of law, since, significantly more than was the case with other social facts, the Durkheimians were interested in the origins of legal phenomena. For all these reasons, in sum, it seems clear that a study of the Durkheimians' sociology of law is crucial to an understanding and/or evaluation of their sociology.

References

Bouglé, C. 1899. *Les Idées égalitaires: étude sociologique*. Paris: Alcan.
  1935. *Bilan de la sociologie française contemporaine*. Paris: Alcan.
Carbonnier, J. 1978. *Sociologie juridique*. Paris: Presses Universitaires de France.
  1979. *Flexible Droit: textes pour une sociologie du droit sans rigueur*, 4th edition. Paris: Librarie Générale de Droit et de Jurisprudence.
Davy, G. 1917. Review of J. Durand, 'Remarques sur la notion contractuelle du mariage', *Revue philosophique*, vol. 84, pp. 283–90.
  1922a. *La Foi jurée: étude sociologique du problème du contrat*. Paris: Alcan.
  1922b. *Le Droit, l'idéalisme et l'expérience*. Paris: Alcan.

W. Paul Vogt

1931. 'L'Unité de fondement de l'obligation juridique', *Archives de philosophie du droit et de sociologie juridique*, vol. 1, pp. 87–95.

1933. 'Le Problème de l'obligation chez Duguit et Kelsen', *Archives de philosophie du droit et de sociologie juridique*, vol. 3, pp. 7–36.

Duguit, L. 1911. *Traité de droit constitutionnel*. Paris: Boccard.

Durkheim, E. 1886. Les Etudes de science sociale, *Revue philosophique*, vol. 22, pp. 61–82.

1893a. *De la division du travail social*. Paris: Alcan.

1893b. Review of Richard (1892), *Revue philosophique*, vol. 35, pp. 290–6.

1901. 'Deux lois de l'évolution pénale', *Année sociologique*, vol. 4, pp. 65–95.

1975. *Textes*, vol. 1. Paris: Editions de Minuit.

Fauconnet, P. 1900. Review of Lévy (1899), *Année sociologique*, vol. 3, pp. 425–8.

1920. *La Responsabilité: étude sociologique*. Paris: Alcan.

Gurvitch, G. 1947. *Sociology of Law*. London: Routledge.

Hauriou, M. 1916. *Principes de droit public*, 2nd edition. Paris: Tenin.

Huvelin, P. 1907. 'Magie et droit individuel', *Année sociologique*, vol. 10, pp. 1–47.

Lévy, E. 1899. *Responsabilité et contrat*. Paris: Librairie Cotillon.

1933. *Les Fondements du droit*. Paris: Alcan.

Lévy-Bruhl, H. 1961. *Sociologie du droit*. Paris: Presses Universitaires de France.

Mauss, M. 1896. 'La Religion et les origines du droit pénal', *Revue de l'histoire des religions*, vol. 34, pp. 269–95; vol. 35, pp. 31–60, in Mauss 1969. *Oeuvres*, vol. 2, pp. 651–98. Paris: Editions de Minuit.

1906. 'Essai sur les variations saisonnières des sociétés eskimos: étude de morphologie sociale', *Année sociologique*, vol. 9, pp. 39–130.

1925. 'Essai sur le don: forme et raison de l'échange dans les sociétés archaïques', *Année sociologique*, 2nd series, vol. 1, pp. 30–186.

Pickering, W.S.F. 1979. 'Gaston Richard: collaborateur et adversaire', *Revue française de sociologie*, vol. 20, no. 1, pp. 163–82.

Richard, G. 1892. *Essai sur l'origine de l'idée de droit*. Paris: Thorin.

1898. 'La Philosophie du droit et la sociologie juridique', *Revue philosophique*, vol. 46, pp. 645–60.

1899. 'Philosophie du droit', *Revue philosophique*, vol. 48, pp. 615–41.

1901. 'Philosophie du droit et droit économique', *Revue philosophique*, vol. 51, pp. 173–201.

1906. 'La Philosophie du droit au point de vue sociologique', *Revue philosophique*, vol. 61, pp. 63–87.

1909. 'Philosophie du droit, la contrainte sociale et la valeur du droit subjectif', *Revue philosophique*, vol. 67, pp. 285–318.

1912. 'La Sociologie juridique et la défense du droit subjectif', *Revue philosophique*, vol. 73, pp. 225–47.

Segond, J. 1911. 'La Renaissance idéaliste et néo-kantienne de la philosophie du droit', *Revue philosophique*, vol. 71, pp. 168–86.

Tarde, G. 1894. *Les Transformations du droit*. Paris: Alcan.

Vogt, W.P. 1976. 'The Uses of Studying Primitives: a Note on the Durkheimians, 1890–1940', *History and Theory*, vol. 15, pp. 33–44.

8. The absence of political sociology in the Durkheimian classifications of the social sciences

PIERRE FAVRE

This research note could not pretend to present – and even less to resolve – the considerable problem of the conception of politics held by the Durkheimian sociologists (on Durkheim himself one should refer principally to Filloux 1977 and Lacroix 1981). Even less could it have the ambition of elucidating the relations between the 'French school of sociology' and what one called at the time 'the political sciences' or 'political science' (or, much more rarely, 'political sociology'). Nor will it concentrate upon describing the relationships that could have existed at the end of the last century among the *agrégés* in philosophy who oriented themselves toward sociology, the professors in the faculties of law, and the instructors of diverse origins called to give courses at the Ecole Libre des Sciences Politiques. This note seeks only to inject, into a largely open debate, a new element based on the examination of the diverse classifications of the social sciences set out by the Durkheimians. Accordingly, in order to emphasise the appropriately documentary aspect of this research, we must specify the full limits of the problem with which we will be dealing. To do that, it suffices to make two observations.

At the moment when the Durkheimians were working to constitute a 'new science' (Durkheim 1909, r. 1970: 137),[1] there was among all the sciences of society – at the margins of economics, for example – a speciality the existence of which appeared natural to all: the science of politics. This is not the place to relate how Durkheim's contemporaries understood such a science. It is important only to be assured that this science was considered by everyone to be both possible and in the process of being constituted. If one is not satisfied by the indications of this provided in official nomenclature – such as, the Ecole Libre des *Sciences Politiques*, the section of the Catholic Faculties of Lille devoted to the sciences sociales et *politiques*, the doctorate in the faculties of law in *sciences politiques* et économiques, etc. (Hauser 1903, Rain 1963, Rosenbauer 1969) – a reading of the works of the epoque leave no doubt of it. Thus, in Edmond Goblot's essay on the classification of the sciences (1898:

[1] 'r.' signifies 'republished in', in this case, republished in Durkheim 1970.

216–18), he made room – among the sciences that 'have begun' and that 'pertain to sociology' – for 'sociology of the State' (note that Goblot thus spoke of a *sociology*). Similarly, in his book on the philosophy of the social sciences, René Worms (1903) distinguished the anatomy and physiology of societies and situated 'political science' among those sciences having physiological studies as their object. Or, if one prefers an indication of a different sort, one can recall that, when in May 1903 the publisher Félix Alcan inserted an extract from a review of Tarde's *Les Transformations du pouvoir* into his list of published works, the review cited indicated at the outset that 'this book is in part an essay in political sociology'. The case was made. Durkheim could not have been unaware – he obviously was aware[2] – that among the social sciences that 'have begun', as Goblot put it, there was a science of politics.

As Durkheim undertook to constitute a new science – and as he wavered as to its name, 'social science'? 'moral statistics'? 'sociology'? (Lacroix 1976: 213) – one particular task seems always to have called forth his efforts, i.e. that of providing 'as clearly as possible an idea of what constitutes the domain' of that science, of acquiring a 'higher consciousness of its object', of 'more exactly accounting for the terrain on which [sociology] engages itself' (Durkheim 1900, r. 1975: 13–14). But, because sociology's 'sphere of action' was immense, that task immediately called forth another: to organise, on the basis of a new principle conforming to the orientations of the new science, the 'multitude of specialised disciplines' (Durkheim and Fauconnet 1903, r. 1975: 121) which, up to then, had dealt with social facts that were themselves rather specialised. As early as 1888, Durkheim wrote that 'a science is truly constituted only when it divides and subdivides itself' (1888, r. 1970: 100). He did not vary on that point, since, twenty years later, he could come back to the same idea:

If sociology is a positive science, one may be certain that it does not restrict itself to a single problem, but that on the contrary it is comprised of different parts, of distinct sciences that correspond to the diverse aspects of social life. There are in reality as many branches of sociology, as many specialised social sciences, as there are different species of social fact. (Durkheim 1909, r. 1970: 147)

The fact that sociology was constituted by Durkheim as the corpus of the social sciences – and that this 'implies and indicates a radical change in ... the organisation of those sciences' (Durkheim and Fauconnet 1903, r. 1975: 121) – leaves no doubt of the importance Durkheim attached to the classification of the sciences that he proposed; the same is true of the classification of the bibliographic notices and the analyses that constitute the major part of the *Année sociologique*.

[2] Compare, for example, a polemical reference to the political sciences: they are 'bastardised speculations, half theoretical and half practical, half science and half art' (Durkheim 1890, r. 1970: 225).

The problem that will concern us is, then, readily circumscribed: in the frequent presentations by Durkheim, and subsequently by the Durkheimians, of the organisation of the different specialised social sciences, was room made for political sociology, and, if so, where? I will confine myself here to supplying the documentary evidence allowing for a response to that question. The importance of this seems to me to go far beyond simple historical information, since what is in fact at stake is the very existence of a sociology of politics in France during the century following Durkheim's theoretical choices. I will successively examine Durkheim's articles relative to the division of sociology, then the classificatory plan of the *Année sociologique*, to which the major part of this article will be devoted, and, finally, several texts will be examined dating from the period after Durkheim's death – notably, the important contributions of Marcel Mauss.

Durkheim, political sociology, and the divisions of sociology

If one refers first to the numerous texts in which Durkheim explained sociology – its domain, its divisions, and the diverse schools that one encountered therein – one easily observes that political sociology was not designated by him as a constituent branch of the discipline 'which has just been born' (Durkheim 1900, r. 1975: 13).

In one of Durkheim's very first works, published in 1886 – in which he probably wanted to end a series of book reviews with a conclusion that integrated the contributions and objectives of the books analysed into a harmonious synthesis – he scarcely isolated a sociology of the political, since he differentiated:

a general sociology that has as its objective the study of the general properties of social life;

a sociology of the normal, which is composed of three specialised sciences, the first of which studies the State, another, the regulatory functions (law, morality, religion) and, finally, the third, the economic functions of society;

a sociology of the pathological, of which criminology is the most developed part. (Durkheim 1886, r. 1970 : 213–14)

In subsequent works, references to political phenomena became more and more rare, when they did not altogether disappear. From 1888, his suggested division of sociology no longer made room for sociology of the State, and no longer for a political sociology that could, for example, be the equal of economic sociology.[3] In 1900, and again in 1909, Durkheim confined himself

---

[3] This is so even though Durkheim still mentioned political facts or institutions here and there; as when he cited 'political beliefs' (1888, r. 1970: 101) as being among the objects of social psychology; or, again, when he observed that the military and diplomacy 'are social phenomena of which it should be possible to build a science'; but he then added, 'but that science does not yet exist, even in an embryonic state' (p. 103).

to the now classical simple classifications, in which the rubrics were close to those progressively established in the *Année sociologique*, and in which political sociology was definitively absent. Durkheim effectively distinguished social morphology, social physiology (essentially comprised of sociology of religion, sociology of morality, sociology of law, economic sociology), and general sociology. There was thus no reference to a possible political sociology (although place was made for linguistic sociology and sociology of aesthetics), nor was mention made, even as an example, of any political phenomenon whatsoever. Reading these texts, and only these texts, one cannot fail to notice how much politics appears to have been the blind spot of Durkheimian sociology. The few allusions (for example, in Durkheim and Fauconnet 1903, r. 1975: 131, 135, 139, 142) to the science of the State, to political science, to political organisation, to the formation of political parties are made only in the course of discussions of theses that Durkheim rejects. Furthermore, that absence of the political was so natural for Durkheim that it manifests itself in the very texture of his writing: when he enumerated the phenomena of which sociology must take possession – and as he wove his sentences within the limits imposed by style – he never cited political phenomena, but always religious, moral, legal, and economic phenomena.

The reasons for such a systematic eviction of the political from Durkheim's texts defining the field of sociology cannot be advanced here: indeed, one could not pretend to offer such an explanation without taking into account the totality of Durkheimian sociology in its relationships with political questions; and that goes far beyond the framework of this note. We will simply mention three possible explanations for Durkheim's silence about the political. 1. The most simple reason – and the very one Durkheim advanced – would be that sociology should consider political facts as most often being fortuitous, as being the 'product of contingent combinations'; they could not, therefore, be the objects of a science. Naturally, one would still have to explain why Durkheim had this notion of political facts as being contingent, why he considered contemporary facts not to be possible objects for a science. 2. The second reason would be along the lines of the strategies laid out by Durkheim to gain recognition for sociology as a university discipline. Having to assert himself in the faculties of letters and to differentiate himself essentially from philosophy, Durkheim was led to do battle at the outset on the front of the sociology of morality and religion. The science of the State, the political sciences, had been claimed by other institutions – the faculties of law and the Ecole Libre des Sciences Politiques – against which Durkheim did not intend to take up combat immediately. This explanation would imply only a strategic withdrawal by Durkheim: his sociology would remain in spirit and in practice no less the founder of *all* the social sciences, including the sciences of the political, even if the concrete development of research in that domain was momentarily suspended.[4] 3. The third explanation for the absence of the political in the Durkheimian classifications of the social sciences would involve looking into things from the perspective of the itinerary followed by our sociologist. Although in his first writings Durkheim was not far from putting the phenomenon at the centre of his concerns (Lacroix 1976) and although he even constructed a veritable political sociology between 1887 and his course on socialism, after the 'rupture of 1895' (Lacroix 1981) and for reasons of an essentially biographical nature, he abruptly affirmed the primacy of religious facts and consecrated himself to the study of the social in that one of its dimensions which seemed to him the most general: the religious dimension.

It matters little which was the determinant reason (in fact the explanation could be a combination of these reasons – see Lacroix 1978): Durkheimian sociology never explicitly assigned a definite place in its classifications to political sociology, and it could not, therefore, be accepted by its contemporaries as the direct founder of a science of the political. Our investigation would not, however, be complete if it left aside the work which doubtless contributed the most to set the course of Durkheimian sociology – the *Année sociologique*.

The place of political studies in the classificatory plan of the 'Année sociologique'

In a study of the place of the political in the Durkheimian classifications of the social sciences, the *Année sociologique* incontestably represents a fundamental source, even if it is curiously under-exploited. Durkheim certainly attached considerable importance to the *Année*'s undertaking of specifying, volume after volume, the divisions of sociology. 'One can look forward', he wrote in the preface to volume 2, 'to the determination by sociology of a new, more methodical, redistribution of the phenomena with which [the specialised sciences] concern themselves; and that is not the least of the services that it is destined to render. For nothing is more contrary to the progress of science than a faulty classification of the problems it treats' (p. iv). One can thus legitimately conclude that the divisions of the *Année* were an object of Durkheim's particular attention and that the part played in them by editorial improvisation was slight. And this is even more the case since the team united around Durkheim in no way constituted an editorial committee discussing the problems of the journal; they did not, for example, confront

---

[4] Yet many problems remain unresolved here: if Durkheim, for strategic reasons, did not mean to place himself on the terrain of the faculties of law, how does one explain the important place given to sociology of law? If Durkheim wished to ignore the Ecole Libre des Sciences Politiques, why did he open the collection *Travaux de l'Année sociologique* to Lucien Lévy-Bruhl who had been teaching at that school for ten years?

each other over the order in which the sections were to be laid out (see Besnard's article, this volume). One can add that the *Année sociologique* is also interesting because of its continuity: the division of sociology that was implemented, not only in theory but in action, through the practical negotiations that took place day after day concerning concrete matters (under which rubric will a particular book be placed?) was produced in such a manner – at first slowly established by successive emendations and then progressively institutionalised – that it is necessarily significant.

Some precious lessons as to the place given to the political in the Durkheimian edifice can be drawn from a simple examination of the contents of the twelve volumes of the *Année sociologique*, first series: the separation into rubrics, their order of succession, their relative importance, the typographical formats employed are all indications worth deciphering. Our more-or-less preliminary formal study authorises four observations.

(1) Political sociology was not considered in the *Année* to be identifiable. From the first year, some inviolable sections were constituted: 'general sociology', 'sociology of religion', 'economic sociology'. 'Sociology of morality and law', which existed from the first volume, became with the fourth 'sociology of law and morality' and was accompanied by a subtitle: the 'study of legal and moral rules considered in their genesis'. 'Criminal sociology', which existed from the outset, was also modified beginning with volume 4 to become 'criminal sociology and moral statistics'. The section 'social morphology' appeared in the second volume and became permanent after that. But, of political sociology nothing at all! Apart from a single exception, things political saw the light of day in merely one sub-section, which, under the restrictive sub-title 'political organisation', became independent only beginning with the fifth volume. The constitution of that sub-section came at the close of a revealing evolution: in volume 1 there existed only the sub-section 'social organisation'. In volumes 2, 3, and 4, that sub-section became 'social and political organisation' (or inversely 'political and social' organisation). That sub-section finally gave birth to two independent sub-sections only from the fifth volume. Thus, political sociology was not considered to be a 'branch of sociology'; it was not an individualised 'special science' (in the expression very often used by Durkheim).

(2) A second indication of Durkheimian sociology's uncertainty regarding a sociology of political phenomena is found in the frequent changes in the place assigned to the sub-section 'political organisation'. From volume 5 on, the general categories of classification that were utilised in the *Année* had become stabilised. The contested designations (as, for example, 'criminal anthropology' or 'anthroposociology') had disappeared, and the narrow designations ('customs according to habitat' or 'sexual morality, women') had ceded place to more general labels. But, despite this stabilisation of

rubrics, the place of the sub-section 'political organisation' fluctuated constantly within its section: sometimes 'political organisation' followed 'social organisation' and preceded 'domestic organisation' (vols. 5, 9, 10); sometimes the sub-section followed the other two rubrics just cited (vols. 6, 7, 11, 12), which were themselves put into one sequence or the other. Moreover, on three occasions, the rubrics were further individualised: the rubric 'war' in the fifth volume, the rubric 'socialism' in the sixth, and a sub-section 'functioning of political institutions' in the ninth. The Durkheimian classification thus failed to provide a logical and definitive place into which to insert the political rubric.

(3) Next, one cannot fail to notice the dissymmetry in the *Année sociologique* characterising the subject that the Durkheimians did not as yet call political sociology. In fact, beginning with the fourth volume, the central part of the *Année* was based on a division between *genesis* and *functioning*. This was specified in the sub-titles of the third and fourth sections: 'the study of legal and moral rules considered in their genesis' and 'the study of legal and moral rules considered in their functioning'. Durkheim explained himself clearly here: 'That which one seeks in the third section is the manner in which [the rules of law and of morality] have progressively constituted themselves; it is their origins that we have tried to arrive at. The study has been genetic.' In the fourth part, by contrast, 'one takes [the rules] fully constituted and observes the manner in which, once formed, they are applied by men. It is the conditions, no longer of their formation, but of *their functioning*, that one is undertaking to determine' (vol. 4, p. 435). The natural consequence of such a division is that 'in principle, each chapter of section three should have ... its counterpart [in section four]' (*ibid.*). In fact, in a consistent manner, the sub-section 'domestic organisation' corresponded to the sub-section 'statistics of domestic life', the study of law corresponded to the study of criminality, etc. By contrast, with the sole exception of volume 9, the chapter consecrated to political organisation never had its 'counterpart' in the fourth section. This is a further indication of the difficulty the Durkheimians had in constituting a complete science of the political.

(4) Our final observation has its source in two very simple computations. On the one hand, we find that the number of collaborators who participated in the rubric 'political organisation'[5] was exceptionally high, since a list of them includes Bouglé, G. Bourgin, Davy, Durkheim, Fauconnet, Gernet, Hourticq, Lapie, Laskine, Parodi, Richard, Stickney. Thus, 12 of the 46 collaborators on the *Année*, that is, more than one quarter, were called upon to contribute to the political rubric. If one considers the great stability of the sub-sections continuously supervised by Mauss or Simiand, for example, one

[5] I include here the political part of the sub-section 'social and political organisation' of volumes 3 and 4 and the single sub-section on 'the functioning of political institutions'.

can see that the political rubric was a problem, and that the team did not include any real specialist who could take charge of it. The large number of collaborators writing in that sub-section is even more revealing when one considers that those 12 contributors were called upon to take care of a mere 49 book reviews! Indeed, one observes – with the second computation – that the number of reviews of more than 25 lines placed under that rubric was very low: of the *Année*'s 2,097 reviews of which Nandan (1974) has made an inventory, 49 constitutes scarcely more than 2 per cent.

We cannot conclude, however, without first resolving a preliminary question: did things political have so little place in the *Année* simply because at the time there were few books published that could have been interesting for political sociology? In order to respond with full precision, one would have to be able to establish *by rubric* the relation between the books published (especially in France and Germany) and the books reviewed in the *Année*. This work has not been done, even in a preliminary way. Nonetheless, some close studies allow one to confirm that the rubric 'politics' could have accommodated many more books than were the subject of reviews in the Durkheimian publication. Consider, for example, the imposing *Traité de droit politique, électoral et parlementaire* by Eugène Pierre (of which an important edition appeared in 1902), or Woodrow Wilson's *The State. Elements of Historical and Practical Politics* (1889; French translation 1902), or the *Introduction à l'étude de l'ethnographie politique* (1907) by Henri Gaidoz, or Boutmy's *Etudes politiques* (1907), etc. One could doubtless cite many other titles. Even if one presumes that certain works of this sort were not received by the editorial staff of the *Année*, or that Durkheim could not find a collaborator to review them, it still appears certain that the meagre expanse of the political rubric is attributable to a Durkheimian bias, and not to the scarcity of books published.

These remarks about form are clearly insufficient; we must now examine the content of the different rubrics concerned. I have decided to distinguish that which was included and that which was excluded from the *explicitly* political rubric. That decision is obviously debatable: the classification of such different works in the *Année*'s categories could not have been easy; the uncertainties and the gropings are very perceptible.[6] However, in the twelve issues, the rubric 'political organisation' appears to have been endowed with a coherence sufficient to make its content significant.

[6] Thus, why did the rubric 'general theories of the law and morality' in the first volume of the *Année* open with Lapie's long review of Antonio Labriola's *Essais sur la conception matérialiste de l'histoire* (original: *La concezione materialistica della storia* 1895)? In a later volume that review would doubtless have appeared either in 'the object and method of sociology' part of the section on general sociology (as did, for example, the Salvemini–Croce–Sorel debate which was reviewed in volume 6, pp. 123–5) or under the rubric 'socialism' (as were the works of Marx, the third essay of the same Labriola, other works of Benedeto Croce, etc.).

(1) Reviews of three categories of works occurred with great regularity in the sub-section on 'political organisation'.

a. Of them, about half were *historical* books: such as Jakob Burckhardt's book on the history of Greek civilisation (in volume 3), or Ferdinand Lot's *Fidèles et vassaux*, which dealt with the period from the ninth through the twelfth centuries (vol. 8), or a book on the Byzantine Empire (vol. 9), or another on the pharaonic monarchy (vol. 8), and no less than five books on ancient Russia (vols. 4, 5, 7). Gernet's joining the *Année* perhaps added slightly to the place given to historical works, notably those dealing with ancient Greece,[7] but the tendency had already been fully established. There is nothing very surprising in this. Since the third section was consecrated to legal and moral (read also: political) rules *considered in their genesis*, it was quite natural for historical works to be accommodated there.

b. Next, more than one-quarter of the books inventoried were books on constitutional law or constitutional theory. Many dealt, directly or indirectly, with the State: for example, Jellinek's *Le Droit de l'Etat moderne*, Duguit's *L'Etat, le droit objectif et la loi positive* (both in vol. 5), and several other more specialised works (on the Italian head of state, on the Swiss *Landsgemeinde*, on the constitution of City-States). The rubric remained, however, rather narrow. Certain fundamental works such as Hauriou's *Principes de droit public* or Duguit's *Traité de droit constitutionnel* were relegated to a general rubric (in this case, in vol. 12, 'general theories of law') and treated from a legal perspective. We would also be tempted to put into this category books that dealt with the debate about democracy in terms more doctrinal than descriptive: such as Bouglé's *La Démocratie devant la science* (in vol. 8) and *De l'esprit du gouvernement démocratique* by Prins (vol. 10).

c. The slightly less than one-quarter of the sub-section remaining dealt with books that could be said to be part of political science as it is presently conceived. Certain of these books have in addition become 'classics' of political science, such as those of Ostrogorski (vol. 7) and Michels (vol. 11) on the oligarchical tendencies in political parties, or that of Bentley, *The Process of Government: a Study of Social Pressures* (vol. 11). Certain of the books we are dealing with here were even intended to be treatises in political science, such as G. Tarde's *Les Transformations du pouvoir* (vol. 3), Deslandres's *La Crise de la science politique et le problème de la méthode* (vol. 6), or, finally, Garner's *Introduction to Political Science* (vol. 12). The rarity of this type of work will, however, become evident if one observes that there was less than one book per volume explicitly indicated as being in political science.

---

[7] Gernet was in fact a Hellenist who specialised in the history of Greek law. At the same time as his studies at the Ecole Normale Supérieure, which concluded with his *agrégation* in grammar, he followed courses in law and obtained the *licence* in law (information provided by Philippe Besnard).

Pierre Favre

(2) On the other hand, certain works explicitly referring to themselves as political or explicitly called political by the writers of the book reviews were placed in other rubrics. The harvest is richer than one might have expected given that there are four categories of works that were thus reviewed.

a. Books on political psychology were reviewed in the 'general sociology' section. That fact is worth noting since among them are to be found two books by Emile Boutmy: *Essai d'une psychologie politique du peuple anglais au XIXe siècle* (vol. 5) and *Eléments d'une psychologie politique du peuple américain* (vol. 6). Both were reviewed by Bouglé. Did Boutmy's preference for collective psychology naturally lead Bouglé to place him in a section where he had several times discussed the relations between sociology and psychology, and where place was subsequently made for 'the mentality of groups' and for 'collective ethology'?

b. The problems of war and of revolution are more revealing. By their very nature, these subjects fit badly into the adopted plan: there was here no 'political organisation' but, rather, disorganisation; and, if there was a question of a 'functioning', it was hardly one of 'legal and moral rules'. Further, no solution to the problem was found. One year (vol. 5) a rubric 'war' was created; it oddly concluded the 'diverse' section, following sociology of aesthetics, technology and language. But, that rubric did not survive: books on war were later placed under the 'international morality' rubric (for example, Constantin's *Le Rôle de la guerre, étude de sociologie générale* in volume 10). At the same time, an *Essai sur les révolutions* foundered in the rubric 'diverse and general questions' (vol. 11); Hourticq, the author of the review, noted at its outset that 'of the questions relative to political life, this one is doubtless one of those least susceptible of being well resolved from the sociological point of view' (p. 31).

c. Books coming from socialist authors or devoted to socialism were fully as much of a problem. In the first volume, a rubric in the 'economic theories' sub-section was consecrated to 'socialism and economic science'. In the three following volumes, books on socialism continued to be placed in the 'economic sociology' section – either in the distinct 'socialist doctrine' rubric (vol. 2) or in a sub-section entitled 'social theories, socialism' (vols. 3 & 4). The books surveyed there were numerous: one finds mentioned the French translations of Marx's works, the publication of Labriola's third *Essai*, the publication of the books of Vandervelde, Bernstein, Kautsky, Jaurès, and those of the Italian philosopher briefly tempted by Marxism, B. Croce, etc. In the fifth volume, the rubric disappeared, but only to be reborn the following year when an autonomous sub-section was opened by Fauconnet, but at the tail end of the 'diverse' section – the same place where, the previous year, the ephemeral rubric on 'war' had been placed! Then the rubric disappeared completely; the rare books on socialism that were mentioned were placed either in the 'political organisation' section (as in the case of Anton Menger's book, *Neue Staatslehre*, vol. 7: 441–3) or in an economic rubric called 'economic science and practical social doctrines' in volume 8 and 'economic systems' in volume 9. That the existence of the rubric caused a problem is attested to by the introductions that preceded it. In the third volume, Simiand specified that socialism was considered 'as a social phenomenon, and to that extent, it is studied or can be studied sociologically' (p. 543). In the sixth volume, Fauconnet went further:

One gives the name socialism to a whole ensemble of contemporary phenomena: economic transformations, the appearance and development of new institutions, the political action of the organised working class, the emergence and propagation of new moral and legal doctrines. All these facts can be studied by the sociologist from a purely scientific point of view. (p. 578)

It will suffice for the moment to stress that in the *Année* these facts enumerated by Fauconnet did not fit within the limits assigned to political sociology.

d. Finally, studies of political morphology were the object of a distinct treatment, since they were accounted for in the important section that, beginning with the second volume, was devoted to social morphology. Besides, in the first volume, in the 'socio-geography' rubric, Durkheim reviewed at length a book by Ratzel, *L'Etat et son sol étudiés géographiquement* (pp. 533–9). In the second volume, a second book by Ratzel, *Géographie politique*, was the subject of a new ten-page text by Durkheim in which he applied himself to defining the object of the specialised social science that political geography would constitute. Durkheim's interest was great enough that in the following year the *Année* opened with an 'original paper' – brief, it is true – by Ratzel. This was the only paper explicitly about politics in the entire first series: 'Le Sol, la société et l'Etat' (vol. 3: 1–14). In the same volume there was another review by Durkheim of one of Ratzel's books and yet another in the fourth volume. After that one has to wait until the eleventh and twelfth volumes to see the reappearance of books on political morphology: Ratzel again (vol. 11: 720–3), Tonnelat's *L'Expansion allemande hors d'Europe* (vol. 11: 761–5), and *Géographie sociale. Le sol et l'Etat* by Vallaux (vol. 12: 814–18).

If we now gather together all the indications that we have obtained from the examination of the *Année sociologique*, we can only emphasise the fragmentation and the degradation of that which could have constituted a political sociology. That fragmentation (or repulsing?) particularly manifests itself in three ways.

(1) In the first place, the institutional aspect was favoured. The *Année* dealt with 'political organisation' and did not fulfil its program of also dealing with 'public life' (Durkheim, vol. 5: 436). Most often the political was

209

understood in the sense of the organisational rules of the State; and in order to study those rules, the Durkheimians preferred 'to turn towards the past ... the only means of discovering the elements of which they are composed' (vol. 5: 435). From this came the preference shown for history and also the impossibility of determining a logic of classification treating either of revolution, of class struggle or of war – all of which found no place to reside in the plan of the *Année*.

(2) In the second place, that which in the very terminology of the *Année*'s writers was called 'political' obviously eluded the classificatory work undertaken by Durkheim. In his elaboration of the classificatory plan of the social sciences, Durkheim most often searched for analytical re-classifications. Thus, when he constituted the 'social morphology' section, Durkheim first sought a logical object for that science; then he observed that that object 'is presently the concern of different disciplines' (geography, history, demography); and he concluded: 'there is, we believe, an interest in drawing these fragmentary sciences out of their isolation and in putting them in contact with one another by uniting them under the same rubric' (vol. 2: 520–1). But, political studies did not receive that classificatory attention from Durkheim. Explicitly political works were scattered in diverse rubrics without any manifest desire for organisation.

One could imagine, for example, that politics could have been considered as an element or an aspect of each 'special science' or as a 'problem to be dealt with' (Durkheim 1909, r. 1970: 148) by each branch of sociology. Politics could thus have been a vertical slice through the strata of sociology. If one follows that image and uses by way of example the divisions of sociology presented by Durkheim in 'Sociologie et sciences sociales' (1909), that vertical classification can be done in the following way:

Different types of social fact	Specialised political sociologies
Social substratum	Geopolitical studies
Religious beliefs, practices and institutions	Sociology of political beliefs and types of membership in political communities
Moral ideas and customs	Sociology of political practices
Legal institutions	Sociology of political institutions
Economic institutions	Sociology of public policy

But nothing of the sort was done, even though some non-dominant tendencies to see things in this way appeared here and there in the *Année*.

210

The manifest uncertainty that ruled over the distribution of political works in the various sub-sections is demonstration enough that the problem had not been thought of by Durkheim in this form.

(3) Finally, one should note the differences between the *Année*'s collaborators in this domain, even if the fact of such differences is not specific to the reviews of books on political science and political history. On the question of the State, for example, Durkheim tended to minimise its role in his book reviews, to make a derivative institution of it. Thus, he chose to treat feudal organisations and those on which clans were based as social organisations and not as political organisations – even though he called the latter *politico*-familial (vol. 5: 343). Likewise, he criticised Frazer for calling magicians 'political chiefs'; according to Durkheim, they should have been seen as priests or as properly religious chiefs (vol. 10: 415). Bouglé's approach was quite the opposite. The expression 'political science', which flowed but rarely from Durkheim's pen, was used naturally by Bouglé. He recounted without criticism the positions of the German author Mayr who practically identified the science of the State with the science of society (vol. 5: 136–7). In the same volume, Gaston Richard could with no greater hesitancy refer to the definition by the Spanish sociologist Posada: 'political science has the State as its object, such as it is and such as it has developed in history' (vol 5: 355). And P. Lapie appeared to be far from Durkheim when, in reviewing Tarde's *Transformations du pouvoir*, he enumerated the following questions without troubling himself with sociological precautions: 'How are the attributions of the State modified? How is the domain in which those attributions are exercised modified? How are the means of action of power transformed? How are the relationships between the rulers and the ruled transformed?' (vol. 3: 362).

After Durkheim: Mauss, Davy, Bouglé, and some others

All of these difficulties of situating the political within Durkheimian sociology will become clearer for us, *a posteriori*, by referring to certain subsequent texts by Marcel Mauss (1927a, 1927b, 1934) in which the nephew so visibly and sometimes so maladroitly took the place of his deceased uncle. What did Mauss in fact say either about political matters or politics?

His first affirmation: 'politics is not a part of sociology' (1927a, r. 1969: 232). Mauss said this over and over again: politics is 'that other discipline . . . in which we do not engage'. The reason Mauss gave is that politics is an *art*, it is a practice, and one must never confuse a science with its applications.

But, Mauss continued, confusion can stem precisely from the fact that politics is 'the practical art corresponding' to sociology. 'Politics and sociology have but one and the same object: societies' (1927a, r. 1969:

211

233–4); the task of the first is to administer societies, of the second, to know them. Because of that identity of their object, it is important to distinguish with full rigour *pure* sociology – from which politics is 'ruthlessly eliminated' – and *applied* sociology, which, very simply, is politics.

The connection between politics and sociology does not stop there, since, for Mauss, politics, or applied sociology, is the ultimate justification for pure sociology. Sociology, said Durkheim, would not be worth 'an hour of trouble' if it had no practical utility. And that utility, according to Mauss, will find itself realised in those political studies which should 'crown and conclude' sociology. By such studies, the sociologist should 'aid in directing opinion, that is to say, the government' (1927a, r. 1969: 243) and clarify the knowledge, the predictions and the judgements on which the art of politics is based.

We are thus left with the possibility of a sociology of politics. Mauss hesitated as to whether to label it: 'sociology of politics', 'science of the social arts', 'theory of the political arts', 'pragmatics', 'the very specialised part of the sociology of action', etc. However, he clearly described the science that remained to be constituted: 'it consists simply of seeing ... how, in terms of political behaviours, men act, have known or believed one another to act, have divided themselves in diverse surroundings and groups, have reacted to other societies or to the physical milieu' (p. 237).

On the other hand, Mauss admitted that he was not sure where, within the classificatory plan of the social sciences, to put that sociology of the political. Should one consider that the political is so tied to the legal phenomenon of the State that political sociology will be a rubric within sociology of morality and law?[8] On the other hand, since the State, the constitution, and the establishment of a sovereign power are 'convergent in the whole of society' (p. 237), should one make political sociology the fourth group of research within general sociology (after the study of systems of social facts, the study of social systems, and the categories of knowledge)? Or, inversely, since 'everything converges' upon political facts (but to an extent that 'we do not know how to specify'), should one acknowledge that at the heart of each division of sociology a political rubric must be opened?

The manner in which Mauss dealt with the political question in 1927 (although his 1901 text, written with Fauconnet, contained nothing more than Durkheim's works at the time) is particularly enlightening, in a retrospective way, about the Durkheimian attitude. First, it confirms that the problem had been obscured by Durkheim, since Mauss had to devote an

[8] Mauss continued to maintain that solution in his 'Fragment d'un plan de sociologie générale descriptive', but, however, concluded as follows: 'Thus, with Durkheim, having ourselves, perhaps with a rather great risk of error, classed the State among legal phenomena, we continue to persist in that somewhat partial view and to reserve the study of political organisation and its functioning to the description of the law in the societies studied' (1934: 310).

entire chapter of his paper to a question that Durkheim did not even mention. It also confirms that Durkheim indeed had a bias against constituting a political sociology and a tendency to reduce political phenomena to their legal expression. Finally, it allows one to see the consequences the Durkheimian options had for the development of political sociology in France: political sociology, never designated by Durkheim as a branch of sociology, was late in constituting itself and in making itself recognisable. Is it not revealing that, although Durkheim tended to orient his disciples in such a way that they covered the ensemble of the territory of sociology, before 1914 *not one* of his young disciples had worked toward becoming a specialist in the study of political facts?

This is so much the case that we can complete our study of the place of the political in the Durkheimian classifications of the social sciences by observing that in the interwar period the surviving Durkheimians did not succeed in integrating political studies and sociology in a satisfying manner. Thus, Mauss's explicitly political works remained uncompleted. In the same way, Davy's *Sociologie politique* (1924), which would require a separate study,[9] did not succeed in marking out a sociological territory – for several reasons. First, his choice of sovereignty as the central concept of political sociology,[10] besides leading Davy to devote one hundred pages to legal theories of sovereignty, did not orient him toward precise studies of the functioning of contemporary political societies. Next, the entire second part of Davy's book was consecrated to the subject in which he had specialised in previous works: 'elementary social organisations', especially totemic societies, tribal societies, and civilisations characterised by the potlatch. Thus, his work was more of an introduction to political anthropology than to political sociology. Finally, Davy abruptly finished his book, without troubling himself about intermediate stages, with some reflections on the problems of national unity and patriotism and by a discussion of the theses of Renan (in 'What is a nation?') and Fustel de Coulanges. The echoes of the Great War were thus so pervasive in the work that it could doubtless not by itself have given birth to a specifically political sociology, even supposing that all the other social conditions of the emergence of the discipline had been filled. Fifteen years

---

[9] Note, for example, that Davy began his *Eléments de sociologie* with *political sociology* and intended to continue that work with a *domestic sociology*, which never appeared (but to which the political sociology referred from time to time). There was in this a noteworthy reversal of perspective, since the habitual Durkheimian order prescribed 'beginning' sociology either logically, by social morphology or pedagogically, by general sociology or, in terms of importance, by sociology of religion.

[10] See the definition of the object of political sociology (p. 13): political sociology 'deals essentially with the nation and the State and with their relations to individuals: it asks what are the diverse ways in which the group or its qualified representatives exercise their sovereignty over individuals, and, reciprocally, in what ways and by what rights do individuals demand their own liberty as against the diverse groupings which unite them'.

later, another Durkheimian, Halbwachs, devoted a short chapter of his *Morphologie sociale* (1938) to political morphology, which he defined as 'the study of the diverse systems of government and administration in their relations with the exterior forms of the groups over which they rule' (1938, r. 1970: 27). But, if Halbwachs indeed wished to encourage sociologists to renounce the apparent Durkheimian indifference to political facts, he over-emphasised the great dependence of those facts on the phenomena of social morphology.

But the most revealing example, not leaving the domain of classifications of the social sciences, is that of Célestin Bouglé. Among the original Durkheimians, Bouglé might seem to be the one who was most sensitive to the political question. In his works, he sociologically elucidated democratic concepts (*Les Idées égalitaires*, 1899; *La Démocratie devant la science*, 1903), and he devoted several studies to social reformers such as Proudhon and Saint-Simon. But the place of political sociology in his pedagogical works was marked by an astonishing disassociation. In the *Guide de l'étudiant en sociologie* (1921, written with M. Déat) and in the *Eléments de sociologie* (1926, written with J. Raffault), the first of which was a bibliography and the second a collection of texts, political sociology was in fact presented as such. In the *Eléments* it even carved out a choice place for itself: nearly one hundred of the 506 pages of the collection! On the other hand, when it was no longer a matter of citing titles of works or of compiling extracts, but of explaining sociology – for example, in *Bilan de la sociologie française contemporaine* (1935) or in *Qu'est-ce que la sociologie?* (1907) – political sociology disappeared, and not a single reference was ever made to political phenomena. The table of contents of the *Bilan* is worth reproducing:

Sociology and psychology
Ethnology and sociology
Social morphology
Sociology and history
Sociology of law
Economic sociology.

Moreover, when by way of conclusion the author cited the other human sciences that he could have discussed, he mentioned aesthetics, linguistics, and studies of technol gy – one again sees here the content of the 'diverse' section of the *Année* – and did not think to mention political sociology. Thus, political sociology appeared as a bibliographical category and not as a natural division of sociology; it was not a constituent sub-discipline that was impossible to avoid mentioning.

The same remark could be made regarding the relation between educational programs and the works of sociologists. In the Official Program of the Ecoles Normales Primaires of 18 September 1920 (reprinted in

Hubert 1930: xiii-xiv), political sociology made up the longest paragraph; but in the book by Daniel Essertier (1930), a sociologist rather close to the Durkheimians, political sociology nowhere appears, even though Essertier dealt with linguists, geographers, historians, jurists, and economists in addition to recognised sociologists.

The nature of the contest between Durkheim and politics as a possible object of sociological study without doubt had durable effects on the distribution of the social sciences in France. Excluded from the classification of those sciences, absent from the *Année sociologique* (the plan of which certainly was for many French sociologists a veritable categorisation of knowledge, a formula for the systematic apprehension of the real), political sociology saw itself deprived of one of the preliminary conditions for existence: not even the recognition that it was legitimate, but the simple recognition that it was possible. Political sociology was the victim in the great scientific struggle engaged in at the end of the nineteenth century between nascent sociology, the political sciences (the monopoly of which was claimed with some consistency and pugnacity by Boutmy for the Ecole Libre des Sciences Politiques), and the social sciences that the professors in the law faculties imagined themselves to be teaching. The result would be to defer for a half-century the constitution of political phenomena as objects of scientific study.

References

Bouglé, C. 1907. *Qu'est-ce que la sociologie?* Paris: Alcan.
 1935. *Bilan de la sociologie française contemporaine.* Paris: Alcan.
Bouglé, C., and Déat, M. 1921. *Le Guide de l'étudiant en sociologie.* Paris: Garnier.
Bouglé, C., and Raffault, J. 1926. *Eléments de sociologie. Textes choisis et ordonnés.* Paris: Alcan.
Davy, G. 1924. *Eléments de sociologie. I. Sociologie politique.* Paris: Delagrave.
Durkheim, E. 1886. 'Les Etudes de science sociale', *Revue philosophique*, vol. 22, pp. 61–80 (republished pp. 184–214 in Durkheim 1970).
 1888. 'Cours de science sociale: leçon d'ouverture', *Revue internationale de l'enseignement*, vol. 15, pp. 23–48 (republished pp. 77–110 in Durkheim 1970).
 1890. 'Les Principes de 1789 et la sociologie', *Revue internationale de l'enseignement*, vol. 19, pp. 450–6 (republished pp. 214–25 in Durkheim 1970).
 1900. 'La sociologia ed il suo dominio scientifico,' *Rivista italiana di sociologia*, vol. 4, pp. 127–48 (French translation pp. 13–36 in Durkheim 1975).
 1909. 'Sociologie et sciences sociales', pp. 259–85 in *De la méthode dans les sciences.* Paris: Alcan (republished pp. 137–59 in Durkheim 1970).
 1970. *La Science sociale et l'action.* Paris: Presses Universitaires de France.
 1975. *Textes*, vol. 1. Paris: Editions de Minuit.
Durkheim, E., and Fauconnet, P. 1903. 'Sociologie et sciences sociales', *Revue philosophique*, vol. 55, pp. 465–97 (republished pp. 121–59 in Durkheim 1975).
Essertier, D. 1930. *La Sociologie.* Paris: Alcan.

Pierre Favre

Fauconnet, P., and Mauss, M. 1901. 'Sociologie', pp. 165–76 in *La Grande Encyclopédie*, vol. 30. Paris: La Grande Encyclopédie (republished pp. 139–77 in Mauss 1969).

Filloux, J.C. 1977. *Durkheim et le socialisme*. Genève: Droz.

Goblot, E. 1898. *Essai sur la classification des sciences*. Paris: Alcan.

Halbwachs, M. 1938. *Morphologie sociale*. Paris: Colin (new edition 1970).

Hauser, H. 1903. *L'Enseignement des sciences sociales; état actuel de cet enseignement dans les divers pays du monde*. Paris: Chevalier-Maresq.

Hubert, R. 1930. *Manuel élémentaire de sociologie; programme des écoles normales primaires, baccalauréat, certificat de morale et sociologie pour la licence ès lettres*, revised edition. Paris: Delalain.

Lacroix, B. 1976. 'La Vocation originelle d'Emile Durkheim', *Revue française de sociologie*, vol. 17, no. 2, pp. 213–45.

1978. 'A propos des rapports entre Durkheim et Marx: de l'analyse de texte à l'analyse sociologique', pp. 329–50 in *Etudes offertes au Professeur Eméren-tienne de Lagrange*. Paris: Librairie Générale de Droit et de Jurisprudence.

1981. *Emile Durkheim et la politique*. Paris: Presses de la Fondation Nationale des Sciences Politiques.

Mauss, M. 1927a. 'Divisions et proportions des divisions de la sociologie', *Année sociologique*, new series, vol. 2, pp. 98–176 (republished pp. 178–245 in Mauss 1969).

1927b. 'Note de méthode sur l'extension de la sociologie, énoncé de quelques principes à propos d'un livre récent', *Année sociologique*, new series, vol. 2, pp. 178–92 (republished pp. 283–97 in Mauss 1969).

1934. 'Fragment d'un plan de sociologie générale descriptive', *Annales socio-logiques*, série A, fasc. 1, pp. 1–56 (republished pp. 303–54 in Mauss 1969).

1969. *Oeuvres*, vol. 3. Paris: Editions de Minuit.

Nandan, Y. 1974. 'Le Maître, les doctrines, les membres et le magnum opus. Une étude critique et analytique de l'école durkheimienne et de l'*Année socio-logique*'. Thesis, Université de Paris V.

Rain, P. 1963. *L'Ecole libre des sciences politiques*. Paris: Fondation Nationale des Sciences Politiques.

Rosenbauer, M. 1969. 'L'Ecole libre des sciences politiques de 1871 à 1896. L'enseignement des sciences politiques sous la IIIe République'. Dissertation, Universität Marburg/Lahn.

Worms, R. 1903. *Philosophie des sciences sociales*, vol. 1. *Objet des sciences sociales*. Paris: Giard et Brière.

9. Education and social mobility: Paul Lapie's pathbreaking work

MOHAMED CHERKAOUI

It is a well-known fact that the organisation of the *Année sociologique* was criticised on several occasions by Durkheim's own collaborators, who pointed to the artificiality of the classification, the absence of any system, and the incomprehensible gaps (cf. Mauss 1927). The most surprising of these seems to be the absence of the sociology of educational systems. Admittedly, there are occasional reviews of works on education, but they are not systematically grouped under the same heading.[1] This could not have been due to any lack of interest in the subject, since the evolution of ideas and institutional innovations in the field of education had been intense from the end of the seventies,[2] whilst the very involvement of Durkheim and the Durkheimians in the teaching of pedagogy at the faculty of arts, as well as their work in the people's universities,[3] demonstrate how much importance they actually attached to the subject. Nor could it have been a paucity of writing in the field that prevented the founder of educational sociology from devoting even so much as a regular sub-section to this area of study, since a

[1] These reviews are to be found under several headings: *Année sociologique* 1899, 1st section, general sociology, 2nd sub-section, social philosophy, pp. 171–4, a review by Parodi; 1899, vol. 3, moral and juridical sociology, 10 various, 394–9, by Lapie; 1900, vol. 3, 10 questions, 446–7 and 447–8, two reviews by Durkheim; p. 448, 1901, vol. 4, criminal sociology and moral statistics, 3, on morality and criminality in general according to the countries, 443–5, by Durkheim; 1904, vol. 7, various, 4 education (the only time a section is devoted to education), 684–6, by Durkheim.

[2] For an account of the changes that took place from 1870 onwards, see Marion's thesis, 1889. Courses on pedagogy began to develop in the arts faculties from the beginning of the eighties. The first, set up in Paris in 1883, was taught by Henri Marion. The provincial universities were quick to follow suit. The first chair was created in the Sorbonne in 1887. It should not be forgotten that many Durkheimians – starting with Durkheim himself – taught pedagogy.

[3] Durkheim and many Durkheimians lectured in the people's universities. Several universities and university lecturers were associated with this process of transmitting knowledge to the lower classes. The movement, which took its inspiration from the English experiment 'University Extension', began modestly enough in 1895 and reached its peak in 1906 when there were 169 people's universities. See Pelisson 1911a and 1911b. It should be remembered, however, that the adult education given by 'University Extension' in England was intended for those who were unable to gain admission to university. The system was instituted by the University of Cambridge in 1873, and Oxford in 1878. Other universities followed suit.

Mohamed Cherkaoui

considerable number of publications, articles, books and even journals devoted to educational systems appeared both in France and elsewhere between 1898 and 1914. If Durkheim neglected this research, it is probably because he believed it belonged more to the realm of psychology than of sociology. Indeed, psychology already occupied the whole of the territory conventionally called experimental pedagogy, whereas for Durkheim sociology should be oriented more towards an analysis of the genesis, functions and transformations of educational institutions and their relationships with the other social agencies, rather than being a microscopic and metrological study of the optimum conditions for learning and of the understanding of the effects of school on the professional future of the pupils.[4]

The same reason would account for the remarkable fact that, contrary to the usual practice of the *Année sociologique* of reviewing the works of its contributors, there was no mention of the works of Paul Lapie (1869–1927) on the sociology of education and social morphology which will form the basis of the present paper.[5] It is true that to Durkheim Lapie's theoretical position might, to say the least, have appeared marginal and ambiguous in relation to the institutional and scientific orthodoxy that the new intellectual field had to conquer. In reality, both in his research and in his epistemological professions of faith, Lapie never broke with psychology, nor indeed with the other competing schools of sociology. One has only to read his correspondence, remember his initiating role in the creating and financing of a laboratory of psychology, and examine his research activities in Bordeaux, which are in many ways related to those of Alfred Binet, to realise the importance he attached to the study of psychological phenomena and the theoretical benefits he hoped to derive from them for sociology.[6] One then has only to remember the interest he displayed in the sociology of Tarde and the detailed study entitled 'La Hiérarchie des professions', which was a discussion of Tarde's *La Psychologie économique*, to realise that his intellectual orientation was completely free of all doctrinal prejudice (Lapie 1902).

[4] A brief account of several works on experimental pedagogy is to be found in Binet's article (1900). On the institutional relationships between psychology and the science of education see for example Lapie 1926, especially the first text entitled 'pédagogie française' which gives its name to the work as a whole. The role to be assigned to sociology is described on pages 26 ff. On the relationship between pedagogy on the one hand and psychology and sociology on the other, see Durkheim 1922: 88–90, and 125–6. A presentation of the principles of analysis used in Durkheim's educational sociology is to be found in Cherkaoui 1976, 1977, 1978 and 1980.

[5] The following references were made, however: Lapie 1898 in *Année sociologique*, 1899, pp. 557–9, review by Durkheim; Lapie 1899 in *Année*, 1900, pp. 328–30, review by Lapie himself; Lapie 1908 in *Année*, 1910, pp. 371–3, review by Bouglé.

[6] It was Paul Lapie who had the idea of setting up a laboratory of psychology. He requested financial aid from the dean of the arts faculty for the purchase of equipment and instruments (letters dated 12 November, 10 and 13 December 1910 and 22 March 1911). This correspondence is in Lapie's administrative file in Bordeaux. Lapie's empirical research dates from this time.

218

So Lapie's pluri-disciplinary essays must have seemed like living antinomies both to his friends from the *Année sociologique* and to his colleagues in psychology whose methods and results he knew and used. These few but remarkable studies are nothing less than original investigations into (1) the psychological and social determinants of school attainment, (2) the effects of school on juvenile crime, and (3) the connections between social morphology, educational variables and mobility. The pioneering nature of this research undertaken more than sixty years ago is sufficient to justify its presentation here. The sociological problematic which it develops is, apart from the nuances, the same as that of contemporary sociologists; the type of demonstration deployed and the use made of the new methods of investigation are remarkable for their rigour.[7]

The research, it will be noted, is entirely centred on the relationships between school and society. Lapie had, in fact, shown an early interest in the problems of education, and in particular in all aspects of primary schools, where, under his father who was also a teacher, he began his apprenticeship.[8] Between 1898 and 1902, in Rennes, where he lectured in philosophy, he maintained close links with the primary-school teachers at the college of education and at public lectures. From these various contacts came the slim volume entitled *Pour la raison*. In 1902–3, in Aix, where he also taught philosophy, he gave two important lectures at the local college of education on the scientific mission of primary-school teachers, urging them to apply the rules of psychological and sociological method to an observation of their own school and commune.[9] In Bordeaux, between 1903 and 1911, where he was, in succession, lecturer in the history of philosophy, lecturer in social sciences, professor of philosophy, and, secondarily, lecturer to candidates for the inspectorate of primary schools, Lapie undertook original empirical research into the sociology and psychology of education.[10]

[7] The originality of these studies was not sufficiently noticed even later. Laubier, R., 1925, *Année sociologique*, p. 216, gives a brief account of Lapie (1923) (1926).

[8] At that time, primary schools were – and long remained – the schools for lower-class children. Middle-class children were educated at home by a private tutor in the very wealthy families, or attended fee-paying elementary classes in the grammar schools. These classes were completely separate from primary school proper. The primary branch on the one hand, with its elementary primary, higher primary and professional schools, and the secondary branch on the other, with its elementary classes and grammar schools, constituted two autonomous, closed worlds. It was theoretically possible to go from primary to secondary, and the very small number of grants enabled lower-class children to go to grammar school, as was Lapie's case.

[9] The text of the two lectures was reprinted in Lapie 1923.

[10] Lapie, it should be noted, had a liking for empirical research. In Tunis, between 1893 and 1896, when he was a young philosophy teacher, he gathered precise data on the customs, institutions and law of Jews and Muslims which provided the material for Lapie 1898. When the *Année sociologique* began, it was his wish that it should commission surveys not only of so-called primitive or traditional societies, but of others too, and in particular contemporary France. See his letter to Bouglé of 20 November 1896 in this volume and Lapie 1923: 111.

Mohamed Cherkaoui

His interest in education in schools can better be measured from the number of his contributions to the *Année sociologique* which were concerned with pedagogical problems. As well as reviews of works on moral and juridical sociology, Lapie, in fact, contributed substantial analyses of recent publications concerned with education. And, even during his long administrative career as rector of the Toulouse educational district from 1911 to 1914, as director of primary school education from 1914 to 1925, and finally as vice-rector of the Paris educational district from 1925 till his death in 1927, he maintained his special interest in schools, in teachers and in pedagogical problems, by running the *Revue pédagogique* (Lapie 1937).

The determinants of educational success

To the question 'how to explain success at school', already explored in the first works of Binet, Lapie answered by a survey, admittedly limited to 24 subjects between the ages of 8 and 14 picked from the quickest and slowest learners in the intermediate class of the first year in primary school, but a survey which was rigorously conducted for all that.[11] The framework in which Lapie carried out his survey was the classic one of psychology, that of faculties, which is why he begins by asking what differences there might be between the so-called elementary psychological functions, such as sight and hearing, in the fast and slow learners, before coming to the 'higher' functions such as imagination, will or judgement. No significant differences appear between fast and slow learners for the 'elementary' functions, but slow learners score less than fast learners on tests for the 'higher' psychological functions. Lapie is also interested in the physiological basis of the differences observed, noting height, weight, respiratory capacity, and so on, and comparing them to the averages for each age group as calculated by Binet. The existence of a correlation between physical and intellectual development refers back to social differences between the families and calls for a sociological study. This direction had already been explored by Binet and his collaborators from the Société Libre pour l'Etude Psychologique de l'Enfant,[12] towards 1907, but the sociological survey led Lapie to results which are far more significant and more relevant to modern times.

The sociological variables he chose are, in fact, the ones normally used in

[11] This study of slow and fast learners constitutes the first chapter of the first part of Lapie 1923. It was first published in volume 18 of the *Année psychologique*, 1912: 233–70.

[12] It was in relation to certain observations of anthropometric variations found in schools in socially different parts of Paris that Binet and his collaborators demonstrated the effect of the socio-economic environment. See Avanzini 1970: 149–55, which remains the most substantial work on Binet in spite of Wolf's unsuccessful attempt (1973). The Société Libre, founded on 9 November 1899, was inspired, presided over, and had its program of work largely defined by Binet from 1901 until his death in 1911.

research by educational sociologists: economic status, level of education of the parents, composition of the phratry, presence of both parents in the home, parental interest in the child's education, the importance they attach to schooling, the socialisation of the child in all its forms, from the exercise of paternal authority to diffuse social control, the socialising agents, role of the mother, and so on.

Lapie observed that the families of fast learners have a much higher economic status and fewer children than the families of slow learners. The latter are also more frequently incomplete, with one of the parents being dead in some 50 per cent of cases. Compared with the fathers of the slow learners, those of fast learners have a higher level of education, as measured by qualifications and the number of years of schooling. The latter also attach more importance to the education of their children than do the former, with the result that fast learners are rarely absent from school and their school work is much more closely controlled. In this respect, Lapie stresses the role of the mother in the child's success at school. It would not be going too far to consider Lapie's explanations as the discovery of two groups of independent and complementary variables which have an influence on the child's progress at school, the first group of variables being linked to the control of school work and the second group being linked to social control or socialisation.

So, in spite of the limitations of the survey and the doubtful nature of the results, the underlying problematic reveals an acute understanding of the relationships between family and school that Lapie had already analysed in his earlier research, either by integrating them into his study of juvenile crime, or by reformulating them into two constituent elements of a theory of social mobility.

School and crime

That Lapie should have devoted one of his empirical studies to the relationship between school and crime is scarcely surprising, given the importance and the relevance of the debate that was then taking place on this subject.[13] The State schools were accused, by their political opponents and by some criminologists, of being an instrument of corruption. Lapie's data were compiled from the files on 102 young people aged 18 or below who, between December 1908 and January 1910, had been the object of a court order in Bordeaux. The information concerning their schooling was compiled from the records of the schools they had attended and the subjects were divided into five groups according to the number and gravity of their offences.

A comparison of the average level of education of the delinquent

[13] Lapie's article 'L'Ecole publique et la criminalité juvénile' was first published in *La Revue du Mois* in February 1911: 144–68, reproduced in Lapie 1923: 176–9.

population under study and the general population of young people of the same age groups reveals that the first contains two to three times more illiterates than the second. Furthermore, there is a correlation between the degree of ignorance and the gravity of the offences: the least serious offences were committed by those with more schooling.

But Lapie goes beyond the rather rudimentary indicator of educational level to look more closely at the *kind* of schooling received by delinquents. The average duration turns out to be not seven but four years, but, more especially, the attendance of delinquents is much more irregular: on average, they are absent a third of the time. Finally, a survey conducted by Lapie on delinquents' attitudes leaves no doubt as to their lack of interest in the teaching provided and reveals that they show strong resistance to any kind of socialisation. All of these observations demonstrate that school had no useful effect on these children.

Lapie was also able to refute a second accusation that the State schools promote delinquency by not providing religious education. In fact, there is as much delinquency amongst pupils at denominational schools as there is amongst pupils of State schools. Not only that, but a more accurate calculation leaving out girls, who are more numerous at denominational schools, leads to the conclusion that the latter have a less fortunate 'influence' on delinquency than the State schools.

In a third phase, Lapie attempted to analyse the correlations between school, social ambition and criminality. According to opponents of the State schools, the increase in crime could be attributed to the thwarted ambitions of young people, a frustration largely fostered by the schools. Lapie's answer to this is that the delinquents' failure at school could have left them with no illusions as to their future. It is not, he adds, frustration, but educational and occupational instability which characterise these delinquents. The number of unstable subjects in this particular group is four-and-a-half times greater than in the group which was the object of his study on choice of occupation discussed below.

According to Lapie, educational instability, which is a probable determinant of occupational instability, can be explained by material poverty. In fact, outside the 20 per cent of families who are guaranteed the economic minimum, the remainder is composed of unqualified working-class families faced with chronic unemployment, or the *Lumpenproletariat* living at the limits of legality or in open illegality. Absenteeism from school can be quite simply explained by the fact that these children are needed to give economic assistance to their parents.

Moreover, careful observation of the families of these delinquents reveals that free union was not, as had been wrongfully claimed, the source of the problem,[14] since in this respect there was no difference between the delinquent population studied and the population as a whole, but that the incidence of broken homes is higher amongst such families. More than 50 per cent of young delinquents come from incomplete families. Lapie's explanation of juvenile delinquency here is based on the concept of social disorganisation.

Economic structure, school and social change: outline of a theory of mobility

Of all of Lapie's psychological and sociological research, the most original and the most relevant to modern times is, without doubt, the study of social morphology entitled 'Les Effets sociaux de l'école', published in *La Revue scientifique* in 1904.[15] Lapie begins his study of the problem of the distribution of people in the occupational structure by a detailed critique of the two methods used at the time. The first consisted in asking pupils if they would like to go into the same occupation as their mother or father. For example, Lefèvre, professor in educational science at the faculty of arts in the University of Lille, concluded from a questionnaire sent to 37,000 pupils in the intermediate classes of primary schools in the North[16] that two thirds of boys wanted to do the same job as their father and three quarters of girls wanted to do the same job as their mother.

The second method consisted in comparing the father's occupation with the one that the son went into straight after school and noting the variations in the total number of people in each occupation. Lapie underlined the inadequacies of this method by analysing a report by René Leblanc (1901), containing a statistical breakdown of pupils from higher primary schools in all the departments except the Seine and Algeria for the years 1889–99 and comparing the fathers' occupations with those of the sons. Amongst other things, Leblanc (1901: 124) arrived at two conclusions: firstly, 'higher primary education tends to direct working-class children towards more menial jobs or towards primary school teaching'; secondly, the difference between gains and losses to the three economic sectors, agriculture, commerce and industry, tends essentially to be to the detriment of the first. Lapie (1923: 117–18) contests this kind of interpretation:

[14] This thesis – as also the thesis concerning the relationship between schooling, frustration and crime – was maintained in particular by some members of the Société d'Economie Sociale, who were the successors of Le Play.

[15] Reproduced under another title in Lapie 1923.

[16] All Lapie's references are disarmingly laconic. The use of precise references to the articles and works under discussion was rare at the beginning of the century. This usually causes much fruitless searching before finding the reference text necessary for a careful examination of the argument of the author one is studying. The article Lapie is referring to is by Lefèvre 1900.

Mohamed Cherkaoui

Certainly, we are told how many farmers each generation contains, how many industrialists, tradesmen and civil servants, but we are not told, for example, if the 6,824 farmers of the second generation are all sons of farmers ... Although the equality of the numbers might suggest it, it is not likely that all the boys who went into industry had fathers who were also in industry. Statistics may make us believe that movement is in one direction whereas in reality it is in the opposite direction ... It is impossible to grasp the social reality behind this kind of statistic.

In other words, this second method may well show structural mobility from one generation to the next in so far as that can be read from marginal cases, but it tells us nothing at all about overall mobility and the complex phenomena of occupational variation. Lapie's problem is not to analyse the effects of school on changes in occupational structure but rather to measure the influence of educational level on overall mobility.

On the basis of these clearly formulated requirements, Lapie strives to define a new method which will account for the jobs actually done by individuals and not for their aspirations. But he also asks to what extent the initial choice is definitive or provisional, given the increased frequency with which individuals change jobs during their lifetime. As a result, one should not restrict oneself to noting job distribution at school-leaving age, but also take into account any changes that may have taken place after ten years.

Given the inadequacy of available means and the material difficulties

Table 1 *Comparative occupational distribution of parents and the pupils leaving a given school between 1872 and 1893 (taken from Lapie, 1923, p. 121)*

	Occupation		
	Parents	Children	
Viticulture	323	271	−52
Wine production	63	118	+55
Food	49	35	−14
Clothing	27	27	=
Building	84	84	=
Transport	28	28	=
Luxury goods	11	12	+1
Civil service and liberal professions	31	34	+3
Domestic	22	3	−19
Occupation unknown	53	45	
Parents died before children reached school age	31		
Further study		48	
Deceased before choosing an occupation		17	
	722	722	

involved in collecting this kind of longitudinal data, Lapie restricts his survey to 722 school-leavers between 1872 and 1893 in a commune in the department of the Marne, in the heart of the Champagne vineyards. He begins by applying the analytical technique commonly used to calculate demographic movements.

What can be learnt from Table 1? It would seem that school deflects pupils from the agricultural profession towards industry, since there is a drop of almost 16 per cent in wine growing and an increase of 87 per cent in wine production. But Lapie points out that this kind of calculation is misleading, since, out of the 323 sons of wine growers, 8 died, 21 went on to further study, and 55 chose not to go into the same job as their father. Moreover, there were 32 new recruits to agriculture. What is needed, then, is a new technique which more adequately records demographic movements: such is the origin of the mobility tables, an example of which is given from Lapie's article (See Table 2).

The originality of this discovery should be underlined: Lapie was the inventor of the tables of social mobility, as can be shown from a study of all research in any way connected with jobs and mobility undertaken in France or anywhere else.[17] In this respect, we may draw on the first global study of social mobility, *Social and Cultural Mobility*, in which Sorokin (1927) attempts to synthesise all the work done on the problem of vertical mobility in industrial societies. His intentionally exhaustive bibliographical research takes him back to the beginning of the century. The oldest study, with which Lapie was certainly acquainted, was due to an initiative of the members of the Société de Sociologie in Paris. The way in which the subject was approached, the hesitation in defining it, and the outline of the solution put forward by the sociologists in this Société over three meetings enable us to appreciate more clearly Lapie's contribution to the study of the problem of social mobility.

The three meetings were devoted to the question of occupational heredity. What is meant by this term? Is it a case of heredity of skills, in the genetic sense of the term as René Worms (1900) maintains, or simply a continuity due to economic and psycho-sociological causes, as other members of the Société believed? Are we to adopt the nomenclature used by the census and shall we classify occupations according to 'the utilitarian nature of their activity', in

[17] Lapie (1911) was to publish a paper entitled 'L'Ecole et la société' which reproduced the main data and hypotheses of the 1904 article which he corroborated from two other studies: the first was written by A Binet (1909) and A. Limousin ('La Cote de moralité à l'école primaire'). The second was by a primary school teacher, F. Maumy, who published his results in a pamphlet entitled 'Une Ecole rurale pendant un demi-siècle (1850–1900). L'Ecole de St Domer (Creuse)', in Montluçon in 1902. Wishing to compare several mobility tables relating to different school populations, Lapie was obliged to compile for himself the information concerning the occupations of the parents of the children from the school of St Domer, since Maumy's pamphlet did not provide it.

Table 2 Table of inter-generational mobility (reproduced from Lapie, 1923: 136)

Occupation of parents \ Occupation of Children (1st choice)	Landowners	Farming landowners	Farm workers	Wine industry	Food	Clothing	Building	Transport	Luxury goods	Civil Service, clerical and liberal professions	Domestic	Further study	Disappeared before 1st choice	Deceased before 1st choice	Totals
Viti-culture — Landowners	*1*											17			18 ⎱ 323
Farming Landowners		*70*										4		3	79 ⎰
Farm workers		1	*168*	32	4	2	6	1	1	8		6		5	226
Wine industry			2	*43*	1	3	1	2	1	3		3		1	63
Food			2	7	*21*	2	2	6	2	2	1	1			49
Clothing			2	6		*10*			2	3		6	1	1	27
Building			3	10	2	3	*51*			4	1	1	3	1	84
Transport			2	2	1	1	2	*14*	1	2			3		28
Luxury goods			1				1		*5*				4		11
Civil Service, clerical and liberal professions			2	1		2	3	2		*10*		9	2	1	31
Domestic			2	10			2	1		1	*1*	1	2		22
Occupation unknown			9	4	1		6	1		1			28	2	53
Orphans			6	3	5	4	10	1					2	3	31
Totals	1	71 ⎱ 271	199 ⎰	118	35	27	84	28	12	34	3	48	45	17	722

* Figures in italics show the number of children taking up the parental occupation

other words by sector, or according to 'analogy of function between different occupations', such as two engineers working in two different sectors? For the choice of criteria will influence the results of the analysis. Can general laws be derived from the statistical analysis of the determinants of occupational change, such as education, ambition, the kind of job (possibly implying inheritance of property)? Clearly, these discussions are basically centred on the definition of the subject. And even the two surveys carried out by two members of the Société were undertaken simply to illustrate the difficulties involved in a study of inheritance. In the first, Adolphe Coste restricts himself to an analysis of an inventory of 97 addresses in order to show that, according to the classificational criteria chosen, a smaller or greater number of sons will be shown to be doing the same 'job' as their fathers. The second, undertaken by Charles Limousin, comes down to the following observation: out of the 64 people surveyed, 38 do the same job as their father or mother, 28 do a different job, and 4 changed from the same job to a different one. No details are given on the kind of people surveyed and no analytical method is proposed.

According to Sorokin (1927), we have to wait for the demographic works of Chessa (1912) and Gini (1912) – both after the work of Lapie – to find a clear exposition of some of the problems of mobility between generations and a construction of mobility tables. The conclusion is that, in every respect, Lapie's work is innovatory: theoretically, as we have already seen, in that it formulates in particular an entirely new problematic of the distinction between the two types of mobility and their causes, and methodologically in that it constructs an index of heredity and an analytical tool, namely the mobility table, and proposes a way of reading it that is adequate to the problems of the relationships between school and transformation of occupational structure, and in particular to the rural exodus.

Let us now come back to the analysis of individual movements to test the hypothesis that school deflects pupils away from agricultural work. In actual fact, we observe that all the occupations suffer losses from one generation to the next. To measure these, Lapie constructs an index of immobility or heredity which is equal to the ratio of the sum of sons doing the same job as their father to the total number of fathers. In the example given, the overall index is equal to 0.60. If we base ourselves on the value of this index, which is equal to 0.74 for agriculture, we can conclude that the hypothesis that school deflects children away from agriculture is false. The relative immobility of the agricultural classes can be explained by their status as landowners. But the fact remains that it is the only social category not increasing in size. Is school to blame for this, as René Leblanc suggested (1901: 121)? Ideally, an answer to the problem of the effect of school on occupational change should be based on a comparison (which cannot be

Mohamed Cherkaoui

made) between two communes with an identical socio-economic structure but of which only one would have a school.

According to Lapie, there is an indirect method which would involve an individual study of all those who have left agriculture. If the total number of wine growers is divided into three classes according to size of farm and work (non-farming landowner, farming landowner, farm labourer), we find that 53 out of 55 who leave farming come from wine-growing families owning less than 2½ acres and having, as a result, to work for somebody else. The two other cases were due to physical incapacity. All the rest followed in their father's footsteps. Such a result surely justifies an explanation by purely economic causes. The same kind of explanation can be applied to the new recruits to agriculture, all of whom come from families with an even lower social status and for whom the move to wine growing represents the first step up in the social ladder.

Lapie also bases his conclusions on a longitudinal study of complete and parallel statistical series concerning produce per acre of vine and the number of sons leaving wine growing. He finds a strong correlation between mobility and price fluctuations. In other words, schooling can in no way be considered a cause of what, today, we understand by structural mobility. The conclusion is the same no matter what methodology is chosen.

Lapie takes the analysis further by studying those individuals who, after the first study, stayed on at school (higher primary or secondary education). This means that he studies the relationships between the variables (social category of the father, level of education and son's occupation) at two different points of time. Does the fact of staying on at school deflect the child from doing the same job as his father? In actual fact, 90 per cent of the sons of wine growers who stayed in education beyond primary school did go into the same job as their fathers. All of them came from landowning families, for the most part not farming the land themselves. In other words, the same economic explanation of mobility applies.

The longitudinal study also reveals that of the 34 individuals who, after primary school, joined what Lapie calls the 'bureaucratic army', only 25, or 74 per cent, were in the same job ten years later. The reason, according to Lapie (1923: 144–5), is that a period of service in the bureaucracy

is often the equivalent, for lower-class children, of secondary education for middle-class children. Many rich people send their children to college without the slightest intention of preparing them for the administrative or 'liberal' professions. They simply acquire an education while waiting for the time when they will be old enough to manage the land or the business. In the same way, lower-class children go to work in the town hall or the tax office, for a bailiff or tradesman, until the time when they are able to choose a firm career.

The observation that out of the 18 individuals who, after post-primary school education, went into the liberal professions or the civil service, only 4 came from poor families and had to depend on grants to make their way, leads Lapie to reflect on the social policy of equality of opportunity in education and the waste of intelligence and talent.

Half a century later, this theme was to become the main argument of the social and educational reformers and a subject of study for the sociologists. But the conclusions on social policy suggested by Lapie's empirical research were to remain a dead letter for half a century. On this point, as on others, Lapie was to remain, in France at least, ahead of his time.

References

Avanzini, G. 1970. *Alfred Binet et la pédagogie scientifique: la contribution de Binet à l'élaboration d'une pédagogie scientifique*. Paris: Vrin.
Binet, A. 1900. 'Revue générale sur la pédagogie expérimentale en France', *Année psychologique*, vol. 6, pp. 594–606.
    1909. 'Ce que vaut l'école primaire comme préparation à la vie', *Bulletin de la société libre pour l'étude psychologique de l'enfant*, April–May.
Buisson, F. 1911. *Nouveau dictionnaire de pédagogie et d'instruction primaire*. Paris: Hachette.
Cherkaoui, M. 1976. 'Socialisation et conflit: les systèmes éducatifs et leur histoire selon Durkheim', *Revue française de sociologie*, vol. 17, no. 2, pp. 197–213.
    1977. 'Two Theories of Change in Educational Systems', *Harvard Educational Review*, vol. 17, no. 4, pp. 556–67.
    1978. 'Système social et savoir scolaire: les enjeux politiques de la distribution des connaissances selon Durkheim', *Revue française de science politique*, vol. 28, no. 2, pp. 313–48.
    1980. 'Consensus or Conflict? Return to Durkheim's Proteiform Theory', *Theory and Society*, vol. 8.
Chessa, F. 1912. *Trasmissione ereditaria dei professioni*. Turin: Fratelli Bocca.
Durkheim, E. 1922. *Education et sociologie*. Paris: Presses Universitaires de France.
Gini, C. 1912. *I Fattori demografici dell'evoluzione delle nazioni*. Turin: Fratelli Bocca.
Lapie, P. 1898. *Civilisations tunisiennes. Musulmans, Israélites, Européens. Etude de psychologie sociale*. Paris: Alcan.
    1899. *La Justice par l'Etat. Etude de morale sociale*. Paris: Alcan.
    1902. Le Hiérarchie des professions, *La Revue de Paris*, pp. 390–416.
    1902. *Pour la raison*. Paris: Cornely.
    1904. 'Les Effets sociaux de l'école', *La Revue scientifique*, pp. 6–12, 42–6, (reproduced in Lapie 1923).
    1908. *La Femme dans la famille*. Paris: Doin.
    1911. 'L'Ecole et la société, *Année psychologique*, vol. 17, pp. 80–96.
    1923. *L'Ecole et les écoliers*. Paris: Alcan.
    1926. *Pédagogie française*. Paris: Alcan.
Lapie P.O. 1937. *Paul Lapie. Une vie. Une oeuvre*. Paris: Sudel.
Laubier, R. 1925. *Année sociologique*, p. 216.
Leblanc, R. 1901. *Rapport – classe I. Education de l'enfant – Enseignement primaire – Enseignement des adultes*. Paris: Imprimerie Nationale.

Mohamed Cherkaoui

Lefèvre, G. 1900. 'Une Enquête pédagogique dans le cours moyen des écoles primaires du Nord', *Revue Pédagogique*, vol. 36, pp. 4–26.

Marion, H. 1889. 'Le Mouvement des idées pédagogiques en France depuis 1870', *Recueil des monographies pédagogiques publiées à l'occasion de l'exposition universelle de 1889*, vol. 1, pp. 3–83. Paris: Imprimerie Nationale.

Mauss, M. 1927. 'Divisions et proportions des divisions de la sociologie', *Année sociologique*, new series, vol. 2, pp. 98–176.

Pelisson, M. 1911a. 'Les Universités populaires', in Buisson 1911.

1911b. 'Extension universitaire', in Buisson 1911.

Sorokin, P. 1927. *Social and Cultural Mobility*. New York: The Free Press, 2nd edition, 1959.

Wolf, T. 1973. *Alfred Binet*. Chicago: The University of Chicago Press.

Worms, R. 1900. *Revue internationale de sociologie*, pp. 196–207, 370–5, 443–54, 519–27.

10. Durkheimian sociology versus philosophical rationalism: the case of Célestin Bouglé

W. PAUL VOGT

During his lifetime, Célestin Bouglé was amongst the best known, influential, and academically successful members of the Durkheimian group. An early adherent of what he termed 'the Bordeaux school', Bouglé supported its cause for four decades, both through his expositions of Durkheimian doctrine[1] and in his administrative career. By the interwar years, his writings had won him wide recognition as one of the main figures in modern French thought. J. Benrubi (1933) included Bouglé in his account of the 'sources and currents' of French philosophy, while Paul Nizan (1932) vilified him as one of the bourgeoisie's academic 'guard dogs'. In short, Bouglé was one of the most important members of the Durkheimian team and one of the most famous. Yet Bouglé's relationship to 'sociologism' was always somewhat ambivalent, and he several times dissented from some of Durkheim's central methodological doctrines. Furthermore, Bouglé, one of the best-known university scholars of his time, is today largely forgotten. These two features of his work – that it is not widely known and that it was sometimes critical of, and usually ambivalent towards, Durkheimian methodology – are related. They are the central theme of this essay.

Bouglé was born in Saint-Brieuc (Côtes-du-Nord) in 1870. After the death of his father, he went to Paris in 1884 to attend the Collège Rollin and the Lycée Henri IV where he successfully prepared for the entrance examination to the Ecole Normale Supérieure (entering the class of 1890). After having been ranked first in the philosophy *agrégation* of 1893, he obtained a scholarship for work in Germany, where he studied the teachings of Simmel, von Jhering, Wagner, and Lazarus. These studies appear to have greatly influenced the course of his thought and were the subject of his first book (Bouglé 1896), written while he was professor of philosophy at the Lycée of Saint-Brieuc. In 1898, he became Maître de conférences at the faculty of letters at Montpellier. In 1899, he obtained the doctorate for his work on the

[1] The two most important are: *Qu'est-ce que la sociologie?* (1907) and *Bilan de la sociologie française contemporaine* (1935).

W. Paul Vogt

social origins of egalitarianism. In 1900, he moved to the faculty of letters at Toulouse and, in 1908, to the Sorbonne (Weisz article, this volume).

Although he continued to publish at a remarkable rate after World War I, his interests increasingly turned from research to academic administration. He was founder and director of the Centre de Documentation Sociale, adjunct director (1927–35) and then director (1935–40) of the Ecole Normale Supérieure. Throughout these years he maintained an active involvement in national politics. He was one of the earliest adherents of the Ligue des Droits de l'Homme formed during the Dreyfus Affair, and he was vice-president of that organisation from 1911 to 1924. As a member of the Radical and Radical-Socialist Party, he ran, unsuccessfully, for a seat in the Chamber of Deputies in 1901, 1906, 1914, and 1924. He was a regular contributor to the *Dépêche de Toulouse*, and several of his books were collections of lectures delivered to various social and political action groups.[2] He was apparently a powerful orator and a welcome and frequent guest at political meetings.

There are several probable reasons for the relative obscurity today of a man who was so eminent only forty years ago. Bouglé was uncommonly eclectic,[3] too eclectic to be an unqualified adherent of the Durkheimian sociological consensus. He could appreciatively cite Simmel, Tönnies, Spencer, Tarde, and Durkheim – all in the same article. Given the breadth of his appreciations, it is not surprising that, while he believed that Durkheimian sociology was extraordinarily important and while he always remained associated with the school, he also frequently maintained that sociology had to be supplemented, often by doctrines most other Durkheimians considered to be at best without sociological interest.[4] In some ways, Bouglé was too 'old fashioned', too much a generalist and synthesiser in an age that increasingly remembered and rewarded specialists. He may also have been something of a sociological outsider because he wrote with uncommon grace and charm at a time when 'literary' fashions in scholarly writing were coming under attack. For whatever reasons, he seemed unwilling to follow either of the two main Durkheimian routes to academic and scientific respectability: (1) developing the special linguistic competencies needed to study 'primitive' societies in the manner of Mauss and Granet; (2) acquiring the technical skills of the sort used by Halbwachs and Simiand to analyse the statistical regularities of modern social facts.

Bouglé's contribution and his originality, if it can be called that, lay

[2] For example, see Bouglé 1904 and 1923a. On Bouglé's liberalism see Logue 1979. I owe much of the information in this and the preceding paragraph to M. Philippe Besnard and the late Mlle J. Bouglé.

[3] This was perhaps more the case at the end than at the beginning of his career. See, for example, Bouglé 1938b.

[4] See, for example, his very sympathetic analysis of Tarde (Bouglé 1905).

232

elsewhere. While always remaining an advocate of Durkheimianism, he maintained close personal and intellectual ties with the more-or-less neo-Kantian rationalists so important in French academic philosophy at the time. Most of these, like Bouglé, were frequent contributors to the *Revue de métaphysique et de morale*.[5] Bouglé's continued affiliations with philosophy provided the grounding for most of his significant criticisms of Durkheimian sociology. These were usually muted versions of harsher objections to sociological method made by philosophers such as Boutroux, Brunschvicg, Lalande, and Parodi. Bouglé disagreed with Durkheim about the relation between theoretical and practical reason, the origins of conceptual categories, the relative independence from social influences of human reason, the importance of 'teleology' (understood as the study of the desires of social actors), and the uses of psychological introspection in sociological explanation.

His understanding of these matters was based in large part on his appreciation of philosophers' rejoinders to sociologism, and that often led him to make important methodological distinctions. But that may also partly explain why his scholarly contributions were comparatively rare during the last two decades of his career. Caught between a philosophical belief in the limits of sociological determinism and a sociological awareness of the weaknesses of an asocial, ahistorical philosophical rationalism, he was unable to contribute significantly to either form of scholarship. Thus, after World War I, he wrote mostly popularisations, texts for students, and histories of social doctrines – in a word, summaries of the work of others. Nonetheless, his writings remain important for understanding the development of Durkheimian sociology. Because Bouglé never quite broke intellectually with philosophy, his work provides an instructive example of what was involved in severing sociology from philosophy, an operation many thought crucial to establish the independence of sociology.

Nearly all of Bouglé's major criticisms of Durkheim can be found in his first book, *Les Sciences sociales en Allemagne* (1896). Although he later modified and moderated some of his criticisms of Durkheim contained in that work, he never fully abandoned any of them. Hence the book merits our careful attention.

Like many promising young *agrégés*, Bouglé won a government scholarship to study in Germany. Assessment of German moral philosophy was clearly an important matter for French academics around the turn of the century, as it was for the educational administrators who provided the funds

---

[5] Between 1894 and 1938, Bouglé published 24 items in it. The average number of articles contributed to that journal by any one author from 1900 through 1939 was 2.7. For an important account of the reasons for the continuation of Durkheimian links with academic philosophy see Karady 1979.

W. Paul Vogt

for travel to Germany. The only open question was which German thinkers were most worthy of study. Bouglé's choices were not widely approved by other members of the Durkheimian group. Marcel Mauss, for instance, contended that Bouglé had chosen poor exemplars, men who were representatives of rather narrow and isolated tendencies in German thought. Mauss (1897) believed that Wundt and Schäffle (that is, scholars studied by Durkheim a decade earlier) would have been better subjects of study. Maurice Halbwachs (1941: 27–9) was also critical. Bouglé, he said, 'was at that time a little intoxicated by all that German philosophy'. The influence of that German philosophy, Halbwachs concluded, explained why Bouglé was 'within the sociological camp, a moralist who retained his sympathy for metaphysical psychology'.

On the basis of his study of German social science and moral philosophy, Bouglé challenged Durkheim in four ways: he rejected the notion of the methodological unity of the social and natural sciences; he denied that social facts could be understood only by an 'external' study of them; he thought that introspection and psychology were fundamental to social science; and he contended that social science was not directly useful for the determination of the ends men ought to pursue.

Bouglé agreed with all Durkheimians that, for a discipline to become scientific, it had to move beyond description to explanation. But, he maintained, the principles of explanation differ according to whether one is studying social or physical phenomena. Physical phenomena repeat themselves ceaselessly. Social phenomena, because they are much more complex, recur with less regularity and are characterised by greater variety. From this dichotomy Bouglé somewhat naively concluded that description is more easily converted into explanation in the physical than the social sciences. In sum, even though the natural and physical sciences have more precise methods, sociologists are wrong in trying to imitate them closely. Method in the social sciences must be different, for 'the most precise and certain procedures do not work equally well for all data' (Bouglé 1896: 36–8, 155–6).

These reflections led Bouglé to assert that Durkheim's desire to copy the methods of natural science was a bit fetishistic. In his attempt to study only exterior, objectively observable signs or indices of social facts, Durkheim had adopted the dubious procedures of mechanism. The exactitude gained in this way was false, for, Bouglé insisted, externally observable things 'do not always carry a true imprint of social phenomena'. That is why the exterior observation of social facts, while simplifying the task of the sociologist, is inadequate: 'it will not take us far if it is not illuminated and guided by interior observation'. Bouglé (1896: 149–50) concluded that Durkheim insisted on the priority of external observation because he confused his methodological convenience with the ontological character of his subject-matter.

234

The introspection Bouglé called for to supplement observation of exterior indices rested on psychology. Here, Bouglé explicitly sided with Tarde and Le Bon against Durkheim, for he believed that the primary need for sociology was a psychological base. This base would be a social not an individual psychology. It would be a psychology of groups or peoples, a *Völkerpsychologie*. Bouglé did not explain the nature of the link between an *individual* scholar's introspection and a *social* psychology. That gap was a major weakness in his methodological alternative to Durkheim's procedures. Despite this vagueness, his general point was plain enough. In his view, Durkheim's major error was desiring to avoid all psychological explanation. This was impossible, for the 'reactions to which the consciences of individuals find themselves yielding, due only to the fact of their association, are clearly psychological phenomena ... Awareness of these particular reactions can lead ... to the idea of a social psychology distinct from individual psychology, but not to the idea of a sociology without psychology' (Bouglé 1896: 18–20, 42, 151–2).

More specifically, Bouglé thought that the kind of psychological data needed was 'teleological' – dealing with people's ends, aspirations, or desires. Most Durkheimians objected to the study of desires, for they believed that it could not yield true causal laws, which were always statements of the determinant relationships of a single cause to a single effect. Bouglé agreed that such was the nature of a causal law in the physical sciences, but insisted that determinant relationships or mechanical laws were simply not possible in the social sciences. While Bouglé conceded that analyses of ends and desires would be very speculative and easily open to abuse, he nonetheless asserted that they must be undertaken. Shunning all 'metaphysical' procedures and having strictly limited ambitions, his teleology would be 'scientific'. It would offer neither the certitude possible in the natural sciences nor sufficient conditions of understanding, but, he thought, it would allow sociology to escape a sterile mechanism.

In fact, Bouglé maintained, as Tarde (1895) had, that even Durkheim, despite himself, was forced to resort to teleological explanation. When Durkheim said that the increasing volume and density of societies produced the division of labour by stimulating 'the struggle for life' and making the satisfaction of needs more difficult, he had introduced a teleological element into his explanation. And, without that element, Durkheim would have had no explanation at all: 'bring together as many men as you like; make their societies as voluminous and as dense as possible: if they do not wish to live, and to live well, the division of labour will never be produced "of itself"'. Taken alone, neither social volume and density nor the desire to satisfy needs were sufficient explanations; but together, Bouglé (1896: 154–5) concluded, they could provide a satisfactory account of social phenomena.

The final objection Bouglé made to Durkheim's works concerned the role of social science in the determination of the proper ends of, and the useful means for, moral life. Durkheim had maintained that, science, by enabling us to anticipate the course of socio-moral development, would direct us toward the ends we ought to pursue. Foreseeing those developments, we would desire them, and we would have scientific grounds for making them our ends. The means helpful to attain those ends, however, were in the realm of the practical social and political arts; they were not the province of the theoretical sciences. Bouglé reversed this formula, and in so doing sounded more like Weber than Durkheim. Science, he held, could determine what ends were in fact dominant in a given society, but it could not attribute any value to them. And when, as is inevitably the case, ends are chosen extra-scientifically, science could then 'indicate to us the proper means for realising them'. The only systematic way to evaluate our moral *ends*, the only way these could be more than the result of our whims, would be to study morals metaphysically. Science, he averred, 'only gives us the matter of morality. From where are we to take its form? If we want final criteria for good and evil other than our personal feelings, must we not ask for them from metaphysics?' (Bouglé 1896: 170–2.)

While the subject of *Les Sciences sociales en Allemagne* naturally leads one to note the German inspiration of much of Bouglé's methodological critique, it is important also to recognise that there were more than ample French sources from which Bouglé could have drawn, and almost certainly did draw, some of his conclusions. Emile Boutroux had long insisted on the limits of natural science, there was no more fierce adherent of a psychological approach to sociology than Gabriel Tarde, and André Lalande had concluded that an autonomous 'constituent reason' was the final arbiter in moral valuation. Among these and the many other sources that could be cited, probably the most important figure for Bouglé was his friend Dominique Parodi. Parodi's main concern was the 'anti-intellectualism' he believed to be characteristic of most significant schools of French thought in the years after 1890, including Durkheimian sociology, which Parodi believed was guilty of scholarly anti-intellectualism through its attempt to explain the mental by the social. Parodi (1907 and 1919), like many other rationalists critical of Durkheim, maintained that any system of explanation not assuming the independent and self-justifying role of the rational intellect thereby undermined its own premises. Members of the dominant school of French academic philosophy, in short, argued that Durkheimian sociology was conceptually flawed in a very basic way, and Bouglé was always somewhat swayed by this argument.[6]

One must be careful not to overemphasise the importance of Bouglé's disagreements with Durkheim at this stage. The differences between them

[6] See Bouglé 1938a for his assessment of Parodi, Boutroux, and Lalande.

were real, and Bouglé persisted in stressing them in several of his subsequent writings; but, upon closer examination, they sometimes seem more matters of emphasis than of fundamental principle. At least, they were not great enough to prevent Bouglé from being a contributing editor, from the first volume, to *L'Année sociologique* (chapter 1, this volume).

The basis of the collaboration between the two sociologists was in part established by Durkheim's letter to Bouglé of 14 December 1895 (see this volume). Bouglé had sent Durkheim a copy of *Les Sciences sociales en Allemagne*. Durkheim, after thanking Bouglé for the book and for 'the great courtesy of your very interesting discussion', firmly indicated that he was 'desirous of diminishing the distance that separates us, or appears to separate us' and that he thought it would be quite possible to do so.[7]

Bouglé apparently accepted the validity of some of the comments Durkheim went on to make in his effort to 'diminish the distance' between them. Three years later, in his doctoral thesis, Bouglé admitted that certain differences separated him from Durkheim, but he added that he suspected that these were differences of expression rather than of thought (Bouglé 1899: 20). That seems accurate, for when Bouglé actually applied the rules of method outlined in *Les Sciences sociales en Allemagne* to his study of egalitarianism, the differences between his and Durkheim's methods were not very striking. Bouglé repeatedly said that after demonstrating 'historically' the constant conjunction of two phenomena, one then needs to verify 'psychologically' and 'deductively' that the two are causally related, that the conjunction is not a mere coincidence (Bouglé 1899: 88–9, 125). Other than the somewhat strident terms in which he put the second of these two methodological steps (sociology 'will be deductivist or it will not be'), his procedure seems quite routine. It adds up to saying that, after we have established a correlation, we ought to give it some thought so as to be sure that it is reasonable to posit a causal connection between the correlated phenomena. It is hard to see why Durkheim, or anyone else, would object to that method.

While it is true that every one of the points made in *Les Sciences sociales en Allemagne* as rejoinders to Durkheim were repeated in *Les Idées égalitaires*, they were not offered as criticisms of Durkheim in the latter work, and they had a less central place in the exposition. Indirect evidence of this change of tone and emphasis is to be had by looking at some of the objections raised by philosophers on Bouglé's examination jury. A central issue that had separated Bouglé and Durkheim, and would do so again, was Bouglé's according greater importance to the independent force of rational thought in

---

[7] This letter was printed in Durkheim 1976: 166–7. Other letters from Durkheim to Bouglé printed there, plus those in Durkheim (1975), give ample evidence of the close collaboration between the two sociologists.

his explanations of the actions of his subjects. But several members of the jury chided Bouglé, as they had Durkheim, for slighting the importance of rationality as a cause of social phenomena: 'you omit too much of that necessary intermediary between social causes and the success of egalitarian ideas – rationalism' (A. Croiset); 'the egalitarian idea proceeds from the human soul, not from social forms' (E. Boutroux); 'you attribute too much importance to social forms' (H. Michel); and G. Séailles even accused Bouglé of mechanism on grounds similar to those Bouglé had used earlier to charge Durkheim with the same fault (Bouglé, *et al.* 1900: 13–8).

In the nine years between his doctoral examination and the completion of his *Essais sur le régime des castes* (1908) Bouglé published little indicating strong divergences from or differences with the Durkheimian school. Decades later, when Halbwachs (1941) assessed Bouglé's works and when Bouglé (1935) discussed his own contributions to contemporary sociology, the books on egalitarian ideas and the caste system were the two considered most worthy of mention. Both were in large part essays in what would come to be called the sociology of knowledge and, as such, accorded well with Bouglé's main interest: the relation of ideas to social structures and social action.

The central problem in *Les Idées égalitaires* was determining the sort of social conditions that influenced the appearance of and the diffusion of egalitarian thought: 'among the social forms that we can differentiate, which are those that favour the expansion of egalitarianism, such that their mere presence in a country or an era would furnish a partial explanation for the progress egalitarian ideas made' in that country and era? If he could answer this question, Bouglé contended, that would constitute a demonstration of its analytical power (Bouglé 1899: 19).

Democratic ideas of the sort that Bouglé studied were, he concluded, most widespread in the societies of modern Western Europe and North America, for 'the social forms particular to Western civilisation are also those most favourable to the success of egalitarian ideas'. The dominant 'morphological' characteristics of those societies, in short, were conducive to the growth and diffusion of egalitarianism (Bouglé 1899: 237). Bouglé divided the features of Occidental civilisation leading to the flourishing of egalitarian ideas into three general categories: (1) a great increase in 'dynamic density', which resulted in the multiplication of social contacts among members of these societies; (2) a similarly large growth of social 'complexity', which enabled individuals to belong simultaneously to many social groups or 'circles'; (3) a significant degree of social 'unification', which through developments like an increase in the power of the State, insured equality before the law for the entire population. Each of these morphological factors was composed of several subsidiary developments, and each of them encouraged the extension of the other two. Together they assured the triumph of egalitarianism.[8]

Of more general interest is Bouglé's conception of the proper method for conducting a sociological study of ideas and of the field open to such a study. Some sorts of ideas, he believed, were more open to sociological explanation than others, and some types of questions about the ideas were more readily than others answered by recourse to sociological procedures. This can best be represented schematically.

KINDS OF IDEAS:

aesthetic → scientific → industrial → social

KINDS OF QUESTIONS ABOUT THE IDEAS:

| were they correct or justified? | → | why were they invented or discovered? | → | what caused their diffusion? |

As one moves from the left to the right of either spectrum, sociological explanation becomes both easier and more appropriate. Thus, for example, social ideas, 'which allude to the organisation of the society itself', are more closely bound to, and hence explicable by, social conditions than are scientific ideas; it is easier to give a sociological account of the spread of an idea than of its discovery, and so on. In *Les Idées égalitaires*, Bouglé concentrated most heavily on the *diffusion* of *social* ideas, but he excluded on principle no one of the 'kinds of ideas' and only one of the 'kinds of questions' about them: sociology could not decide, he concluded, whether an idea was correct, whether an individual or a society was justified in believing it.[9]

While it is clear from Bouglé's political activities and from many of his other writings that he advocated egalitarianism as well as studied it, he steadfastly insisted that science could not justify it or prove it to be an end one ought to strive to attain. He maintained that 'if egalitarianism seems clearly today to be the prime mover of our civilisation, that is because it is its natural product'. Had he followed Durkheim here, Bouglé could have concluded

---

[8] Bouglé 1899: second part. The notion of 'density' was based heavily on Durkheim's writings, that of 'complication' on Simmel's. Bouglé's conclusions about causation clash with Durkheim's dictum that a single effect is always to be explained by a single cause. Bouglé postulated a multiplicity of causes leading to a single effect (egalitarian ideas) and insisted that to do otherwise would be to offer 'as their sufficient cause one of their many conditions' (p. 246). This 'error' he often called *Einseitigkeit*.

[9] Bouglé 1899: 78–80. While Bouglé did not systematically treat questions of method in the sociology of knowledge, this schema (the terms of which I have supplied in part) is a faithful representation of his conclusions. For a fuller treatment of Durkheimian work in the sociology of knowledge see Vogt 1979.

that this was a condition sufficient to justify egalitarianism. But he did not. Rather he averred that 'consciousness retains the ability to scorn that which science explains. If might does not make right, the grounds of the value of a tendency remain distinct from the conditions of its success. That is why knowledge of the social forms that contribute to the progress of egalitarianism prohibit no one from making an effort to stem it.' But that effort would have to be immense. Because the morphological traits supporting the ideas were so deeply ingrained in modern Western societies, one would have to alter radically, perhaps even destroy, those societies in order to check the advance of democracy (Bouglé 1899: 248–50). This conclusion, if not a justification for egalitarianism, is obviously a persuasive argument in its favour.

One possible objection to his procedures that Bouglé took great care to answer proleptically was what he called the 'ideological explanation'. It might be said, and members of his examination jury did say it, that his sociological explanation could be turned around. The cause of the concomitance of egalitarian ideas and the social forms he described would then be that the ideas produced the forms. If that were so, the social forms would be only the necessary *effect* of egalitarian ideas. In reply, Bouglé admitted that it was often difficult to distinguish cause and effect, that concomitance was easier to demonstrate than anteriority. Often, causally linked phenomena 'react incessantly on one another and become by turns, through a sort of perpetual exchange of roles, cause and effect of one another'. But in this case, Bouglé affirmed, the very massiveness and pervasiveness of the social forms make it inconceivable that they could have been produced by ideas alone. Thus the alternative is between a sociological explanation and no explanation at all. The ideological explanation resulted only in 'the adoration of a mystery' – the mystery of the *sui generis* workings of Reason (Bouglé 1899: 241–4, 80).

Similar considerations shaped the writing of Bouglé's study of the dominance of the caste system in India. This work enabled him to construct a 'natural experiment' – to test comparatively the validity of the conclusions he had reached in *Les Idées égalitaires*. Indian society displayed morphological characteristics exactly opposite to those he had used to explain egalitarianism: it had a low level of dynamic density because social circles did not overlap and because there was no centralisation or social unity. This resulted in inequality before the law, in different legal sanctions for members of different socio-religious groups.

Essais sur le régime des castes is Bouglé's most characteristically Durkheimian work. The form and content of his exposition closely parallels that of other Durkheimian studies of non-Western societies. It is also the only one of Bouglé's books widely regarded as significant by modern specialists.[10] Yet there is one major difference. Unlike Durkheim, Granet, Mauss, and many other Durkheimians, Bouglé found little to admire in the non-Western society he studied. He could see no practices which, suitably updated, could serve as guides to modern man.[11] Rather, he was plainly horrified by the caste system. This can best be seen in the concluding essay on 'Literature', which, like the whole of *Les Idées égalitaires*, was an essay in the sociology of knowledge.

If the caste system could be shown to have shaped even Hindu literature, Bouglé thought, his theses about its overwhelming influence in Indian society would 'receive a final and striking confirmation'. The confirmation would be striking because literary styles were aesthetic ideals and practices (on the far left of the above spectrum of 'kinds of ideas'), which were often too individual to be easily analysed with sociological methods: 'Above all, when it is a question of the "superstructure" of a civilisation, it is only too clear that social forms are not alone at work. Forces of all sorts converge with them, the mixed action of which remains so mysterious that it is perforce well to retain, here more than elsewhere, the margin of the inexplicable' (Bouglé 1908a: 190–1).

But the crushing, oppressive force of the caste system was so great that it could decisively mould even aesthetic life. The roots of the religiously inspired caste system were so deeply sunk into Indian society that all literature was sacred. There was no 'profane literature' in the land of the Brahmans. All literature was written by and for the initiated and was, consequently, burdened with an excessive formalism. Its authors were impelled by a desire to obscure rather than to clarify, to bedazzle rather than to communicate. It was characterised by enigmatic formulations and 'sibylline word games'. Why was this so? Because, in short, it served the self-interested motives of the members of the Brahmanic elite who wrote it. The priestly caste wishes 'to defend ... its privileges'. The 'bizarre complications' of the Veda were 'more-or-less intentional: esoterism served the cause of those priestly families in the process of surrounding themselves with the walls of caste'. In sum, Hindu literature was obscure and formalistic because of the opportunism of those born into the intellectual caste who used it to conserve their dominance (Bouglé 1908a: 196, 200, 212).

These conclusions are really very surprising. They involve a major shift in Bouglé's method for the sociology of knowledge. In *Les Idées égalitaires* theories were explained in terms of their function as an integral part of Western civilisation and were related to morphological facts. But here, aesthetic works are 'unmasked' as part of the tactics of a self-serving ruling

[10] See Louis Dumont's preface to the fourth edition (Paris 1969) and D. F. Pocock's introduction to the English translation (London 1971).
[11] For a discussion of this point see Vogt 1976.

W. Paul Vogt

class. Bouglé's assessment is especially striking because he had in an earlier chapter expressly warned against 'attributing the creation of the caste system to the interested calculations, the artifices, the conspiracy of the Brahmans' (Bouglé 1908a: 65). Only his profound repugnance for this society, for this quintessence of inequality, can explain his methodological *volte face*.

Between the publication of *Les Idées égalitaires* and *Essais sur le régime des castes*, Bouglé wrote his longest and in many ways his most powerfully argued book. In it, his political values, his passion for a certain kind of equality stand out. His work on biology's challenge to democracy (1903) was a refutation of the pseudo-science of various sorts of political reactionaries, especially those who buttressed their anti-egalitarian values with biological analogies. With the possible exceptions of his friends Paul Lapie and Dominique Parodi, Bouglé devoted more effort than any other scholar associated with the Durkheimian group to demolishing the arguments of the racists in scientific clothing who wrote much of what passed for social science at the time.

La Démocratie devant la science was not strictly speaking a sociological study. An interesting study could have been written (and still could be) about the social origins of biologism in social thought. Bouglé did not write it. He neither analysed the social forms which could account for the immense popularity of pseudo-scientific books on biological sociology nor attempted to unmask the self-interested motives of those who wrote them. He simply sought to refute their arguments. His book had an unambiguously political purpose: to safeguard 'democratic ideas ... from the verdict of a so-called "science"' (Bouglé 1923b: vii).

Bouglé set out to combat a three-headed biological enemy of democracy: 'anthropo-sociology' stressing the inheritance of traits; organismic theories relying on the concept of differentiation of species; and Social Darwinism emphasising the competition amongst organisms. Each of these three – differentiation, heredity, and competition – had been used as descriptive and prescriptive models for human societies. Bouglé rejected each in turn. His task was essentially negative. In destroying the validity of biological sociology, he felt, he would not be directly proving the justice of democratic theories, but he could perhaps succeed in freeing social thought from its 'naturalist obsession'.

The conclusion Bouglé drew was relatively simple: the biological and social worlds are different orders of being; hence, laws derived from one cannot accurately be applied to the other. Two general considerations were more important in leading him to this conclusion. First, he contended, the real method of the biological sociologists was *not* to misapply to human behaviour concepts drawn from the study of other species. Rather it was to squeeze the study of other species into categories derived from prejudicial views of human life, claiming all the while that 'science' had thereby justified these prejudices. Second, Bouglé contended, Darwinian biology, or any other kind, is incapable of yielding objective criteria of progress for animal populations. Thus it cannot do so for human societies. Progress is an evaluative, not a scientific, notion: 'value judgements ... that biological observation can neither confirm or quash' are crucial to all discussions of progress. In short, based on his appreciation for the distinctness of the social realm and even more on his insistence on the differing methods of explanation appropriate for natural science, social science, and moral philosophy, Bouglé rejected all forms of biological sociology, even those supporting his own political beliefs. It is worth stressing Bouglé's conclusion here, in part because of the continued influence of the 'naturalist obsession'. 'That which stands out most clearly from our research on the lessons of biology is the extreme difficulty man has in "letting nature speak" in order to record its counsel; the counsellor speaks several languages and varies its responses according to the preconceived ideas of its interlocutors.'[12]

The undeniably political purpose of this, Bouglé's longest, book and the fact that he published many others in the same vein provide ample indication that he was at least as interested in defending his conception of democracy as in sociological scholarship. And, in fact, the volume of his strictly sociological writing does begin to decrease by the end of the first decade of the twentieth century. While we need not fully accept Halbwachs's assessment (1941) that, after 1910, Bouglé ceased altogether to contribute to 'our science', it is true that the bulk of Bouglé's most significant sociological work was completed prior to World War I.

Following his book on the caste system, Bouglé published (1908b) one of the few serious Durkheimian analyses of Marxism. In the next four years he wrote, among other things, several articles and a book on Proudhon's sociology (1910b, 1910c, 1912b), another assessment of Darwinism in sociology (1910a), and a discussion of the parallels between Rousseau's thought and socialist theory (1912a). By this time it was already evident that his interests had taken a turn away from sociology toward the history of social theory and the problems of education.[13] Yet, he did introduce, in 1914, one new sociological concept, *polytélisme*, i.e. the multiplicity of ends. With this he once again tried to deal with a problem he had first taken up a quarter-century before: the importance of the ends of human action as a determinant of social life (Bouglé 1914).

World War I, during which Bouglé, like many other French intellectuals,

---

[12] Bouglé 1903: 132–4, 185–6, 228. It is interesting to note that Bouglé had similarly argued against the 'naturalism' implied in studies of primitive societies (1899: 52–3).

[13] In the interwar years, he devoted much time to editing a scholarly edition of Proudhon's complete works. See also Bouglé 1932.

wrote patriotic tracts, undoubtedly accounts in part for the eight-year gap between his first 'remarks on *polytélisme*' and the publication of his book incorporating them. *Leçons de sociologie sur l'évolution des valeurs* (1922) shows how strongly the war influenced his thinking by raising anew for him the issue of the moral unity of French society. Indeed, his pride over the patriotic zeal of French youth during the conflict was a major theme in his writings for several years following the signing of the treaty (Bouglé 1923a). He repeatedly pointed out, for example, that the willingness of French soldiers to sacrifice themselves for a higher, patriotic end showed that laic moral education had not weakened the moral fibre of the nation as advocates of religious moral instruction had predicted. His task in the *Evolution des valeurs* was to explain the sociological conditions of this moral unity.

The inevitable tendency of modern societies, Bouglé maintained, was toward the differentiation of values in the moral realm as it was toward specialisation in the economic. Yet that differentiation did not produce a congeries of disunited, unrelated groups. It was, in fact, the condition of a new, higher sort of moral unity. This was possible because several ends pursued by adherents of different value systems (Catholics, Protestants, and 'free-thinkers', for example) could all be attained by the same means. It was this 'multiplicity of ends that the same means allows one to attain' that Bouglé designated *polytélisme*. However, this same means, because it was used by many different individuals and groups, became in its turn a value or an end. Hence, the major moral duty of the schools was to inculcate respect for such common means, which had become ends. In that way the moral unity of the nation could be forged and maintained. But it would be a moral unity allowing for – no, indeed, requiring respect for a diversity of ends and for individual differences. Thus, Bouglé concluded, it is today possible for 'groups to be less numerous than ideas' because *polytélisme* 'allows individuals inspired by divergent ideas to conjoin their efforts' (Bouglé 1922: 90, 278–9).

These conclusions do not differ widely from those of Durkheim, who also frequently maintained that a higher unity could, in fact had to, grow out of the diversity characteristic of the modern era, as, for example, in his ideas of organic solidarity and the 'cult of the individual'. But there is an important difference between their verdicts and the tones in which they pronounced them. Again and again Durkheim concluded that the morals of modern society were in a state of 'crisis' or at least 'mediocrity'. New forms of unity were to be hoped for. They were not already with us, and this concerned Durkheim greatly. Such worries are conspicuously absent from Bouglé's work. Even after World War I and through the troubled 1930s he remained convinced, at least in his published works, that the happy outcomes he had described were so deeply embedded in the structure of modern societies that there was little cause for the alarm that led Durkheim in *Les Formes élémentaires de la vie religieuse* or Mauss in *Essai sur le don* to hope that modern man would somehow be able to revive part of the spirit of primitive societies and recapture some of their glorious moral unity.

But *Evolution des valeurs* contains a more important, though perhaps related, difference that Bouglé had with Durkheim, and one that shows the full measure of his ambivalence toward Durkheim's most fundamental theories. In his chapters on the 'origins of rational thought' and on the 'social conditions of scientific progress', Bouglé explicitly and repeatedly vacillated between the theses of neo-Kantian rationalism on the one hand and Durkheimian sociologism on the other.

In order to explain how modern scientific and rational thought could have arisen out of the confused magico-religious thinking of primitives, Bouglé asserted, it was necessary to postulate in man 'a certain capacity for precise observation and for reasoning about his observations'. Durkheim and Mauss in their essay 'De quelques formes primitives de classification' (1903) had also postulated some innate mental capacities such as the ability to distinguish left from right and past from present. But these simple abilities of *observation* were quite rudimentary in comparison to the abilities of *reasoning* that Bouglé insisted were necessary for the emergence of science and rationality. Bouglé set severe limits on the sociological account of the origins of concepts and the categories of rationality. No number or intensity of social phenomena could have produced the categories of reason 'if man does not react to his experiences according to certain modes predetermined by his very nature'. That nature was not only something built up by social forces, which always have to exert their influence 'on a certain number of given forms'. Social forces aid in the development of innate capacities. They are not the 'unique creators' of them. In short, society could not have constructed the mental categories if a certain 'embryo of reason' had not been given in the individual (Bouglé 1922: 176, 193–5).

One can hardly over-emphasise the importance of these conclusions. They were, in a word, a summary of the standard rationalist objection to Durkheim; and they were written not by Boutroux, or Brunschvicg, or Lalande, or Parodi, but by one of the best-known members of the Durkheim group. And, unlike Bouglé's earlier criticisms, these cannot be explained away as the exuberance of a young scholar perhaps a little intoxicated by German philosophy. Bouglé's politics played some role in his departure from Durkheim's conclusions. He believed that unless one granted some powers to reason in political thought, a reason independent of social determinism – unless one rejected what he called 'illusionism' – a free, democratic political life was inconceivable (Bouglé 1908b). Whatever the cause, Bouglé ended in what might be called a 'theory of the *yes, but*'. Does one admit, Bouglé

W. Paul Vogt

asks, that there are social determinants of rationality? Yes, but ... Does one therefore conclude that rationality is independent of social forms? Yes, but ...

Bouglé's break with Durkheimian sociology was not sharp. As founder and director of the Centre de Documentation Sociale, he aided the careers of many sociologists and anthropologists whose sociologism was stronger than his own. Throughout the remaining years of his life, he maintained the same delicate balance between two seemingly irreconcilable positions. His continued ambivalence can be seen in two of his last books: *Bilan de la sociologie française contemporaine* (1935) and *Les Maîtres de la philosophie universitaire en France* (1938). There is little need to summarise these two books, for they are mostly summaries – often excellent and instructive summaries, it is true – of the works of others. We need only note here that in them Bouglé expressed considerable agreement with what were to some extent two antagonistic camps in French Academe. In each book, the scholars who were the subject of the other are, as it were, always present in the background murmuring their criticisms.

The central theme of the two books is a phenomenon that Bouglé rightly saw as one of the main divisions in French thought in his lifetime and which he more or less embodied: 'sociologism against rationalism'. Bouglé was a sociologist. He was also a philosophical rationalist, and his rationalism was, as Georges Davy (1967) justly pointed out, 'the key to the oscillations in the degree of warmth of his adhesion to sociology'. During the years spanning Bouglé's academic career, one could not be a fully integrated member of the Durkheimian school without denying the theses of philosophical rationalism. Bouglé would not deny them. But he would not deny sociology either. Hence the ambivalence that to some extent paralysed his scholarly abilities.

References

Benrubi, J. 1933. *Les Sources et les courants de la philosophie française contemporaine*, 2 vols. Paris: Alcan.
Bouglé, C. 1896. *Les Sciences sociales en Allemagne. Les Méthodes actuelles*. Paris: Alcan.
1899. *Les Idées égalitaires. Etude sociologique*. Paris: Alcan.
1903. *La Démocratie devant la science. Etudes critiques sur l'hérédité, la concurrence, et la différenciation*. Paris: Alcan.
1904? (n.d.). *Solidarisme et libéralisme*. Paris: Rieder.
1905. 'Un Sociologue individualiste: Gabriel Tarde', *Revue de Paris*, vol. 3, pp. 294–316.
1907. *Qu'est-ce que la sociologie?* Paris: Alcan.
1908a. *Essais sur le régime des castes*. Paris: Alcan.
1908b. 'Marxisme et sociologie', *Revue de métaphysique et de morale*, vol. 16, pp. 723–50.

1910a. 'Le Darwinisme en sociologie', *Revue de métaphysique et de morale*, vol. 18, pp. 72–92.

1910b. 'La Méthode de Proudhon dans ses premiers mémoires sur la propriété', *Revue d'économie politique*, vol. 24, pp. 712–31.

1910c. 'Proudhon sociologue', *Revue de métaphysique et de morale*, vol. 18, pp. 614–48.

1912a. 'Rousseau et le socialisme', *Revue de métaphysique et de morale*, vol. 20, pp. 341–52.

1912b. *La Sociologie de Proudhon*. Paris: Colin.

1914. 'Remarques sur le polytélisme', *Revue de métaphysique et de morale*, vol. 22, pp. 595–611.

1922. *Leçons de sociologie sur l'évolution des valeurs*. Paris: Colin.

1923a. *De la sociologie à l'action sociale*. Paris: Presses Universitaires de France.

1923b. 'La "Sociologie monarchiste"', preface to the 3rd edition of Bouglé 1903.

1932. *Socialismes français*. Paris: Colin.

1935. *Bilan de la sociologie française contemporaine*. Paris: Alcan.

1938a. *Les Maîtres de la philosophie universitaire en France*. Paris: Maloine.

1938b. 'Convergences des sciences sociales', *Revue de métaphysique et de morale*, vol. 45, pp, 89–103.

Bouglé, C. *et al.* 1900. 'Summary of Bouglé's (1899) Doctoral Thesis Defence'. *Revue de métaphysique et de morale*, vol. 8, January supplement, pp. 9–18.

Davy, G. 1967. 'Célestin Bouglé, 1870–1940', *Revue française de sociologie*, vol. 8, no. 1, pp. 3–13.

Durkheim, E. 1975. 'Lettres d'Emile Durkheim', pp. 389–487, in E. Durkheim, *Textes*, vol. 2. Paris: Editions de Minuit.

1976. 'Textes inédits ou inconnus d'Emile Durkheim', *Revue française de sociologie*, vol. 17, no. 2, pp. 165–96.

Halbwachs, M. 1941. 'Célestin Bouglé, sociologue', *Revue de métaphysique et de morale*, vol. 48, pp. 24–47.

Karady, V. 1979. 'Stratégies de réussite et modes de faire-valoir de la sociologie chez les durkheimiens', *Revue française de sociologie*, vol. 20, no. 1, pp. 49–82.

Logue, W. 1979. 'Sociologie et politique: le libéralisme de Célestin Bouglé', *Revue française de sociologie*, vol. 20, no. 1, pp. 141–61.

Mauss, M. 1897. Review of Bouglé 1896, *Devenir social*, vol. 2, pp. 369–74.

Nizan, P. 1932. *Les Chiens de garde*. Paris: Rieder.

Parodi, D. 1907. 'Morale et sociologie', *Revue d'économie politique*, vol. 21, pp. 241–70.

1919. *La Philosophie contemporaine en France*. Paris: Alcan.

Tarde, G. 1895. 'Criminalité et santé sociale', *Revue philosophique*, vol. 39, pp. 148–62.

Vogt, W. P. 1976. 'The Uses of Studying Primitives: a Note on the Durkheimians, 1890–1940', *History and Theory*, vol. 15, pp. 33–44.

1979. 'Early French Contributions to the Sociology of Knowledge', pp. 101–21 in *Research in the Sociology of Knowledge, Sciences and Art*, ed. R. A. Jones and H. Kuklick, vol. 2. Greenwich, Conn.: JAI Press.

11. The epistemological polemic: François Simiand

PHILIPPE BESNARD

The appearance of a new discipline – sociology – in the field of the social sciences, the beginnings of its institutionalisation in the university, could not fail to give rise to controversies with neighbouring disciplines. In those territorial struggles, the role of François Simiand (1873–1935) was decisive. He was in the front lines in the polemics the Durkheimians conducted – especially those with historians, geographers, and economists – in order to gain recognition for the scientific legitimacy of sociology. One can even say that he was always on the offensive, acting as a sort of leader of the attack, while other Durkheimians, such as Bouglé, played rather more defensive roles.

Simiand's singular position at the heart of the Durkheimian group is explained in large part by his specialisation, and also in part by the particular circumstances of his career. If, at its beginning, his course of studies was the classic one (Ecole Normale Supérieure, first place in the philosophy *agrégation* of 1896), he very quickly oriented himself towards economics and defended in 1904 as his doctoral thesis in the faculty of law a study of the wages of coal-mine workers in France (Simiand 1907). Unlike his two closest collaborators, Hubert Bourgin and Maurice Halbwachs, he neglected to obtain a doctorate in letters, which could have opened the doors of the university to him. From 1901 to 1914, he held a post of librarian at the Ministry of Commerce and the Ministry of Labour. At the same time, from 1910 on, he taught economic history at the Ecole Pratique des Hautes Etudes. During the war, he worked in the Ministry of Armaments where he was the principal collaborator of the socialist minister, Albert Thomas; and, from 1919 to 1920, he was director of labour in Alsace-Lorraine. Also in 1919, he became professor at the Conservatoire National des Arts et Métiers where he taught labour organisation and, subsequently, political economy. In 1931, he was elected to the Collège de France as professor of labour history. That belated recognition must not lead one to forget the overall marginal character of a career like Simiand's. It is particularly astonishing to see Simiand, whose intellectual authority was recognised quite early, holding a librarian's post. Perhaps his choice was influenced by the example of Lucien Herr, the prestigious librarian at the Ecole Normale Supérieure with whom Simiand had very close ties. In any case, his position outside the university certainly afforded him great freedom in the polemics he had with those in it. It is also true that a position of relative institutional marginality was not rare among the most eminent Durkheimians (see the article by Karady in this volume). Mauss provides another example, since, like Simiand, he did not obtain a doctorate in letters and, also like Simiand, he was an unsuccessful candidate for the Collège de France before World War I and entered there only much later (Besnard 1979).

That parallel between Mauss and Simiand can be pushed even further, for both of them occupied a central position in the Durkheimian team. Like Mauss, Simiand reveals the typical characteristics of the principal members of the group, whether in terms of his intellectual training or of his commitment to socialism. He was a member of the team from the very first and remained to his death a major factor in all the collective enterprises of the Durkheimians: the *Année sociologique*, first and second series, the *Annales sociologiques*, and the Institut Français de Sociologie. One can even say that Simiand was one of Durkheim's few collaborators without whom the Durkheimian school would not be conceivable, while one can conceive of it without a Richard or a Bouglé.

However, the position of Simiand is distinguished from that of Mauss by his greater autonomy with regard to Durkheim. He was, although at the heart of the group, the uncontested leader of a sub-group composed of H. Bourgin, Halbwachs (and, to a lesser degree, G. Bourgin), a group of collaborators that he had recruited and whose works he guided. He was also editor, from 1901 to 1906, of the journal *Notes critiques. Sciences sociales*, which could appear to have been to some degree competing with the *Année sociologique*. In addition, the importance of his role within the deployment of Durkheimian troops was due not to his proximity to but rather to his distance from the principal themes sounded by the team's nucleus, a distance that was tied to his specialisation in economics.

The specialisation, which was in perfect conformity with the Durkheimian project of annexing the principal sectors of the social sciences, was in large part the cause of the controversies that Simiand carried on with disciplines neighbouring on and competing with sociology. Those controversies are the central focus of the present article.[1] Simiand was not only the Durkheimian

---

[1] It is obviously not possible in a few pages to discuss Simiand's work in its entirety. The overall revaluation that his work would merit remains to be done. I could thus only allude to the positive aspects of his work. Besides, this paper deals principally with the years before the war, during which Simiand was in the front lines of the Durkheimian offensive. That is hardly a

Philippe Besnard

group's economist, but he was also, along with Halbwachs, its principal expert in statistics: thus, in 1921, he was president of the Paris Statistical Society. If one also takes into account his initial training in philosophy and his early interest in the theory of knowledge,[2] one understands how it is that Simiand was among the Durkheimians both the best-armed and the most motivated to put forth arguments of a methodological and epistemological nature in the debate between sociology and the other social sciences. The term 'epistemological', although anachronistic, is legitimate in this context, since Simiand's criticisms of history, human geography, and economics fundamentally questioned the scientific status of those disciplines. Finally, let us add that, of all the Durkheimians, Simiand's positions on methodological questions were the most coherent, but also the most extreme.

At the turn of the twentieth century, the question of the domain and the method of history, of its relations with the other social sciences, was the object of an international debate. In France, that debate was not uniquely tied to the appearance of Durkheimian sociology, since, from 1894, the historian Paul Lacombe had raised questions about certain of his discipline's methodological principles. But, the forcefully announced ambitions of Durkheimian sociology gave the debate special form and vigour. The confrontation between the Durkheimians and certain historians was very quickly pushed to extremes since each camp laid claim to a position of hegemony in the field of the social sciences. The controversy was not confined to a question of the frontiers between the two disciplines, but pertained to the right of each to exist.

Durkheim's preface to the first volume of the *Année sociologique* (1898), devoted in good part to the relations between sociology and history, is a well-known example. Apparently pleading for the interpenetration of the two disciplines, Durkheim in fact denied all scientific status to history as it was practised at the time and reduced its role to that of the principal supplier of the materials upon which sociologists could draw. He admitted that history could be a science if it explained, that is, if it compared; but, he added, 'from the moment it begins to compare, history becomes indistinguishable from sociology' (1898: iii).

metaphor, since Simiand carried the debate into scholarly societies and congresses: for example, it was before the Society of Modern History that in 1903 he attacked historical method; he continued that critique before the French Society of Philosophy in 1906. He was also the Durkheimians' delegate to the International Congress of Philosophy at Heidelberg in 1908 where he presented one of his most radical critiques of economics. In the interwar period, his close collaborator and friend, Halbwachs, more or less replaced him in that role of critic and often reasserted analogous arguments (see the article by Craig in this volume). Among the secondary sources on Simiand, I have used especially Halbwachs (1936), Vogt (1976), Bouglé (1936).
[2] Halbwachs 1936: 292 indicated that a work written by Simiand when he was a student dealt with Kant's theory of knowledge.

Durkheim's taking such a position could not leave the historians indifferent. Among them, the principal protagonists in the ensuing debate were Charles Seignobos (1854–1942), Henri Hauser (1866–1946), a specialist in social history, and the economic historian Paul Mantoux (1877–1956), who had a more flexible position and who responded to Simiand in 1903.[3] The principal adversary and the principal target of the Durkheimians was, without any doubt, Seignobos, who was the best embodiment of the type of history that they impugned. Seignobos was professor of modern history at the Sorbonne and specialised in the political history of nineteenth-century France. He was also interested in methodological questions and had published, in 1898 with Langlois, an *Introduction aux études historiques* – a methodological manual that had given rise to an elaborate critique by Simiand (1898). But it was in his book on the historical method applied to the social sciences (Seignobos 1901) that he conducted his counter-attack against sociology. In the first place, he began by excluding sociology from his definition of the social sciences, and even went on to specify that the word sociology, invented by philosophers, was destined to disappear after a period of fashionableness (1901: 7). In the second place, he assigned to history the role of organiser of the federation of the specialised social sciences. He gave two arguments: the historical method must be utilised by all the social sciences because they all deal with indirect data; only history enables one to study a social whole in its totality and in its reciprocal relations with simultaneous phenomena. Although Hauser disagreed with Seignobos on some points (see the article by Weisz in this volume), in his inventory of the teaching of the social sciences (1903), he restricted his criticisms to Durkheimian sociology, which he accused of manipulating abstractions and arbitrarily isolating a particular institution from the mass of social facts.

Hauser's book was published in 1903, that is to say, at the moment the polemic reached its peak. Indeed, it was in 1903 that Simiand presented his paper. 'Méthode historique et science sociale', and published it in two instalments in the *Revue de synthèse historique* – a journal created in 1900 by Henri Berr to promote encounters between history and the other social sciences. And, it was in the same year that Durkheim and Fauconnet (1903) defined sociology as 'the system of the social sciences' (history included). That new offensive by the Durkheimians was probably not unrelated to the very recent arrival of Durkheim at the Sorbonne. Simiand's intervention in the debate was thus part of a whole, and one in which other members of the. team took part, notably by criticising the books by Seignobos and Hauser: Durkheim, Fauconnet, and Bouglé did so in the *Année sociologique*; H. Bourgin in historical journals (see Weisz's article, notes 52 and 53). However, Simiand's response was by far the most developed and the most

---

[3] For more detailed information about the intervention of historians in the debate and their reactions to the Durkheimians' criticisms, see Rébérioux (forthcoming).

Philippe Besnard

destructive. His article, 'Méthode historique et science sociale' (one should note that Simiand wrote of social science in the singular because, in his eyes, there was only one social science), appeared under the guise of reflections on the points of view about history expressed by Seignobos and Lacombe. In fact, it was an almost point-by-point refutation of Seignobos's arguments[4] – Lacombe was cited only with praise – and also, in the second part of the article, a response to Hauser. Most generally, Simiand's article is a radical denunciation of a conception of history that he called 'historicising history' (*l'histoire historisante*), and which has also been called 'positivist'. His critique often has the tone of a philosophy course for historians considered to be novices in the subject, despite their methodological pretensions.

Simiand's work has often been remembered for its famous denunciation of the 'tribe of historians' who worshipped the three 'idols': the idol of politics, the idol of the individual, and the idol of chronology. But that denunciation only imperfectly summarises a much more complex series of arguments, arguments which can be but briefly outlined here.

Simiand began by affirming, against Seignobos, the possibility of a social science, and he did so in a manner completely in conformity with Durkheimian orthodoxy: in order for a science of human phenomena analogous to the sciences of nature to be possible, that science must deal with an objective domain. One can define as objective all that which comes to us from society (rules of law, religious dogmas, forms of property, etc.) and which is independent of our individual spontaneity. Simiand responded also to the 'over facile nominalist pleasantries' that were applied to sociology, even though, taken seriously, they would imply the impossibility of any science. All scientific facts are abstractions. Sociology must therefore utilise abstractions without according them a metaphysical existence, and it must concentrate on selecting 'fortunate abstractions', that is to say, those which reveal regularities and, if possible, laws. Traditional history prohibits itself from being scientific through its fascination with the single and concrete event and by its obsession with the individual, which, moreover, is itself only an abstraction.

Furthermore, such fascination with the individual is tied to an erroneous notion of causality. Historians understand by 'cause' either one or several anterior facts chosen without method (i.e. selected by following their personal tastes or intellectual fashions), or they mean by 'cause' their reconstructions of the motives of human actors. But according to Simiand, one cannot establish a causal tie between an actor and an act, but only between two phenomena of exactly the same order. The cause of a pheno-

[4] Three years later, in Simiand's presentation on 'causality in history', Seignobos would still be his target (Simiand 1906). And it was again Seignobos that Durkheim took to task in 1908 at the French Society of Philosophy (Durkheim 1908).

menon is nothing other than an invariable and unconditional antecedent phenomenon. Social science, if it wishes to be a science, must therefore, while not ignoring contingent and individual elements, eliminate their effect in order to bring to light the stable relationships between phenomena.

The same absence of principled criteria rules over the choice of the frameworks in which the historian puts his research: these are the frameworks implied by chronology, by the division of subjects according to political regime, and by studies limited to a single society. In order to justify that last choice, Seignobos and Hauser argued from the interdependence of all the facts in a society. To this Simiand replied that history practised in such a framework in fact limits itself to describing: that, like any social phenomenon, the general bond Seignobos and Hauser postulated is an abstraction; and that only the comparative study of a phenomenon in several societies enables one to establish constant relationships, and thus to explain.

Simiand thus denied *en bloc* the principles and practices of 'historicising history'. Such history devoted itself to the task of establishing the facts, and fancied itself as being an exact and impartial representation of the past. But, that alleged empiricism in fact rested on non-explicit choices, for there can be no such photography of the past. If history wished to become scientific, it had to accept that its practice had to conform to that of all science, that is to say, that it had to formulate hypotheses and verify them. If it did not do that – Simiand suggested, going further here than other Durkheimians – history would be limiting itself to accumulating data not even utilisable by sociology. And this would be all the more regrettable since the scientific study of the past is one of the rare means by which sociology can put its hypotheses to the test.

Such a brutal attack had little chance of ending in a diplomatic success, even though Simiand tried to rally certain historians to his point of view by making his target Seignobos's conception of history. However, his challenge to historicising history, and the appeal to the new generation of historians that Simiand issued in the concluding lines of his article, were not without echo. It is well known that much of Simiand's program has been taken up again as its own by the *Annales* school (see Burguière 1979, Revel 1979, and Craig's article in this volume).

Among the Durkheimians, Simiand was also the one who challenged in the most radical way the scientific status of human and regional geography – a discipline that was in full vigour in France due to the impetus given it by Vidal de la Blache and his disciples. Simiand defiantly reviewed, in the *Année sociologique* (1910), five doctoral theses published between 1905 and 1909 – respectively, by Demangeon, Blanchard, Vallaux, Vacher, and Sion. Simiand was not alone in criticising the bases and the ambitions of human

Philippe Besnard

geography; rather, that was the task of Durkheim and then of Halbwachs, who had induced the debate with the anthropo-geography of Ratzel and who affirmed the pre-eminent rights of 'social morphology' in the sixth section of the *Année sociologique*.[5] It even seems odd at first glance to see Simiand intervene in that section, since his forays outside of the section on 'economic sociology' were quite rare.

That intervention is more easily understood when one looks at the nature of the criticisms Simiand addressed to those studies, which were all regional monographs. In the first place, a comparison of those books showed the indeterminacy of the very object of human geography. That discipline abusively extended its field of investigation to all physical or human facts that were localisable, that is to say, to all that one could represent on a map. Since such facts were innumerable, the choices made among them appeared to be either arbitrary or to be following tradition or intellectual fashion. Geographic facts should have been defined as those 'of which the localisation is the constitutive or essential element' (1910: 726). Only Vacher's work corresponded to that criterion. In the second place, geography revealed itself incapable of demonstrating the cogency of its explanatory principle, namely, the essential action of the physical milieu on social facts, on economic facts, or even on habitat. That incapacity to explain was tied to what constituted for Simiand the major flaw of those studies, that is to say, the choice of the narrow framework of the regional monograph. To limit oneself to a region, to the observation of a single case, is to 'condemn oneself in advance to being unable to prove anything' (1910: 731). Only the comparative study of a phenomenon in rather numerous different sites enables one to distinguish random coincidences from true correlations. Simiand thus exhorted geographers to reverse their procedure completely: studying a region in its totality can only be the result of a 'science of social morphology', and not the means to establish it.

It is difficult to imagine a more negative epistemological critique. Human geography did not have a specified object of study, it had no explanatory power, and, above all, its unit of analysis, the regional area, could not constitute the legitimate framework of a scientific study. But, the notion of 'natural regions' was the very basis of the methodology of Vidalian geographers and the means by which they distinguished themselves from the anthropo-geography of Ratzel.

It is tempting to relate – as Chartier (1980), basing himself on the work of Karady (1976, 1979), has recently done – that vigorous methodological attack to the respective institutional positions of the Vidalian geographers and the Durkheimian sociologists. The two schools had more than one point in

[5] On the relations between social morphology and human geography see Berdoulay 1978, Craig's article in this volume, and the research in progress of Howard Andrews.

254

common: an elevated academic recruitment (former students of the Ecole Normale Supérieure, *agrégés*); the existence of a journal (the *Annales de géographie* were created in 1891); the open search for marks of scientificity. But, while Durkheimian sociology remained peripheral in the university, there was a veritable institutional breakthrough by geography at the beginning of the century (Karady 1976: 275–7). In that context, according to Chartier (1980: 35), the Durkheimian rejection of the region as a framework for research had a double significance: on the one hand, it was a shady attempt to acquire for the benefit of social morphology the 'simultaneously utilised and denied' attainments of human geography; and, on the other hand, it enabled sociology to play one of the only trump cards at its disposal in the French university system – especially against regional geography, which was 'mired in the concrete' – namely, its status as a theoretical and abstract science, a status tied to its proximity to philosophy and even to its ambition of replacing philosophy.

Such an interpretation certainly has a good deal of validity, and one can in addition document it more precisely. The five books examined by Simiand were all doctoral theses (that was also true of the book by R. De Felice which Simiand limited himself to citing in a note). Of the five authors, four had obtained university posts. The element of rivalry is even manifest in Simiand's text where he brought up the 'great ambitions' of the discipline. Similarly, one could emphasise that, precisely because of Simiand's extra-academic position, he was the spokesman of the Durkheimians when being such involved criticising French academics. It is even possible to relate the *Année sociologique*'s change of attitude toward the Vidalians to the very recent success of these latter in the university. In fact, in volume 8 (1905), just before the emergence of those doctoral theses on regional geography, the *Année* had given to Vacher the task of reviewing Vidal de la Blache's *Tableau de la géographie de la France* and E. de Martonne's doctoral thesis. Vacher was a student of Vidal, and E. de Martonne was Vidal's son-in-law. Vacher's reviews were rather flat and destitute of any critical comment, although, in the next volume, he felt himself much more free to argue with books by German geographers.

There is thus no shortage of material to support a strategic interpretation of Simiand's attack. Yet, it is equally possible to indicate its limits. Karady (1976: 305) describes Durkheimian strategy towards the human sciences that were well established in the university (philosophy, history, geography) as being simultaneously a strategy of alliance with them, of the offering of services, and as an attempt to substitute itself for them, to occupy their domain by criticising their epistemological presuppositions. That ambivalence can be clearly seen in the case of sociology's relations with philosophy, and Karady (1979: 54–8) has well demonstrated it, especially in regard to

Durkheim. But the strategic interpretation seems to me much less obvious for sociology's relations with history, and it is hardly perceptible as far as human geography is concerned. If the Durkheimian strategy was to establish relationships of interdependence between sociology and the other social sciences, one must admit that the radical critiques that Simiand addressed to academic historians and geographers were a tactical error. It is equally certain that the accumulation of regional monographs could only have clashed profoundly with the methodological convictions of Simiand, who, on this point, again took up his criticism of the research frameworks of historicising history. The very identity of that criticism, addressed on the one hand to a form of history that Simiand considered obsolete – and which was debated even within the historians' camp – and, on the other hand, to the rising school of Vidalian geographers – who were of the same generation as Simiand, who had the same education, and several of whom had the same commitment to socialism – is another indication that for Simiand the content of the argument was not reducible to tactical considerations.

It would probably be a vain exercise, in assessing Simiand's critique, to attempt to distinguish the part of it attributable to conviction from the part motivated by strategy. It is better simply to acknowledge that Simiand's methodological convictions were in complete conformity with the Durkheimian ambition of establishing sociology as the system of the social sciences, and that those convictions could thus be put at the service of that ambition. But, there was in this no exceptionally subtle strategy. The very term strategy evokes a conscious and coherent overall plan of action. But, is it coherent to try to gain recognition from neighbouring disciplines, all the while demonstrating to them that they have no reason to exist? Besides, if strategy there was, it ended in a diplomatic failure. Perhaps that failure was one of the reasons that caused academic sociology in France long to remain an appendage of philosophy.

It would, moreover, be an error to believe that the principal means utilised by the Durkheimians to legitimate sociology as against other social sciences was to put it forth as an abstract and conceptual science and to invalidate empirical observation. In Simiand's case, that would even be to look at things exactly backward – by forgetting his scientific works and the second section of his epistemological critique, that which dealt with economics. For the battle that Simiand conducted was a battle on two fronts, and his critique of 'abstract' economics occupied him much more than his polemic with history and geography. Indeed, he developed that critique in some hundreds of pages – not without a bit of repetition – in his articles, in the methodological parts of his books (notably, Simiand 1932a), and above all in his very numerous reviews in the 'economic sociology' section of the *Année sociologique*.[6]

In taking as his general target 'traditional political economy', Simiand in fact aimed at the diverse currents within marginalism (a term that was not used at the time). In his reviews of authors such as Walras, Jevons, Effertz, Pareto, Marshall, Fisher, Landry (and through the latter Böhm-Bawerk), he focused on that economics which referred to itself as 'abstract', 'pure', or 'mathematical', and that Simiand preferred calling 'hypothetical', 'ideological', 'conceptual', 'normative', or 'finalist'.[7] The 'positive' economic science that Simiand extolled was opposed to such traditional economics, but was also opposed to its opposite – that 'economic historicism' which was very often only a simple description of facts. And Simiand took care, when for example he criticised the Austrian 'psychological school', to distinguish its argument from those of the German 'historical school'. We will consider here only his critique of traditional abstract economics, for the objections that he addressed to economic historicism are analogous to those he addressed to history in general. Besides, that choice is true to the one Simiand himself made when, in 1912, he assembled his articles and several of his principal reviews from the *Année* into a small book of methodological combat called *La Méthode positive en science économique* wherein the essence of his argument is presented.

Traditional economics maintains that it is deductive and that it proceeds from certain psychological postulates: more specifically, it assumes that the principal motive of human action is personal interest, which pushes the individual to maximise his advantages at the least possible cost, effort, or risk. Simiand demonstrates with several examples that one can deduce contradictory behaviours, all from that selfsame principle. Thus, it is not only by deduction proceeding from simple and abstract hypotheses that economists account for behaviours. Their theories in fact express the unconscious result of their empirical dealings with economic life. In the place of such non-systematic and thus divergent observations, one must substitute methodical observation and experiment. Furthermore, if economic theory were purely deductive and sought only to be a logically coherent edifice, it could base itself on other postulates: it could, for example, begin with the

---

[6] The general conception of that section, its frequently revised and justified scheme of classification, would merit a separate study.

[7] Later (1932a), Simiand regrouped traditional economics under two rubrics: applied or finalist economics; conceptual or ideological economics. But, he was thus distinguishing mostly intellectual practices and trends; he cited no economist by name. I have cited above the authors that Simiand criticised before the war in the *Année sociologique*, first series. To this one should add that Simiand criticised, several times and quite vehemently, the work of Keynes, which was for Simiand an example of a finalist theory (see especially Simiand 1934c). On the reactions of some economists to Simiand's critique, see the article by Craig in this volume.

Philippe Besnard

hypothesis that work is a pleasure, not a pain or, going still further, that the individual seeks to satisfy the fewest needs possible, and with the most trouble possible.[8]

The method that the economists intend to be abstract and scientific is in reality 'ideological' and normative. One sees that very clearly when they relate their theories to the facts. When the observation of certain facts corresponds to their theses, they use that as an argument to prove the excellence of their theories. When they do not coincide, they explain that the phenomena are too complex and that the observation of them is too difficult. Or, further, they explain that the individuals are not behaving in a 'reasonable' way, that they do not clearly perceive the true nature of their own interests. Hence, economics claims to prescribe the 'reasonable' ends that men ought to pursue; it is thus finalist and normative, and not explanatory.

This normative preoccupation could be found behind the majority of the postulates of that economic theory which referred to itself as 'pure' or 'mathematical'. The fundamental question it posed for itself as it proceeded in that manner was to determine the conditions of equilibrium of an ideally defined market called the free market. Simiand saw in that obsession the finalist postulate that equilibrium is the ideal state of an economic market. Furthermore, such a postulate would be useless if, upon examination, it turned out to be the case that the essence of economic life was a succession of disequilibria. And one of Simiand's well-known principal contributions was to bring to light the long-term fluctuations, the alternating phases of expansion and depression that characterised economic life (Simiand 1932a, 1932b, 1932c, 1934a). But, those phases are not movements around a point of equilibrium. Each is the condition of the other, and that alternation is the condition of economic progress.

Finally, there remains the major complaint that Simiand, as a sociologist, directed toward economics: it claimed to explain social facts while leaving aside society. To seek to explain essential economic phenomena (price, market, trade) by individual psychology is to go against the grain of reality. This is the origin of the principal basis for Simiand's rejection of the marginalist theory of value. Individual needs are merely qualitative elements. But, the notion of value, if it is in fact psychological, is also essentially quantitative, because it is expressed in price; it is 'an opinion which is a quantity', and that characteristic comes from the fact that it has its source in collective opinion. On the basis of these considerations, Simiand criticised

[8] Simiand enunciated that argument in 1899 in order to show the arbitrary and 'ideological' character of a procedure that attempted to be purely deductive. In 1907, in his review of Effertz, the argument was slightly modified and became a criticism of the habitual postulate of economics: referring to Max Weber, Simiand pointed out that labour could be a moral and religious duty (Simiand 1912: 89).

the theory of the determination of prices by the play of supply and demand. That theory is circular since, allegedly explaining the setting of prices, it implies that prices already exist, because the individual estimates of buyers and sellers derive from a price that is already known and put into monetary terms. 'The fundamental defect of that theory is thus ultimately that it tries to explain a phenomenon that is social in nature by some individual phenomena which derive precisely from that social phenomenon itself and which exist only because of it' (Simiand 1908: 901). More generally, the so-called universal law of supply and demand presupposes, for its existence and operation, the conjoining of certain highly specific social conditions, the combination of certain very singular legal and economic institutions.

In brief, for Simiand, economic science remained entirely to be constructed, and it had to be based on a truly 'positive' method, a method that would necessarily be experimental and sociological.

That double critique of 'theories without facts' and 'studies of facts without theory' (Simiand 1932a: x) did not only have a negative aspect. It was obviously tied to a definite conception of sociological method to which Simiand was faithful throughout his scientific career and which he endeavoured actually to put into practice. It is thus necessary to present here, in broad outline, that 'positive' method.[9]

If it wishes to be a science, sociology must conform to the same principles of method as do the already constituted sciences, such as physics or biology. But, these latter progressed thanks to laboratory experimentation, and that seemed impossible in the study of social facts, which is irrevocably dependent upon observation. However, Simiand rejected the classical opposition between experimentation and observation and saw in the statistical method the sociological equivalent of experimentation in the sciences of nature. Undoubtedly, the two differ in that in the one case one works with material entities and in the other with intellectual entities. But the statistical method, properly employed, is a procedure of abstraction as efficacious as the factoring out of a single element by the experimental method. Besides, if the statistical method can play only a secondary role in the natural sciences, it is, on the contrary, especially adapted to the study of social facts, that is, to the study of the characteristics and variations of groups. Statistical research is experimental research applied to 'facts that one determines quantitatively by means of a more or less large number of individual observations, but which are distinct from those individual elements and which do not exist as such in any of them' (Simiand 1922: 19). The statistical method thus became in Simiand's eyes the model for all sociological method.

In order to seize that collective reality, the statistical method must be used

[9] For more details see Simiand 1922, 1932a; Halbwachs 1923, 1936; Bouglé 1936.

and applied in an especially rigorous manner. It is first advisable to neutralise the biases contained in the statistical sources,[10] to reconstruct the series so that they bear upon groups of data which are relatively homogeneous, which have a sufficient scope and which are rather distinct from one another. One must also follow the phenomenon being considered in its continuous development rather than limiting oneself to taking more or less arbitrarily chosen slices of this development; for the study of the variations in a phenomenon over time is one of the best bases for comparative analysis. The construction of homogeneous groups that are rather extensive in space and duration implies without any doubt that one is proceeding by abstraction. But that abstraction is legitimate if it is only a means to test the reality of those groupings, to see if they truly constitute real social entities. Finally, in order to bring to light the regularities in the series of facts and to delimit the causes of the evolution of a phenomenon, one must first pass in review, without any preconceived idea, all the factors susceptible of making it vary.

The 'integral empiricism' that Simiand demanded in fact characterised his works on prices and wages, from his 1902 article on the price of coal through his monumental work on wages of 1932. Thus, in *Le Salaire, l'évolution sociale et la monnaie* (1932a), Simiand first, in volume 1, reconstructed the series of wages and prices; then, in volume 2, passed in review all the phenomena that could have had a relation to the movement of wages: non-economic facts (demographic, technical, religious, legal, political, etc.); economic facts (the systems of and forms of production, the rate of resource use, institutions of distribution, fluctuations in production, of prices, etc.). Only then did he bring to light the decisive role of money, more precisely, the movements of acceleration or of slow-down in the rate of growth of monetary media. Clearly, Simiand's empiricism did not mean that he renounced explanation. As Halbwachs noted (1936: 311), his empiricism had 'its counterpart in a true rationalism' – because, in order for integral observation of the facts to enable one to render them intelligible and to discover regularities, it is very necessary that there be a sort of latent reason in the facts themselves.

But, in order to characterise fully Simiand's methodological thought, one must add to his 'rationalist empiricism' his 'sociologism' (Bouglé 1936: 25), for the powerful role that Simiand attributed to monetary factors – not only in the movement of wages and prices, but in the totality of economic life and its long-term fluctuations – came from the collective representations which attach themselves to money. In his last work, Simiand forcefully emphasised that money, far from being a convention, is a 'real social entity', that it has as its basis a 'social belief', a 'social faith' and that, consequently, all money, including gold, is fiduciary (1934b: 46).

Through this too allusive review of Simiand's scientific work, we can see

[10] As early as 1898, Simiand had criticised Durkheim's use of official suicide statistics.

that he indeed sought to apply the methodological principles in the name of which he denied scientific status to historicising history, to human geography, and to abstract economics. His methodological convictions, formed quite early on, did not vary; they inspired his work, which developed in a continuous line, by increasing depth and breadth, without a notable break or deviation. Thus, it was both by his epistemological critique and by his scientific works that Simiand played an essential role in the Durkheimian enterprise of establishing sociology. He first served that project by occupying the territory of a particular social science – economics.[11] Furthermore, his conviction that there is only one method possible in the study of social facts was perfectly adapted to sociological imperialism. The term imperialism is even perhaps too weak to characterise Simiand's position on the relations between sociology and the other social sciences. One can say that, for him, sociology is more than the system of the social sciences. Since there is only one social science, it is sociology.

References

Berdoulay, V. 1978. 'The Vidal–Durkheim Debate', pp. 77–90 in D. Ley, M. Samuel (eds.), *Humanistic Geography: Prospects and Problems*. Chicago: Maaroufa Press.

Besnard, P. 1979. 'Durkheim, les durkheimiens et le Collège de France', *Etudes durkheimiennes*, no. 3, pp. 4–7.

Bouglé, C. 1936. 'La Méthodologie de François Simiand et la sociologie', *Annales sociologiques*, série A, vol. 2, pp. 5–28.

Burguière, A. 1979. 'Histoire d'une histoire: la naissance des *Annales*', *Annales*, vol. 34, no. 4, pp. 1347–59.

Chartier, R. 1980. 'Science sociale et découpage régional. Note sur deux débats, 1820–1920', *Actes de la recherche en sciences sociales*, no. 35, pp. 27–36.

Durkheim, E. 1898. Préface, *Année sociologique*, vol. 1, pp. i–vii.

1908. Comments at session 28 May 1908: 'L'Inconnu et l'inconscient en histoire', *Bulletin de la société française de philosophie*, vol. 8, pp. 229–47 *passim*.

1909. 'Sociologie et sciences sociales', pp. 259–85 in *De la méthode dans les sciences*. Paris: Alcan.

Durkheim, E., and Fauconnet, P. 1903. 'Sociologie et sciences sociales', *Revue philosophique*, vol. 55, pp. 465–97.

Halbwachs, M. 1923. 'L'Expérimentation statistique et les probabilités', *Revue philosophique*, vol. 96, pp. 340–71.

1936. 'La Méthodologie de François Simiand. Un empirisme rationaliste', *Revue philosophique*, vol. 121, pp. 281–319.

Hauser, H. 1903. *L'Enseignement des sciences sociales*. Paris: Chevalier-Maresq.

Karady, V. 1976. 'Durkheim, les sciences sociales et l'Université: bilan d'un semi-échec', *Revue française de sociologie*, vol. 17, no. 2, pp. 267–311.

---

[11] Thus, when in 1909 Durkheim dealt again with the relations between sociology and the separate social sciences, he used Simiand's early works on wages to show what an economic science conceived of as a 'branch of sociology' could be (Durkheim 1909).

Philippe Besnard

1979. 'Stratégies de réussite et modes de faire-valoir de la sociologie chez les durkheimiens', *Revue française de sociologie*, vol. 20, no. 1, pp. 49–82.

Lacombe, P. 1894. *De l'histoire considérée comme science*. Paris: Hachette.

Langlois, C. V., and Seignobos, C. 1898. *Introduction aux études historiques*. Paris: Hachette.

Mantoux, P. 1903. 'Histoire et sociologie', *Revue de synthèse historique*, vol. 7, pp. 121–40.

Rébérioux, M. (forthcoming). 'Aux origines des *Annales*. Le débat de 1903: historiens et sociologues'.

Revel, J. 1979. 'Histoire et sciences sociales: les paradigmes des *Annales*', *Annales*, vol. 34, no. 4, pp. 1360–76.

Seignobos, C. 1901. *La Méthode historique appliquée aux sciences sociales*. Paris: Alcan.

Simiand, F. 1898. 'L'Année sociologique 1897', *Revue de métaphysique et de morale*, vol.-6, pp. 608–53.

1899. 'Déduction et observation psychologiques en économie sociale', *Revue de métaphysique et de morale*, vol. 7, pp. 446–62.

1902. 'Essai sur le prix du charbon en France et au XIXe siècle', *Année sociologique*, vol. 5, pp. 1–81.

1903. 'Méthode historique et science sociale', *Revue de synthèse historique*, vol. 6, pp. 1–22; 129–57.

1906. Lecture and comments at session 31 May 1906: 'La Causalité en histoire', *Bulletin de la société française de philosophie*, vol. 6, pp. 245–72, 276–90 *passim*.

1907. *Le Salaire des ouvriers des mines de charbon en France. Contribution à la théorie économique du salaire*. Paris: Société Nouvelle de Librairie et d'Edition.

1908. 'La Méthode positive en science économique', *Revue de métaphysique et de morale*, vol. 16, pp. 889–904.

1910. Review of A. Demangeon, *La Picardie et les régions voisines*, R. Blanchard, *La Flandre. Etude géographique de la plaine flamande en France, Belgique et Hollande*, C. Vallaux, *La Basse-Bretagne. Etude de géographie humaine*, A. Vacher, *Le Berry. Contribution à l'étude géographique d'une région française*, and J. Sion, *Les Paysans de la Normandie orientale*, *Année sociologique*, vol. 11, pp. 723–32.

1912. *La Méthode positive en science économique*. Paris: Alcan.

1922. *Statistique et expérience. Remarques de méthode*. Paris: Rivière.

1932a. *Le Salaire, l'évolution sociale et la monnaie. Essai de théorie expérimentale du salaire*, 3 vols. Paris: Alcan.

1932b. *Les Fluctuations économiques à longue période et la crise mondiale*. Paris: Alcan.

1932c. *Recherches anciennes et nouvelles sur le mouvement général des prix du XVIe au XIXe siècles*. Paris: Domat-Montchrestien.

1934a. *Inflation et stabilisation alternées: Le développement économique des Etats-Unis*. Paris: Domat-Montchrestien.

1934b. 'La Monnaie réalité sociale', *Annales sociologiques*, série D, vol. 1, pp. 1–58.

1934c. 'Sur une théorie finaliste et britannique de la monnaie', review of J.M. Keynes, *A Treatise on Money*, *Annales sociologiques*, série D, vol. 1, pp. 158–72.

Vogt, W.P. 1976. 'The Politics of Academic Sociological Theory in France, 1890–1914'. Doctoral dissertation (Ph. D.), Indiana University.

12. Sociology and related disciplines between the wars: Maurice Halbwachs and the imperialism of the Durkheimians

JOHN E. CRAIG

After World War I the Durkheimians were less interested than before in discussing general principles and issuing dogmatic pronouncements, and more committed to specialised scholarship. Their emphasis shifted from the abstract to the specific, from the philosophical to the positivistic. This was to be expected, perhaps, and it was consistent with Durkheim's own intentions.[1] But the events of the war, including the deaths of Durkheim and many of his most promising disciples, accelerated the trend. They contributed to the demise of the institution that had best represented the school, the *Année sociologique*. They also transferred leadership within the school – to the extent leadership continued – to scholars less abstract and dogmatic than Durkheim and more sensitive to their school's critics. In addition the general intellectual climate was less favourable to sociology after the war than before, a change reflected in the school's limited success in attracting new recruits. No doubt this reinforced the Durkheimians' sense that emphasising their school's grandiose ambitions, an effective strategy earlier, was no longer appropriate. Sociology would suffer if it claimed too much too soon. Priority must now go to specific accomplishments.[2]

But the break with earlier practices was not complete. A few Durkheimians combined specific scholarship with an attempt to keep alive the more generalising and assertive traditions of the prewar years. Through essays on methodological questions and reviews of the literature in several disciplines they continued Durkheim's efforts to define sociology and its domain and to clarify its relationship to the other social sciences. Of these scholars the most conscientious and wide-ranging was Maurice Halbwachs. Others may have been closer to Durkheim in their specific scholarly interests and in their talents as teachers and institution-builders, but when it came to defining sociology and to advancing its claims to hegemony over other disciplines Halbwachs was without equal. At least in this regard he was the most Durkheimian of the interwar Durkheimians.

[1] Durkheim 1898: i-ii.
[2] See, for instance, Mauss 1927: 188–92, and Mauss 1933: 37–8, 46.

John E. Craig

It is with Halbwachs's efforts between the wars to promote sociology and to shape its development that this essay is concerned. The emphasis is on Halbwachs's opinions concerning the relationship between sociology and related disciplines, but attention is also given to his opinions concerning rival schools of sociology, and concerning his own.[3]

That Halbwachs became a leading spokesman for the French school of sociology is hardly surprising. He was the very model of a dedicated scholar, an industrious and prolific worker not easily distracted from his academic responsibilities. He was also, as a colleague once observed, a 'man of astonishing curiosity – always engrossed, when one encountered him, by some new intellectual passion which he would disclose to you with that sort of quiet enthusiasm that was his distinguishing feature ...' (Febvre 1946a: 289n.). And thanks largely to this intellectual curiosity and capacity for enthusiasms, he had already acquired a range of scholarly interests and skills unusual even by Durkheimian standards. In the 1890s Halbwachs had come under the spell of Henri Bergson, one of his teachers at the Lycée Henri IV, and while his Bergsonianism proved short-lived, the related taste for grappling with philosophical and psychological questions endured. At the Ecole Normale Supérieure (1898–1901) he had become a socialist, and although this did not distinguish him from many other *normaliens* – or from many Durkheimians, a group he soon joined – the consequences for his intellectual development were distinctive. He had acquired a knowledge of economic theory matched among the Durkheimians only by that of his close friend and mentor, François Simiand. Profiting from two extended stays in central Europe, he had familiarised himself with the German literature on economic and social questions, including the Marxist contributions. He had devoted several articles and two of his most important books, *Les Expropriations et le prix des terrains à Paris (1860–1900)* (1909) and *La Classe ouvrière et les niveaux de vie* (1913), to the empirical analysis of aspects of urban and working-class life in contemporary societies, themes virtually ignored by the other Durkheimians. And, motivated by Simiand and by the requirements of his own research, he had become an authority on methodological questions and the Durkheimians' most sophisticated statistician, a distinction consolidated by his critical studies of Leibniz (1907) and of François Quetelet and the development of social statistics (1912). It was a unique combination of interests and talents, one that left Halbwachs well prepared for his later efforts to promote the Durkheimians' cause.

Halbwachs's personal situation after the war also facilitated these efforts. Late in 1919 he moved from Caen, where he had recently become a *chargé*

---

[3] For more comprehensive surveys of Halbwachs's work, see Verret 1972 and Vromen 1975. Useful shorter studies include Alexandre 1968, Canguilhem 1947, Duvignaud 1968, Friedmann 1955, and Karady 1972.

de cours in philosophy, to the new university in Strasbourg. He remained in Strasbourg for sixteen years, first as professor of sociology and pedagogy, and then, from 1 March 1922 on, as France's first professor of sociology.[4] In 1935 he moved to the Sorbonne, where in quick succession he occupied positions in the history of social economics (1935–7), the methodology and logic of the sciences (1937–9), and sociology (1939–44).[5] He thus spent most of the interwar period as a professor of sociology, and much of it as the only one in France. He also spent all but the first year at universities offering unusually favourable environments for productive scholarship and for shaping the development of one's discipline. There is no need to elaborate on the significance of the move to the Sorbonne; suffice it to note that it put Halbwachs at the centre of the nation's intellectual life and into close proximity with many of France's leading social scientists and most promising students. Yet in some respects the conditions in Strasbourg, Halbwachs's base for most of his academic career, were even more conducive to scholarly work. In this case elaboration is in order.

Throughout the interwar period the University of Strasbourg was distinguished both by its physical facilities and by the quality and spirit of its faculty. The institution inherited the spacious buildings, the excellent library, and the numerous laboratories and institutes established before the war for its German predecessor, and it received generous support from the government to improve them. The result was a collection of resources for teaching and research superior to that of any other French university, the University of Paris included. Perhaps more distinctive, however, was the institution's academic climate. The professors appointed in 1919, many of them young army veterans occupying their first university positions, shared a sense of mission and a commitment to reform rarely found even at new institutions. They were determined to give greater emphasis to research than was then common at French universities, and to this extent were in the tradition of the prewar movement to modernise and to 'Germanise' the French universities, a movement identified with 'la nouvelle Sorbonne'. Yet their admiration for what this movement represented, and for what the German universities represented, was not complete. They associated the reform movement and German higher education with the proliferation of increasingly narrow and isolated academic disciplines, and they wanted to counter this trend. They hoped to make their university a centre not only of research but also, to borrow Henri Berr's expression, of 'the spirit of synthesis'. There was, in short, a commitment to collaboration among the disciplines and a consciousness of belonging to a team, an *esprit de corps*, without counterpart at other French universities.[6]

[4] For the background see Craig 1979a: 8–12.
[5] Craig 1979b: 290, and Weisz's article, this volume.
[6] Berr 1921: 1–13, Berr 1922: 1–6.

John E. Craig

Halbwachs was not a leader of this team – a mild and almost timid man, he was never among the faculty's dominant figures – but he was an important member. He was a mainstay of such collaborative ventures as the *réunions du samedi*, a faculty forum for the discussion of recent scholarly works, and he numbered among his friends and debating partners not only colleagues in philosophy (Martial Guéroult and Maurice Pradines) and the social sciences (Charles Blondel, Marc Bloch, Lucien Febvre, Georges Lefebvre), but also a Germanist (Edmond Vermeil), a jurist (Gabriel Le Bras), a mathematician (Maurice Fréchet), and a physiologist (Emile Terroine).[7] It is obvious, too, that he found the environment conducive to scholarship. It was in Strasbourg that he wrote some of his most important works, including *Les Cadres sociaux de la mémoire* (1925), *Les Causes du suicide* (1930), and *L'Evolution des besoins dans les classes ouvrières* (1933). And while some of the subjects he examined had concerned him earlier – social classes and the social morphology of cities, for example – in certain areas his work appears to have been strongly influenced by his Strasbourg colleagues. Thus his interest in reconciling some of Bergson's insights with the analysis of social facts, first manifested in Strasbourg, was shared and presumably reinforced by Blondel and Pradines.[8] And his collaboration with the mathematicians Georges Cerf and Maurice Fréchet – he taught courses in statistics with both men and wrote *Le Calcul des probabilités à la portée de tous* (1924) with Fréchet[9] – no doubt reinforced his interest in quantitative research. By 1932 Halbwachs was insisting that 'if it is possible in sociology to find quantitative relations of causality, it is to them that we should adhere first and above all' (Halbwachs 1932a: 322). And a year later he suggested that with the aid of statistics sociologists could establish laws as valid as those of the natural sciences.[10] His association with the mathematicians had presumably contributed to this optimism.

But the support Halbwachs received from colleagues was not complete. Despite their friendly relations and mutual respect, there were matters on which Halbwachs and his colleagues disagreed. The most important related to a single general theme: the alleged imperialism of Durkheimian sociology.

Durkheim had considered sociology to be not a restricted discipline, like

[7] My information concerning Halbwachs's close friends on the faculty is from Jean Gagé, Roger Mehl, and Robert Minder (personal communications); Maurice Halbwachs to Albert Thomas, 6 January 1924, Fonds Albert Thomas (94 AP 381), Archives Nationales, Paris; the notes of Earle E. Eubank on his interviews with Maurice Halbwachs, les Houches (Haute-Savoie), 1934, Earle E. Eubank Papers (box 2, folder 13), The University of Chicago Library, Chicago; and the notes of Terry N. Clark on his interview with Mme Y. Halbwachs, Paris, 1965, Terry Clark Papers (folder 74), The University of Chicago Library, Chicago. On Halbwachs's participation in the *réunions du samedi*, see 'Réunions du samedi' 1922–35.
[8] See Thibaudet 1925: 483–4.
[9] Fréchet and Halbwachs 1924, and *Index Generalis* 1923–4: F 153 *et seq.*
[10] Halbwachs 1934a: 173–4.

the other social sciences, but rather a general one, one that synthesised the results of the others and hence was superior. That Halbwachs shared this opinion when he came to Strasbourg is clear from his conclusion to an article on Durkheim written shortly before his appointment:

> If Durkheim had the idea of bringing together, within the framework of the *Année sociologique*, the facts studied by the most varied disciplines – by social philosophy, by law, by the history of religions, by political economy, by demography, etc. – it was because he thought that each concerned itself with one part of the domain of the new science, and that the best way to make them fully conscious of their common objective was to bring them into contact with one another. One can now say that he succeeded, and that there is no field of study relating to human nature that should not soon feel the organising and invigorating influence of his doctrine. (Halbwachs 1918: 411)

Halbwachs's Strasbourg colleagues disagreed. To be sure, many had been strongly influenced by Durkheim and his movement. Thus it was largely through reading the *Année sociologique* that the psychologist Charles Blondel and the historians Marc Bloch and Lucien Febvre had become interested in studying social phenomena and in collaboration among the social sciences. But they refused to believe that their own disciplines were subservient to sociology. On the contrary, Durkheim's claims had only convinced them of the need to reform these disciplines so that they could better resist the sociologists' imperialism. This meant that Halbwachs often found it necessary to defend sociology's claims. The result was a series of friendly but serious debates between Halbwachs and his colleagues, debates pursued in private conversations, at the *réunions du samedi*, and in print.[11]

Of course the contest between Durkheimian sociology and its foes was not confined to Strasbourg. After the war the Durkheimians found themselves on the defensive everywhere.[12] But nowhere else was the contest as visible as at the University of Strasbourg, through much of the period the one French university with a chair of sociology; nowhere else was a prominent Durkheimian so directly exposed to such formidable adversaries. For a sociologist interested in defining the limits and distinguishing features of his discipline – for a sociologist like Halbwachs – the situation was close to ideal. As for the results, they can best be considered with reference to the specific debates in which Halbwachs participated.

One debate concerned sociology's relations with psychology. At the root of the dispute was Durkheim's refusal to acknowledge that psychology could

---

[11] Among works discussed by Halbwachs at *réunions du samedi* were M. Granet, *La Religion des chinois* (Paris: Gauthier-Villars, 1922), G. Davy, *La Foi jurée* (Paris: Alcan, 1922), and R. Hertz, *Mélanges de sociologie religieuse et de folklore* (Paris: Alcan, 1928); see 'Réunions du samedi' 1922–3: 107, 193–4 and 1928–9: 200–1.

[12] See, for example, König 1931: 485–7.

John E. Craig

contribute to the understanding of social phenomena. His position had been that collective psychology was merely a branch of sociology while individual psychology was corrupted by subjectivism and in any case had nothing to say about the ultimate determinants of human behaviour, which were social rather than individual.[13] Halbwachs was more generous. He had once considered becoming a psychologist himself – he had decided against it, he later confided to a student, because he had concluded that after Bergson there was little left to say[14] – and he always acknowledged that physiological psychology (*psycho-physiologie*) 'has its domain, just as sociological psychology has its' (Halbwachs 1925a: xi). But in his own works on themes of special interest to psychologists, notably *Les Cadres sociaux de la mémoire* and *Les Causes du suicide*, he was a complete Durkheimian. He insisted that memory and suicide were appropriate subjects of sociological study and that sociology must defend itself against psychological determinism. Thus, after considering psychiatric theories of suicide, he observed that Comte 'warned scholars against that sociological materialism which claims "to explain everything in sociology by the merely secondary influences of climate and race", and, we can add, by the organic and nervous constitution of individuals. Thus can we understand the conflict which today pits sociologists against psychiatrists . . .' (Halbwachs 1930: 449).

Halbwachs's opinions, while more conciliatory than Durkheim's, did not satisfy his leading critic among the psychologists, his colleague Charles Blondel. Of course Blondel, who had also been strongly influenced by Durkheim, found much to admire in his friend's work. He described *Les Cadres sociaux de la mémoire*, for· instance, as 'a new and important demonstration of the services that sociology can offer psychology' (Blondel 1926: 298). But he criticised Halbwachs for commenting on matters that were in the neurologists' domain, observing that 'sociology does not have to settle, in passing, questions that are so manifestly beyond its competence' (Blondel 1926: 298). And he added a warning with which many of their Strasbourg colleagues would have agreed: 'Bold claims and imprudent language should be avoided. They are less appropriate than ever at a time when, not without reason I believe, many would be happy to see constituted a Society of Moral Sciences with sociology occupying one of its council's leading positions, but do not wish to hear any talk of sociological imperialism or of pan-sociology' (Blondel 1926: 298). Blondel believed, more specifically, that sociology and psychology should not only recognise each other's domain but also learn to collaborate. Thus, in his own book on suicide (1933), he attempted to reconcile the sociological and psychological theses.[15] And in a speech in 1937

[13] See Blondel 1946: 66–7.
[14] Roger Mehl (personal communication).
[15] Blondel 1933. In his review of this book Halbwachs indicated their differences succinctly: 'In

268

he appealed for closer relations between the two disciplines: 'natural history and history *per se* concur in inviting sociology not to forget space and the individual for the sake of the group ... autarky is dangerous for the human sciences. It would be in their interest for *homo sociologicus* to rejoin *homo psychologicus* in the gallery of abstractions' (Blondel [1938]: 124).

Did Halbwachs agree? Judging from his later writings he did not. With time he acquired greater respect for psychology's potential as a science, not least because psychologists seemed increasingly willing to give sociology its due. Thus in 1938 he praised Blondel and others for discovering 'that a collective mentality exists and that it is not like a lost, isolated or negligible province, but exerts an influence upon all the functions of individual mentality which cannot be understood or explained without it' (Halbwachs 1938a: 616). But he did not share Blondel's belief in the possibility of close collaboration between individual psychology on the one hand and collective psychology or sociology on the other, since, like Durkheim, he thought the former had nothing to offer the latter: 'As for the aspect of the mental life which is related to society and to its institutions and customs' – the aspect of concern to the sociologist – 'it can be only collective, for it is in union with the collective realities which pervade it, which it finds reflected in its own nature' (Halbwachs 1939: 822).

A second debate concerned the relations between sociology and geography or, to be more precise, between social morphology and human geography. The debate had its origins in Durkheim's reaction in the late 1890s to the environmental determinism of the German geographer Friedrich Ratzel. In distinguishing his own position from Ratzel's, Durkheim insisted that:

In effect it is a question of studying not the forms of the land but rather the forms which affect societies as they establish themselves on the land, which is quite different. No doubt watercourses, mountains, etc. figure as elements in the constitution of the social substratum; but they are not the only elements, nor the most essential. But the very term geography leads almost fatally to assigning them an importance they do not have ... The number of individuals, the way in which they are grouped, the character of their dwellings do not in any sense constitute geographical facts. Hence why retain a term which is so distorted from its usual meaning? For these reasons a new rubric appears necessary. (Durkheim 1899: 521)

The rubric Durkheim proposed was 'social morphology'.

Over the next few years Durkheim and his disciples, particularly Simiand and Halbwachs, refined their arguments and intensified the attack. They

sum, Blondel is very close to recognising that suicide as a collective phenomenon is one thing and that suicide as an individual act is another. From this it would follow that the debate on the matter between sociologists and psychiatrists is irrelevant, since it appears that the two parties are actually not studying the same facts even though they both refer to and concern themselves with suicide. Blondel has not gone this far, since for him the two types of study, however distinct they are proving to be, are necessarily interdependent' (Halbwachs 1933a: 474–5).

rejected the human geographers' explanatory pretensions, insisting that 'the true explanatory fact is human and psychological, and the physical fact is only, at most, a condition' (Simiand 1910: 729). And they faulted their lack of methodological sophistication when assessing the impact of the physical environment. Specifically they criticised the predilection for regional studies that characterised the students of France's leading human geographer, Paul Vidal de la Blache, contending that 'in so complex a matter to limit oneself to a single case is to condemn oneself in advance to proving nothing' (Simiand 1910: 731).[16] The geographers were claiming more than they should, and proving less than they might.

The task of defending the human geographers fell to one of Halbwachs's Strasbourg colleagues, the historian Lucien Febvre. In his *La Terre et l'évolution humaine*, published in 1922, Febvre fought what amounted to a two-front battle. He defended human geography against the social morphologists' suspected ambitions, arguing that 'social morphology cannot lay claim to suppressing human geography to its own advantage, for the two disciplines have not the same method nor the same orientation nor the same objective' (Febvre with Bataillon 1922: 79). But he also attacked the environmental determinism identified with Ratzel. He did so with particular verve for he believed that the Ratzelians' excesses had done much to discredit human geography, thus making it more vulnerable to the Durkheimians' imperialism. Febvre's own solution was to support the 'possibilism' of Vidal de la Blache and his school (arguing that the environment does not determine social behaviour but does limit possibilities) and to recommend that scholars concerned with the relations between man and his environment – 'even sociologists, indeed even "social morphologists"' – base their work 'on the conclusions of human geography' (Febvre with Bataillon 1922: 443).

Halbwachs, once described by Febvre as 'the convinced propagandist' of social morphology (Febvre 1946b: 350), responded to these arguments both at a *reunion du samedi* (those present included Febvre and the geographer Henri Baulig, another Vidalian) and in the first volume of the revived *Année sociologique*. He of course sympathised) Febvre's opposition to the geographic determinists. He was less happy, however, with Febvre's remarks about social morphologists and particularly his suggestion that they base their work on the conclusions of human geography. If they did, Halbwachs insisted, 'when one reaches the social facts one will see them only from a geographical perspective ...' But, he continued: 'The facts of social morphology are essentially social facts. It is toward their social side that one must look: it is to social facts of the same sort that they must be linked. Where

[16] Also see Halbwachs 1910: 722.

geography sees differences, morphology will quite often find identical facts, and vice versa. Each of these sciences can develop only if neither of them tries to encroach on the other' (Halbwachs 1925b: 908).

Following this exchange, the debate declined in intensity. Each side became more limited in its ambitions and more willing to acknowledge its rival's contributions. The human geographers began to recognise that social morphology had a domain distinct from their own and to admit that the sociologists' criticisms 'have certainly helped to put geographers on guard against certain deterministic explanations and against extreme theories of the direct influence of the environment' (Demangeon 1923: 168).[17] And, led by Halbwachs, the social morphologists put more emphasis on 'the constraints that the environment places on human arrangements', and, by focusing their own attention on demographic questions, tended to redefine social morphology along narrower and less threatening lines (Halbwachs 1970: 49). Symptomatic of the improved relations was the participation of two of the most distinguished human geographers, Albert Demangeon and Jules Sion, in the production of the section of the *Annales sociologiques* devoted to social morphology, presumably at the invitation of Halbwachs, the section's editor. Also symptomatic was Halbwachs's contributions on social morphology to the *Encyclopédie française*, presumably at the invitation of its editor, Febvre.[18]

A third debate concerned the relations between sociology and history. It was a debate provoked by the Durkheimians' contention that history was subordinate to sociology. This does not mean the Durkheimians had a low opinion of historical explanations. On the contrary, they believed that contemporary institutions could not be fully understood without considering their origins and evolution; 'to my knowledge', Durkheim once observed, 'there is no sociology deserving the name that does not have a historical character' (Durkheim 1908a: 229). But, while the Durkheimians respected historical explanations, they did not respect those offered by historians. The function of historians, in their opinion, was to provide facts for the sociologist to interpret.[19] At least this should be their function. As it was, some Durkheimians believed, historians were incapable of doing even this. The foremost proponent of this view was François Simiand. In a series of debates with historians and philosophers between 1900 and World War I, Simiand argued not only that historians' explanations were unscientific – the basis for sociology's claims to superiority – but also that historians could not even be relied upon to fill the role assigned them by the Durkheimians. The

[17] Also see Bloch 1924: 238–9.
[18] See *Annales sociologiques*, série E, vol. 1 (1935) – vol. 4 (1940) *passim*, and Halbwachs *et al.* 1936.
[19] See Durkheim 1898: ii–vi, and Bellah 1965.

John E. Craig

implication was that, if the historians did not correct their ways, the sociologists would have to ignore them entirely and collect their own evidence.[20]

Most historians dismissed these criticisms as mere manifestations of the arrogance of an upstart and suspect discipline. But some were more sympathetic. Noteworthy was a diffuse group associated with the philosopher Henri Berr and the journal he founded in 1900, the *Revue de synthèse historique*. All were avid readers of the *Année sociologique*[21] and agreed with many of the Durkheimians' observations concerning their own discipline and the social sciences generally. In particular they shared the sociologists' disdain for what Berr labelled 'historicist history' (*histoire historisante*) and agreed that the study of the past should become more scientific and, to this end, that there should be more collaboration among the disciplines that studied man and society. But they rejected the claim that history was subservient to sociology. Their position – at least as represented by Berr and his journal – was that claims to primacy among the social sciences were obstacles to the collaboration they all desired. What was required, instead, was a general recognition that each discipline was of equal standing and had a distinctive and important contribution to make.[22]

But for two historians associated with Berr and his journal, Marc Bloch and Lucien Febvre, this was not enough. In the 1920s, when they were colleagues in Strasbourg, Bloch and Febvre became convinced that Berr's general objectives could be pursued more effectively. In their opinion, Berr and his journal were too philosophical, insufficiently combative, and, perhaps most serious, of limited influence among historians. It was with this in mind that they decided to establish a journal of their own. It appeared in 1929 and was entitled *Annales d'histoire économique et sociale*.[23]

The declared objective of the *Annales* was to develop and to promote a new approach to social and economic history, an approach rooted in a readiness to innovate and to borrow from other disciplines. But the editors' intentions were not as limited or innocent as their occasional public pronouncements implied. For behind their interest in developing a new kind of history lay a desire to strengthen history's position among the social sciences. In their opinion the Durkheimians' imperialism had been a more-or-less natural response to the failure of the *historiens historisants* dominant in the discipline to cultivate all parts of history's domain and to use up-to-date methods. Viewed in this light, one of the underlying objectives of Bloch and Febvre was to reclaim for history the territory expropriated by the

---

[20] See, in particular, Simiand 1903, 1906 and 1907.
[21] See, for instance, Piganiol 1955: 246.
[22] See, among others, Faublée 1964 and Leuilliot 1964.
[23] Leuilliot 1973, Morazé 1957: 4.

272

sociologists. Beyond this, though, they also sought to challenge sociology's claim to primacy among the social sciences. Admittedly, it is difficult to reconstruct the evolution of their ideas on these questions, partly because of their distaste for theoretical discussions and partly, perhaps, because they did not think it prudent to reveal their ultimate goals. But Bloch and Febvre apparently believed that there were only two potential rivals for primacy among the social sciences, history and sociology, and that history's claims were – or could be – more legitimate. Looked at another way, they apparently thought that history's best defence against its neighbours' imperialism was for history to become imperialistic itself.

But what about Bloch's and Febvre's more specific intentions concerning sociology? To what extent did they plan to open the *Annales* to sociologists and to sociological articles? These were among the questions their publisher raised a few months before the first issue appeared. In his response Febvre noted that: 'We have no intention of presenting general sociological articles in the journal. The sociologists have their own organs; the only ones in France working systematically and in the scientific spirit have in particular the *Année sociologique* at their disposal.' Febvre added, however, that historians should be kept informed of the developing literature in sociology and indicated that they might consider publishing articles in the field of economic sociology.

It is for such reasons that we are anxious that this French school of Durkheim, which has for all men of our generation had an undeniable influence, sometimes positive it must be added and sometimes negative, have a representative among us. He is not there to do the work of a man of party or of doctrine, but as an informant and, to a certain extent, a critic. (Quoted in Leuilliot 1973: 320)

The man to whom he referred was his Strasbourg colleague Maurice Halbwachs.

During the first decade of the *Annales* – the period that most concerns us – the journal's treatment of sociology was in accord with the policy indicated in Febvre's memorandum. The *Annales* published only six articles by sociologists, three by Halbwachs and three by a non-Durkheimian, Georges Friedmann.[24] But throughout the decade Halbwachs was a valued member of the editorial committee and contributed dozens of book reviews and short notes. Worthy of particular attention are his comments on statistical methods in the first few volumes; these were among the first discussions of the merits and techniques of statistical analysis to appear in any journal directed primarily at historians.[25]

[24] The articles by Halbwachs were Halbwachs 1929, 1932b and 1934b.
[25] For a virtually complete list of Halbwachs's contributions to the *Annales*, see Karady with Thiébart 1972. The only important item missing from this bibliography is Halbwachs 1946.

Halbwachs's collaboration reflected the high regard in which Bloch and Febvre held their colleague. They admired 'his ingenious intellect, even-handed and always alert', and they considered him a good example of the Durkheimians' growing willingness to moderate the dogmatism of their *maître*. Consider, for instance, Bloch's reaction to Halbwachs's *L'Evolution des besoins dans les classes ouvrières* (1933):

> How can one refuse to note, from one book to the next, the growth of a mind, one of the best qualities of which is that it always remains extremely flexible and lively? For that matter it would not be difficult – I have already made this observation elsewhere – to discern among other scholars trained in the same school, the signs of an analogous development. More and more, French sociology is tending to give the temporal dimension its due. It is not for the *Annales* to complain. (Bloch 1935a: 83)

It was not just the retreat of Halbwachs and of other Durkheimians from earlier claims, not just their adoption of positions more compatible with their own that impressed the historians of the *Annales*. So did the sociologists' methodological advances. Although the *Annales* historians were hardly positivists, they agreed that the research methods and the reasoning of historians were much less scientific than they should be, and they believed that in this area there was much to be learned from sociologists. Febvre, for instance, argued that historians could profit from the Durkheimians' interest in establishing taxonomies.[26] Bloch praised the efforts of Halbwachs, Mauss, and Simiand to develop more precise and workable definitions of such terms as 'lifestyle' (*genre de vie*), 'civilisations', and 'class'; these efforts, he noted, responded to the needs of all historians who shared his own dissatisfaction with such traditional but imprecise concepts as 'nobility' and 'bourgeoisie'.[27] Both Bloch and Febvre acknowledged that Simiand's harsh criticisms of historians' approaches to causation were justified.[28] And both praised the quantitative methods employed by Halbwachs and Simiand and urged historians to familiarise themselves with them. He longed for the day, Bloch once commented, when historians would recognise that statistics was one of the most important of their auxiliary sciences.[29]

But while they found much to admire in the Durkheimians – more than they had found earlier – they still had misgivings. Essentially their complaint was that, while the sociologists were moving in the right direction, they had a long way to go. As this suggests, their specific criticisms were similar to those historians had been making since the emergence of the Durkheimian school. Thus Bloch complained that the sociologists gave too much attention to primitive societies and too little to Europe, that the book reviews in the

[26] Febvre 1930: 583.
[27] Bloch 1931: 592.
[28] Bloch 1934a: 2–3, Febvre 1930: 585, Febvre 1935: 391.
[29] Bloch 1929a: 429.

Annales sociologiques tended to be too abstract, that the Durkheimians continued to over-emphasise the collectivity and to take liberties with other disciplines, and that Halbwachs distinguished too sharply between the historical and sociological approaches.[30] Another contributor to the *Annales*, André Piganiol, suggested that the sociologists were too impatient, offering syntheses without undertaking the necessary preliminary studies.[31] Febvre noted that the Durkheimians – he specifically mentioned two of those most sympathetic to history, Célestin Bouglé and Marcel Mauss – continued to regard the discipline of history with condescension.[32] And in a two-part article published during World War II a new addition to the *Annales* team, Charles Morazé, attacked the methods and pretensions of Simiand in particular and the Durkheimians in general. Morazé maintained that the Durkheimians had limited their potential through their obstinate belief in the legitimacy of isolating social facts, that they continued to be more interested in annexing other disciplines than in assisting them, and that despite Simiand's efforts and claims he had not succeeded in developing a scientific methodology for the social sciences. The root of the problem, he continued, was the Durkheimians' preoccupation with emulating the physical sciences.[33] In Morazé's opinion the sociology of Max Weber opens 'a route that is frankly broader and more productive' (Morazé 1942: 35).

These criticisms, even Morazé's, were well intentioned. The objective was not to undermine the Durkheimian school, but to reform and strengthen it. The *Annales* historians frequently expressed the hope that the Durkheimians would remain vigorous and influential, and there is no reason to question their sincerity.[34] Their motives, however, were far from altruistic. They realised that in many respects they and the Durkheimians were fighting the same battles and, as noted above, that the historian prepared to borrow selectively could learn much from the sociologists. In other words the discipline of history, at least as defined by the *Annales*, would profit if the Durkheimian school remained healthy.

But how much room was there for collaboration? To what extent did the two disciplines share domains and interests? On these questions the *Annales* historians, like the Durkheimians, were not united. One of them, Piganiol, thought sociology was the limit toward which history was moving, and once expressed the hope that the two disciplines would merge.[35] But others, including Bloch and Febvre, were less radical. Bloch believed that the

---

[30] See Bloch 1927: 176, 1929b: 435–6, 1934b: 510, and 1936: 458.
[31] Piganiol 1933: 324–5.
[32] Febvre 1949: 229.
[33] Morazé 1942. For a defence of Simiand against some of Morazé's criticisms, see Halbwachs 1943: x–xi.
[34] See Bloch 1935b: 393, and Febvre 1934: 220.
[35] Piganiol 1933: 324 and 1955: 245–6.

John E. Craig

Annales historians differed from the Durkheimians both in the methods they used and in the problems they examined, while Febvre argued that the disciplines had distinct orientations and, on another occasion, that they examined the same problems but approached them differently.[36] Whatever their differences, though, they agreed that close collaboration was essential. 'It is by scholarly exchanges of this sort', Bloch argued, 'that one can hope to see the sciences of man progress. There would not be a worse danger for them than a dogmatic partitioning which causes the sociologists and the historians to ignore each other or to regard each other with mutual disdain' (Bloch 1925: 82).

Halbwachs was not in full accord. To be sure, he had a high regard for the work of historians such as Bloch and Febvre. Indeed, after moving to the Sorbonne he even agreed to join Bloch – who had followed a year later – in establishing and directing an institute of economic and social history.[37] Yet Halbwachs never modified his negative opinions concerning Bloch's discipline. He continued to criticise historians for emphasising description rather than explanation and for being unscientific and hence unreliable in their approaches to both. The historian's understanding of causation, he argued in 1936, 'is poorly developed. Historians think of a cause as one or several anterior facts selected unsystematically, on impulse, in accord with the ideas of the historian himself and his environment, in accord with intellectual fashions' (Halbwachs 1936: 287). In practice this usually meant that the historian gave too much emphasis to the influence of contingent events. And Halbwachs made similar criticisms of historians' efforts at description. Here he was less generous than Durkheim, for like Simiand he did not even think sociologists could rely on the descriptive materials provided by historians.[38] He contended that the methods that he and Simiand advocated for the study of the past – and that Simiand employed in his studies of the history of price and wage trends – were far more sophisticated than those used by historians.

But, it should be emphasised, Halbwachs did not consider these methods the exclusive property of sociologists and natural scientists. He insisted, rather, that they were appropriate to all of the social sciences, history included. Thus he left the door open for closer collaboration between history and sociology. If the two disciplines were to move closer, however, history would have to concede the most, for historians could not take full advantage of the methods favoured by Halbwachs and Simiand without abandoning their preoccupation with the unique and learning to share the sociologists' concern with the general, with regularities and laws. In sum, if there was to

[36] Bloch 1945: 31, and Febvre 1934: 220.
[37] Bloch 1938: 53.
[38] Halbwachs 1936: 287–8, 290–1, 307–8, 317–18.

276

be closer collaboration it would have to be on sociology's terms. Halbwachs made his position clear at the thesis defence of Raymond Aron. At one point he remarked to the candidate: 'On several occasions you use the expression "difference between the microscopic and the macroscopic levels" to indicate, I think, the historical and the sociological, but you seem to assign more value to the former than to the latter. But sociology is superior to history' (quoted in Fessard 1971: 66–7).[39]

The last of the major debates concerned the relations between sociology and economics. Durkheim's position, articulated in 1908 at a meeting of the Société d'Economie Politique, was that economic facts such as the values of commodities and modes of production were in part matters of opinion and taste and in this respect were like the facts analysed by the other social scientists. Seen from this perspective 'Political economy loses ... the hegemony that it assigns itself and becomes a social science alongside the others, in close association with them yet without being able to claim dominance over them' (Durkheim 1908b: 66). It was a position seconded and elaborated by the leading economic sociologists in the Durkheimian camp, Simiand and Halbwachs. In the *Année sociologique* and elsewhere they repeatedly attacked the assumptions, methods, and pretensions of the economists, directing particular criticism at their deductive approaches and at the concept of *homo economicus*. And in many of their articles and books they attempted to exemplify what was needed. Simiand's studies of fluctuations in wages and prices contended that the expectations and desires of individuals are basically determined by social and collective psychological factors. Halbwachs argued similarly in his studies of consumption patterns in the working class, insisting that one's perceptions of what is necessary – of the values of commodities – are shaped by the nature of one's work and by one's social environment and cultural traditions.

The position of the pure economists – the thorough-going individualists at whom the Durkheimians directed their attacks – was summarised by the president of the Société d'Economie Politique, Paul Leroy-Beaulieu, following Durkheim's remarks to the society. While acknowledging that opinions could modify certain economic factors, Leroy-Beaulieu asserted that they could have no bearing on the laws of economics, which are manifestly objective and 'have the force of physical laws'. He concluded by claiming that 'political economy occupies the top rank among the social sciences; it alone rests on indestructible and material foundations, and its laws are fixed regardless of changes in opinion' (Leroy-Beaulieu 1908: 73). After this the pure economists generally ignored the Durkheimians'

---

[39] For a fuller discussion of the relations between the Durkheimians and the *Annales* school, see Craig 1981.

criticisms, but two exceptions are worth noting. A few months after the confrontation at the Société d'Economie Politique, Clément Colson publicly took issue with Halbwachs's laudatory review of Simiand's study of the wages of French coalminers (a book Colson had not read). He accused Halbwachs of not understanding the law of supply and demand, argued that collective factors have no impact on wage levels, and, implying guilt by association, suggested that Halbwachs and Simiand had become immersed 'in abstractions that are much more in harmony with recent German political economy than with the traditional political economy of France and England' (Colson 1908: 730). And in the 1930s, Georges and Edouard Guillaume, among the most abstract and mathematical of French economists, emphasised the dangers inherent in the empirical and statistical methods employed by Simiand, rejected all efforts to relate economic trends to psychological factors, and noted that Simiand's laborious calculations had yielded no results incompatible with those of their own more parsimonious approach.[40]

But these critics did not speak for all French economists. As with the psychologists, the geographers, and the historians, there were a number who agreed with much of what the Durkheimians said about their discipline and with some of the suggested remedies. Among them were many of those identified with the *Journal d'économie politique*, the most eclectic of France's major journals of economics. Particularly sympathetic was Gaëtan Pirou, one of the journal's editors. In the late 1920s he praised Simiand's methodological contributions, accepted the essence of his argument concerning the determinants of coalminers' wages, and noted that Simiand had already had a significant impact on many younger economists.[41] Two years later he praised Simiand's *magnum opus*, *Le Salaire*, describing it as 'a work which will certainly represent a landmark in the history of the theory of wages, but which also and above all will permit us to observe to what extent the positive method, of which M. F. Simiand has become the brilliant theorist, is capable of reforming economics' (Pirou 1931: 1708). And subsequently Pirou and others often commented favourably on the contributions of sociology, and particularly the work of Simiand and Halbwachs, to the development of economics. Although hardly prepared to set aside deductive theorising, they stressed the importance of complementing it with empirical research of the sort advocated by the Durkheimians. Thus in his review of Halbwachs's *L'Evolution des besoins dans les classes ouvrières* one economist concluded that 'It is precisely by books like the one by M. H. that a bridge can be built between reality and mathematical abstractions' (Bousquet 1935: 237). And in 1938 Pirou observed that 'the debate over the best means to construct the science of economics' was between the

[40] Guillaume 1933: 16, 19; G. and E. Guillaume 1937: 11–14 and *passim*.
[41] Pirou 1929: 10, 115–18, 143–7, 156. Also see Labrousse 1980: 112–13.

deductive school and the positivist school – the latter best represented by Simiand – and that the outcome was in doubt: 'I do not believe that as things stand one is authorised to decide which of the two methods is better. Accordingly it is appropriate to let the partisans of each work freely. They will be judged by their results' (Pirou 1938: ix, x).

These economists conceded more than the Durkheimians. Indeed, with the exception of a young scholar on the fringes of the group, Robert Marjolin, the latter conceded next to nothing.[42] Simiand was certainly familiar with the pure economists' deductive theories, and he once acknowledged that one of them had yielded results similar to his own.[43] Yet he never employed these theories in his own work, and apparently never admitted that they might contribute to the development of economics. Halbwachs, his successor as the Durkheimians' leading spokesman on economic questions (Simiand died in 1935), was hardly more generous. He expressed dismay over the popularity of mathematical approaches to economics at English and American universities and at the Centre Polytechnicien d'Etudes Economiques in Paris.[44] He published harsh critiques of much of the literature that resulted, including works by the Guillaumes, A. C. Pigou, and John Maynard Keynes.[45] And he criticised those generally sympathetic to empirical research for not recognising that 'to treat economic phenomena "as things", one must observe them from without and not from the perspective of the agents themselves, which is necessarily practical and technical and always limited' (Halbwachs 1940b: 48). To be sure, he once observed – in a speech at the Centre Polytechnicien d'Etudes Economiques, an unsympathetic forum – that 'mathematical economics, which is a good instrument of analysis, can admittedly force us to see aspects of economic reality which would otherwise escape us' (Halbwachs 1937a: 30). But he immediately added that it had more to offer mathematicians than economists, and argued that the latter should direct their energies elsewhere. Specifically, they 'would do better to bring us new materials, to collect facts with which we are not yet familiar, to carry further and further the positive exploration of reality as it is' (Halbwachs 1937a: 30). It was a mission similar to that which the Durkheimians assigned the historians.

Between the wars Halbwachs manifested considerable interest – more than most Durkheimians – in the potential and limits of his discipline. He did so under the influence of a variety of challenges that came from outside the circle of Durkheim's disciples. Some, as we have seen, came from scholars in

[42] For Marjolin's position, see Marjolin 1941.
[43] Simiand 1933: 19–22.
[44] See Halbwachs 1937a: 23–30, and 1940a: 7–9 and *passim*.
[45] Halbwachs 1938b: 39–48, 1937b: 62–70, 116–24, and 1940a: 9–19.

John E. Craig

neighbouring disciplines. But others came from fellow sociologists who were not Durkheimians, particularly from German and American sociologists. And yet another came from Marxism. If we are to understand the development of Halbwachs's ideas concerning sociology, his responses to these challenges must also be considered.

As noted above, Halbwachs's interest in Germany and in German literature in the social sciences antedated World War I. It may be assumed, accordingly, that he would have followed the development of German social thought between the wars even if he had not accepted a position at the University of Strasbourg. But once in Strasbourg, he found an environment particularly conducive to studying Germany and German scholarship. Although the university, like its German predecessor, was basically a bastion of a national culture rather than a bridge between two cultures, many of its professors had a special interest in German questions and considered it their responsibility to introduce German scholarship to France. In addition there were a few Alsatian professors who had studied at German universities and come under the influence of such scholars as Georg Simmel and Max Weber, and there were facilities and opportunities for studying Germany not available at any other French university. These environmental factors help to explain why Halbwachs did more between the wars than any other Durkheimian to introduce German sociology to France.[46]

Halbwachs's interest in Germany did not distinguish him from his Strasbourg colleagues, but his attitude toward the country did. Of the professors 'from the interior' he was, until the advent of Hitler, among the most Germanophile. He was one of the first to contribute to a German scholarly journal (in 1926 to the *Jahrbuch für Soziologie*).[47] He was in the minority that favoured inviting German exchange professors to the University of Strasbourg.[48] And he and Blondel appear to have been the only Strasbourg professors to participate in the Franco-German conferences at Davos of 1928–31. (Among the German scholars with whom Halbwachs became acquainted in Davos was the sociologist Werner Sombart.)[49] In short, Halbwachs was a good European and, at least until the 1930s, a proponent of Franco-German reconciliation. It was in this spirit that he interpreted the work of the German sociologists in courses – including one on 'The principal representatives of German sociology'[50] – and in publications.

[46] It should be noted, too, that Halbwachs was affiliated with the university's Centre d'Etudes Germaniques and accordingly journeyed frequently to Mainz, the centre's base until 1930, to lecture. See Vézian 1930: 389–90.
[47] Halbwachs 1926.
[48] See the minutes of the Faculté des lettres (Conseil) of the University of Strasbourg, 24 Nov. 1928, Archives départementales du Bas-Rhin (Strasbourg): AL 154, no. 3.
[49] Halbwachs 1933b: 52.
[50] See Vézian 1930: 390.

280

The German sociologist to whom Halbwachs gave the most attention was Max Weber. In fact Halbwachs was the first French sociologist to appreciate the importance of Weber's work, the first to attempt to popularise it in France, and the only Durkheimian to evaluate it systematically. As for his opinion of Weber's work, it was very favourable. He admired Weber's thesis on the origins of capitalism, employed it in his own work more than once, and defended it against its critics in Germany (Lujo Brentano and Werner Sombart) and in England (H. M. Robertson).[51] He also praised and used Weber's ideas concerning charisma and bureaucratisation.[52] What most impressed him, however, were Weber's methodology and integrity. Halbwachs welcomed the theory of ideal types, observing that: 'Behind this somewhat uncertain concept one at least discerns a quite justified sense of the inadequacy of traditional notions' (Halbwachs 1929: 87).[53] He approved of Weber's commitment to interdisciplinary research. He praised his efforts 'to eliminate from the social sciences everything that might remotely resemble value judgments' (Halbwachs 1929: 83–4). And he admired Weber's lack of dogmatism and his intellectual daring (traits, it might be added, that also characterised Halbwachs):

What is striking about him ... is that he never ceased revising his ideas. Each time he finished a project, it seems that he found a new impetus to go even further. One could easily compare him to one of the industrial capitalists of the heroic era, so well described by him, who felt naturally obligated to reinvest everything they had earned in new enterprises. (Halbwachs 1929: 88)

Halbwachs had less to say about other German sociologists, and most of what he said was less generous. There were a few whose work he admired, including Karl Mannheim, Georg Simmel ('a gifted sociologist'), and Werner Sombart.[54] But generally speaking he considered German sociologists to be preoccupied with theoretical questions and with *Geist* and *Kultur*, and hostile to empirical and interdisciplinary research. And he disapproved. He would not accept the argument, suggested by Raymond Aron in *La Sociologie allemande contemporaine* (1935), that 'the two sociologies, the French and the German, both well express "the national spirit"'. He considered this 'too simple a way of sanctifying an opposition that may be temporary; it is to run counter to the sentiments of those who believe that sociology is a science (and not a philosophy, in the traditional sense)'. Halbwachs's own thesis was that sociology in Germany reflected the difficulties through which

[51] See Halbwachs 1925a: 342–5, 1925c, and 1935: 97–9.
[52] Halbwachs 1925a: 303 1929: 87, and 1934c: 260–1.
[53] Also see Halbwachs 1925d: 727.
[54] See Halbwachs 1932c: 364–5, 1955: 91–3, 100, and, for the quotation, Pradines and Halbwachs 1924–5: 229. A former student, G. Erwin Ritter, recalls that Halbwachs 'did his best in his lectures ... to make intelligible the theories of Max Weber and Werner Sombart' (personal communication).

John E. Craig

the country was passing on the road to modernity: 'the Germans have a great deal of difficulty comprehending the situation in which they find themselves and adapting themselves to new circumstances. This explains the passion for self-analysis and the metaphysical excesses that are the most striking features of these sociological systems' (Halbwachs 1937c: 622–3). Once Germany had adjusted to modernity, he implied, its sociologists would adopt the more scientific outlook identified with French sociology.

Halbwachs's opinions about American sociology were also largely formed during his Strasbourg years. More precisely, they were largely formed during the few months in 1930 that he spent as a visiting professor at the University of Chicago, at the time the leading American centre of sociological research.[55] This experience stimulated his interest in American sociology, and after returning to France he followed its development closely. In fact after 1930 Halbwachs was, by French standards, an authority on the subject.

Halbwachs was more sympathetic to American sociology than to German. He particularly approved of the Americans' emphasis on urban and industrial sociology and their diligence in collecting data. But he also found room for criticism. He thought the Americans gave too little attention to the potential contributions of neighbouring disciplines; like most Germans, they defined sociology too narrowly. And he considered their methods insufficiently scientific. He insisted that the monographs of the Chicago school were 'books of description, no doubt, rather than of science' (Halbwachs 1932b: 18), and suggested that Americans should give more attention to statistics and to the formulation of hypotheses.[56] If the Germans went too far in one direction, the Americans went too far in the other: 'while the German sociologists hardly ever leave theorising behind, the Americans are perhaps not sufficiently concerned with guiding ideas and perspectives' (Halbwachs 1932d: 81).

Halbwachs did not respond as systematically or explicitly to the Marxist challenge, perhaps because he took it less seriously. Of course, in some respects his interests were close to those of Marxist theorists and scholars. Like the Marxists – and more than any other Durkheimian – he concerned himself with the analysis of social classes and the causes of social change. But the hypotheses he advanced and the conclusions he reached had little in common with the Marxists'. Halbwachs considered position in the occupational order to be only one of the factors determining class identity, and class

[55] In responding to the invitation to visit the University of Chicago, Halbwachs wrote: 'I would find it very rewarding to study the organisation of your department of sociology. There is much that we can learn from you.' Halbwachs to Ellsworth Faris, 30 April 1930, The University of Chicago Library, Chicago. Halbwachs was at the university for one trimester (autumn 1930), and taught courses, in English, on 'Modern French Sociology' and 'Suicide'. See Faris to Halbwachs, 6 June 1930, *ibid.*

[56] Halbwachs 1932b: 18, 20–30.

identity to be only one of the factors determining individual thought and behaviour. He insisted that the most fundamental cleavage in modern societies was that between the urban and rural worlds and their respective lifestyles (*genres de vie*), not that between the industrial working class and the bourgeoisie.[57] He noted that the Marxist theory of the progressive proletarianisation of the middle classes did not conform to reality.[58] And he claimed that, while the industrial working class currently had greater solidarity than any other class, this solidarity was far from complete and could be expected to decline with time.[59] Indeed, for Halbwachs the progressive democratisation of tastes and patterns of consumption was tending to erode all class distinctions and, hence, the potential for class conflict. In this regard he looked for guidance concerning the future of European societies not to the works of Marxist theorists but rather to contemporary trends in the United States.[60]

These confrontations with German and American sociology and with Marxism had an effect on Halbwachs similar to that of his debates with scholars in other disciplines: they increased his interest in epistemological and methodological questions and his concern over his discipline's future. More specifically, they reinforced his desire to see sociology become more scientific. Of course the other Durkheimians had also wanted their discipline to be scientific, but Halbwachs believed that, with the partial exception of François Simiand, they had not understood what was necessary or possible. They had not always succeeded in separating their values from their work, for instance, and they had not fully appreciated the importance of using quantitative methods. Halbwachs, the most accomplished statistician among the Durkheimians, gave particular emphasis to the latter. He insisted that statistical analysis was 'the only means of identifying social regularities' (Halbwachs 1944: 114), and once suggested that the fields of sociology best able to utilise quantitative methods – namely two of his own fields, economic sociology and social morphology – were more advanced than the others.[61]

But were there limits? How advanced or scientific could sociology become? With time the Durkheimian whom Halbwachs considered 'our methodologist' (Halbwachs 1937a: 25), François Simiand, became rather restrained. Thus in 1933 Simiand concluded that social scientists could not aspire to the objectivity of the natural scientists or to their opportunities for controlled experiments, and hence that it was presumptuous to think in

[57] See Halbwachs 1955: 59–88.
[58] See Halbwachs 1934c: 706–7, and 1934d: 335–6.
[59] Halbwachs 1926: 384–5, and 1934c: 32.
[60] Halbwachs 1931: 79–81, 1933c: ix-x, and 1933b: 80–1.
[61] Halbwachs 1940a: 3.

terms of laws of social behaviour.[62] But Halbwachs disagreed. He referred to laws rather than to regularities, Simiand's preferred term, and he remained convinced that with improvements in statistical methods and in the collection of data the social sciences could become genuinely scientific. Indeed he argued, somewhat ironically, that Simiand's *Le Salaire* exemplified the possibilities: 'we have nothing to regret, nor any reason to envy other scholars, if it is true, as the book of M. Simiand seems to me to establish, that it is now possible to raise the science of man and of human societies exactly to the level already reached by the natural sciences' (Halbwachs 1932a: 363).

Obviously the challenges Halbwachs faced from other disciplines and from other schools of sociology – and from other Durkheimians – had not undermined his positivism. In fact they apparently had the opposite effect. They seem to have strengthened his belief that through a greater reliance on quantitative methods sociology could become more like the natural sciences. And they apparently helped to convince him that sociology had to become more like the natural sciences if it was to consolidate its gains and justify its claims to leadership among the social sciences.

Halbwachs's opinions on these matters went beyond those of his contemporaries. Fellow Durkheimians were less ambitious while younger French sociologists, influenced by Weber or by phenomenology or by Marxism, rejected the positivism advocated by Halbwachs. But the next generation was to be more sympathetic. Indeed, in many respects the recommendations Halbwachs made between the wars were consistent with the course that the mainstream of French sociology was to follow after World War II. This does not mean that his influence was decisive or even significant. It is clear, however, that Halbwachs and many postwar sociologists responded similarly to a common sense of crisis in their discipline: by giving greater emphasis to methodological questions, to separating values and scholarship, to empirical research, and to statistical analysis. Because of this it is legitimate to consider Halbwachs the closest link between the Durkheimians and contemporary French sociology.

References

Alexandre, J.-M. 1968. 'Maurice Halbwachs (1877–1945)', pp. xvii-xxii in M. Halbwachs, *La Mémoire collective*, 2nd edition. Paris: Presses Universitaires de France.

Bellah, R. N. 1965. 'Durkheim and History', pp. 153–76 in R. A. Nisbet *et al.*, *Emile Durkheim*. Englewood Cliffs, N. J.: Prentice-Hall.

Berr, H. 1921. 'L'Esprit de synthèse dans l'enseignement supérieur, I. L'Université de Strasbourg', *Revue de synthèse historique*, vol. 32, pp. 1–13.

[62] Simiand 1934: 197-9.

1922. 'L'Esprit de synthèse dans l'enseignement supérieur, II. L'Université de Strasbourg – vue d'Allemagne', *Revue de synthèse historique*, vol. 34, pp. 1–6.

Bloch, M. 1924. Review of Lucien Febvre with Lionel Bataillon, *La Terre et l'évolution humaine. Introduction géographique à l'histoire* (Paris: La Renaissance du Livre, 1922), *Revue historique*, vol. 145, pp. 235–40.

1925. 'Mémoire collective, tradition et coutume à propos d'un livre récent', *Revue de synthèse historique*, vol. 40, pp. 73–83.

1927. Review of *L'Année sociologique*, second series, vol. 1 (1923–4), *Revue historique*, vol. 155, p. 176.

1929a. 'Un Choix de statistiques', *Annales d'histoire économique et sociale*, vol. 1, pp. 428–9.

1929b. 'Le Développement de Paris depuis le milieu du XIXe siècle', *Annales d'histoire économique et sociale*, vol. 1, pp. 434–6.

1931. 'Un Symptôme social: le suicide', *Annales d'histoire économique et sociale*, vol. 3, pp. 590–2.

1934a. 'Le Salaire et les fluctuations économiques à longue période', *Revue historique*, vol. 173, pp. 1–31.

1934b. 'Histoire, doctrine économique, sociologie', *Annales d'histoire économique et sociale*, vol. 6, p. 510.

1935a. 'La Répartition des dépenses comme caractère de classe', *Annales d'histoire économique et sociale*, vol. 7, pp. 83–6.

1935b. 'Les Annales sociologiques', *Annales d'histoire économique et sociale*, vol. 7, p. 393.

1936. 'La Sociologie et le passé du droit', *Annales d'histoire économique et sociale*, vol. 8, p. 458.

1938. 'A l'ombre de la Sorbonne', *Annales d'histoire économique et sociale*, vol. 10, p. 53.

1945. 'Témoignages sur la période 1939–1944', *Annales d'histoire sociale*, no. 1, pp. 15–32.

Blondel, C. 1926. Review of M. Halbwachs, *Les cadres sociaux de la mémoire* (Paris: Alcan, 1925), *Revue philosophique*, vol. 101, pp. 290–8.

1933. *Le Suicide*. Strasbourg: Librairie universitaire d'Alsace.

[1938]. 'Psychologie et sociologie', pp. 123–4 in *Les Convergences des sciences sociales et l'esprit international* (Travaux de la conférence internationale des sciences sociales, Paris, July 1937). Paris: Paul Hartmann.

1946. *Introduction à la psychologie collective*, 4th edition. Paris: Colin.

Bousquet, G.-H. 1935. Review of M. Halbwachs, *L'Evolution des besoins dans les classes ouvrières* (Paris: Alcan, 1933), *Revue d'économie politique*, vol. 49, p. 237.

Canguilhem, G. 1947. 'Maurice Halbwachs (1877–1945)', pp. 229–41 in *Faculté des Lettres de l'Université de Strasbourg : Mémorial des années 1939–1945*. Paris: Les Belles Lettres.

Colson, C. 1908. 'La Théorie économique du salaire et l'économie politique traditionnelle', *La Revue du mois*, vol. 6, pp. 728–30.

Craig, J. E. 1979a. 'France's First Chair of Sociology: a Note on the Origins', *Etudes durkheimiennes*, no. 4, pp. 8–13.

1979b. 'Maurice Halbwachs à Strasbourg', *Revue française de sociologie*, vol. 20, pp. 273–92.

John E. Craig

1981. 'Die Durkheim-Schule und die *Annales*', pp. 298–322 in Wolf Lepenies (ed.), *Geschichte der Soziologie. Frankfurt a. M.: Suhrkamp.*

Demangeon, A. *1923. 'Introduction géographique à l'histoire', Annales de géographie, vol. 32, pp. 165–70.*

Durkheim, E. 1898. Préface, *Année sociologique*, vol. 1, pp. i–vii.

1899. 'Morphologie sociale', *Année sociologique*, vol. 2, pp. 520–1.

1908a. Comments at Séance du 28 mai 1908: 'L'inconnu et l'inconscient en histoire', *Bulletin de la société française de philosophie*, vol. 8, pp. 217–47.

1908b. Comments at Société d'économie politique : Reunion of 4 April 1908, *Bulletin de la société d'économie politique*, pp. 65–7, 70–2.

Duvignaud, J. 1968. Préface, pp. vii–xv in M. Halbwachs, *La Mémoire collective*, 2nd edition. Paris: Presses Universitaires de France.

Faublée, J. 1964. 'Henri Berr et *L'Année sociologique*', *Revue de synthèse*, vol. 35, pp. 68–74.

Febvre, L. 1930. 'Histoire, économie et statistique', *Annales d'histoire économique et sociale*, vol. 2, pp. 581–90.

1934. 'Intervention de M. Lucien Febvre – Discussion', pp. 216–20 in *Science et loi* (5ème semaine internationale de synthèse, 1933). Paris: Alcan.

1935. 'François Simiand (1873–1935)', *Annales d'histoire économique et sociale*, vol. 7, p. 391.

1946a. 'Note on Maurice Halbwachs', p. 289 in M. Halbwachs, 'Réflexions sur un équilibre démographique. Beaucoup de naissances, beaucoup de morts. Peu d'enfants, peu de décès, *Annales. Economies – Sociétés – Civilisations*, vol. 1.

1946b. 'Une Sociologie de la pratique religieuse', *Annales. Economies – Sociétés – Civilisations*, vol. 1, pp. 350–1.

1949. 'Vers une autre histoire', *Revue de métaphysique et de morale*, vol. 54, pp. 225–47.

Febvre, L., with Bataillon, L. 1922. *La Terre et l'évolution humaine. Introduction géographique à l'histoire*. Paris: La Renaissance du Livre.

Fessard, G. 1971. 'Raymond Aron, philosophe de l'histoire et de la politique', pp. 49–88 in *Science et conscience de la société. Mélanges en l'honneur de Raymond Aron*, vol. 1. Paris: Calmann-Lévy.

Fréchet, M., and Halbwachs, M. 1924. *Le Calcul des probabilités à la portée de tous.* Paris: Dunod.

Friedmann, G. 1955. 'Maurice Halbwachs', pp. 9–23 in M. Halbwachs, *Esquisse d'une psychologie des classes sociales*. Paris: Rivière.

Guillaume, G. (?) 1933. Comments in report of session 19 May 1933, *X-Crise*, no. 5, pp. 16, 19.

Guillaume, G. and E., *et al.* 1937. *Economique rationnelle*, 5 vols. Paris: Hermann et Cie.

Halbwachs, M. 1910. Review of F. Ratzel, *Raum und Zeit in Geographie und Geologie* (Leipzig: Barth, 1907), *Année sociologique*, vol. 11, pp. 720–3.

1918. 'La Doctrine d'Emile Durkheim', *Revue philosophique*, vol. 85, pp. 353–411.

1925a. *Les Cadres sociaux de la mémoire*. Paris: Alcan.

1925b. Review of L. Febvre, Le Problème de la géographie humaine à propos d'ouvrages récents (*Revue de synthèse historique*, vol. 35 [1923], pp. 97–116), *Année sociologique*, 2nd series, vol. 1, pp. 902–8.

1925c. 'Les origines puritaines du capitalisme', *Revue d'histoire et de philosophie religieuse*, vol. 5, pp. 132–54.

1925d. Review of Max Weber, *Wirtschaft und Gesellschaft* (Tübingen: J. C. B. Mohr [Paul Siebeck], 1922), *Année sociologique*, 2nd series, vol. 1, pp. 724–8.

1926. 'Beitrag zu einer soziologischen Theorie der Arbeiterklasse', *Jahrbuch für Soziologie*, vol. 2, pp. 366–85.

1929. 'Max Weber: un homme, une oeuvre', *Annales d'histoire économique et sociale*, vol. 1, pp. 81–8.

1930. *Les Causes du suicide*. Paris: Alcan.

1931. 'Dans les Etats-Unis d'aujourd'hui: impressions d'un ouvrier français', *Annales d'histoire économique et sociale*, vol. 3, pp. 79–81.

1932a. 'Une Théorie expérimentale du salaire', *Revue philosophique*, vol. 114, pp. 321–63.

1932b. 'Chicago, expérience ethnique', *Annales d'histoire économique et sociale*, vol. 4, pp. 11–49.

1932c. Review of Karl Mannheim, *Die Gegenwartsaufgaben der Soziologie* (Tübingen: J. C. B. Mohr [Paul Siebeck], 1932), *Revue critique*, vol. 100, pp. 364–5.

1932d. 'La Sociologie en Allemagne et aux Etats-Unis', *Annales d'histoire économique et sociale*, vol. 4, pp. 80–1.

1933a. Review of C. Blondel, *Le Suicide* (Strasbourg: Librairie universitaire d'Alsace, 1933), *Revue philosophique*, vol. 116, pp. 473–5.

1933b. 'Budgets de famille aux Etats-Unis et en Allemagne', *Bulletin de l'institut français de sociologie*, vol. 3, pp. 51–82.

1933c. *L'Evolution des besoins dans les classes ouvrières*. Paris: Alcan.

1934a. 'La Loi en sociologie', pp. 173–96 in *Science et loi* (5ème semaine internationale de synthèse, 1933). Paris: Alcan.

1934b. '"Gross Berlin": grande agglomération ou grande ville?', *Annales d'histoire économique et sociale*, vol. 6, pp. 547–70.

1934c. 'Les Classes sociales', *Revue des cours et conférences*, vol. 35, no. 1, pp. 213–20, 325–33, 538–47, 713–22, and no. 2, pp. 23–32, 260–9, 450–60, 697–707.

1934d. Review of Emil Grünberg, *Der Mittelstand in der kapitalistischen Gesellschaft* (Leipzig: Hirschfeld, 1932), *Annales sociologiques*, série D, vol. 1, pp. 333–6.

1935. 'Une Controverse: puritanisme et capitalisme', *Annales d'histoire économique et sociale*, vol. 7, pp. 97–9.

1936. 'La Méthodologie de François Simiand. Un empirisme rationaliste', *Revue philosophique*, vol. 121, pp. 281–319.

1937a. 'Le Point de vue de la sociologie', *X-Crise*, no. 35, pp. 23–30.

1937b. Review of A. C. Pigou, *The Economics of Welfare*, 4th edition (London: Macmillan, 1932), *Annales sociologiques*, série D, vol. 2, pp. 62–70, 116–24.

1937c. 'Les Courants de la pensée sociologique en Allemagne', *Annales d'histoire économique et sociale*, vol. 9, pp. 622–3.

1938a. 'Individual Psychology and Collective Psychology', *American sociological review*, vol. 3, pp. 615–22.

1938b. Review of G. and E. Guillaume *et al.*, *Economique rationnelle*, 5 vols. (Paris: Hermann et Cie, 1937), *Annales sociologiques*, série D, no. 3, pp. 39–48.

1939. 'Individual Consciousness and Collective mind', *The American journal of sociology*, vol. 44, pp. 812–22.

1940a. *Sociologie économique et démographie*. Paris: Hermann.

John E. Craig

1940b. Review of B. Nogaro, *La Méthode de l'économie politique* (Paris: Librairie générale de droit et de jurisprudence, 1939), *Annales sociologiques*, série D, vol. 4, pp. 46–8.

1943. Préface, pp. vii–xi in B. V. Damalas, *L'Oeuvre scientifique de François Simiand*. Paris: Presses Universitaires de France.

1944. 'La Statistique en sociologie', pp. 113–34 in *La Statistique, ses applications, les problèmes qu'elle soulève* ($7^{\text{ème}}$ semaine internationale de synthèse, 1935). Paris: Presses Universitaires de France.

1946. 'Réflexions sur un équilibre démographique. Beaucoup de naissances, beaucoup de morts. Peu d'enfants, peu de décès', *Annales. Economies – Sociétés – Civilisations*, vol. 1, pp. 289–305.

1955. *Esquisse d'une psychologie des classes sociales*. Paris: Rivière.

1970. *Morphologie sociale*, 2nd edition. Paris: Colin.

Halbwachs, M., *et al.* 1936. 'Le Point de vue du nombre', pp. 7.76–3, – 7.94–4 in *Encyclopédie française*, vol. 7. Paris: Comité de l'encyclopédie française.

Index Generalis. 1923–4. *Index Generalis*, vol. 4. Paris: Gauthier-Villars.

Karady, V. 1972. 'Biographie de Maurice Halbwachs', pp. 9–22 in M. Halbwachs, *Classes sociales et morphologie*. Paris: Editions de Minuit.

Karady, V., with Thiébart, A. 1972. 'Bibliographie des oeuvres de Maurice Halbwachs', pp. 409–44 in M. Halbwachs, *Classes sociales et morphologie*. Paris: Editions de Minuit.

König, R. 1931. 'Die neuesten Strömungen in der gegenwärtigen französischen Soziologie', *Zeitschrift für Völkerpsychologie und Soziologie*, vol. 7, pp. 485–505.

Labrousse, E. 1980. 'Entretiens avec Ernest Labrousse', *Actes de la recherche en sciences sociales*, nos. 32–3, pp. 111–25.

Leroy-Beaulieu, P. 1908. Comments at Société d'économie politique: 1908, *Bulletin de la société d'économie politique*, pp. 72–3.

Leuilliot, P. 1964. 'Henri Berr dans l'historiographie française', *Revue de synthèse*, vol. 35, pp. 93–7.

1973. 'Aux origines des "Annales d'histoire économique et sociale" (1928). Contribution à l'historiographie française', pp. 317–24 in *Mélanges en honneur de Fernand Braudel*, vol. 2. Toulouse: Privat.

Marjolin, R. 1941. *Prix, monnaie et production*. Paris: Alcan.

Mauss, M. 1927. 'Sur l'extension de la sociologie', *Année sociologique*, 2nd series, vol. 2, pp. 177–92.

1933. 'La Sociologie en France depuis 1914', pp. 36–46 in *La Science française*, vol. 1. Paris: Larousse.

Morazé, C. 1942. 'Essai sur la méthode de François Simiand', *Mélanges d'histoire sociale*, no. 1, pp. 1–24, and no. 2, pp. 22–44.

1957. 'Lucien Febvre et l'histoire vivante', *Revue historique*, vol. 217, pp. 1–19.

Piganiol, A. 1933. 'Celtes ou Celtisés?', *Annales d'histoire économique et sociale*, vol. 5, pp. 322–5.

1955. 'Qu'est-ce que l'histoire?', *Revue de métaphysique et de morale*, vol. 60, pp. 225–47.

Pirou, G. 1929. *Doctrines sociales et science économique*. Paris: Sirey.

1931. Review of F. Simiand, *Le Salaire*, *Revue d'économie politique*, vol. 45, p. 1708.

1938. Préface, pp. v–x in H. Guitton, *Economie rationnelle, économie positive, économie synthéthique*. Paris: Sirey.

Pradines, M., and Halbwachs, M. 1924–5. 'L'Institut de philosophie', *Bulletin de la faculté des lettres de Strasbourg*, vol. 3, pp. 227–31.

'Réunions du samedi'. 1922–35. *Bulletin de la faculté des lettres de Strasbourg*, vols. 1–13.

Simiand, F. 1903. 'Méthode historique et science sociale', *Revue de synthèse historique*, vol. 6, pp. 1–22, 129–57.

1906. Lecture and comments at session 31 May 1906 : La causalité en histoire, *Bulletin de la société française de philosophie*, vol. 6, pp. 245–72, 276–90 *passim*.

1907. Comments at session 30 May 1907 : Les conditions pratiques de la recherche des causes dans le travail historique, *Bulletin de la société française de philosophie*, vol. 7, pp. 291–306 *passim*.

1910. Review of A. Demangeon, *La Picardie et les régions voisines*, R. Blanchard, *La Flandre. Etude géographique de la plaine flamande en France, Belgique et Hollande*, C. Vallaux, *La Basse-Bretagne*, A. Vacher, *Le Berry. Contribution à l'étude géographique d'une région française* and J. Sion, *Les Paysans de la Normandie orientale*, *Année sociologique*, vol. 11, pp. 723–32.

1933. Comments in report of session 19 May 1933, *X-Crise*, no. 5, pp. 19–22.

1934. 'Intervention de M. François Simiand – Discussions', pp. 197–200 in *Science et loi* (5ème semaine internationale de synthèse, 1933). Paris: Alcan.

Thibaudet, A. 1925. 'Dans le monde de la mémoire', *La Nouvelle Revue française*, vol. 25, pp. 483–92.

Verret, M. 1972. 'Halbwachs ou le deuxième âge du durkheimisme', *Cahiers internationaux de sociologie*, no. 53, pp. 311–36.

Vézian, E. 1930. 'Le Centre d'études germaniques', *L'Alsace française*, vol. 10, pp. 389–90.

Vromen, S. 1975. 'The Sociology of Maurice Halbwachs'. Doctoral dissertation (Ph.D.) New York University.

Index

Index

Index

Index

For EU product safety concerns, contact us at Calle de José Abascal, 56–1°,
28003 Madrid, Spain or eugpsr@cambridge.org.

www.ingramcontent.com/pod-product-compliance
Ingram Content Group UK Ltd.
Pitfield, Milton Keynes, MK11 3LW, UK
UKHW042153130625
459647UK00011B/1315